Introduction to
FORENSIC
PSYCHOLOGY
Essentials for Law Enforcement

Introduction to
FORENSIC PSYCHOLOGY
Essentials for Law Enforcement

Stephanie Scott-Snyder

CRC Press
Taylor & Francis Group
Boca Raton London New York

CRC Press is an imprint of the
Taylor & Francis Group, an **informa** business

CRC Press
Taylor & Francis Group
6000 Broken Sound Parkway NW, Suite 300
Boca Raton, FL 33487-2742

© 2017 by Taylor & Francis Group, LLC
CRC Press is an imprint of Taylor & Francis Group, an Informa business

No claim to original U.S. Government works

Printed on acid-free paper
Version Date: 20160719

International Standard Book Number-13: 978-1-4987-5550-4 (paperback)

Library of Congress Cataloging-in-Publication Data

Names: Scott-Snyder, Stephanie, author.
Title: Introduction to forensic psychology: essentials for law enforcement/ by Stephanie Scott-Snyder.
Description: New York: CRC Press, 2017. | Includes bibliographical references and index.
Identifiers: LCCN 2016030828| ISBN 9781498755504 (pbk.: alk. paper) | ISBN 9781315298559 (ebk)
Subjects: LCSH: Forensic psychology. | Law enforcement
Classification: LCC RA1148 .S36 2017 | DDC 614/.15--dc23
LC record available at https://lccn.loc.gov/2016030828

Visit the Taylor & Francis Web site at
http://www.taylorandfrancis.com

and the CRC Press Web site at
http://www.crcpress.com

Printed and bound in the United States of America by
Edwards Brothers Malloy on sustainably sourced paper

CONTENTS

PART II Crimes and Criminals

PREFACE

Research indicates that there are psychological principles at play in the situations encountered by law enforcement personnel. This book fulfills an important need in the ever-evolving field of criminal justice by providing officers with comprehensive foundational knowledge of forensic psychology. It places interview strategies, emotional disturbance, homicide, sexual and domestic violence, hostage negotiation, and other critical scenarios into psycholegal context. This book offers police (patrol officers, dispatchers, investigators, and correctional/community correctional professionals) a working knowledge of psychology, thus assisting them in better understanding the individuals with whom they come into contact on a daily basis. This book will help law enforcement to interpret and anticipate behavior, while responding safely and effectively.

In addition to serving as training material for police professionals, this text applies to various university courses. It provides students with strong theoretical knowledge of forensic psychological concepts and places those theories within the unique framework of their real-life application to criminological and policing scenarios.

AUTHOR

Stephanie Scott-Snyder is a forensic mental health clinician. She has provided court-mandated therapy to offenders, conducted risk assessments, worked closely with law enforcement, and provided crisis intervention to victims of violent crime. She is an adjunct faculty member at two renowned New York City metro area colleges, where she teaches Forensic Psychology, Psychology of Law, and Social Psychology, in addition to supervising student internships. Scott-Snyder graduated first in her class from Fairleigh Dickinson University with a Master of Arts degree in Forensic Psychology and is an associate member of the American Psychological Association, a lifetime member of Psi Chi the International Honor Society in Psychology, a clinical member of both ATSA (The Association for the Treatment of Sexual Abusers) and New Jersey ATSA, and is a Clinically Certified Forensic Counselor (CCFC) by the National Association of Forensic Counselors (NAFC). Prior to her work within the criminal justice system, Scott-Snyder was a Writer-Producer and Creative Director for network television, with specific expertise in true crime projects.

Part I
Background

1

Introduction

THE CHIRENO MURDER

On April 18, 2008, the residents of New Jersey witnessed one of the most horrific crimes in their state's history—an ax murder. After buying both an ax and a knife at the local hardware store, 34-year-old Fernando Chireno drafted a letter to his mother and children. In it, he apologized for the fact that he was going to kill his estranged wife, Luisa Chireno. Later that night, he broke into the apartment where Luisa resided with the couple's three young children (Petrick, 2010).

When police responded to the scene, they found a trail of blood leading from the victim's home out into the street. After Chireno had struck her multiple times with the ax, Luisa desperately fled her apartment. With the children still cowering inside their mother's home, Chireno chased his wife into the middle of the street where he repeatedly stabbed her. Luisa later died in surgery with more than 15 wounds (Petrick, 2010; Valdes, 2010).

Aside from the obvious (and obscure), which is that Chireno was armed with an ax, this case involves an amalgamation of both physical and psychological dynamics. On the surface, this was a violent and heinous crime. In fact, you've probably already begun to formulate opinions about the perpetrator and perhaps even the victim. However, when we dig deeper and examine the pertinent psychological principles, we can begin to better understand the offense and the experience of those involved. In addition, we can also identify important issues for law enforcement to consider.

3

By identifying the offender's motivations and psychological makeup, police officers can begin to answer questions such as:

- What precipitated Chireno's desire to murder his estranged wife?
- What triggered him to act on that desire at that particular time?
- How long had Chireno been planning Luisa's murder? Did anyone else know or suspect that he had homicidal intent? Were there any warning signs?
- Why did Chireno choose to break into his wife's apartment in the middle of the night? Whom did he expect to find there at that time?
- Was Chireno aware that his children would be in the apartment on the night of the attack? Did he knowingly force them to bear witness to their mother's murder? If so, why had he written a letter of apology to them?
- Was Luisa the only person that Chireno intended to harm that night? Or had he planned to kill another family member or even an intervening police officer?
- Did Chireno perhaps intend to die at the scene?

Fernando Chireno's actions created a multitude of questions for investigators. By understanding the point of view and the psychological composition of suspects, witnesses, and victims, police are better equipped to respond effectively and safely. That is where forensic psychology comes in.

OVERVIEW OF FORENSIC PSYCHOLOGY

For many years, the term *forensic psychology* was something that was most often heard in movies and on TV rather than in the day-to-day workings of our legal system. It was loosely associated with films such as *The Silence of the Lambs* and was viewed as an esoteric discipline, something incomprehensible—and almost mysterious. Within the past decade, forensic psychology has gained popularity and has become part of the vernacular. As a scientific discipline, it has made enormous strides to become an integral part of our legal process.

Stated very simply, **forensic psychology** is the application of psychological principles to any task faced by the justice system (Fulero & Wrightsman, 2009). This basic definition is purposely broad, as psychology can be used to assist in an array of situations encountered at various

4

points in the civil and criminal justice system. The following is a list of scenarios commonly faced by law enforcement, in which a solid understanding of psychology is extremely useful:

- Investigating violent and/or serial crimes (profiling)
- Gang violence
- Interrogating suspects
- Interviewing witnesses
- Responding to and supporting crime victims
- Sexual and domestic violence
- Appropriate use of force
- Threat assessment (pertaining to stalking, school violence, mass shootings, terrorist acts, etc.)
- Hostage negotiation

This list is by no means exhaustive, but it paints an important picture: psychology and policing are inextricably linked. By developing an understanding of the principles that govern cognition and human behavior, you will improve your skills as a criminal justice professional.

PSYCHOLOGY TRAINING FOR LAW ENFORCEMENT

Right now, you may be wondering why such heavy emphasis is being placed on obtaining a solid background in psychology when law enforcement academies focus their curricula on activities such as firearms training, first aid/cardiopulmonary resuscitation (CPR), self-defense, tactical measures, criminal law, crime scene investigation, emergency vehicle operation, patrol procedures, and so on. Why do law enforcement officials and other justice professionals need to be well-versed in psychology? Why is procedural training simply not enough?

To answer these questions, let's revisit our initial example about the attack on Luisa Chireno. Prior to the night of the murder, there was a documented history of domestic violence between the victim and her husband. A final restraining order (FRO) was in place, which Chireno violated by entering his wife's apartment. In addition, Chireno suspected that Luisa had become sexually involved with another man shortly before the murder (Valdes, 2010).

These historical details reveal that the domestic homicide of Luisa Chireno was likely the tragic culmination of a significant pattern of marital violence. Such contextual clues are vital pieces of information for law enforcement. Clearly, the crime scene was a hostile and potentially volatile environment, where violence had escalated to an extreme over a period of time. In what appeared to be an emotionally-driven act, Chireno had violated an FRO, which was initially granted because a judge had agreed that Luisa had cause to fear for her own safety. These factors illustrate the relationship between homicide, DV, and behavioral profiling, which will be discussed in further detail in Chapters 5, 7, and 8 respectively.

Similarly, the presence of the Chireno children adds an additional psychological component to this investigation, as it is a clear indicator of the mental state of the perpetrator—Chireno was determined to carry out the murder regardless of whether his children were present or not. Additionally, the history of family violence to which the children were exposed, in combination with the fact that the killer was their father, creates a complex set of dynamics for officers tasked with interviewing these children. Avoiding further trauma to victims and witnesses while eliciting truthful information is crucial to an investigation. Both interview and interrogation strategies will be explained in Chapter 9, and how to successfully work with victims and minors will be addressed in detail in Chapters 10 and 11, respectively.

Let's continue with the Chireno case. At the trial, Chireno's attorney attempted to present an insanity defense. Although the defense was rejected by the court, evidence was presented that Chireno had a history of mental illness. Specifically, expert testimony indicated that he had been treated for schizophrenia and miscellaneous behavioral problems from an early age. At the time of the murder, Chireno reportedly believed that the voice of God was directing him to kill his wife (Valdes, 2010).

The presence of mental health difficulties in a suspect's life highlights a critical consideration for law enforcement: how to safely apprehend someone who is experiencing symptoms of mental illness—and how this scenario might differ from arresting someone who is simply noncompliant. A suspect's mental health is an important issue for police to recognize and understand as it impacts how he or she is most likely to respond to them. It also informs the tactics used by police when approaching/confronting a particular suspect. Interacting with psychologically disordered offenders will be discussed in Chapter 3. Furthermore, Chapters 4 and 12 will build upon this information to enhance readers' understanding of psychopathy and the relationship between mental illness and threat assessment.

Forensic psychology is not an exact science. However, through empirical data we have developed a better understanding of human behavior and its relationship to the law. As you continue to read this book, you will gain foundational knowledge of forensic psychology from the unique perspective of its usefulness to the law enforcement community. When we seek to understand the psychological dynamics of any given situation, we are better equipped to protect and serve.

2

Overview of Forensic Psychology Concepts

WHAT IS FORENSIC PSYCHOLOGY?

What comes to mind when you hear the phrase *forensic psychology*? Perhaps you envision a brilliant psychologist providing insight about a serial killer's behavior in order to profile a bizarre crime. Or maybe you think of Eddie Ray Routh pleading not guilty by reason of insanity (NGRI) to the murders of Chris Kyle and Chad Littlefield in the widely publicized American Sniper trial. In this case, forensic psychological experts provided hours of testimony regarding Routh's state of mind on the day of the murders. Alternatively, you might think of any one of numerous cases of child sexual abuse that have made headlines, where psychologists have weighed in on the veracity of "recovered" memories.

In Chapter 1, the term forensic psychology was broadly defined as the application of psychological principles to a task faced by the legal system. Not only is this a rather loose definition, but it fails to acknowledge an ongoing controversy within the field as to how the definition of forensic psychology should be conceptualized. Additionally, experts debate who should qualify as a forensic psychologist and what constitutes appropriate forensic psychological training.

Professor Jack Brigham, the former president of the American Psychology–Law Society, addressed the divisive issue of who should be considered a forensic psychologist by both professional and training standards in his presidential address entitled "What is forensic psychology, anyway?" He discussed both the broad definition of forensic psychology as well as a narrower definition, which views the discipline as a subspecialty of clinical psychology. Defining forensic psychology from such a strict clinical viewpoint would limit its scope to include only clinical practice issues relevant to the legal system (Brigham, 1999). Some examples might include assessing insanity, evaluating competency, or providing court-mandated mental health treatment to offenders as these activities rely heavily upon a skillset in clinical or counseling psychology.

The narrow focus of the clinical definition would exclude the categorization of research-based endeavors, such as expert testimony on topics including memory, false confessions, and eyewitness identification, from falling within the purview of forensic psychology. It would also fail to recognize trial consultation as a legitimate forensic psychological activity.

Due to the justice system's increasing reliance on both clinical *and* research-oriented activities, there is an ongoing debate in the field as to whether the narrow clinical definition of forensic psychology is too restrictive. Should psychological research pertaining to the legal system be considered forensic psychology?

One reason why it is imperative to operationalize the definition of forensic psychology is so that psychologists can communicate effectively with the legal system. Imagine being asked to testify about your research on eyewitness identification in a major murder trial. The trial hinges on one witness's identification of the suspect, making your research particularly salient. Once on the stand, you are asked, "Are you a forensic psychologist?" How would you answer that question? Would you say, "It depends," or "I don't know?" This type of vague answer would likely frustrate a judge and confuse (or infuriate) a jury (Brigham, 1999).

Another reason that we need to consider the definition of forensic psychology is for training purposes. Kirk Heilbrun (as cited in Fulero & Wrightsman, 2009) developed a comprehensive training model that encompasses two approaches and three training areas. It includes both applied and academic activities in which psychologists participate within the justice system (Fulero & Wrightsman, 2009). A conceptualization of this model is outlined in Table 2.1.

Table 2.1 Heilbrun's Conceptualization of Training in Forensic Psychology

	Law and Psychology Interest Areas (with Associated Training)		
	Experimental (Clinical, Counseling, School Psychology)	**Clinical (Social, Developmental, Cognitive, Human Experimental Psychology)**	**Legal (Law, Some Training in Behavioral Science)**
Research	1. Assessment tools 2. Intervention effectiveness 3. Epidemiology of relevant behavior (e.g., violence, sexual offending) and disorders	1. Memory 2. Perception 3. Child development 4. Group decision making	1. Mental health law 2. Other law relevant to health and science 3. Legal movements
Applied	1. Forensic assessment 2. Treatment in legal context 3. Integration of science	1. Consultation re jury selection 2. Consultation re litigation strategy 3. Consultation re "state of science" 4. Expert testimony re "state of science"	1. Policy and legislative consultation 2. Model law development

Source: Brigham, J. C., *Law and Human Behavior*, 23, 282, 1999, table 3. Reprinted by permission of Kluwer Academic/Plenum Publishers.

ROLES OF FORENSIC PSYCHOLOGISTS

There are myriad ways for psychologists to obtain legitimate training that is applicable to the legal system, as various subspecialties of psychology intersect the forensic arena. For example, a neuropsychologist may be asked to examine a patient who has sustained frontal lobe damage resulting in a loss of impulse control. If the patient's impulsivity has led him or her to commit subsequent criminal acts, the psychologist's expert opinion will be used to inform the jury so that they may determine criminal culpability. In essence, the psychologist will be using psychological evidence to help the triers of fact (judge and/or jury) to determine whether there is a medical/psychological reason why this individual should not be held *criminally* responsible. Thus, in this example, neuropsychology overlaps the legal system and the psychologist is acting in a forensic capacity.

Other clinical roles often assumed by psychologists within the legal system include assessing a defendant's sanity or competence, providing offense-specific therapy to offenders, counseling victims of domestic and sexual violence, evaluating potential police candidates, completing fitness for duty evaluations, and conducting risk assessments. Although this text mainly focuses on issues relevant to the criminal justice system, it should be noted that psychologists additionally engage in civil forensic activities, such as completing child custody evaluations or assessing an individual's competence to execute a will.

Experimental or research-based roles for forensic psychologists encompass trial consultation (i.e., evaluating the effects of pretrial publicity, preparing witnesses for trial, assisting with voir dire, etc.), and acting as an expert witness with regard to research findings on confessions, perception, memory, violence and race, and the veracity of eyewitness testimony. Psychologists in some states may also engage in behavioral evidence analysis (i.e., profiling).

As you can see, forensic psychologists work very closely with law enforcement today … but what about in the past?

BRIEF HISTORY OF FORENSIC PSYCHOLOGY

The activities performed by forensic psychologists today are diverse and the history of the intersection between psychology and the law is riddled with contention. To better understand the development of the relationship between social science and the legal system, let's examine some milestone issues at the very crossroads of psychology and the justice system.

As long as society has seen a need to regulate human behavior by instituting laws, courts have been tasked with the burden of having to determine how to handle individuals who are unwilling or, due to mental disease or disorder, unable to conform their behavior to the requirements of the law (Fulero & Wrightsman, 2009).

In 1843, Daniel McNaughten attempted to assassinate British Prime Minister Robert Peel. Instead, he inadvertently shot and killed the prime minister's secretary, Edward Drummond. When questioned, McNaughten said that he had been persecuted by Tories who had compelled him to commit the murder. McNaughten's mental state became an issue during his trial and he was found not guilty on the grounds of insanity. The verdict created widespread upset and resulted in the House of Lords posing several psychologically based questions to the British judiciary. Among them: What is the proper standard for insanity? (Frederick, Mrad, & DeMier, 2007). Answering this question is of prime importance to dispensing justice, as a successful affirmative defense results in a not guilty verdict; in other words, an insanity defense seeks to decriminalize and thus legally excuse an offender's behavior.

The McNaughten case was one of the earliest and most significant attempts to merge psychological principles with law-making and the legal system. The psychological issue of the defendant's mental state at the time of the crime and its bearing on the insanity defense became standardized in the landmark decision, which eventually became known as the "McNaughten Rule." Still in force today, McNaughten stipulates that an individual meets criteria for insanity if it is clearly proved that he was acting under "a defect of reason, from disease of the mind, as not to know the nature and quality of the act he was doing; or, if he did know it, that he did not know he was doing what was wrong" (Frederick et al., 2007).

The early part of the twentieth century was interspersed with several more significant attempts to infuse the legal system with psychological insight. In 1906, Sigmund Freud made a speech before a group of Austrian judges in which he proposed that psychology could be of use to the court. Freud's developing theories of personality and psychopathology strongly influenced his thinking about the etiology of criminal behavior, and he likened working with the unconscious mind to detective work. He warned judges and others involved in the judicial system that they would likely be influenced by their unconscious when making decisions (Horowitz & Willging, 1984).

In 1908, however, psychology gained wide recognition for its potential impact on the legal system. Researcher Hugo Munsterberg wrote the controversial book *On the Witness Stand*. It covered topics such as memory, eyewitness accuracy, confessions, hypnosis, and crime detection and prevention. Munsterberg's purpose in writing the text was to advise the legal system, much as Freud had done, that psychology had much to offer their profession. Munsterberg's viewpoint regarding the need for forensic psychological expertise was summed up in his statement: "the individual could not accurately judge the real world that existed outside him, or for that matter the nature and processes of his own mind" (Fulero & Wrightsman, 2009, p. 7). Therefore, he posited that in order for investigative and courtroom matters to be completed accurately, assistance from a psychologist should be sought.

Despite his unpopularity for making such remarks, Munsterberg engaged in crucial forensic psychological activities such as demonstrating

Table 2.2   Important Dates in the Study of Law and Psychology

Year	Event
1843	Daniel McNaughten's affirmative defense (NGRI) is successful, following expert testimony about his mental health.
1906	Freud implores the court to recognize and utilize the benefit of psychological insight into the legal system.
1908	Hugo Munsterberg's *On the Witness Stand* is published.
1909	Munsterberg's work is publicly chastised by legal scholars.
1968–1969	The American Psychology–Law Society (AP-LS) is established.
1980–1981	APA Division 41 (Psychology and Law) is founded.
1984	AP-LS merges with APA Division 41.
1991	An ethics code is established specifically for forensic psychologists, which recognizes the unique discipline in which they work. It is known as *The Specialty Guidelines for Forensic Psychologists*.

Source: Brigham, J. C., *Law and Human Behavior*, 23, 273–298, 1999.

the fallibility of memory as well as providing expert testimony in highly publicized trials. He would later become known as the father of forensic psychology. For a comprehensive overview of the critical historical events in the study of law and psychology, see Table 2.2.

Criticisms of Psychology by the Legal System

The spirited advocacy by Munsterberg and other social scientists for psychology's utility in the courtroom drew sharp criticism from the legal system. Legal scholars characterized the use of psychological tenets as an interference and an intrusion into the justice system. The following specific critiques were made (Fulero & Wrightsman, 2009):

- Psychological experiments have no bearing on real life.
- Psychologists often go beyond their empirical findings in order to make judgments.
- Psychologists' activities (e.g., trial consulting) often interfere with the necessary and legitimate activities of the legal system.

Was Freud Right?

Both Freud and Munsterberg made bold statements about the need for psychological science in the courtroom—and the legal system fired back.

14

Now, it's your turn to decide. Examine the following case, keeping both sides of the argument in mind.

On February 11, 1987, the body of 37-year-old Peggy Hettrick was discovered in a field in Colorado. She had been stabbed to death and sexually mutilated with surgical precision. Fifteen-year-old Timothy Masters became a suspect early in the investigation because he had seen the body on his way to school, but had failed to report it to the authorities. During the course of the investigation, police found depictions of violence in sketches and stories created by Masters prior to the murder. They had these analyzed by a board-certified forensic psychologist, who without interviewing Masters, made assumptions about both his motivations and guilt. Dr. Reid Meloy testified that Masters' drawings and writings should be considered a "fantasy rehearsal" for the murder of Peggy Hettrick. He opined that Masters had violent fantasies and deep hostility toward women. He therefore concluded that the teenager fit the profile of a killer (see Figure 2.1).

Let's consider Freud's statement for a moment. Were the investigators in this case influenced by subconscious or unconscious bias? In other words, did they unknowingly allow suppressed preconceptions to determine the extent to which Masters' drawings caused them to focus on him as the primary suspect? What about Dr. Meloy? Did unconscious influence have any bearing on his testimony? Did he go beyond the data and overreach—perhaps based on his own preconscious interpretations of Masters' sketches?

Timothy Masters was convicted largely based upon the testimony of Dr. Meloy, despite the fact that there was no physical evidence linking him to the crime. Investigators found no blood, fiber, hair, skin, or fingerprints in his home, at his school, or at the crime scene to indicate that he was involved in the murder. Masters was exonerated based on DNA evidence in 2008—after spending nearly a decade in prison. Perhaps retired FBI Agent Roy Hazlewood said it best: "Fantasy is not motive" (Perri & Lichtenwald, 2009).

To further understand the endorsements and criticisms of psychologists in and around the courtroom, we must take a closer look at the competing goals and values of psychology and the justice system.

LAWS VERSUS VALUES

Haney states, "Psychology is descriptive and law prescriptive" (as cited in Costanzo & Krauss, 2012, p. 7). This means that psychology seeks to explain how people *actually* behave, while the law tells us how people

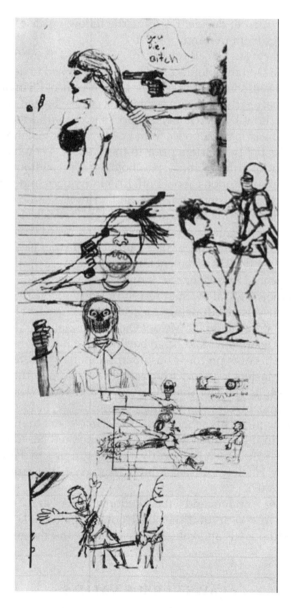

Figure 2.1 Timothy masters' sketches. (Perri, F. S., & Lichtenwald, T. G., *Forensic Examiner,* summer ed., 52–69, 2009. Retrieved from: http://www.all-about-forensic-psychology.com/support-files/criminal-profiling.pdf. With permission.)

should behave. Psychology is mainly focused on accurately describing human behavior and its causes. Conversely, the primary goal of the law is to set specific guidelines and consequences for that behavior. How then are these two disciplines interrelated?

Due to a need to regulate human behavior, we have created laws—or necessary rules by which society must abide. Typically, a law is preceded by troubling behavior that leads to a disagreement that then needs to be resolved by authorities. Instituting a law serves to set a precedent for future incidents.

How do we determine what should be written into law? Very simply, this decision is centered on our values. Values are the standards set by the societal consensus surrounding which behaviors are acceptable and which are unacceptable. Another way to view values is as the standard for decision making. When a society's values change, so does the law (Fulero & Wrightsman, 2009).

For example, prior to the late 1970s, a married man could *legally* force his wife to engage in sexual relations with him under what was codified as the "marital rape exemption." According to the Rape, Abuse, and Incest National Network or RAINN (2009), it was not until 1993 that society viewed consent as necessary for sex between married partners and criminalized spousal rape in every state in the United States.

Another more recent example of society's values igniting change in the law has to do with the expansion of social and mobile media, and minors' access to it. Fearing an increase in "sexting," prosecutors have begun to bring criminal charges against children and teens caught sending indecent pictures of themselves to one another, under the umbrella of child pornography laws. The *Michigan Journal of Law Reform* cites a specific case in 2010, whereby two minors in Indiana, aged 12 and 13, were charged with child exploitation and possession of child pornography for sending each other nude photos.

Hinckley and the Influence of Values

To further illustrate the influence that values have had on our legal system, we need to travel back to 1981 when John Hinckley, Jr. attempted to assassinate former president Ronald Reagan. When he went to trial, Hinckley pleaded NGRI. His defense was predicated on the idea that although he had planned and purposely executed the attack, he was not acting of his own volition. Rather, his actions were the result of severe pathology. Hinckley's attorneys argued that he had developed a delusional preoccupation with the film *Taxi Driver* and its star Jodie Foster. Unable to get Foster's attention despite obsessively stalking her, Hinckley reportedly began to identify with the hero in the film who stalks and shoots the president; he viewed the assassination attempt as a desperate way of ensuring that Foster would notice him. Hinckley's affirmative defense was successful and he was found not guilty by reason of insanity and mandated to a psychiatric institution in June of 1982 (*Cornell Law Review*, 1982). Hinckley was released on August 5, 2016 by order of the court, as it was determined that he no longer posed a threat to himself or others.

As in the McNaughten case, public outrage erupted following the announcement of the verdict in the Hinckley trial. In the firestorm that followed, the insanity defense came under attack. Both the American Psychiatric Association (APA) and the American Bar Association (ABA) fought for more stringent standards by which to determine insanity. Some states decided to abolish the insanity defense entirely, while others adopted a guilty but mentally ill (GBMI) verdict that would result in punishment for the crime in tandem with mental health treatment (Fulero & Wrightsman, 2009). The American Psychological Association (1984) argued for an empirical approach "in which both existing standards and proposals for change would be carefully examined for their scientific merit" (as cited in Rogers, 1987, p. 841).

HOW IS TRUTH DETERMINED?

As you have learned, the aim of psychology is fundamentally different from that of law. This disparity is sharply highlighted when we examine how each discipline arrives at an understanding of the "truth."

Given the APA's response following the Hinckley verdict, it is clear that psychology bases its vision of truth on empirical evidence. Questions about human behavior are answered by collecting data. That data is gathered via observation and experimentation and is then objectively measured.

How does law enforcement determine truth? Have you ever seen investigators on crime dramas say that they are going to "go with their gut?" In general, law enforcement personnel employ intuition and rely on personal observation. Additionally, police are more willing than psychologists to resort to a more extensive array of methods for determining truth. For example, police use a combination of observation, forensics, deduction, intuition, and alternative methodologies such as consulting with psychics in particularly difficult missing persons cases (Fulero & Wrightsman, 2009).

Now let's go into the courtroom. Attorneys, including judges, are thought to rely heavily on both intuition as well as legal precedent in order to arrive at their notion of truth. J. Alexander Tanford (1990) argued that the Supreme Court is inclined to "approve legal rules based on intuitive assumptions about human behavior that research by psychologists has shown to be erroneous" (p. 138). Illustrating this point is the majority decision in *Schall v. Martin* (1984), where the Supreme Court opined, "Judges *can* predict dangerous behavior, no matter what the relevant research says" (Melton, 1987, p. 489).

Aside from relying upon intuition, one could argue that for defense attorneys, the truth is irrelevant as all defendants, despite their guilt or innocence, are entitled to competent legal representation. Because our justice system is adversarial in nature, both the prosecution and the defense zealously advocate for their client (the state or the defendant) before an impartial group of people (the jury). It is then up to the jurors to sort through the evidence and come to a fair decision (the verdict).

Although the adversarial nature of our justice system is meant to find the truth, unfortunately, innocent people *can* be accused, arrested, convicted, and even executed. Historically, police and prosecutors were resistant to the idea of post-conviction DNA testing due to the belief that their investigations yielded accurate results. Now, Conviction Integrity Units are becoming a consistent part of prosecutors' offices around the country in order to appropriately address defendant requests to review convictions on various grounds. Our justice system, while effective, is also flawed. Therefore, it is incumbent upon all criminal justice professionals to strive to reach a thorough understanding of human thoughts, feelings, and behavior, and to apply that knowledge to the legal system.

THE IMPORTANCE OF PSYCHOLOGY IN LAW ENFORCEMENT

You may be asking yourself, "How common is it for law enforcement to utilize psychological principles?" Following are several examples of how understanding various disciplines of psychology can be of assistance to criminal justice professionals.

Did you ever see the TV show *To Catch a Predator*? Imagine that you are part of a sting operation to catch an adult male who has been grooming a 12-year-old girl for sex. The target of your operation chatted with the potential victim online for days—maybe even weeks—before asking her to meet him. Before the perpetrator has a chance to touch the victim (who is of course an undercover officer), you and your team move in and make the arrest. You'd probably be excited—and rightfully so. However, when you interview the suspect, he states that he is not a sex offender, nor is he a pedophile. He never laid a hand on the "girl." So, really, who was he hurting?

A firm grasp of cognitive psychology will help you understand where this person is coming from *and* how to talk with him. Cognitive psychology is the examination of cognition (thinking) and how errors in thinking, called *cognitive distortions*, are related to criminal behavior.

Some other domains that overlap the legal system are clinical, developmental, and social psychology. Clinical psychology deals with the diagnosis of mental illness. With regard to law enforcement, it is important to understand how to safely and effectively approach someone who is suffering from a mental disorder. Developmental psychology encompasses the study of children and adolescents. Have you ever had an interest in joining a gang violence task force? If so, you will need to be well-versed in developmental psychology. Social psychology examines how people act in groups versus how they act individually. Social psychological research pertains to jury decision making, school and workplace violence, and even terrorism.

As you can see, psychology in its many forms can serve to inform police work and the justice system as a whole. Therefore, it is important to blend these cultures. The goal for this text is to incorporate psychology's empirically supported understanding of human behavior with the observation and instinct so skillfully utilized throughout the law enforcement community.

3

Effective Intervention

THE RELATIONSHIP BETWEEN MENTAL DISORDERS AND CRIME

According to the *Diagnostic and Statistical Manual of Mental Disorders*, 5th ed., or DSM-5 (American Psychiatric Association, 2013), the term *mental disorder* is defined as:

> A syndrome characterized by clinically significant disturbance in an individual's cognition, emotion regulation, or behavior that reflects a dysfunction in the psychological, biological, or developmental processes underlying mental functioning. Mental disorders are usually associated with significant distress in social, occupational, or other important activities. An expectable or culturally approved response to a common stressor, such as the death of a loved one, is not a mental disorder. Socially deviant behavior (e.g., political, religious, or sexual) and conflicts that are primarily between the individual and society are not mental disorders unless the deviance or conflict results from a dysfunction in the individual as described above.

The DSM-5 conceptualizes mental disorders as being the product of a dysfunction of internal processes, meaning that an abnormality exists within the individual that affects thought, emotion, or development. This dysfunction most likely results in the afflicted individual experiencing distress and/or difficulty in professional or social arenas. Additionally, in order for something to be considered a disorder, the resulting thoughts, feelings, or behaviors cannot be expected, or culturally appropriate, given the situational stressor(s). For example, depressed mood is a typical or expected response to a traumatic event, such as the death of a loved one, and is therefore not considered a symptom of disorder in this context.

Does the presence of a mental disorder make an individual more likely to commit a crime? What about a violent crime? There is a common belief in our society that criminal behavior, especially bizarre or violent criminal behavior, is committed by people with mental illness. However, as you will learn in this chapter, that is not accurate.

THE CRIMINALIZATION OF MENTAL ILLNESS

There has been some speculation regarding the development of a disturbing trend within the criminal justice system: the incarceration of individuals who would previously have been treated in a psychiatric (or hospital) setting. The result is that our jails and prisons are becoming de facto mental hospitals (Teplin, 1983). According to a 2004 survey conducted by the Treatment Advocacy Center, there are 3 times more individuals diagnosed with severe mental disorders in jail than there are in psychiatric hospitals across the United States. Take a moment to absorb that—and consider its implications. This processing of mentally ill individuals through the justice system has become known as the "criminalization of mental illness."

According to Teplin (1983), police decision making is relevant to the issue of criminalization. She notes that in some cases, law enforcement's ability to resolve mental health calls is restricted due to limited psychological resources—for example, a lack of potential community referrals or even a shortage of available hospital beds in psychiatric facilities can severely limit options for responding officers. Research has revealed that police may therefore be more apt to arrest persons who exhibit symptoms of mental disorder, as these individuals may present as verbally abusive, belligerent, or disrespectful (Bartol & Bartol, 2008). Other times, due to unclear or inconsistent protocols, it is simply easier for police to exert authority and control the situation once an arrest has been made. Officers may, therefore, consider arrest to be a more efficient way to resolve situations involving persons experiencing psychiatric crises.

DEBUNKING MYTHS

In society's collective unconscious, there exists an assumption that symptoms of mental illness are inextricably linked to patterns of criminal behavior, especially when that behavior is bizarre or violent. Jillian Peterson, PhD, explains: "When we hear about crimes committed by people with mental illness, they tend to be headline-making crimes so they get stuck in people's heads. The vast majority of people with mental illness are not violent, not criminal and not dangerous" (American Psychological Association, 2014).

Early studies have shown that mentally disordered individuals—even those who are severely mentally disordered—are no more likely than the general population to commit serious crimes against others (Bartol & Bartol, 2008). However, more recent research has shown that there *is* a relationship between crime and mental illness. For the most part, this association is limited to individuals currently experiencing a serious mental disorder. Those who have been symptomatic in the past but are not currently experiencing symptoms are unlikely to engage in violent behavior.

Research conducted by Peterson, Skeem, Kennealy, Bray, and Zvonkovic (2014) found that 7.5% of crimes committed by people diagnosed with a serious mental disorder were directly related to and correlated with the symptoms of their illness. Of the 429 crimes analyzed in the study, 3% were directly related to symptoms of major depression, 4% to symptoms of schizophrenia spectrum disorders, and 10% to symptoms of bipolar disorder. This study did not find a causal connection between criminal behavior and symptoms of mental disorder over time. In other words, the research did not bear out a finding that individuals with mental illness repeatedly commit crimes as a direct result of psychiatric symptoms. However, the subjects involved in the study did self-report having been motivated to commit crimes for reasons such as poverty, homelessness, and unemployment, which they viewed as unrelated to their diagnoses (Peterson et al., 2014).

As you can see in Table 3.1, society subscribes to a number of myths regarding the relationship between crime and mental illness. One thing to be considered is that specific mental disorders have been identified as being more closely associated with criminal behavior than others (Bartol & Bartol, 2008).

PSYCHOLOGICAL DISORDERS AND ASSOCIATED CRIMINAL BEHAVIOR

Symptoms of mental disorder are exhibited as a continuum of behaviors that range from the fairly innocuous to the extremely dangerous. Bartol and Bartol (2008) provide the following insightful examples to illustrate

Table 3.1   Common Myths about Mental Illness

Myth	Fact
The majority of people with mental disorders are violent.	The majority of psychologically disordered people do NOT engage in violence.
Individuals with mental illness commit violent crimes at a much higher rate than do people who do not suffer from mental illness.	While the research on the statistics is conflicting, the major risk factors for violent criminality are sociodemographic, socioeconomic, and environmental—not psychological (Stuart, 2003).
Male and female psychiatric patients are at the same risk to reoffend following release from hospitalization.	Mentally disordered *males* with a history of at least one violent incident have a high probability of being violent within a year following their release.
A diagnosis of schizophrenia is a precursor to random violence.	When violent, individuals diagnosed with schizophrenia typically hurt family members and are experiencing hallucinations and/or delusions at the time. A diagnosis of substance abuse (with or without the presence of a concurrent mental health diagnosis) appears closely linked to violence (Stuart, 2003).

this behavioral range: If a person walks into a hotel elevator, faces the back wall, and proceeds to stare blankly at it, while other passengers face the front of the elevator, this behavior would be considered strange. However, if upon reaching the desired floor, the elevator opens from the "back" door, then there is a rational explanation: this person is familiar with the operation of this particular elevator. This context normalizes what would otherwise be deemed odd behavior. In the absence of this reasonable explanation, however, this behavior would likely be alarming to the other people on the elevator. Additionally, a clinician might view this behavior as indicative of an anxiety or dissociative disorder, absent this enlightening narrative.

If the same individual walks into the hotel lobby, appearing highly agitated, brandishing a weapon, and states that the hotel employees are Satan's minions and must die, there would be no logical explanation

(Bartol & Bartol, 2008). The latter example of course would be considered irrational and dangerous behavior. In one situation, the behavior initially seems peculiar, but harmless. However, in the second situation, the abnormal behavior creates a highly volatile environment. With that distinction in mind, let's consider the following disorders and their relationship to crime.

SCHIZOPHRENIA SPECTRUM AND PSYCHOTIC DISORDERS

According to the DSM-5 (American Psychiatric Association, 2013), psychotic disorders including schizophrenia are characterized by certain key features: delusions, hallucinations, disorganized thinking/speech, disorganized and/or abnormal psychomotor behavior, and negative symptoms such as diminished emotional expression.

Delusions are fixed beliefs that are not amenable to change, despite evidence to the contrary. They conflict with the generally accepted view of reality. Delusions can be classified as either bizarre, meaning that they are clearly implausible and do not derive from everyday life experiences, or nonbizarre, meaning that they *could* at least be somewhat plausible. An example of a bizarre delusion is that the Central Intelligence Agency (CIA) has implanted microchips in people's brains in order to gain mind control over the human race. A nonbizarre delusion would be suspecting the presence of consistent police surveillance despite a lack of supporting evidence.

Hallucinations are false perceptions that occur without external stimuli. They are sensory experiences that take place without independent stimulation, and can involve any of the five senses. Most often, they manifest as auditory hallucinations (hearing voices). These voices may seem either familiar or unfamiliar to the individual experiencing the hallucination, but they are clearly distinguished from the person's own thoughts. They are just as vivid as externally motivated perceptions, such as listening to the radio or carrying on a lively conversation. When the voices are perceived as giving orders, they are referred to as *command hallucinations*. Although not as common, visual, olfactory, tactile, and gustatory hallucinations can also be experienced.

Overview of Schizophrenia

Clinically, *schizophrenia* involves a distorted sense of reality, inappropriate expression of emotion, and disordered thinking. However, public perception of schizophrenia is that it involves irrational or unpredict-able behavior. Therefore, people more often associate violent and bizarre crimes with schizophrenia than with other psychological disorders. Although early research indicated that people living with schizophrenia were no more likely than the general population to engage in violence, more recent studies suggest that individuals diagnosed with the disorder are more likely than the general public to carry out aggressive and violent acts (Buchanan, Fahy, & Walsh, 2002).

Schizophrenia is diagnosed when, over a significant period of time, an individual exhibits two or more of the key features described at the beginning of this section. At least one of the two symptoms *must* be delu-sions, hallucinations, or disorganized speech, which includes tangential or incoherent speech (American Psychiatric Association, 2013). Although often accompanied by nonbizarre delusions, schizophrenia patients typi-cally experience delusions that are bizarre in nature, such as believing that aliens have invaded their town.

Schizophrenia and Crime

On June 21, 2000, Officer Jeffrey Moritz was shot and killed in Flagstaff, Arizona, after responding to a routine noise complaint. Residents of the upscale neighborhood had reported that a pickup truck was driving up and down the street repeatedly while blaring loud music. While in uni-form and driving a marked police car, Officer Moritz approached the truck. Moments later, he made an emergency radio call that he had been shot.

The shooter, 17-year-old Eric Clark, fled the scene on foot, but was later captured. Clark pleaded not guilty by reason of insanity, stating that at the time of the murder, he had been acting under the delusion that Flagstaff had been inhabited by aliens that could only be stopped by bul-lets (Arrillagaap, 2006; Frederick et al., 2007).

Records indicate that Eric Clark suffered from untreated schizo-phrenia. Months before he shot and killed Officer Moritz, Clark had been arrested for drunk driving and possession of a controlled danger-ous substance after police found LSD in his car. This exemplifies the significant relationship that often exists between schizophrenia and substance abuse. It is not uncommon for individuals with schizophre-nia, as well as other debilitating psychological disorders, to use street drugs and other mind-altering substances to self-medicate. Because schizophrenia impairs judgment and insight, affected individuals have difficulty anticipating the consequences of their actions, including drug use. Research tells us that when a person with schizophrenia abuses alcohol or drugs, his or her risk of engaging in violent behavior increases (Buchanan et al., 2002).

It is possible—and likely probable—that Eric Clark was experiencing command hallucinations at the time he killed Officer Moritz. Another more famous case where command hallucinations resulted in violence is that of serial killer, David Berkowitz, aka Son of Sam. Berkowitz began terrorizing New York City in the summer of 1976. By the time he was captured in 1977, he had slain at least eight victims. Berkowitz claimed that he had been commanded to kill attractive young girls by the voice of a demon that spoke to him through his neighbor's dog.

Although it is rare for people with schizophrenia to kill strangers or commit random acts of violence, such as in the cases of Eric Clark and David Berkowitz, research is beginning to indicate that people afflicted with this disease are possibly at an increased risk of engaging in violent criminal behavior, including homicide (Naudts & Hodgins, 2005). When offenders with a diagnosis of schizophrenia do commit murder, they most often kill relatives or caretakers while actively experiencing psychotic symptoms (Bartol & Bartol, 2008).

When trying to understand the relationship between schizophrenia and crime, it is important to remember that although an individual's behavior may appear bizarre to an outside observer, his or her actions are consistent with his or her own (false) beliefs and perceptions. For example, it is not uncommon for people with schizophrenia to buy multiple locks for their doors or to board up windows. To an observer, this may seem odd, but when we put some context around these behaviors, we see that these individuals often feel extremely paranoid. They may believe that someone or something is trying to harm them, or that their body or mind is being taken over. For example, a rather common tactile hallucination is that there are bugs crawling underneath their skin. Those experiencing this hallucination will sometimes scratch or scrape their skin until they draw blood. Additionally, family members or caretakers may be hurt when trying to intervene in such instances.

When discussing the interaction between law enforcement and individuals with schizophrenia, we must acknowledge that suicide, as a form of violence, is likewise a serious concern for this population (American Psychiatric Association, 2013). Persons with schizophrenia have a higher rate of suicide as compared with the general population. Command hallucinations may direct these individuals to inflict self-harm. Clearly, if someone attempts or threatens suicide, professional help should be sought immediately.

Delusional Disorder

Unlike with schizophrenia, the delusions experienced by persons diagnosed with delusional disorder are considered to be nonbizarre. The DSM-5 classifies them into five subtypes (American Psychiatric Association, 2013):

- *Erotomanic type*: Someone with this delusion believes that someone else, often someone famous or of a higher social status, is in love with him or her. This belief may often lead to stalking or attempting to directly contact the object of the delusional thinking.
- *Grandiose type*: People with this delusion have an overinflated sense of self. They may believe that they possess special talent or insight that others do not (or cannot) appreciate.
- *Jealous type*: The central theme of this delusion is that the afflicted person's spouse or romantic/sexual partner is unfaithful.
- *Persecutory type*: Individuals suffering from this subtype of delusion think that they are being mistreated or that someone is planning to harm them. These beliefs often involve thinking that they are being conspired against, cheated, spied on, followed, poisoned, harassed, and so on. This delusion often results in repeated, unfounded complaints to police.
- *Somatic type*: This type of delusion involves the false belief that the individual has a medical problem and/or a physical disability.

It is essential to recognize that people with delusional disorder tend to function well in society—outside the realm of their delusion, that is. Additionally, not all types of delusions are strongly associated with a risk of violence toward others. According to William Reid, MD, MPH (2005), individuals whose delusions consist of erotomanic, jealous, or persecutory features are at a significantly higher risk of engaging in violent behavior. Of the individuals experiencing these three subtypes of delusions, those who have previously come to the attention of law enforcement appear to be at an even higher risk.

Let's examine erotomanic delusions more closely. Reid (2005) cites an example whereby a woman with no known history of mental health treatment develops a delusional belief that a TV news personality is secretly in love with her. Despite having never met in person, she believes that he is communicating his love to her via signals hidden in his broadcasts. The delusion results in the woman harassing the newscaster's wife, showing up at the TV station, and subsequently being arrested. Following a brief psychiatric hospitalization, she is released and begins to make harassing phone calls to the newscaster's home, despite multiple police contacts and mental health referrals. Ultimately, the newscaster and his family are compelled to move to another city.

When encountering persons with delusion disorder, it is important for law enforcement to keep in mind that these individuals are unlikely to experience their delusion as troublesome during reality testing (e.g., when confronted with proof to the contrary). Most other facets of their life will appear "typical" or "functional." Therefore, police involvement will most often be focused on de-escalating situations specifically related to their delusion.

Think back to Chapter 2 when we discussed John Hinckley, Jr. and his delusional obsession with actress Jodie Foster. You will recall that Hinckley developed an infatuation with her and made an assassination attempt on former president Ronald Reagan in order to gain Foster's affection. In this case, Hinckley's erotomanic delusion took the form of violence toward a third party (see Figure 3.1).

Unlike people with other classifications of delusions, individuals with persecutory-type delusions may actively seek help from law enforcement because they believe that someone is conspiring against them. On February 20, 2003, Avery County sheriff's deputies Hicks and Coffey arrived at the home of Elijah Puckett in response to a "mental patient" call. When they pulled up to the residence, Puckett shot and killed Hicks as he exited the squad car. He then shot Coffey in the face with a shotgun and fled the scene. Despite his injuries, Coffey was able to call for backup; Puckett was later taken into police custody.

Upon further investigation, law enforcement learned that Puckett had shot the deputies with weapons that had previously been seized by the court due to complaints from his family about his psychological instability. Because Puckett's family had refused to testify against him, the weapons had been returned to him by court order only days prior to the shooting. Puckett stated that he had shot the officers because he became afraid when two strangers approached his home.

In the aftermath of the shooting, Puckett's family disclosed that he had been suffering from persecutory delusions. He believed that people, specifically government workers and Federal Bureau of Investigation (FBI) agents, were spying on him. In response to this belief, Puckett put tape over the eyes of a deer's head that hung on his living room wall so

Dear Jodie:

There is a definite possibility that I will be killed in my attempt to get Reagan. It is for this very reason I am writing you this letter now.

As you well know by now I love you very much. Over the past seven months I've left you dozens of poems, letters and love messages in the faint hope that you could develop an interest in me... I know the many messages left at your door and in your mailbox were a nuisance, but I felt that it was the most painless way for me to express my love for you...

Jodie, I would abandon this idea of getting Reagan in a second if I could only win your heart and live out the rest of my life with you... I will admit to you that the reason I'm going ahead with this attempt now is because I just cannot wait any longer to impress you. I've got to do something now to make you understand, in no uncertain terms, that I am doing this for your sake! By sacrificing my freedom and possibly my life, I hope to change your mind about me. This letter is being written only an hour before I leave for the Hilton Hotel. Jodie, I'm asking you to please look into your heart and at least give me the chance, with this historic deed, to gain your respect and love.

I love you forever.

John Hinckley

Figure 3.1 "Dear Jodie": Hinckley's letter to Foster. (From Buss, M., *The dangerous passion: Why jealousy is as necessary as love and sex*, Simon & Schuster, New York, 2000.)

that people could not see into his house to spy on him. He also listened carefully to a police scanner, placed toothpicks over door hinges to alert him of intruders, and lost sleep over his fear that people were trying to alter the deeds of his property (Wood, 2013). As you can see, the effects of persecutory delusions can be significant.

Now, let's consider jealous-type delusions. It is important to clarify that as a feeling, jealousy is a natural part of the human condition. However, jealousy as a delusion is rooted in the fictional yet stringent belief that one's spouse or lover is being unfaithful. Despite this notion not standing up to reality testing, the person experiencing the delusion is likely to become preoccupied with this belief, seek to confirm it, and use even insignificant instances, such as his or her partner's slightly disheveled appearance, as proof of infidelity. Delusional jealousy has been linked to both aggression and hostility. It can manifest as threats of violence against the allegedly unfaithful spouse, acts of domestic violence, or more extreme behavior, such as killing the spouse, or less commonly, murdering the spouse's perceived lover (Silva, Ferrari, Leong, & Penny, 1998).

A study of the correlation between delusional jealousy and violence found that 65% of the individuals in the test sample had threatened to kill their spouses due to alleged infidelity. Of these, 66% subsequently acted out violently against their spouses, suggesting that threats of bodily harm or homicide should be taken seriously by law enforcement as indicators of potential violence. Sixty percent of the overall sample physically harmed their spouses as a result of their delusion. If we extrapolate from this data, we can see that there is a dangerous connection between jealousy-based delusions and the risk of violent crime (Silva et al., 1998).

MOOD DISORDERS

Previously, diagnoses such as bipolar disorder, mania, and depression were collectively classified as affective or mood disorders. The DSM-5 now separates bipolar and related disorders from depressive disorders, thus recognizing bipolar-type diagnoses as a bridge between the diagnostic classes of psychotic and depressive disorders, in terms of symptomology, genetics, and family history (American Psychiatric Association, 2013).

Bipolar Disorders

Bipolar disorders encompass multiple diagnostic labels, including bipolar I and bipolar II. For our purposes, we are going to focus more on the association between symptomology and crime, rather than differential diagnoses.

Bipolar I disorder criteria embody the modern conceptualization of "manic depression." That is, an individual with this disorder will present with episodes of severe mood that fluctuate between mania and depression. A *manic* episode is a period of abnormally and persistently elevated mood (American Psychiatric Association, 2013), during which individuals experience extreme bouts of energy, including sexual energy. Persons in this mood state may appear irritable, impulsive, easily distracted, or extremely goal-directed. Additionally, they may make bad business investments, go on shopping sprees, be excessively talkative, or have floods of creativity. Mania presents specific challenges for law enforcement, as individuals experiencing such episodes often engage in increasingly risky behavior, which can lead to nonviolent crimes such as prostitution, drug use, and shoplifting (Bartol & Bartol, 2008). Because individuals with bipolar disorder are prone to agitation, mania can also lead to impulsivity resulting in aggression and subsequent violence. Aggression born from impulsivity is common in people diagnosed with bipolar disorder; this behavior is a response to a perceived threat (fight or flight). A decrease in the person's ability to control his or her impulses is the underpinning of the increased aggression (Lee, Galynker, Kopeykina, Kim, & Khatun, 2014).

Bipolar II disorder is a milder form of mood elevation, wherein the individual's moods fluctuate between milder episodes of mania, known as *hypomanic episodes*, and periods of (major) depression. *Major depression* is characterized by depressed mood, diminished interest in everyday activities, insomnia or hypersomnia, fatigue, feelings of worthlessness, diminished ability to think or concentrate, indecisiveness, and recurrent thoughts of death or suicide (American Psychiatric Association, 2013).

Research indicates that females are more likely than males to experience *rapid cycling*, or rapid shifting between mania/hypomania and depression. Rapid cycling increases an individual's risk of committing suicide—a crucial element for police to be aware of when responding to a call involving someone with bipolar disorder. Additionally, women with bipolar disorder are more likely to experience *mixed states*, which refers to having both manic and depressive symptoms at the same time. For example, an individual may report experiencing sleeplessness and racing thoughts, while feeling hopeless, irritable, and suicidal. Individuals in this state are prone to agitation that can result in impulsive aggression (Lee et al., 2014).

Depressive Disorders

The category of depressive disorders includes a host of conditions, the common feature of which is the "presence of a sad, empty, or irritable mood, accompanied by somatic and cognitive changes that significantly affect the individual's capacity to function" (American Psychiatric Association, 2013). Arguably the most well known of these disorders is *major depressive disorder*, the hallmark features of which are an extremely depressed mood (i.e., feeling sad, empty, hopeless, worthless) and anhedonia (i.e., losing interest in or having the inability to find pleasure in previously enjoyed activities). Symptoms persist for a period of no less than 2 weeks. As mentioned earlier, other symptoms may include changes in sleeping and eating patterns, difficulty concentrating, fatigue, feelings of unwarranted guilt, and recurrent thoughts of death or suicide.

You may be wondering what the connection is between depression and criminal behavior. Does it perhaps seem counterintuitive that depression would be linked to crime or even violence? Research conducted by Modestin, Hugg, and Ammann (1997) found no *direct* link between major depression and crime. However, episodes of depression *can* involve an intense feeling of dysphoria (i.e., a negative mood state marked by dissatisfaction, restlessness, or anxiety), accompanied by agitation or irritability, which can subsequently increase the risk of violence (Lee et al., 2014). Modestin et al. (1997) described acting on such hostility as "anger attacks"—or intense, inappropriate, and rage-filled outbursts associated with physiological responses such as sweating, flushing, and abnormal heart rate. Anger attacks are also accompanied by an "out of control" feeling. The apathy and hopelessness so inherent to depression combined with this irritability and loss of control may explain why depression likely plays a significant role in violent acts such as mass murder, workplace violence, and "suicide-by-cop," which can be defined as a situation where an offender threatens law enforcement, thus forcing officers to end his or her life by shooting (Bartol & Bartol, 2008).

Research indicates that depression in teens, especially females, is correlated with delinquency (Kovacs, 1996; Obeidallah & Earls, 1999; Teplin, 2000). The logic behind this is that when depressed, people stop caring. They stop caring about what happens to them or to those around them. Additionally, when someone becomes apathetic to this degree, legal consequences cease to be a deterrent to criminal activity. Teenagers who are prone to impulsive behavior by nature become indifferent to matters of personal safety, which may increase their likelihood of engaging in criminal activity and being adjudicated delinquent (Bartol & Bartol, 2008).

One study, conducted by Fazel et al. (2015), did not find a causal connection between depression and crime. Rather, it found an association between depression and criminal conviction. Perhaps this link can be explained through sociological factors such as poverty, unemployment, and early trauma. Another explanation may be that when offenders are depressed, they don't exert much effort toward their own defense—because they just don't care! This indifference plays a role in their criminal conviction.

A discussion of the relationship between depression and criminal behavior would not be complete without referencing *postpartum depression*. The DSM-5 uses a *peripartum onset* specifier, meaning that a depressive episode may begin during pregnancy or in the weeks following childbirth (American Psychiatric Association, 2013):

Peripartum-onset mood episodes can present either with or without psychotic features. Infanticide is most often associated with postpartum psychotic episodes that are characterized by command hallucinations to kill the infant or delusions that the infant is possessed, but psychotic symptoms can also occur in severe postpartum mood episodes without such specific delusions or hallucinations. Postpartum mood (major depressive or manic) episodes with psychotic features appear to occur in from 1 in 500 to 1 in 1000 deliveries and may be more common in primiparous women. (p. 187)

Perhaps the most widely publicized (and tragic) crime attributed to a postpartum depressive episode in recent years was that committed by Andrea Yates. She suffered from postpartum depression with psychotic features. On July 20, 2001, Yates drowned her five children, one by one, in the bathtub of the family's home in Clear Lake, Texas. Following the murders, she called 9-1-1. When police arrived, they discovered one child still floating face down in the bathtub, and the bodies of the other four children laid out on the bed.

According to her attorney, Yates was operating under the delusional belief that she was possessed by the devil and that the mark of Satan was hidden on her head underneath her hair. The only way for her to be free of this burden was to be executed. Additionally, Yates' children had to die so that their souls could be saved.

Andrea Yates was eventually found not guilty by reason of insanity, meaning that due to a mental disease or defect, she was unable to distinguish right from wrong at the time that she committed the murders. She was subsequently remanded to inpatient psychiatric care.

PERSONALITY DISORDERS

Personality disorders represent another category of psychological disturbance that is often associated with criminal activity. The American Psychiatric Association (2013) defines *personality disorder* as "an enduring pattern of inner experience and behavior that deviates markedly from the expectations of the individual's culture, is pervasive, and inflexible, has an onset in adolescence or early adulthood, is stable over time, and leads to distress or impairment."

We can view personality disorders as extreme examples of normal personality traits. For instance, we are all paranoid at times; however, individuals who suffer from paranoid personality disorder exhibit maladaptive and enduring patterns of distrust that significantly impact their ability to function.

Studies have established that personality disorders are overrepresented in forensic populations. That is, there are fewer people in the general population who have been diagnosed with a personality disorder than there are in jails, prisons, and forensic mental health facilities (Fazel & Danesh, 2002). Because these disorders are incurable and pervasive, the very traits that resulted in the initial criminal act often result in reoffense.

The DSM-5 identifies 10 specific personality disorders, which have then been classified into three distinct categories (Clusters A, B, and C) based upon their common characteristics (see Table 3.2). Research indicates that each cluster of personality disorder is associated with different forms of criminal behavior (Davison & Janca, 2012). A clear understanding of the nature of the relationship between these disorders and criminal activity will enhance law enforcement's ability to address criminogenic needs and best utilize risk management procedures.

Research has consistently shown a primary diagnosis of personality disorder to be the most common among individuals convicted of homicide (Shaw et al., 2006). In order to evaluate the relationships among personality disorder subtypes and various forms of criminal behavior, Roberts and Coid (2010) used logistical regression to conduct a meta-analysis of data (self-report, conviction history, and Structured Clinical Interview for Axis II Disorders or SCID-II) collected from 391 prisoners in England and Wales. They found that antisocial personality disorder (ASPD) was strongly correlated with a wide array of criminal offenses, including most violent crimes as well as obstruction of justice, firearms possession, theft, fraud, robbery, and burglary. This information is not surprising given the blatant disregard for and pattern of violating the rights of others that is central to ASPD. Conduct disorder was also strongly related to criminal behavior in all spheres. (For an overview of the trajectory of ASPD through the lifespan, see Table 3.3.)

Roberts and Coid (2010) also found that of the Cluster C disorders, the avoidant classification was most associated with nonviolent offenses such as criminal damage, but not at all related to the commission of firearms charges. This makes sense given the "hands-off" characteristic of this subtype. Dependent personality disorder, on the other hand, was strongly correlated with both firearms offenses as well as violent crime, although it was negatively associated with criminal damage.

Of the Cluster A disorders, paranoid personality disorder was associated with robbery and blackmail, while schizotypal personality disorder was significantly associated with arson, but negatively correlated with

Table 3.2   Personality Disorders by Cluster

Cluster A	
Odd or eccentric behavior	Paranoid personality disorder
	• Characterized by distrust and unwarranted suspicion of others; interpretation of others' intentions as malevolent
	Schizoid personality disorder
	• Lack of interest in/detachment from socialization; limited affective range
	Schizotypal personality disorder
	• Cognitive and perceptual distortions, including "magical thinking;" social deficits
Cluster B	
Dramatic, emotional, or erratic behavior	Antisocial personality disorder
	• Blatant disregard for and violation of the rights of others; lack of remorse; pattern of aggressive, violent, and criminal behavior
	Borderline personality disorder
	• Pervasive pattern of unstable interpersonal relationships; excessive impulsivity
	Histrionic personality disorder
	• History of attention-seeking and dramatic/excessive displays of emotion
	Narcissistic personality disorder
	• Grandiose sense of self; arrogance; need to be admired by others
Cluster C	
Anxious or fearful behavior	Avoidant personality disorder
	• Hypersensitivity to rejection; feelings of inadequacy; shyness in social settings; isolation
	Dependent personality disorder
	• Excessive dependence on others; a constant need to be taken care of; clingy behavior; fear of disapproval and rejection
	Obsessive-compulsive personality disorder
	• Preoccupation with perfectionism and orderliness; rigidity; neglect of social relationships and hobbies due to lack of flexibility

Source: American Psychiatric Association, *Diagnostic and statistical manual of mental disorders,* 5th ed., Washington, DC, 2013.

Table 3.3 Relationship among ODD, CD, and ASPD

Oppositional defiant disorder (ODD)	A childhood disorder characterized by a persistent pattern of acting out (e.g., anger, irritability, defiance, and vindictiveness) against parents and/or other authority figures. Children with this disorder are likely to lose their tempers and refuse to comply with rules at home or at school as they are resistant to being controlled by authority. When a child's diagnosis has progressed from ODD to CD, he or she attempts to control others via intimidating and coercive means.
Conduct disorder (CD)	A childhood and adolescent disorder characterized by disruptive and violent behavior that violates the basic rights of others. Behavior typically involves one of the following: aggression toward people or animals (e.g., bullying, forced sexual activity, physical fights), destruction of property (e.g., vandalism, fire setting), deceitfulness (e.g., shoplifting, breaking and entering), or serious rule violations (e.g., truancy, running away from home for extended periods of time). CD is often considered a precursor to ASPD.
Antisocial personality disorder (ASPD)	An adult disorder (age 18 and up) characterized by the persistent violation of the rights of others. Individuals with ASPD fail to show respect for social norms (such as laws), disregard the safety of themselves and others, behave irresponsibly with regard to work, finances, and other obligations, exhibit irritability, aggression, and impulsivity, engage in deceitful behavior such as lying, stealing, or conning others, and lack remorse for their actions. A diagnosis of ASPD requires the presence of CD in the individual prior to the age of 15.

robbery and blackmail. Finally, schizoid personality disorder was associated with kidnapping, burglary, and theft (Davison & Janca, 2012).

According to Warren and South (2009), there is a link between a diagnosis of borderline personality disorder (BPD) in females and prostitution. One of the central features of BPD is impulsivity, which perhaps explains the promiscuity involved in prostitution. The other hallmark characteristic of this disorder is a definitive pattern of instability in interpersonal relationships. Think of BPD as the "I hate you—I hate you—don't leave me" disorder because afflicted persons tend to have rollercoaster-like relationships—intense and volatile. However, when they are confronted with the (real or imagined) possibility of being abandoned, sufferers become frantic. In terms of their interaction with the criminal justice system, this

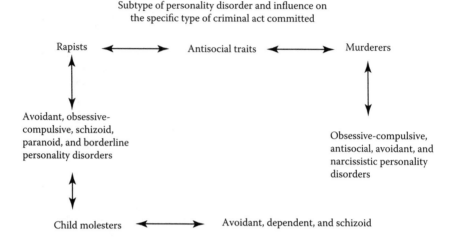

Figure 3.2   Personality disorder subtypes. (From Francia, C. A., et al., *American Journal of Forensic Psychology*, *28*(3), 55–68, 2010; Eher, R. et al., *Z Sexualforsch*, *23*, 23–35, 2010.)

feeling of desperation can result in stalking behavior (Sansone & Sansone, 2010).

Studies demonstrate that personality disorders also play a role in both sexual and violent crimes, and that the subtype of personality disorder appears to influence the specific type of criminal act committed. Research indicates that both rapists and nonsexual offenders (i.e., murderers) exhibit more antisocial traits than sex offenders who molest solely prepubescent children. Contrastingly, child molesters exhibit more avoidant, dependent, and schizoid traits than their nonsexual offending counterparts. Francia et al. (2010) found that nonsexual offenders most often met criteria for obsessive-compulsive, antisocial, avoidant, and narcissistic personality disorders, while sexual offenders were most commonly diagnosed with avoidant, obsessive-compulsive, schizoid, paranoid, and borderline personality disorders. Additionally, rapists had higher rates of Cluster B personality disorders (specifically antisocial and borderline) than did child molesters (Eher, Rettenberger, & Schilling, 2010) (Figure 3.2).

POLICE RESPONSE TO MENTAL ILLNESS

Law enforcement personnel are often the first to respond to mental health emergencies. In fact, as many as 6% of people suspected by police to be involved in criminal activity have been diagnosed with a mental illness (Engel & Silver, 2001; Teplin & Pruett, 1992). Additionally, mental health calls account for between 7% and 10% of all police contacts (Reuland & Margolis, 2003). This percentage increases to nearly 20% when we include individuals experiencing drug- and alcohol-induced psychiatric symptoms (Kaminski, DiGiovanni, & Downs, 2004). Given the frequency of such encounters, it is important to recognize some of the hazards inherent to them:

- When individuals suffering from acute mental illness are not receiving proper treatment, there is an increased risk of injury to both the mentally disordered individual as well as to the responding officer.
- Persons with mental illness may not respond well (or at all) to routine police procedures and/or commands (Engel, Sobol, & Worden, 2000).
- When police lack the requisite knowledge and ability to recognize and de-escalate mental health crises, they may respond with undue force (Ruiz, 1993; Ruiz & Miller, 2004) or fail to provide proper assistance to victims diagnosed with psychological disorders (National Council of State Governments, 2002).
- Using excessive force against someone with a mental illness can significantly damage community relations, as it shakes the public's faith in law enforcement.
- Legal issues can arise when a situation is improperly handled.
- A lack of appropriate resources means that mental health calls can result in the arrest of the person in crisis, thus over-tasking the correctional system. People who have committed relatively minor offenses are jailed while requiring exorbitant amounts of psychiatric care.

In order to ensure the most efficient resolution with the least potential for injury, some police departments have developed protocols for handling mental health calls. Ultimately, these procedures are meant to connect individuals with mental illness, as well as their family members and caretakers, with the appropriate resources, thus enhancing their quality of life and increasing the safety of the community (Watson, Morabito, Draine, & Ottati, 2008).

The New York Police Department (NYPD) argues for safe interactions between law enforcement and "persons in crisis" or "emotionally disturbed persons" (EDPs), as they were previously called:

> EDP calls are difficult as well as frequent ... Most EDP calls turn out to involve people who are neither a danger to themselves or others. Nevertheless police are called to respond to a large number of cases that are dangerous or that, if improperly handled, could quickly become

dangerous. As police, we are responsible for getting such people to mental health professionals, but we also have other responsibilities. We must protect the lives and safety of EDPs as well as the lives and safety of other innocent people, including ourselves. We also have an obligation to protect EDPs' rights and dignity. (As cited in Chappell, 2010)

Use of Force

As you can see, contact with individuals who have mental illness presents a multitude of issues for law enforcement. One such issue is the decision to use force, and more specifically deadly force. It is legally permissible for law enforcement to use reasonable force to impede a dangerous subject. As there is no "shoot-to-wound" mandate, this means that police can legally apply deadly force. This is understandable given the fact that a crisis situation can turn fatal in a matter of seconds. However, this can also be very frightening considering the fact that people with mental illness who require police intervention may lack the capability to either control their actions or to conform their behavior to the requirements of the law. These individuals may have difficulty understanding or adhering to officers' commands and may therefore be viewed as threatening by police.

According to the Office of the Public Advocate—Queensland (2005):

The person with a mental illness will most likely be highly distressed and fearful of his/her own safety, may be experiencing paranoia or delusions involving police, and may have a history of contact with law enforcement. Combined with this is the response of the police officer, an officer who may have received only cursory mental health training, who may be fearful for his/her own safety and that of others on the scene, and who is acutely aware of the potential for violence that exists in dealing with situations involving behavioral disturbance. (p. 1)

Given the volatility of interactions between law enforcement and individuals experiencing psychiatric crises, it is clear why these situations sometimes result in the use of lethal force. In order to decrease fatalities in such scenarios, the use of nonlethal weapons such as tasers (i.e., stun guns) has been suggested. There is general controversy surrounding this topic because of the inconsistent guidelines for use and more importantly, the labeling of tasers as "nonlethal."

According to a study undertaken by the National Institute of Justice (2008), the use of tasers by police personnel has reduced injuries to both officers and suspects, as well as decreased the use of deadly force. However, medical evidence suggests that deaths have occurred in healthy adults, as well as those suffering from heart problems, substance abuse, and mental illness, subsequent to being tased. Researchers have cautioned officers against the use of a conducted energy device (CED) with "at-risk" populations such as pregnant women, older adults, and individuals with physical impairments. Tasers are to be deployed after an officer has thoroughly analyzed the risk of using the weapon, including any apparent health concerns of the target (Taylor et al., 2009). However, more research is warranted regarding the use of these weapons by police in confronting subjects with mental illness (Chappell, 2010).

RECOGNIZING THE SIGNS AND SYMPTOMS OF MENTAL ILLNESS

Because not all police agencies provide mental health training to their officers, many officers' understanding of how mental illness presents or "looks" is based upon a combination of formal education (high school/ college courses), media representation, societal stigmatization, and personal experience. It is important to keep in mind that not all individuals with a mental disease or disorder act and react the same way. Therefore, reflecting on one's own limited and idiosyncratic experience may not be accurate across multiple situations.

Some police departments provide their recruits with a progressive written directive in order to help them recognize some of the common signs of psychological distress that may be encountered in the field. Officers are reminded that it is crucial to their safety and that of the community to be sensitive to and aware of such indicators. While one instance of thought, feeling, or behavior that interferes with an individual's ability to function does not necessarily constitute mental illness, the Anne Arundel County Police Department (2012) considers the following symptoms to be warning signs of mental disorder:

1. Social withdrawal: It sounds self-explanatory, right? If officers encounter someone who appears to be socially removed from his or her family, friends, or normal activities, such as work or hobbies, he or she may be experiencing social withdrawal.
2. Depression: The symptoms of depression that police are trained to recognize match the DSM-5 criteria discussed earlier in this chapter. Individuals may express extreme sadness (hopelessness,

helplessness, pessimism), or a loss of interest in activities that they once enjoyed. They may express suicidal thoughts. Collateral information may also indicate that they have had changes in eating or sleeping patterns (weight gain or loss, fatigue, or insomnia).

3. Disordered thinking or psychosis: When encountering individuals suffering from delusional disorders, police may notice that they appear to be paranoid. Furthermore, these individuals may believe that they are being threatened or harassed. They may use nonsensical or made-up words, repeat words, or speak very slowly or extremely rapidly. They may experience hallucinations and/or delusions and may appear irrational. Even minor problems can be extremely challenging for them to manage.

4. Inappropriate expression of feelings: "Inappropriate" expressions of emotion can take many forms. Police may notice that individuals appear overly hostile or angry, lack emotion entirely, or express emotion inappropriately, such as by laughing at a tragic event.

5. Inappropriate or unusual behavior: Similar to inappropriate emotion, inappropriate or unusual behavior can be exhibited in a variety of ways. Officers may notice hyperactivity (or mania), inactivity, substance abuse, hoarding, hitchhiking, strange or bizarre movements and postures, excessive staring, ritualistic behavior, forgetfulness, wandering, or a lack of attention to personal hygiene and/or appearance.

6. Cognitive impairment: Cognitive impairments are difficulties in cognitive processes, such as thinking, decision making, and remembering. Such impairments may be expressed as confusion or disorientation to time, place, or person. In other words, an individual may not be able to state who he or she is, what year it is, where he or she is, or who the president is. He or she may present with short-term memory loss or paranoia, may get lost in familiar places, or may be unable to feed, wash, or use the rest room unassisted.

Law enforcement may encounter mentally disordered individuals during a wide range of common situations. For example, individuals with cognitive impairments such as dementia may be found wandering, lost, or engaging in bizarre behaviors in public. Officers may come across individuals with mental illness when responding to routine disturbances or acts of aggression. Persons engaging in self-injurious behavior that is symptomatic of mental health issues may also come to the attention of police. Psychologically disordered individuals may additionally be forcibly uncooperative with caregivers or may display socially inappropriate, aggressive, or threatening behavior in public.

Because many of these symptoms exist internally (as they are emotionally or cognitively based), officers will find that gathering collateral information from family, friends, and neighbors can provide them with necessary insight.

In tandem with, or in addition to the symptoms discussed previously, some individuals may have educational or communication limitations. Therefore, simply giving them an order (e.g., "drop the weapon") or reading them their Miranda rights may not be sufficient to ensure comprehension or compliance (Anne Arundel County Police Department, 2012).

INTERVENTION STRATEGIES AND BEST PRACTICES

Several approaches have been developed in order to better equip police to respond to mental health calls. One such approach is the use of crisis intervention teams (CITs) that are based on a model developed by the Memphis Police Department. These teams employ specially trained officers that, regardless of rank, are given the authority to take the lead on mental health calls. After thoroughly assessing the situation, CIT officers determine the appropriate course of action: de-escalation, negotiation, emergency psychiatric assessment/care, or arrest (Cochran, Deane, & Borum, 2000). These officers additionally act as intermediaries between the police department and mental health resources (Borum, Deane, Steadman, & Morrissey, 1998). Because their objective extends far beyond removing and/or incapacitating the individual, CITs are seen as an effective problem-solving methodology (Thompson & Borum, 2006).

A second intervention strategy is the co-responder model. In this approach, mental health practitioners respond to the scene of a police emergency in order to perform immediate mental health evaluations and consult with police on psychological issues. Currently, there are more than 1050 CIT and co-responder programs in use nationwide (Reuland, Schwarzfeld, & Draper, 2009).

Although not all departments have one of the aforementioned programs, many forward-thinking agencies supplement officer training with a set of parameters, outlining how to handle encounters with persons with mental illness, whether they be victims, witnesses, or perpetrators.

Often, these guidelines will include some or all of the following (Anne Arundel County Police Department, 2012):

- Keeping safety in mind, transport the individual to a calm, distraction-free environment. Mental health symptoms can often be triggered (or exacerbated) by sensory experiences, such as bright lights and loud voices.
- Speak calmly, using short direct phrases.
- Use nonthreatening body language and avoid crowding the person.
- Avoid fast, jerky, or big/dramatic movements, as they may be interpreted as threatening.
- Be mindful not to impulsively label odd or eccentric behavior as disobedient or belligerent.
- Allow the individual to take his or her time—do not rush a mentally disordered person. Cognitive impairments can make it difficult for him or her to process information.
- Do not become angry and/or frustrated with the individual.
- Pay attention to nonverbal communication (i.e., gestures, eye movements, etc.), as some people who suffer from mental illness may experience language or communication deficits.
- Contact family, friends, and caretakers for collateral information and for guidance about how to de-escalate the specific individual in crisis.
- Always keep a safe distance.

As you can see, it is essential for law enforcement personnel to receive training about how to properly and safely interact with mentally disordered individuals. It is important to note, however, that such directives do not apply to mass shootings, even when committed by offenders experiencing severe psychiatric disturbance. For example, when faced with incidents such as the Sandy Hook shooting or the Aurora movie theater shooting, law enforcement's priority is not to negotiate, but rather to stop and debilitate the shooter as quickly as possible. This often results in the perpetrator being shot and killed by police. School shootings will be covered in further depth in the chapter on threat assessment.

Emotion and negotiation are part of most police contacts. However, navigating them appropriately becomes critical when it is a mental health call. Harvard University negotiation expert Dr. Daniel Shapiro (as cited in Meyers, 2008), advises that in order to assuage emotional outbursts, negotiators (police in this instance) should:

- Make the individual feel heard and understood. Do not dismiss him or her.
- Strive to make the person feel as though you're on his or her team. In a state of conflict, people have a tendency to feel at odds with other people. Therefore, feeling a connection or sense of collaboration is essential to a successful negotiation.
- Engage the person. In other words, get him or her to invest in and commit to the decision to seek psychological assessment, counseling, and so on. Encourage him or her to feel as though he or she is distinctly *choosing* to play an important role in the resolution of the negotiation.
- Show the person respect.

Dr. Shapiro reminds negotiators that "the key is building some kind of alliance with the challenging person." The most successful negotiators are able to develop and maintain some semblance of personal connection throughout the encounter. Additionally, it is crucial to employ empathy. "If I approach as if we are adversaries, I'm creating a highly reactive situation," says Shapiro. You may be able to diffuse a potentially dangerous situation simply by asking, "How can I help you?" (Meyers, 2008).

Part II
Crimes and Criminals

4

Psychopathy

THE GREAT IMPOSTER

Ferdinand Waldo Demara, Jr. wore many masks. Throughout his life, he borrowed the names, experiences, and credentials of numerous people. He lived as a monk, a teacher, a zoology student, and posed as a variety of high-profile professionals including a religious psychologist, a dean of philosophy, and even a surgeon in the Royal Canadian Navy. His exploits amass some of the most complex and successful identity hoaxes in history. It is the stuff movies are made of—literally. Demara's scams inspired the 1961 film *The Great Imposter* and more recently, Steven Spielberg's *Catch Me If You Can* (Biography.com Editors, 2016a).

Demara began his "career" by forging documents, including transcripts. This led him to assume the identity of religious psychologist Robert L. French, PhD. Using French's credentials, Demara obtained employment as a professor of psychology in Pennsylvania, although he did not stay for long. Before he could be discovered (and likely to *avoid* being discovered) Demara obtained employment elsewhere—first as an orderly in a psychiatric hospital in Los Angeles and then as an instructor at St. Martin's College in Washington State (Biography.com Editors, 2016a).

The Federal Bureau of Investigation soon tracked Demara down and arrested him—although not for identity theft! He served 18 months in prison for desertion after having gone AWOL from the U.S. Navy. Following his release from prison, Demara chose a new identity—and began studying law at Northeastern University. He then shifted gears and joined a Catholic monastery in Maine, where he was known as "Brother John" (Biography.com Editors, 2016a).

While residing at the monastery, Demara became acquainted with a man named Dr. Joseph Cyr. He admired him, observed him, and ultimately targeted him. Demara enlisted with the Royal Canadian Navy as Dr. Joseph Cyr and was shipped out on the naval destroyer *Cayuga* in the midst of the Korean War—as a trauma surgeon. As a result of having studied medical and surgical texts in order to pass himself off as Dr. Cyr, Demara had mastered basic surgical procedures and actually performed several operations, including amputations and a bullet extraction during major chest surgery. Demara was formally and publicly commended for successfully performing lifesaving surgeries on wounded servicemen. This publicity ultimately drew the attention of the real Dr. Joseph Cyr's mother, who alerted authorities that Demara was an imposter. The Royal Canadian Navy did not press charges and Demara got away with it—again (Biography.com Editors, 2016a).

Once returned to the United States by Canadian officials, Demara continued to impersonate people, although he did not opt for such highly visible identities as that of Dr. Cyr. In 1955, Demara gained employment as an assistant warden in a prison and was arrested when an inmate recognized him from a *LIFE* magazine interview he had given (Biography.com Editors, 2016a).

Demara's schemes ultimately led to criminal charges including fraud, forgery, theft, embezzlement, vagrancy, and public drunkenness. Melvin Belli, the attorney who twice defended Demara against accusations of child molestation, which had resulted from his work at a youth camp, said of him, "The strings all ran out on him.... There was no way to channel or exploit his tremendous talents. But I never heard him say he had any regrets about anything" (*New York Times*, 1982).

Ferdinand Waldo Demara is an example of an individual who lived his life without any regard for the rules or laws of society. He was an imposter and a psychopath.

WHAT IS A PSYCHOPATH?

Have you ever used the word psychopath to describe someone? If so, close your eyes right now and picture that person. What qualities did the individual possess that you felt warranted that label? Was he or she sadistic? Selfish? Remorseless? Manipulative? Cunning? Opportunistic? Compare your image to the following scene set by Pozzulo, Bennell, and Forth (2013):

After 19-year-old J.R. dropped out of college, he found employment at a local convenience store. Unsatisfied with his earnings, he devised a plan. J.R.'s 16-year-old friend Shawn had long been complaining about his folks and had previously expressed a desire to "get rid of them." J.R. seized the opportunity, offering to help Shawn kill his parents and collect on their life insurance. The only caveat was that J.R. insisted he be given half of the insurance money. After enlisting the help of another friend who had access to a car, J.R. began to develop a detailed plan to commit murder for profit.

On the night of the killings, J.R. and his two friends went to a nearby strip club where J.R. instigated a fight with the bouncer to ensure that the three teenagers would be remembered and would therefore have an alibi. The boys then proceeded to Shawn's house, armed with a baseball bat and a tire iron. There, Shawn's parents and 14-year-old sister were brutally beaten. As the threesome exited the premises, J.R. doused the first floor of the house with gasoline before setting it ablaze. As a result, two people died and one was critically injured. J.R. and his friends were subsequently arrested, charged, and convicted of murder in the first degree. At his trial, J.R. *proudly* described himself as the "puppet master" and detailed his ability to manipulate his younger friends. He exhibited no remorse for his actions and clearly lacked empathy for his victims.

As you can see, the story of J.R. differs significantly from that of Ferdinand Waldo Demara. However, both individuals share important psychopathic traits. Hare (1993) describes psychopaths as having no regard for the rights or feelings of others and as frequently targeting vulnerable victims to achieve their own goals. Sometimes they charm others in order to exploit them, while other times they use violence to get what they want. The common thread is their lack of conscience.

Psychopathy can be defined as a cluster of interpersonal, affective, and behavioral characteristics. Psychopaths are social predators who engage in a pattern of serious violations of the rights of others in order to meet their own needs or otherwise attain their desires. They employ charm, manipulation, intimidation, and violence to achieve their goals and lack any sense of remorse. They are cold-blooded and those around them are often left feeling betrayed, brokenhearted, and disappointed due to unmet expectations. These individuals comprise approximately 1% of the general population. However, that number is higher—15%–25%—in the prison population (Hare, 2006).

51

In his book *The Mask of Sanity*, Hervey Cleckley (1976), a psychiatrist and a pioneer in the field of psychopathy, identified and described 16 interpersonal and behavioral traits common to psychopaths (see Table 4.1). Currently, The Psychopathy Checklist–Revised (or PCL-R) developed by Robert Hare (Hare, 1991, 2003) is the universal method for assessing psychopathy in adults. It is a 20-item rating scale that is strongly based upon Cleckley's research and utilizes a two-factor model (see Table 4.2).

Factor 1 traits describe the individual's psychological and emotional constitution, and are linked to an inability to benefit from therapy (Seto & Barbaree, 1999). These qualities have also been correlated with premeditated predatory violence, whereas Factor 2 traits appear to be associated with spontaneous and impulsive violence (Hart & Dempster, 1997). Factor 2 characteristics such as impulsivity, poor planning, and excessive need for stimulation, are related to maintaining a deviant and parasitic lifestyle. While Factor 1 is a better overall identifier of psychopathy, Factor 2 is a stronger indicator of general and violent recidivistic behavior (Walters, 2003).

Psychopathy, Antisocial Personality Disorder, and Sociopathy: Similar But Not the Same

Although the terms psychopathy, sociopathy, and antisocial personality disorder (ASPD) are often used interchangeably in the vernacular, their meanings differ. As you've just learned, psychopathy is the persistent violation of the rights of others due to a constellation of affective, interpersonal, and behavioral deficits. Psychopathy includes characteristics such as lack of remorse, inflated self-concept, flat affect, and objectification of others. It does not include positive psychotic symptoms, such as delusions, hallucinations, and irrational thinking. Psychopathic individuals have poor judgment and do not learn by experience. In addition, they are incapable of experiencing the felt emotion of love.

As discussed in Chapter 3, ASPD is categorized as a personality disorder in the DSM-5. Its behavior-oriented criteria consist of a pervasive pattern of disregard for, and violation of, the rights of others. A diagnosis requires at least three of the following: failure to conform to societal norms with respect to the law, deceitfulness, impulsivity, irritability or aggressiveness, reckless disregard for the safety of others, consistent irresponsibility, or lack of remorse (American Psychiatric Association, 2013). Because ASPD is characterized by criminal behavior, with the additional facet of impulsivity or the failure to plan ahead, it follows that a significant

Table 4.1 Cleckley's Primary Psychopathy Profile

Superficial charm and good "intelligence"	The typical psychopath makes a positive first impression—seeming superficially happy, interested, and well-adjusted.
Absence of delusions	He or she does not exhibit psychosis (hallucinations, delusions), or other signs of irrational thinking.
Absence of anxiety	He or she has an absence of "nervousness" or psychoneurosis.
Unreliability	A psychopath disregards obligations both big and small. He or she cannot be regularly relied upon.
Untruthfulness/ insincerity	Although he or she may appear disarmingly straightforward, a psychopath is insincere and dishonest—especially when it suits his or her own purpose(s).
Lack of guilt or remorse	He or she presents with flat affect and has a lack of deep and lasting emotions.
Inadequately motivated antisocial behavior	A psychopath engages in antisocial behavior (cheating, stealing, etc.) for relatively small stakes. In other words, he or she commits crimes such as theft and fraud with no apparent goal (other than for the sake of doing it).
Poor judgment	He or she fails to learn by experience.
Pathological egocentricity and incapacity for love	A psychopath's world revolves totally around him or herself. He or she is unable to feel love and form attachment.
Poverty of affect	He or she exhibits a general sense of flat affect and blunted emotion (in addition to his or her incapacity for love).
Lack of insight	A psychopath lacks the ability to see him or herself (and his or her behavior) as others do.
Unresponsive in interpersonal relations	A psychopath, despite how others treat him or her, cannot be counted upon to show consistent appreciation or empathy, except in superficial and self-serving terms.
Unusual behavior after alcohol consumption	A psychopath may engage in violent, obscene, or bizarre behavior after drinking even only a little bit.
Impersonal sex life	A psychopath gives in to his or her slightest impulse, resulting in numerous and impersonal sexual contacts.
Failure to follow any life plan	A psychopath is unable to consistently pursue a life goal.
Suicide attempts rarely carried out	Suicidal threats made by psychopaths are often empty. Sometimes suicide attempts are made in an effort to manipulate others to their benefit. It is rare that a psychopath will genuinely desire to commit suicide.

Source: Cleckley, H. M., & Cleckley, E. S., *The mask of sanity: An attempt to clarify some issues about the so-called psychopathic personality*, St. Louis, MO: Mosby, 1988.

Table 4.2   Hare's Psychopathy Checklist–Revised (PCL-R)

FACTOR 1	FACTOR 2
Glibness/superficial charm	Proneness to boredom/need for stimulation
Grandiose sense of self	Parasitic lifestyle
Pathological lying	Poor behavioral controls
Cunning/manipulative	Early behavior problems
Lack of remorse or guilt	Lack of realistic goals
Shallow affect	Impulsivity
Callous lack of empathy	Irresponsibility
Promiscuous sexual behavior	Many short-term relationships
Failure to accept responsibility (for one's own actions)	Juvenile delinquency
	Revocation of conditional release
	Criminal versatility

Source: Hare, R. D., et al., *Psychological Assessment: A Journal of Consulting and Clinical Psychology, 2*(3), 338–341, 1990.

portion (a majority) of the prison population receives this diagnosis. It also stands to reason that those with ASPD tend toward violence.

Sociopathy was explained by Lykken (2000) as "genetically normal children whose failure of socialization was due to their being domiciled with an immature, overburdened, unsocialized, or otherwise incompetent parent or parents." Comparison of the aforementioned terminology highlights several similarities and differences among these conditions. Psychopathy maintains a behavioral component, similar to that of ASPD and its focus on criminality. However, unlike ASPD, personality traits are key to identifying psychopathy. Like psychopathy, sociopathy encompasses both personality and behavioral elements. However, it utilizes a strictly environmental perspective to explain its etiology in contrast to the genetic component present in both psychopathy and ASPD. According to Quay (1965), a significant biological component of psychopathy is that psychopaths have an underaroused cerebral cortex, meaning that they are perpetually understimulated (or "half in the bag"). Therefore, in order to feel satisfied, they must engage in more frequent, varied, and extreme forms of excitement than the average person. Otherwise, they will crave more.

Another difference is that ASPD is a formal diagnosis in the DSM-5, whereas sociopathy has been removed from the text. Currently, psychopathy appears in Section III (Emerging Measures and Models) of the DSM-5 as a specifier for antisocial personality disorder (e.g., with psychopathic features). This inclusion represents the APA Board of Trustees' commitment to preserving current clinical practice, while introducing a new approach which conceptualizes personality disorders as impairments in personality functioning and pathological personality traits (American Psychiatric Association, 2013).

Unlike ASPD, both psychopathy and sociopathy have been divided into several subtypes. The heterogeneity among psychopaths, not only in forensic settings but in the community at large, has implications for law enforcement. Recognizing and understanding these individuals—and knowing how to effectively manage encounters with them—will not only make you better at de-escalating dangerous situations, but could save you hours of exhaustion and frustration!

CLASSIFICATIONS OF PSYCHOPATHS

Hare (1970) developed the following schematic for categorizing psychopaths: primary, criminal, secondary, and dyssocial. ***Primary psychopaths*** exhibit the affective and behavioral deficits measurable by the PCL-R. They also have identifiable psychological and biological traits that distinguish them not only from the general population, but also from the majority of the criminal population. Therefore, they are considered "true" psychopaths.

As you know, psychopaths are overrepresented in prisons, with about one quarter of inmates meeting diagnostic criteria for psychopathy. While psychopathy may predispose someone to commit physical or sexual violence, you may be surprised (and disturbed) to learn that most of these individuals are nonviolent. By the same token, most violent people are nonpsychopathic. In fact, due to their extreme levels of manipulativeness, lack of remorse, and ability to make favorable first impressions, many psychopaths find successful careers in entertainment, politics, or even on Wall Street. However, impulsivity, lack of anxiety, and the inability to learn from their mistakes, make psychopaths more likely to engage in recidivistic behavior. Psychopathy is therefore a key component of serial crimes.

Criminal psychopaths are those primary psychopaths who engage in repetitive criminal (antisocial) behavior (Hare, 1970). It is this subtype that we will focus on in this chapter.

The antisocial or violent behavior perpetuated by ***secondary psychopaths*** is due to acute emotional disturbance. These individuals were previously referred to as neurotic delinquents, symptomatic psychopaths, or offenders with emotional disturbance (Hare, 1970).

Dyssocial psychopaths, like criminal psychopaths, engage in aggressive, antisocial activity; however, these actions are the result of learned behavior, as opposed to innate personality traits. The dyssocial psychopath learns antisocial behavior from his or her subculture (e.g., family, gang, etc.) (Hare, 1970).

With regard to the latter two classifications, the term psychopath is misleading, as it bears little resemblance to the personality and behavioral traits (not to mention deficits and motivations) of the primary psychopath. Regardless, both secondary and dyssocial psychopaths are often mislabeled and mistakenly considered criminal psychopaths due to their high recidivism rates.

CRIMINAL PSYCHOPATHS

As previously noted, the term "criminal psychopath" refers to those primary psychopaths who are "dominant, manipulative individuals characterized by an impulsive, risk-taking and antisocial lifestyle, who obtain their greatest thrill from diverse sexual gratification and target diverse victims over time" (Porter et al., 2000, p. 220). These are prolific and highly versatile offenders, whose crimes range from minor infractions such as passing bad checks or theft, to heinous crimes such as serial homicide. As compared with their nonpsychopathic counterparts, criminal psychopaths begin offending at an earlier age and continue their criminal careers longer. They also engage in a more varied and violent array of offenses and are additionally more likely to reoffend violently after they are released from incarceration (Hare, 2003).

- Take John Wayne Gacy for instance. By all accounts, he was a pillar of the community. He had been named Junior Chamber of Commerce "Man of the Year" and was a successful contractor. He donated his time dressing up as "Pogo the Clown" and entertaining at charity functions and children's hospitals. Gacy also murdered 32 young men in cold blood and buried their bodies in the crawl space underneath his house (Cahill, 1987).

Due to the serious and often violent nature of the offenses committed by these individuals, psychopathy is an important construct for anyone involved in the criminal justice system to understand. The ease and cruelty with which psychopaths exact violence has a significant impact not only on the law enforcement community, but on society as a whole (Hare, 1996).

- Consider Gary Tison. While serving a life sentence for the murder of a corrections officer, Tison manipulated prison officials into housing him in a minimum security unit. He then engaged the aid of his sons, whom he had brainwashed, to take the prison by force in order to facilitate his escape. When the group's getaway car got two flat tires, Tison flagged down another driver for help. He subsequently shot and killed the Good Samaritan and his family before stealing their car (Clarke, 1990). The dynamics of this case made it extremely frustrating for police.

Because they "lack a normal sense of ethics and morality, live by their own rules, are prone to use cold-blooded, instrumental intimidation and violence to satisfy their needs, and generally are contemptuous of social norms and the rights of others" (Gretton, McBride, Hare, O'Shaughnessy, & Kumka, 2001, p. 428), criminal psychopaths are considered to be the most violent and persistent of predatory offenders (Hart & Hare, 1997). As a group, their violent crimes, including sexual assault, homicide, and serial offenses, appear to be significantly more sadistic than violent offenses committed by the general population (Holt, Meloy, & Stack, 1999).

- Let's examine the case of small town dentist Kenneth Taylor. After abandoning his first wife, he remarried and subsequently attempted to kill his second wife. He then remarried again and brutally beat his third wife—on their honeymoon—only to kill her a year later. After the murder, he put her body in the trunk of his car and left it there while he calmly visited with his parents. When his crime was discovered, Taylor claimed that he had killed his third wife in self-defense as she had been sexually abusing their infant child (Maas, 1990).

Psychopathy has a significant impact on the nature of homicide. While nonpsychopaths tend to engage in emotionally-driven violence, such as committing murder in the midst of a heated domestic dispute, this is rarely the case with criminal psychopaths (Hare, Hart, & Harpur, 1991). Instead, these offenders engage in instrumental violence. In other words, their actions are predatory and motivated by an identifiable (and selfish) goal. Criminal psychopaths frequently utilize violence as a form of revenge or retribution, and often become violent while drunk. Attacks committed by nonpsychopaths are typically directed toward female victims; however, criminal psychopaths usually target males or stranger victims. Hare et al. (1991) noted that violence committed by psychopaths was callous, unfeeling, and "without the affective coloring that accompanied the violence of nonpsychopaths" (p. 395).

Murders that involve excessive brutality and sadism (i.e., torture) tend to be committed by psychopaths. Research suggests that psychopaths are more likely to derive pleasure from both the sexual and nonsexual suffering of their victims than are their nonpsychopathic counterparts (Porter, Woodsworth, Earle, Drugge, & Boer, 2003).

PSYCHOPATHS AND SEXUAL VIOLENCE

In the late 1970s the "Hillside Strangler" case monopolized the headlines. A dozen women were raped, tortured, and murdered in the Hollywood Hills. Angelo Buono was arrested in connection with the killings after his cousin and accomplice, Kenneth Bianchi, turned him in. During the course of his conversation with investigators, Bianchi confessed to his involvement in the crimes—sort of.

After carefully studying psychological concepts such as dissociative identity disorder (formerly multiple personality disorder) and the use of hypnosis during police investigations, Bianchi voluntarily underwent hypnosis. While supposedly in a hypnotic state, he told detectives that he had multiple personalities and that the murders were committed by his evil "alter" named "Steve" (O'Brien, 1985). Police and psychological experts alike were conned into believing that Bianchi presented with dissociative identity disorder (DID) instead of psychopathy.

The hallmark of psychopathic violence is callous brutality. Acts of psychopathic sexual violence also exhibit this feature. While research indicates that psychopathy is only weakly correlated with sexual offending in general, it is, however, strongly associated with repetitive (serial) sexual offenses, violent and sadistic sex crimes, and sexual homicide (Brown & Forth, 1997; Porter et al., 2000).

Consider the brutality with which Bianchi raped, tortured, and killed his victims. There is no doubt that these were sexual homicides. Also consider that Bianchi turned his partner (his own cousin) into the police and then developed an elaborate ruse with which to fool investigators and psychologists.

This begs the questions: What motivated him? Was Bianchi afraid of getting caught? Was he suffering from mental illness? Or did he perhaps simply enjoy killing and manipulating the authorities? What do you think? Do you believe Kenneth Bianchi met criteria for psychopathy?

Let's dig a bit deeper. Research reflects that the specific type of sex crime reveals information about the perpetrator's level of psychopathy. For example, it is generally believed that individuals who commit **sexual homicide** (murder with a sexual component) are the most psychopathic, followed by those who offend against both adults and children, followed by adult-target rapists. The lowest psychopathy scores tend to be found among child molesters (i.e., individuals with *only* child victims) (Brown & Forth, 1997; Firestone, Bradford, Greenberg, & Larose, 1998; Porter et al., 2000; Quinsey, Rice, & Harris, 1995).

The acts of psychopathic sexual offenders are likely to be more brutal and unconventional than those of other sex offenders and appear to be motivated by thrill seeking rather than arousal. Additionally, psychopathic sex offenders commit more diverse and severe forms of sexual homicide (Firestone et al., 1998; Porter et al., 2003).

FEMALE PSYCHOPATHS

While the vast majority of psychopathy research focuses on males, evidence suggests that there are female psychopaths in both the general and criminal justice populations. They are not as numerous as their male counterparts and their behavioral patterns differ from those of male psychopaths (Hare, 1991). Mulder, Wells, Joyce, and Bushnell (1994) found that these females are less aggressive and commit less violent acts than psychopathic males. Additional research suggests that female psychopaths fall into two broad categories. The hallmark features of the first group include a lack of empathic concern for others, use of deception in interpersonal relations, sensation seeking, and proneness to boredom. The second category is defined by early behavioral problems, promiscuity, and adult antisocial (although not violent) behavior (Salekin, Rogers, & Sewell, 1997). While male psychopaths exhibit physical violence, females are more likely to engage in relational aggression (Carroll et al., 2010; Crick, 1995). For example, a female may spread rumors, or attack someone verbally or via social networking.

Not only are the behavioral indicators of psychopathy expressed differently in women than they are in men, but the motivations among the sexes may also differ. For instance, manipulation is often expressed as flirting in women, while in men this frequently translates to the commission of fraud. Unlike in men, where the interpersonal markers of psychopathy are characterized by charm and a grandiose self-image (Rogstad & Rogers, 2008), behaviors, such as promiscuity in female psychopaths, may be reflective of an attempt to gain financial wealth or social status (Thornton & Blud, 2007). A recent study conducted by Harenski, Edwards, Harenski, and Kiehl (2014) confirms that both male and female psychopaths are unable to process human emotional information. It also suggests that the brains of female psychopaths process moral judgment information differently than do those of psychopathic males.

Despite the empirically supported correlation between violence and psychopathy, relatively little is known about the impact of psychopathy on women who commit predatory homicide (Arrigo & Griffin, 2004).

Aileen Wuornos

Aileen Wuornos is widely considered the first predatory female serial killer (Ahern, 2001). Wuornos was convicted of killing seven men and was subsequently executed at the Broward Correctional Institution in Florida on October 9, 2002.

Aileen Wuornos was born on February 29, 1956. Until she was 11 years old, she believed that her maternal grandparents were actually her parents. After being abandoned by their mother, she and her biological brother were adopted by their grandparents. Wuornos reported that she and her brother Keith were treated differently than their grandparents' other children. Wuornos described extreme bouts of cruel emotional and violent physical abuse at the hands of her grandfather. She reported having been forced to lie face down and naked while he beat her repeatedly with a belt (Ahearn, 2001). Wuornos also described being sexually assaulted by her grandfather, and friends of Keith recalled witnessing the siblings engaging in incestuous behavior.

By the time that she reached adolescence, Wuornos' temper was highly volatile. She had angry and violent outbursts that were often unprovoked, and therefore unpredictable. She did not socialize well with her peers and engaged in sexual acts with boys in exchange for money and cigarettes. She became a social outcast. As Russell (1992) remarked, "this little girl learned how to disassociate herself from her body; to blank off emotions" (p. 13).

As an adult, Wuornos' aggression increased—especially toward men. When she was aged 20, she married a man, 50 years her senior. During the course of their brief union, Wuornos' impulsivity was exhibited as heavy drinking, staying out all night, and spending exorbitant amounts of money. One month following their nuptials, Wuornos' husband filed a restraining order against her for beating him with his own cane; he subsequently filed for divorce (Russell, 1992). After the divorce was final-ized, Wuornos accrued a string of arrests for assault and battery, disor-derly conduct, driving under the influence, and various weapons offenses (Ahearn, 2001).

Following her release from prison (for an armed convenience store rob-bery), Wuornos' criminal behavior escalated. She was subsequently arrested for forging bad checks and driving a stolen vehicle. She also reported pros-tituting herself sometimes more than 25 times on any given day. It was around this time that Wuornos met Tyria (Ty) Moore, with whom she became romantically and sexually involved. During her relationship with Moore, violence, prostitution, transience, excessive drinking, and grandiosity were an integral part of Wuornos' life. The couple's courtship lasted throughout the duration of Wuornos' killing rampage (Arrigo & Griffin, 2004).

Wuornos began killing when she was in her 30s. Her kills all fol-lowed the same pattern: she would linger along the highway and wait for a male passerby to offer her a ride. Once inside the vehicle, she would openly admit to being a prostitute and needing to make money. After she convinced the man to engage her services, the two would drive to a secluded area, where Wuornos would undress and discuss pricing. She would engage in minimal sexual behavior until she could convince her victim to undress. While the target disrobed, Wuornos would exit the pas-senger side of the vehicle, and shoot him, while often yelling, "I knew you were going to rape me!" (Russell, 1992, p. 149). Sometimes Wuornos would fire multiple shots before watching her victim die. She would then put her clothes back on, steal the victim's personal effects, drive off in the deceased's vehicle, and celebrate by drinking a beer before returning home to her girlfriend (Arrigo & Griffin, 2004).

After her arrest for the murders, Wuornos told investigators varying versions of the offenses. In an interview prior to her execution she stated, "I gotta come clean that I killed those seven men in first degree murder and robbery. As they said, they had it right: Serial killer. Not so much like thrill kill. I was into the robbin' biz." Wuornos justified her kills as neces-sary to "eliminate a witness." Under questioning regarding her motiva-tion, Wuornos admitted, "I pretty much had them (the victims) selected that they were gonna die ... there was no self-defense" (Broomfield & Churchill, 2003).

As you can see from this case example, Aileen Wuornos' crimes were committed in cold blood. During her interview with Court TV (as cited in Arrigo & Griffin, 2004), she admitted to having felt powerless when confronted with physically and sexually abusive males throughout the course of her life. This sense that she lacked power and control mani-fested in acts of preemptive predatory violence. Her attitude significantly shifted after she killed her first victim—and did not experience remorse. Wuornos' psychopathic personality features in tandem with her violent fantasies propelled her forward. Her crimes were rational, planned, and goal-oriented. In other words, Aileen Wuornos' perception of her victims (as potential rapists) allowed her to objectify, dehumanize, murder, rob, and discard them without regret (Meloy, 1992).

PSYCHOPATHS AND LAW ENFORCEMENT

Have you ever met someone who made your hair stand on end—but you couldn't quite put your finger on the reason why? According to Meloy and Meloy (2002), it is not uncommon for people to experience a visceral reaction upon encountering a psychopath. The researchers explain this physical response as the body's way of warning against falling prey to the psychopath's predatory nature. It is this predacious trait of the psy-chopath that poses a very serious—and dangerous—challenge to those who work within the law enforcement community and judicial system including patrol officers, investigators, attorneys, judges, correctional staff, clinicians, and parole and probation officers. As much as 25% of the prison population is psychopathic; it stands to reason, therefore, that law enforcement personnel *will* have face-to-face interactions with these indi-viduals throughout their careers.

While most officers and investigators rely on their ability to read both situational and emotional cues in the field, it is important not to make assumptions based upon intuition alone. When dealing with a psycho-pathic suspect, it can be dangerous to assume that he or she thinks and feels as you do. Such an assumption can result in your becoming the tar-get of the suspect's manipulation (Hare, 2012). It is imperative for law enforcement to be mindful of the fact that psychopaths are highly skilled in the art of deception; they are master manipulators who exploit oth-ers' weaknesses for their own personal gain. Dr. Reid Meloy (1992) warns, "Psychopaths can be adept at imitating emotions that they believe will mitigate their punishment."

As you learned earlier, psychopaths engage in cold-blooded and cal-culated violence. According to the FBI (1992), they comprise nearly half of the group of individuals responsible for killing police officers in the line of duty. Therefore, misconceptions about psychopaths on the part of law enforcement can lead to significant—and sometimes fatal—mistakes. While officers should not be clinically diagnosing psychopathy, it is important that they be equipped to recognize psychopathic personality traits in order to determine and implement appropriate strategies and tactical approaches. This information becomes crucial throughout criminal investigations, interrogations, hostage negotiations, undercover assignments, and so on. Before we delve into effective methods for interviewing an individual with psychopathic traits, let's review what we know about this population (Federal Bureau of Investigation, 2012):

- Psychopathy is a cluster of enduring personality traits that include: glib and superficial charm, impulsivity, lack of remorse, lack of empathy, shallow affect, irresponsibility, stimulation seeking, lying, manipulation, parasitic lifestyle, and criminal versatility.
- BOTH men and women can be psychopathic. However, statistically there are more male psychopaths than there are female ones.
- Psychopathy does not discriminate among race, culture, or socioeconomic status.
- Although some psychopathic individuals are quite intelligent, others have below-average intelligence.
- Psychopaths come from both single- and two-parent households.
- They may be married and/or have children.
- Psychopaths DO know the difference between right and wrong; they simply disregard rules and laws in order to suit their own needs.
- Psychosis (delusions/hallucinations) is not a symptom of psychopathy. Therefore, psychopaths are *not* out of touch with reality. If they are psychotic, it is a symptom of a separate mental illness, or due to substance use/abuse.
- Psychopathy is incurable.

Recognizing Psychopathic Suspects

Picture yourself sitting face-to-face with a man suspected of stabbing his wife to death in the middle of a violent domestic dispute. It is your job to interrogate him and ultimately obtain a confession or other information of evidentiary value. How would you approach him? Perhaps you would say, "Think about your wife's parents—and how much they're hurting. They need closure." Or maybe you would prefer, "You'll feel better once you get this off your chest."

Now imagine that the person sitting across from you is a serial killer. He has terrorized the community by committing acts of unspeakable brutality—and you suspect that he is psychopathic. How would you proceed? Do you think the same types of questions mentioned in the previous scenario would be effective? What behavior do you think the suspect would exhibit?

Quayle (2008), a former police officer in the United Kingdom, provides the following information regarding how psychopathic suspects are likely to present during an interrogation:

- They may try to engage in a game of cat and mouse. In other words, these suspects may try to outsmart the interrogator in order to "win."
- Psychopathic subjects may attempt to control the interrogation. Rather than answering the questions asked, they will attempt to "turn the tables" and interrogate the interrogator.
- These individuals may enjoy being the central focus and may act as though they are in the midst of a press conference, rather than an interrogation.
- They may say things for shock value. Psychopaths may explain matter-of-factly the gruesome details with which they behaved in the past. For example, they may calmly discuss anything from having tortured small animals to having killed, dismembered, and cannibalized human victims.
- They will likely not be fooled by bluffs. Since psychopaths are professional con artists, they can easily see through an interrogator's strategies.

As you can see, it is crucial for law enforcement to recognize and consider whether a suspect exhibits psychopathic personality traits in order to formulate an appropriate interview strategy. Ultimately, the goal of an interview or interrogation is to acquire a confession or other valuable (i.e., truthful) information. When faced with a psychopathic suspect who is unwilling to confess, investigators must adjust both their overall goal(s) for the interview and their strategies, implementing alternative techniques. Failing to acclimate appropriately can result in an interview that yields little or no worthwhile information. To illustrate, let's examine the case of Christopher Porco. The investigator's failure to adapt to the suspect's psychopathic personality yielded neither a confession nor any useful information (Perri, 2011).

CHRISTOPHER PORCO HOMICIDE INVESTIGATION

Christopher Porco had a history of engaging in deceitful behavior, such as falsifying his college transcripts (Karlin, 2006), burglarizing his parents' home, lying about his own personal wealth, and fraudulently obtaining loans by listing his parents as cosignatories without their consent. When his parents found out, they confronted him and threatened to take legal action (Perri, 2011).

During the early morning hours of November 15, 2004, 21-year-old Christopher Porco entered his parents' home in Delmar, New York, and attacked them with an ax as they slept. His father was killed, and his mother Joan Porco was so brutally assaulted that she lost a portion of her skull as well as her left eye, leaving her severely disfigured (Perri & Lichtenwald, 2007). Shortly before losing consciousness, Joan Porco identified her son Christopher as the perpetrator. However, after emerging from a medically induced coma, she asserted that her son was not responsible for the murder of her husband or the attempt on her own life, and begged police to find the real killer (Perri & Licthenwald, 2008).

The Interview

Investigators often attempt to affect suspects emotionally by pressuring them, asking numerous questions, or overwhelming them. Under these conditions, nonpsychopathic killers often exhibit remorse and extreme emotion prior to breaking down and confessing. However, in the case of Christopher Porco, you will see that this approach was ineffective and resulted in important information not being gathered. As you read through the interview that follows, consider the tactics employed by the investigator (Perri, 2011, p. 49):

Detective: Listen to me. It's not—it's not—it's a crime of passion, okay? Like an emotional thing. You know, that's what it is.

Porco: That's not the (inaudible)—

Detective: An emotional flare up or something, you know, maybe. That's what I'm looking for. Give me something to grasp here. Let me get through the night.

Porco: Nothing happened.

Detective: And you understand what I've been telling you, that this is not a robbery. This is a crime of emotions.

Porco: I know what you are telling me. I—I don't know. I have absolutely no idea.

Detective: I mean, like I told you, in my estimation, that situation, the way I'm seeing it, was something that happened out of a passionate moment.

Porco: You told me they were in bed, so I don't know how passionate that could be, honestly.

Detective: And then afterwards, those emotions subside and the thought is, what's happened? What have I done? What has happened here? What an awful thing.

Porco: I agree it's an awful thing.

Detective: Sometimes your emotions get the best of you, overtake you.

Porco: True.

Detective: Your stomach is going to burn a hole in it. The only way to stop it is to be a man.

Porco: I can't help you.

As the investigator attempted to manipulate Porco's emotions in order to elicit a confession, Porco's responses grew flatter; his answers were absent appropriate affect (Quayle, 2008). Porco's statements did not offer insight into the crime itself, nor was he affected by the detective's attempt to make him feel remorseful. Rather than implementing an emotional strategy, the investigator should have mirrored Porco's calm demeanor. When Porco's responses contradicted the evidence, the investigator should have calmly and directly confronted him regarding each inconsistency. This tactic would likely have induced Porco to tell more lies in order to explain away the discrepancies. The multiple contradictions in his story could then have been used at trial (Perri, 2011).

The interviewer incorrectly assumed that Porco's crime had been motivated by emotion. Because the murder was committed in a horrific manner, investigators believed that an excessive amount of rage provoked the killing. They failed to view the crime as instrumental—a solution to a problem. Porco's parents were going to disclose his fraudulent activities. He killed them to avoid detection (Perri, 2011). Because psychopaths do not experience a state of heightened emotional arousal when they commit a crime, as would nonpsychopathic individuals, heated emotional outbursts (i.e., jealousy, rage, etc.) do not precipitate their offenses. Therefore, one cannot assume that they have acted out of anger (Woodworth & Porter, 2002). Law enforcement officers should avoid projecting their own emotions about the disturbing nature of a crime onto a suspect (Quayle, 2008).

The lack of emotion inherent to psychopathic violence is additionally germane to post-offense behavior. In the wake of an offense (including during an interrogation), psychopaths are not likely to be distraught, fearful, or confused (Hakkanen-Nyholm & Hare, 2009). They will not exhibit remorse. It is extremely important for law enforcement to understand the implications of post-offense behavior when considering whether or not a suspect displays psychopathic tendencies. As we continue to dissect the Porco interview, it will become evident that Christopher Porco was not traumatized by the news of his parents' attack, nor did he display the range of emotions one might expect under the circumstances. Instead, he remained in control, never wept, and focused on learning what information police had that could incriminate him (Perri & Lichtenwald, 2008).

About halfway through the interview, another detective was brought in to speak with Porco. He was calm and matter-of-fact, and addressed Porco's history of lying. In the following passage, you will see that the second interviewer did not employ emotional tactics (Perri, 2011, p. 50):

Detective: I'm still not quite understanding why you go around telling people that you have all this money. That kind of baffles me.
Porco: No, I—
Detective:—you put on this façade.
Porco: It is. And I've done it for a couple of years now.
Detective: What does that say about your character—
Porco: Exactly.
Detective:—Chris? Seriously. What—no tell me, what does it say about your character?
Porco: I guess it's insecurity in a way.
Detective: Does it tell you that you're an honest person?
Porco: Not in that respect, no.
Detective: Trustworthy?
Porco: I think of myself as trustworthy, I guess. If we're going to respond in reference to this, no, I guess I'm not.
Detective: I mean, if I—if I'm a student and I meet you and you're telling me you're going to buy a house because you've got millions of dollars from your grandmother.
Porco: True.
Detective: You're basically lying to these people, right?
Porco: Well, it kind of steamrolled away.
Detective: No, let's not color code it.
Porco: I know it's wrong.
Detective: Do you consider it lying?

Porco: Oh, definitely, yeah. You know, I'm telling them something that's not really true.
Detective: Are you a pathological liar?
Porco: I don't think so. I mean, maybe in that respect.
Detective: What other things have you lied about?
Porco: Really one thing. I'm trying to think of anything else. Just money. I don't really know why I got started on it. It was in high school.

As you can see, this non-confrontational approach urged Porco to admit that he had a history of lying. However, because the investigator was not well-versed in fraud detection as a motive for murder, useful information about the details of the crime was not obtained (Brody & Kiehl, 2010). As you've probably noticed, Porco's behavior was reflective of psychopathy and should have alerted investigators to implement a non-traditional interview strategy (Perri, 2011).

GARY RIDGWAY: THE GREEN RIVER KILLER

Much like Christopher Porco, Gary Leon Ridgway's criminal activity and post-offense behavior indicated psychopathy. Ridgway, also known as the "Green River Killer," is considered one of the most prolific serial killers in history. He murdered dozens of women and teenage girls—most of whom were prostitutes or runaway youth. He strangled most of his victims with his bare hands, and then disposed of their bodies in the woods of King County, Washington. He would later return to the burial sites and have sexual intercourse with the corpses. Ridgway pleaded guilty to 48 counts of first degree murder, although some accounts speculate that he may be responsible for nearly twice that many deaths (Biography.com Editors, 2016b).

Unlike the unsuccessful interview of Christopher Porco, the Ridgway interview yielded useful results. Ridgway calmly described the murders and even went so far as to lead investigators to the bodies of several of his victims. Although he made statements like, "I feel bad for the victims," Ridgway lacked genuine remorse and empathic concern as evidenced by the fact that he denigrated and objectified his victims when he spoke about them. Because the investigators employed appropriate strategies that targeted psychopathic traits and used them as tools to elicit information, Ridgway spent approximately six months detailing his sexual homicides for investigators (O'Toole, Logan, & Smith, 2012).

Since many psychopaths are inherently narcissistic and grandiose, they have a tendency to want to brag or extol their exploits to some extent. In one discussion with Gary Ridgway, the interviewer used these qualities to her advantage. By calmly and steadily playing into Ridgway's feeling of superiority and enjoyment of cat-and-mouse games, she garnered valuable information about how he went about hunting and trapping his victims ("Interview with the Green River Killer"):

Interviewer: It sounds to me like you had a series of ruses ... that you'd use to make you appear normal to some of these women .... Explain that process to me.

Ridgway: They would get in the car.

Interviewer: She's already in the car?

Ridgway: Mmmhmm. She's already in the car. We're driving down the road and first she wants to see my ID. So I whip out my ID and ... I'd have my finger over my driver's license to hide my name. And on the opposite side was pictures—and a picture of my son. And they would see my son and know I was a fairly normal person.

Interviewer: But you were really using your son as part of your ruse.

Ridgway: At the time, I didn't want a picture of my ex-wife there, so I had a picture of my son.

Interviewer: Sure, you had to make it sound good.

Ridgway: ... So, every time I opened up my wallet, there'd be a picture of my son ... and that'd lower any big defenses. And kids' toys. 8-year-olds' toys on the dash.

Interviewer: The only thing that would be better than that would be to have your son in the car with you. That would be an incredible ruse.

Ridgway: That happened once.

Interviewer: What happened?

Ridgway: It was July 18th ... I picked up a woman on a back highway. And Matthew was next to me in the seat and she hopped in. I took her over to the South Airport Area. And I took her into an area and my son was there and I killed her. I'm real sure my son didn't see it. But that only happened one time.

Interviewer: But that was a pretty good ruse, so why didn't you do it again?

Ridgway: I didn't want my son to see that happen again 'cause I was really killing a lot of them. And another thing—it never came to the opportunity again to do it.

PSYCHOPATHY AS A BRAIN DYSFUNCTION

After the two interviews you've just read, you are probably envisioning psychopaths as purely evil individuals who purposefully and willingly choose to commit abhorrent crimes. How does this make you feel? Does it disgust or disturb you? Scare you? Make you angry? How might these feelings influence your interactions with psychopathic suspects? It is important for police to be tuned into their own feelings (such as a dislike for the psychopathic personality) in order to prevent personal bias from interfering with the use of appropriate strategies.

New research by Dr. Kent Kiehl (2015) may help investigators mini- mize their frustration when encountering psychopaths, and also better understand why such suspects need to be addressed differently than their nonpsychopathic counterparts. According to Kiehl, psychopaths have a brain deficit that causes them to think differently and which could qualify as a severe mental illness. This dysfunction affects their ability to regulate attention, motivation, self-control, and emotion. Kiehl explains: "I liken it (psychopathy) to an emotional disorder with an adjunctive impulsivity problem. With those two facets, in conjunction with the right environ- ment, psychopaths develop an unstable lifestyle that often leads to crimi- nal behavior."

Therefore, expecting a psychopath to control his or her behavior and then feel remorse for engaging in harmful acts is like asking someone with narcolepsy to control when he or she falls asleep (Ramsland, 2014). The take away message? Investigators should be mindful of their own emotions and not resort to "turning up the heat" on psychopathic sus- pects when they themselves become frustrated. Emotional ploys will not work with psychopaths because emotionality is literally a language that psychopaths cannot process nor understand.

INTERVIEWING PSYCHOPATHS: BEST PRACTICES

So far, you've learned the importance of remaining calm and directly confronting psychopathic suspects on inconsistencies in their stories. Dr. Dorothy McCoy (2005) offers further insight into how to navigate an inter- view with a psychopath once you've identified him or her as such. McCoy encourages investigators to use body language and facial expressions that convey understanding in order to build rapport and relax the subject from the very beginning of the interview. Remember that psychopaths are cunning and adept at outsmarting others. Therefore, the interviewer should be exceedingly familiar with every facet of the case in order to combat the psychopath's deceitful and evasive nature (Quayle, 2008).

Avoid reacting emotionally and always remain professional and in control. Interviewers should command authority and convey experience from the outset (Quayle, 2008). Avoid fidgeting and appearing uncertain, insecure, or nervous even prior to the interview commencing, as a psychopath will view this as weakness. Keeping in mind that psychopaths strive to be the center of attention, ask open-ended questions that allow them to talk. Psychopaths derive pleasure from trying to shock other people and may verbally attack if they feel cornered (McCoy, 2005). Therefore, avoid expressing emotion as psychopathic subjects will use such disclosure to manipulate you (Quayle, 2008).

Quayle (2008) also suggests avoiding criticism, as this may lead a psychopath to become hostile and end the interview prematurely. In the Ridgway interview, you can see that the examiner not only avoided disparaging remarks, but she also played into Ridgway's ego by emphasizing his unique ability to develop a clever ruse. She acted as though she was interested in learning from Ridgway, and then created the opportunity for him to brag. Psychopaths enjoy being complimented and treated as though they are important. Therefore, asking them for their opinion may prompt them to give evidence or even confess (perhaps in the third person). Keep them talking and ask them questions that appeal to their ego such as "Can you help me figure this out?" Remember, even the slightest reproach could derail the interview (McCoy, 2005).

Avoid confronting psychopaths about the seriousness or heinous nature of their crime(s)—they do not care. Likewise, threatening them with consequences such as serving time in prison will have little impact on their decisions. Psychopaths set unrealistic goals and typically believe that they will be able to escape punishment. Because they develop a pattern of avoiding responsibility for their actions, they will minimize the severity of their behavior and/or their involvement in the crime for which they are being questioned. In order to connect with a psychopathic suspect and facilitate disclosure of offense details, investigators should minimize the crime, the behavior, the suspect's involvement in the offense, or the extent of the damage (McCoy, 2005). This will diametrically contradict the normal inclination and instincts of an investigator but is important in order to make headway and elicit information from a psychopathic interviewee.

When interviewing a psychopath, investigators should expect the subject to present as charming and charismatic. He or she will feign emotion and concern when it is in his or her own best interest. Investigators should be aware of feeling as though the suspect is likable and believable. Once a psychopathic suspect perceives that his or her charm is not working, it will quickly dissipate and be replaced by aggression. Interviewers should additionally expect the suspect to attempt to turn the tables on them and hijack the interview. The subject may attempt to raise irrelevant issues or control the flow of the interview. Investigators should be aware that they may be dealing with a psychopath if they feel as though they have become the interviewee. In order to refocus the discussion, investigators could say, "You raise an important point that I had not thought of, but right now I want to get back to talking about the crime" (McCoy, 2005).

Remember, psychopaths are social predators who view others as prey. Because they will use whatever they can to their advantage (emotion, circumstance, etc.), traditional interview and interrogation strategies are inadequate. In order to conduct effective and successful interviews, investigators should remain vigilant and flexible.

5

Understanding Homicide

THE HISTORY OF HOMICIDE

From Ancient Rome to present day, society has overwhelmingly shown an interest in violence—and specifically homicidal violence. News media, TV shows, and box office successes all attest to the fact that Western civilization has a love of the macabre, making murder an intriguing and marketable subject. This enduring preoccupation highlights the existence of a sort of symbiotic relationship between murder and the media: murder inspires Hollywood and the news media and, in some cases, media has been the catalyst for certain murders (e.g., copycat killings). For example, if you think back to Chapter 2, John Hinckley, Jr.'s assassination attempt on former President Reagan was motivated in part by his obsession with the movie *Taxi Driver*.

Media has also been used and manipulated by some killers as a key component of their crime(s). For instance, following the 2007 mass murder at Virginia Tech, Seung-Hui Cho used the news outlets to disseminate video footage, photographs, and his infamous manifesto. Another more graphic example is the broadcasting (via news and social media) of the Islamic State of Iraq and Syria (ISIS) slayings. In both cases, the media was used not only to convey a message, but to help the perpetrator(s) exert power and control by instilling fear in the general public.

Because murder is a global issue—and one that is highly publicized, it is imperative for the law enforcement community to have the tools to understand, solve, and combat it in its various forms. In order to do so, we must trace the evolution of homicide—methods, manners, and motives—throughout history.

According to historians, homicide rates were particularly high in Europe during the Middle Ages. Following her examination of coroners' inquests, Professor Barbara Hannawalt concluded that most medieval murders began as verbal confrontations. Because affronts to honor were taken seriously at that time, and the royal courts were slow and corrupt, violence became the accepted means with which to settle disputes. Additionally, people carried items such as knives or quarterstaffs (for herding animals), which were readily available to them and could be used as weapons (Butterfield, 1994).

Another example of murder as an "acceptable" means of settling disputes, dates back to Vlad Tepe's rule over Transylvania in the 1400s. Tepe—or Vlad the Impaler as he was called—was known for impaling both foreign and domestic enemies on wooden stakes and then watching them die slow and painful deaths. He had a particular distaste for dishonest subjects and noblemen whom he suspected of plotting against him or attempting to usurp his power. Tepe guarded against foreign attack by arranging stakes around the city so that any enemy would literally come face-to-face with a wall of impaled corpses before considering trying to overthrow him. Rumor has it that Tepe even enjoyed dipping his bread into his victims' bloody wounds while eating dinner (Wilson, 2000). Tepe often used the name Vlad Drakula (which is from the Serbian word for "dragon"). Vlad the Impaler became known for his penchant for sadistic murder and torture to ward off enemies, maintain order, and guard his political aspirations; he became famous for having inspired Bram Stoker's *Dracula*.

Contrary to popular belief, research reflects that it was most often villages (and not cities) that were the scenes of deadly violence. These findings directly contradict one of the central tenets of criminology which states that violence is common to densely populated urban areas where traditional social and relational values have broken down (Butterfield, 1994). According to Eric H. Monkkonen, a professor of American Urban History at the University of California at Los Angeles, "violence is not an immutable human problem. There really has been a civilizing process" (Butterfield, 1994). In other words, thanks to the implementation of certain laws as well as a functioning court system, official justice has replaced private vengeance, thus curbing *some* of the impulsive violence of the past. Today, law enforcement is charged with solving homicide cases motivated by reactive (explosive) aggression, extremist beliefs/terrorist agendas, greed, jealousy, hate, and mental illness.

HOMICIDE: THE ULTIMATE ACT OF VIOLENCE

Simply put, *homicide* is a general term, which refers to the killing of one human being by another. Although people often use the words "homicide" and "murder" interchangeably, murder is actually one of two subcategories of criminal homicide—the other is manslaughter. *Criminal homicide* refers to illegally (i.e., without justification or excuse) causing the death of another person. The scope of the broader term homicide includes killings that are regarded as legally justified, sanctioned, or excusable such as self-defense, state-sanctioned executions, or during the course of police or military action (Bartol & Bartol, 2008).

In our justice system, we have specific definitions (or degrees) of murder and associated charges, many of which vary from state to state. For the purposes of this text, we will review generally accepted definitions rather than state-specific distinctions. We will additionally discuss aggravated assault within this context as some experts view such attacks as failed homicide attempts (Doerner, 1988). It should be noted, however, that another school of thought exists, which stipulates that criminal homicide and aggravated assault differ in terms of important variables, including the motive(s) of the perpetrator (Bartol & Bartol, 2008).

Degrees of Homicide and Assault

First degree murder is a term used to describe any homicide that is particularly violent, cruel, malicious, or that is committed with "malice aforethought." That is, the killing is premeditated and deliberate. Additionally, a homicide, whether planned or unplanned, that occurs during the commission of another serious or violent crime (i.e., a felony) is considered felony murder and is a first degree offense (Pozzulo et al., 2013). For example: A robber holds up a bodega at gunpoint. In an attempt to defend himself and his earnings, the store owner grabs for the offender's gun and it goes off; the store owner is killed instantly. The robber, even though he may not have intended for anyone to die, will be charged with first degree murder.

Similar to first degree murder, *second degree murder* is deliberate. However, the difference is that murder in the second degree is *not* planned (Pozzulo et al., 2013). Let's take a look at another example: A married man discovers that his wife is having an affair. After considering his options, he obtains a permit and purchases a gun. He then lies in wait for his wife to return from a rendezvous with her lover. When she comes home, he shoots and kills her.

Now, let's pretend that the same man has no prior knowledge of his wife's affair. He comes home from work early one day and unexpectedly walks in on his wife and her lover in bed together. The husband becomes enraged, grabs the lamp from the bedside table, and bludgeons both his wife and her paramour to death. How do these scenarios differ? They are both murders; however, the first case demonstrates premeditation and would therefore qualify as first degree murder. The second homicide, although deliberate, is spontaneous. It is a "crime of passion" and an illustration of second degree murder.

Perhaps surprisingly, criminal homicide does not account for a large percentage of the crimes reported in the United States (1.2% annually). Additionally, despite over-exaggerations by the media, in most cases there is very little mystery surrounding the identity of the suspect(s) or possible suspect(s). According to the Federal Bureau of Investigation (2005), the suspect is known in over 70% of homicide cases and, further, in 44% of cases, there is an identifiable relationship (acquaintance, relative, friend, colleague, etc.) between the perpetrator and the victim.

Let's move onto manslaughter. Depending on the state, manslaughter may be classified in a multitude of ways including negligent, involuntary, voluntary, or non-negligent. In general, *manslaughter* is the killing of another human being due to recklessness or negligence. Although such crimes do not involve the intent to kill, the guilty party *should have known* that his or her behavior could result in the death of another person. Therefore, the law holds him or her accountable. For example, drunk driving is a form of reckless behavior that could result in the death of another (or several other) individual(s) (Bartol & Bartol, 2008; Pozzulo et al., 2013).

Unlike homicide, which is a statistically rare occurrence, there are between 850,000 to 1,000,000 aggravated assaults and over 600,000 incidents of simple assault each year, comprising 63% of all Part 1 violent crimes reported to police (Federal Bureau of Investigation, 2005). Given the large disparity in the rate of occurrence between homicidal violence and assault, you may be wondering why we are studying them together. The answer is simple: individuals who resort to murderous violence often have a history of assaultive behavior. Similarly, aggravated assault behaviors can lead to murder.

Assault (or simple assault) is the *intentional* inflicting of bodily harm on another person, or the attempt to inflict such injury. Assaultive behavior is labeled as the more serious offense of *aggravated assault* when the assailant's intention is to inflict serious bodily harm, which is often accompanied by the use of a weapon.

AGGRESSION

Aggression is defined as "behavior perpetrated or attempted with the intention of harming another individual physically or psychologically (as opposed to socially) or to destroy an object" (Bartol & Bartol, 2008, p. 145). Research has led to the development of a bimodal classification system, whereby aggression and homicide are categorized as either *reactive* or *instrumental/predatory* (Kingsbury, Lambert, & Hendrickse, 1997). Homicide that results from reactive (or hot-blooded) aggression is precipitated by negative emotionality that occurs in response to provocation. It is impulsive and unplanned. It is a *reaction* to a perceived harmful, hurtful, threatening, or upsetting *action.*

Instrumental homicide is proactive (not reactive), and is premeditated, calculated, and motivated by a specific goal. This goal could be to attain an object (e.g., money, jewelry, etc.), status (e.g., power or control), or even to fulfill a sadistic or sexual fantasy (Meloy, 1997). For example, if someone robs a bank, his or her goal is to obtain money. He or she may have no desire to harm anyone. However, should someone get in the way, such as a guard, a bank employee, or a police officer, the robber may deem it necessary to kill that person so as not to risk losing the desired goal (i.e., the money). Instrumental aggression is also relevant to cases of murder by hire, as these kills are impersonal. The individual pulling the trigger does so for financial benefit. Lastly, as discussed in Chapter 4, predatory violence (such as serial murder) is instrumental because victims are targeted in a cold, calculated manner, in order to provide the killer with emotional or sexual gratification (Table 5.1).

Data compiled by the FBI indicates that in 2002, 28% of reported homicides resulted from arguments (reactive aggression), whereas 16.5% were instrumental aggression in that they occurred during the commission of other felonies such as forcible rape, robbery, arson, or drug trafficking (Federal Bureau of Investigation, 2003) (Table 5.2).

Miethe and Drass (1999) conducted a study of over 34,000 single-victim, single-offender homicides in the United States between 1990 and 1994, which led them to conclude that the majority of homicides are the result of reactive aggression. According to the study, 80% of the cases examined were reactive, while only 20% were deemed instrumental. The

Table 5.1   Types of Aggression

Aggression Type	Characteristics
Reactive	• Hot-blooded • Response to a physical or emotional trigger • Reaction to a perceived threat • Result of negative emotions • Impulsive; unplanned • May result in domestic homicide
Instrumental (Predatory)	• Proactive • Motivated by a specific goal (money, status, fantasy fulfillment) • Cold-blooded • Often impersonal • Premeditated; calculated • May provide the killer with emotional or sexual gratification • Category includes murder for hire

researchers additionally evaluated the victim-offender relationships in each homicide and categorized them as either: strangers, acquaintances, or family/intimate. They found that most (55%) of the homicides involved acquaintances, and 80% of those were the result of reactive aggression. Family members and intimate partners accounted for the victim-offender relationship in 28% of the cases, with 93% of those homicides being classified as reactive. In only 17% of the cases reviewed were the victim and offender strangers, and only 52% of these cases were the result of reactive aggression. Therefore, one can conclude that reactive homicide occurs more often among relatives, whereas instrumental homicide occurs more often among strangers (Daly & Wilson, 1982) (Figure 5.1).

Similar studies have consistently shown that homicide victims are often acquainted with their killer. Dating back to the 1950s, findings indicate that at least two-thirds of all homicide victims knew their attacker (Bullock, 1955). According to Wolfgang (1958), the victim and the perpetrator were strangers in only approximately 14% of such cases. More recent *Uniform Crime Report* (UCR) data reflects that nearly half of all murder victims were either related to their killer (13%) or acquainted with him or her (30%). Stranger murders comprised only 13% of cases, with relationships unknown in 44%. The research also reveals that 33% of female homicide victims were killed by husbands or boyfriends, making them domestic

Table 5.2 Murder Circumstances by Victim Gender

Circumstances	Total Murder Victims	Male	Female	Unknown
Total	14,121	10,990	3,099	32
Felony type total:	2,089	1,718	370	1
Rape	36	0	36	0
Robbery	988	874	113	1
Burglary	77	52	25	0
Larceny-theft	14	12	2	0
Motor vehicle theft	38	33	5	0
Arson	28	12	16	0
Prostitution and commercialized vice	9	3	6	0
Other sex offenses	14	8	6	0
Narcotic drug laws	554	505	49	0
Gambling	7	6	1	0
Other—not specified	324	213	111	0
Suspected felony type	117	95	22	0
Other than felony type total:	6,972	5,227	1,739	6
Romantic triangle	97	76	21	0
Child killed by babysitter	17	7	10	0
Brawl due to influence of alcohol	139	120	19	0
Brawl due to influence of narcotics	98	83	14	1
Argument over money or property	218	190	28	0
Other arguments	3,758	2,761	995	2
Gangland killings	95	90	5	0
Juvenile gang killings	804	776	28	0
Institutional killings	17	17	0	0
Sniper attack	1	1	0	0
Other—not specified	1,728	1,106	619	3
Unknown	4,943	3,950	968	25

Source: Federal Bureau of Investigation, *Crime in the United States 2004: Uniform crime reports.* Washington, DC: U.S. Department of Justice, 2005.

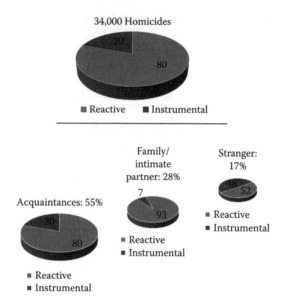

34,000 Homicides

■ Reactive   ■ Instrumental

Acquaintances: 55%

Family/
intimate
partner: 28%

Stranger:
17%

■ Reactive
■ Instrumental

■ Reactive
■ Instrumental

■ Reactive
■ Instrumental

Figure 5.1 Homicidal violence: Reactive versus instrumental. (From Miethe, T. D., & Drass, K. A., *Journal of Quantitative Criminology, 15*, 1–21, 1999.)

homicides, while only 2.7% of male murder victims were killed by wives or girlfriends (Federal Bureau of Investigation, 2005).

Men are victimized by violent strangers more than twice as often as women (Federal Bureau of Investigation, 2005). While the chance of becoming the victim of stranger-perpetrated violence increases with age for women, it remains the same across all ages for men (U.S. Department of Justice, 1989). When the homicide offender is related to or acquainted with his or her victim(s), they typically share similar demographic characteristics. However, in stranger homicides, the offender is often younger and of a different race than the victim.

VICTIM-PRECIPATED HOMICIDE

Wolfgang (1958) found that in approximately 26% of homicide cases, the victim significantly contributed to his or her own murder by violently aggressing against the killer *first*. Studies suggest that minor altercations and domestic disputes more often lead to murder when both parties are acting aggressively. Although verbal quarrels can quickly escalate to physical violence, Wolfgang did not consider taunts, slights, or insults to fall within the parameters of "violence." Therefore, "pure" victim-precipitated homicide, as viewed by Wolfgang, may actually qualify as self-defense on the part of the killer (Bartol & Bartol, 2008).

WEAPONS USED IN VIOLENCE

Not only does the motive for murder differ depending upon the individual offender, but so does the weapon of choice. Research has found that guns and knives (in addition to box cutters and other sharp/cutting instruments) are typically the preferred manner for causing death. This preference is somewhat influenced by the gender, race, and geography of the killer (Bartol & Bartol, 2008). In Philadelphia, for example, stabbing was the most common method of killing in the 1950s (Wolfgang, 1958), while shooting was more common in Chicago during the 1960s (Hepburn & Voss, 1970). Between 1993 and 2004, over 70% of all homicides in the United States were committed with a firearm (Federal Bureau of Investigation, 2003). According to Zawitz and Strom (2000), 58 police officers were killed in the line of duty in 1998. Another 400 were wounded in firearms assaults. In 2014, there were 50 firearms-related officer fatalities, which marked a significant increase (56%) from the 2013 statistics (Chandler, 2014).

When approaching a scene, officers should be aware that the presence of an aggressive stimulus such as a gun, may automatically (and unconsciously) bring about violence-related thoughts. Research has shown a correlation between aggressive thoughts engendered by the presence of a weapon and subsequent aggressive behavior. This phenomenon, known as the *weapons effect*, means that visible weapons promote more aggressive acts, thus creating an increased level of violence (including homicide) and a potentially higher risk to responding law enforcement. In some cases, of course, advancing with a weapon drawn is prudent or necessary; ultimately, the safety of the officer in the face of a violent situation is paramount and so the discretion lies with the responding officer or officers.

MULTIPLE-VICTIM MURDERS

Perhaps some of the most frightening and highly publicized murders are those involving multiple victims. Multiple victim homicide can occur as the killing of a group of people during a singular attack, or the individual killing of multiple people over the course of hours, days, weeks, months, or even years by the same killer or killers.

Spree Murder

Spree murder involves the killing of three or more individuals, typically in at least two locations and without a cooling off period in between. For example, a bank robber who kills two employees inside the bank, followed by a security guard as he flees, and then a police officer during a statewide chase is a spree murderer (Bartol & Bartol, 2008).

In an interview with *LA Times* staff writer Aaron Curtiss (1995), famed FBI profiler John Douglas offered a list of traits shared by many spree killers. Spree murderers' crimes tend to be impulsive and are often preceded by fits of rage, unlike those of serial killers, which tend to be more methodical. Douglas noted that spree killers who stab or strangle their victims likely enjoy the act of killing itself because both of these methods require physical exertion as well as close contact with the victim as he or she is dying.

Mass Murder

Mass murder is the killing of three or more people during one incident at a single location. There is no cooling off period between the kills. The Federal Bureau of Investigation distinguishes between two types of mass murder: *classic mass murder* and *family mass murder* (Douglas & Burgess, 1986). A classic mass murder occurs when an individual targets a public space, sometimes barricading him or herself inside, and randomly kills patrons or other individuals with whom he or she has contact. An example of this was the Luby's Cafeteria massacre in Killeen, Texas.

On October 16, 1991, George Hennard crashed his pickup truck through the plate glass window of the popular restaurant, Luby's Cafeteria. It was lunchtime and Luby's was packed. Hennard exited his truck, took out a 9mm semi-automatic, and began shooting customers. The attack lasted approximately ten minutes, at the end of which 22 people were dead and many more injured. The majority of Hennard's victims were female. Witnesses reported that Hennard appeared to harbor intense hostility toward women and purposely sought them out of the crowd in order to kill them. He was overheard saying, "You bitch," and "Hiding from me, bitch?" to two separate females prior to shooting them.

When police arrived, Hennard used the last bullet in his clip to take his own life (Chin, 1991; Hayes, 1991).

In contrast, during a family mass murder, the targets are not random. This type of homicide occurs when at least three family members are killed during a singular attack and the killer is often another member of the family. In such scenarios, the perpetrator frequently kills him or herself, thus classifying the incident as a murder-suicide.

According to Holmes and Holmes (2001), mass murderers often have a grudge against society which accounts for why they act out against strangers (i.e., victims with whom they were previously unacquainted). Once they have attained their revenge through the initial murderous event, they do not feel compelled to continue killing (as do serial killers). In other words, once their need for revenge is met, mass murderers no longer have a homicidal fantasy yet to fulfill.

Mass murderers can be further classified into eight subtypes (Holmes & Holmes, 2001):

- *Disciple killer*: This individual kills per the directive of a charismatic leader whose acceptance or approval he or she seeks.
- *Family annihilator killer*: This killer murders his or her entire family during one attack. This subtype is similar to the family mass murderer classification.
- *Disgruntled employee killer*: This individual strikes out against his or her current or former place of employment because of a real or perceived injustice. He or she may have been fired, laid off, or passed over for a promotion. This killer's motivation is to right a perceived wrong.
- *Ideological killer*: This individual, also referred to as the "Lone Wolf," amasses weapons in order to lash out against a specific evil in the world. He or she holds stringent political views and often presents as an extremist. He or she may also be affiliated with a cult or terrorist group.
- *Set-and-run killer*: This offender does not plan to die at the scene. Rather, he or she intends to set the crime in motion and escape. This type of killer typically employs methods such as bombing (as did Timothy McVeigh in the 1995 Oklahoma City bombing) or product tampering.
- *Disgruntled citizen killer*: Similar to the disgruntled employee, the disgruntled citizen seeks revenge. Whereas the disgruntled employee lashes out at a specific target (his or her place of

employment), the disgruntled citizen's rage is so intense, that he or she lashes out at the entire world by way of mass murder.
- *Psychotic killer*: This person is often referred to as a mentally disordered multiple murderer.
- *School shooter*: This killer (or team of killers) is usually school-aged and targets their own school. They have a history of social maladjustment and have faced a significant amount of real or perceived peer rejection. Their crimes are also referred to as rampage murders. School shooters will be discussed in Chapter 12.

Sniper Attacks

Another form of multiple victim homicide is the sniper attack. Perhaps the most haunting of such events occurred over a 23-day span in the Washington, DC metro area in October of 2002. A total of 10 individuals selected at random, were killed by sniper fire; six of the victims were killed within the first 2 days of the attacks.

The snipers were 42-year-old John Allen Muhammad and his teenaged accomplice Lee Boyd Malvo. The two had modified a Chevy Caprice in order to enable them to crawl into the trunk via the backseat and shoot a high-powered rifle through a hole above the license plate. Using this method, they terrorized people along the Beltway.

The attacks perpetrated by the "DC Sniper," as Muhammad and Malvo became collectively known, prompted the FBI to study other sniper incidents. The Bureau concluded that sniper violence is a statistically rare occurrence. Of the 364,648 homicides that were reported between 1982 and 2001, only 0.1% were the result of sniper fire. Additionally, nearly 80% of sniper victims were males, and victims' ages varied significantly. In most occurrences (90%), the victim and the sniper were strangers or their relationship was unknown. In 63.6% of reported attacks, a handgun was the weapon used, while the remainder of incidents involved a rifle or a shotgun (Federal Bureau of Investigation, 2003).

SERIAL MURDER

Serial murder is defined as the killing of multiple individuals (minimally three persons) over time. The central characteristic of serial murder is that there is a cooling off period of days or weeks, but more typically months or years, between kills (Bartol & Bartol, 2008). This cooling off period is what separates serial killers from other multiple murderers (Douglas, Ressler, Burgess, & Hartman, 1986). Additionally, serial murders are typically premeditated with a high degree of planning, including specific and purposeful victim selection.

Jack the Ripper

In the fall of 1888, five prostitutes were brutally murdered in the Whitechapel district of London's East End. Their bodies were mutilated in a manner which led law enforcement to suspect that the killer had specialized knowledge of human anatomy. Following the murders, someone claiming to be the perpetrator sent several letters to Scotland Yard, taunting investigators. He signed the memos "Jack the Ripper" and thus originated the nickname for the Whitechapel murderer (Cascio, 1995).

Although Jack the Ripper was never identified, several theories emerged over the years, including claims that the killer was a medical doctor, a famous painter, a Polish immigrant, Lewis Carroll (author of *Alice in Wonderland*), and even a member of the royal family (D. Rumbelow, personal communication, October 2008). Since 1888, countless suspects have been named, contributing to widespread folklore. To this day, Jack the Ripper's identity and motives are unknown. The case remains one of the world's most infamous unsolved crimes—and is often considered the first known instance of serial homicide.

SERIAL KILLERS

Due to the increasing amount of research conducted on and media attention paid to serial killers, the public has become intimately familiar with these notorious criminals. The heinous nature of their crimes has been stored in the public's collective memory, making some of them pop culture icons and household names.

John Wayne Gacy

Between 1972 and 1978, the "Killer Clown" was a menacing moniker all to familiar to Chicago residents. It was the epithet for John Wayne Gacy, a serial killer who sexually assaulted and killed more than 30 teenage boys. Gacy's criminal escapades began with a string of sexual assaults. His first victim was a 15-year-old boy whom he lured into his home by promising to show him pornographic videos (Cahill, 1986). Gacy plied the boy with liquor before convincing him to perform oral sex on him. Gacy tricked several of his subsequent victims into believing that he was authorized to conduct scientific research on homosexuality, which involved their engaging in sexual acts for a payment of $50 (Sullivan & Maiken, 2000).

Gacy was convicted of sodomy and paroled after serving 18 months of a 10-year sentence. While under parole supervision, Gacy was charged with sexually assaulting another teenage boy who claimed that Gacy had invited him into his car at Chicago's Greyhound bus terminal. Gacy then drove the boy to his home where he tried to force him to engage in sexual acts. Because the boy did not appear in court, the complaint was dismissed. Therefore, the Board of Parole never learned of Gacy's charges, which violated the conditions of his supervision (Cahill, 1986).

Following the successful termination of his parole, Gacy continued to employ old tactics to trap new victims. He took some of his victims by force and used deceptive devices to lure others into his home. Once inside the house, Gacy would handcuff (or otherwise restrain) the boys, choke them with a rope, and sexually assault them. He put rags in their mouths in order to muffle their screams and ultimately strangled them before disposing of their bodies. When interviewed, Gacy reported having experienced an orgasm during one of his kills. He stated, "That's when I realized that death was the ultimate thrill" (Cahill, 1986, p. 349). Most of the victims' remains were later discovered in the crawl space beneath Gacy's home.

John Wayne Gacy earned the nickname "Killer Clown" because he was part of a charitable organization whose members dressed as clowns for fundraising events and entertaining at children's hospitals (Cahill, 1986). He created his own performance character, Pogo the Clown. The sharp corners Gacy painted at the edges of his mouth when he dressed as Pogo were contrary to the rounded borders used by professional clowns so as to avoid scaring small children (Linedecker, 1980).

Gacy was convicted of more than 30 murders and subsequently sentenced to death. He was executed by lethal injection on May 10, 1994 (Cahill, 1986).

Ted Bundy

In the mid-1970s, Ted Bundy was another name synonymous with "fear" in homes across the United States. He raped and murdered at least 36 women in seven states. Although it may never be known definitively, the total body count is presumed to be much higher. Bundy was executed via electric chair in Florida in 1989 (Biography.com Editors, 2016c).

By all accounts, Ted Bundy was good-looking, charming, and charismatic—all traits that he exploited in order to gain the trust of his victims before overpowering and ultimately murdering them. He typically approached his victims in public places, feigned illness or injury, and asked for their assistance. His ruse depended upon both the kindness of his victims as well as his own ability to appear nonthreatening. Once he had gained their trust, Bundy subdued his victims, raped, and bludgeoned them. He often disposed of their bodies in remote locations so that he could return to the burial sites and relive his kills. He applied makeup to the decaying corpses and performed sexual acts with them (*necrophilia*). Reports indicate that Bundy decapitated some of his victims and initially kept the severed heads as trophies before deciding to discard them (Keppel, 2005).

Bundy's unusual interests emerged when he was a toddler. His Aunt Julia recalled first noticing his fascination with knives when she awoke from a nap to find herself surrounded by knives. Bundy was standing by her bed, smiling; he was 3 years old (Rule, 2000). As a teenager, Bundy's interests grew darker and he developed habits such as stealing and peeping into neighbors' windows.

Some theorists believe that when Bundy's college girlfriend ended their relationship, the rejection became the catalyst for his crimes. Bundy's rage toward his former paramour was reflected in the appearance of his victims (young, attractive females with long dark hair). However, Bundy remains a suspect in multiple unsolved homicides, some of which predate his college romance. In an interview shortly before his death, Bundy indicated that there were "some murders" he would never talk about because he had committed them "too close to home," or "too close to family," or they involved "victims who were very young" (Keppel, 2010).

Characteristics of Serial Killers

A considerable amount of research has been conducted in order to answer the question: What do serial killers have in common with one another? The somewhat unenlightening answer is that there is no specific set of characteristics that absolutely defines a serial killer; there is no formula or one-size-fits-all profile.

A serial killer's predisposition toward committing crimes of such a heinous nature is biological, sociological, and psychological in nature. These individuals have a biological susceptibility that is molded and reinforced by their psychological constitution and then influenced by social environmental factors at developmentally critical points throughout their lives (Morton & Hilts, 2008). According to an analysis of serial killers conducted by the Federal Bureau of Investigation (1985), each of the 25 subjects evaluated was born into a two-parent household. However, many of the killers reported that their families of origin were dysfunctional on some level. Some indicated that they had family members who abused drugs or alcohol, had trouble with the law, or experienced psychiatric difficulties. Additionally, more than half of the subjects reported that their biological father had left the familial home before they reached the age of 12, and nearly half experienced frequent and/or impactful geographic relocation. Half of the killers studied reported a lack of attachment to their mother—and two-thirds reported a cold or uncaring relationship with both parents. Nearly one-quarter of the subjects reported abuse in at least one sphere: emotional, psychological, physical, or sexual.

TYPOLOGIES OF SERIAL KILLERS

Like other violent offenders, serial killers are driven by a variety of motives, the most common of which have led to four distinct classifications or typologies of serial killers (Holmes & DeBurger, 1988):

- *Visionary*: This type of killer is psychotic and believes that he or she is being commanded (usually by voices or a god or gods) to kill. David Berkowitz, the "Son of Sam" killer, is an example of this subtype. He believed that a demon was communicating with him through his neighbor's dog and was ordering him to kill.
- *Mission-oriented*: These killers see it as their duty to rid society of a particular "evil" or "burden." The problem as they view it, translates to a victim type, such as prostitutes, runaway youth, a specific racial group, and so on.
- *Hedonistic*: These individuals kill for pleasure and are further divided into two groups:
  - *Lust killers*: As the name suggests, lust killers achieve sexual gratification by committing murder.
  - *Thrill killers*: This classification of killer commits murder for the sheer excitement of the kill.
- *Power/control-oriented*: This subtype kills in order to exert dominance and have ultimate control over another human being.

DISPELLING MYTHS ABOUT SERIAL KILLERS

Due in part to the media frenzy surrounding serial murder, many false-hoods and myths have been perpetuated about the psychological facets of this criminological phenomenon. Recent research has helped to clarify some common misconceptions.

Myth: All Serial Killers Are Reclusive and Dysfunctional

When asked to describe the type of individual that might be a serial killer, many people envision a socially inept or isolated person; they report that something about him or her would seem obviously "off." However, serial killers often blend into society. Many of them are married, have families, maintain homes, and are employed. In other words, they literally hide in plain sight. This ordinary façade allows them to go unnoticed by law enforcement (Morton & Hilts, 2008).

- Gary Ridgway, the Green River Killer, who we discussed in Chapter 4, confessed to murdering 48 victims in and around Seattle, Washington. Prior to committing the murders, he had been married three times and was still married at the time of his arrest. Ridgway was also the father of a young son, and main-tained steady employment.
- Dennis Rader, better known as the BTK (Bind Torture Kill) Killer, strangled 10 victims to death in Wichita, Kansas in the 1970s and 1980s. In the 30 years following the final murder, he sent multiple communications to the media, taunting the police. Rader was a husband, father, church elder, Boy Scout leader, public official, and former military officer.

Myth: All Serial Killers Are White Males

There is a common misconception that all serial killers are white males (typically within a certain age range). However, serial killers, similar to other classifications of offenders, are racially diverse. Their races and cul-tures are reflective of the population as a whole (Morton & Hilts, 2008). Following are some examples of non-Caucasian offenders:

- Coral Eugene Watts was an African-American serial killer. He murdered five victims in Michigan before fleeing to Texas, where he subsequently killed another 12 people prior to being arrested.

- Charles Ng, a Hong Kong native, killed numerous people in California with the help of his accomplice Robert Lake.
- Rory Conde was a native of Colombia who murdered six prostitutes in and around Miami, Florida.
- Rafael Resendez-Ramirez was born in Mexico. He killed nine people across three states and later surrendered to law enforcement.
- Derrick Todd Lee was an African-American man who murdered six women in Baton Rouge, Louisiana.

Myth: All Serial Killers Are Sexually Motivated

While many serial murders have a sexual component, there are a variety of other motives such as anger, power/control, thrill, psychosis, extremist ideology, and monetary gain (Morton & Hilts, 2008).

- In the DC Sniper case discussed earlier in this chapter, Muhammad and Malvo were motivated primarily by anger and the excitement they derived from killing. Terrorizing the DC area and mocking both media and law enforcement gave them an emotional high.
- Paul Reid murdered at least seven people in order to eliminate them as witnesses to a series of fast food restaurant robberies that he had committed.

Myth: Serial Killers Cannot Stop Killing

It has been a widely accepted notion that killing is an insatiable passion for serial killers. In other words, once they start killing, they cannot stop of their own volition. Therefore, if a particular killer's series of murders was interrupted, it was previously believed that the offender had been incarcerated or otherwise detained (such as in a psychiatric facility), had moved away, or had died. However, recent research indicates that some serial killers stop murdering before they are caught because there are circumstances in their lives that inhibit them from pursuing additional victims. Such instances might include increased participation in family activities, sexual substitution, or other diversions (Morton & Hilts, 2008).

- Jeffrey Gorton committed his first murder in 1986 and his next in 1991. He was captured in 2002 and engaged in cross-dressing, masturbation, and consensual sex with his wife in the 11-year interim.

- BTK murdered his last victim in 1991. He engaged in auto-erotic activities as an alternative to murder until his capture in 2005.

Myth: All Serial Killers Are Insane

While some serial killers, such as visionary types, suffer from psychosis, most exhibit personality disorders such as ASPD and psychopathy and know that killing is illegal and immoral. Therefore, they typically do not meet legal criteria for insanity (Morton & Hilts, 2008).

Myth: All Serial Killers Were Abused as Children

Popular opinion holds that all serial killers grew up in dysfunctional homes and suffered abuse throughout the course of their childhoods. While it is true that *some* serial killers experienced abuse in one or more spheres, a dysfunctional home life does not predispose someone to commit serial murder (Morton & Hilts, 2008).

SERIAL SEXUAL HOMICIDE

Think back to our discussion of psychopathy in Chapter 4. You will recall that primary psychopaths are impulsive, lack remorse, and experience no fear or anxiety. When criminal, their acts are cold-blooded and result in immediate gratification. By contrast, secondary psychopaths do experience fear and anxiety, and their criminal or antisocial activities are often a result of this intense negative emotionality. Sears (1991) suggests that although it is common for serial killers to simply be labeled as "psychopaths," they actually exhibit a hybrid form of primary and secondary psychopathy as many of them are compelled to kill because of fear, anxiety, or internal conflict, but do not experience guilt. Because psychopaths have an inherent need for excitement, they commit increasingly violent, and sometimes sexual criminal acts, in order to achieve satisfaction.

Sears (1991) hypothesized that most serial killers are sexually motivated and that the vast majority of them are sexual sadists. For these individuals, violent and sexual urges become comingled at some point in their development—the question is "why?"

Perhaps the idea of the hybrid psychopathic serial killer holds the key. One of the most essential characteristics of sexually driven serial homicide is the element of fantasy. These killers have sadistic fantasies and eroticize violence, often as a way of escaping overwhelming fear, anxiety, powerlessness, or other internal stressors (Morton & Hilts, 2008). In that way, fantasy is a coping mechanism. Individuals subjected to abuse and other forms of maltreatment may develop violent fantasies as a means of dealing with poor self-esteem, feelings of helplessness, or the need to exert power and control over their lives. Such fantasies can become almost compulsive in abused children. Having never reached emotional maturation, these children go on to exhibit difficulty managing their violent (and sexual) fantasies as adults (Douglas, Burgess, & Ressler, 1995; Sears, 1991). Through repetitive use of deviant fantasies, these individuals feed their need to achieve emotional and sexual release via violent thought and subsequent violent behavior (Douglas et al., 1995).

Some psychologists liken this increasing intensity of fantasy to brainwashing. For example, serial killer Ed Kemper, the "Co-ed Killer," openly discussed his preoccupation with fantasy: "I knew long before I started killing that I was going to be killing; that it was going to end up like that. The fantasies were too strong. They were going on for too long and were too elaborate" (Vronsky, 2004).

Burgess, Hartman, Ressler, Douglas, and McCormack (1986) developed a motivational model of sexual homicide which has been applied to serial sexual homicide. It denotes five main elements reflective of these offenders' background characteristics, behaviors, experiences, development, fantasies, and cognitive structures. These concepts are critical for law enforcement to understand when investigating such crimes (see Table 5.3).

FEMALE SERIAL KILLERS

Because it is such a rare phenomenon, there has been relatively little research conducted on females who commit serial homicide. In their groundbreaking work *Murder Most Rare: The Female Serial Killer*, Kelleher and Kelleher (1998) suggest that the FBI's organized-disorganized dichotomy of serial killers is insufficient to assist law enforcement in understanding and dissecting the complex motivations of female serial killers. The organized-disorganized scheme has been well-accepted by law enforcement personnel as an investigative tool and categorizes all serial murderers, regardless of gender, race, or motive as either organized or disorganized perpetrators. Organized killers demonstrate planning and control at the crime scene and are typically of above average intelligence,

Table 5.3   Motivational Model of Sexual Homicide

Ineffective social environment	Abuse or neglect perpetrated by parents and caretakers results in the inability to form significant bonds/attachments.
Formative events	Fixation on early trauma causes sexual murderers to develop fantasies as a means of combating feelings of helplessness. As a result, they do not achieve emotional maturation nor do they develop fulfilling interpersonal relationships.
Patterned responses	These early events lead these killers to develop unhealthy social responses such as isolation, hostility, and a preference for autoerotic activity. These offenders come to view the world as a hostile place in which they have no agency, and thus fail to consider the impact of their behavior on others.
Actions toward others	The crimes of sexual murderers are predicated on a need for power and control. As children they likely tortured small animals and bullied classmates. Their behavior becomes increasingly violent as adulthood emerges.
Feedback filter	Because these killers isolate themselves from society, they have a distorted view of their assaults. They are proud of their kills—and easily justify them.

Source: Burgess, A. W., et al., *Journal of Interpersonal Violence*, 1, 251–272, 1986.

socially competent, and gainfully employed. By comparison, disorganized killers leave behind crime scenes that exhibit a lack of planning and organization. They are typically of below-average intelligence, socially inept, and have an erratic work history (Kelleher & Kelleher, 1998). The organized-disorganized classification system will be explored further in Chapter 8, as it is a mainstay of behavioral profiling.

Kelleher and Kelleher (1998) posit that female serial killers fall into two categories: women who act alone and those who kill as part of a team. Of the women who kill solo, the researchers devised five typologies representative of the broad spectrum of potential (or probable) motives *when the perpetrator is legally sane*:

- *Black Widows*: These women systematically kill spouses, paramours, or other family members and are usually motivated by financial gain (Vronsky, 2007).

- *Angels of Death*: These killers murder individuals in their care. This typology often denotes mercy killings, although the motives may be more diverse.
- *Sexual Predators*: These individuals commit serial sexual homicide. While females do kill for sexual gratification, according to Hickey (2006) males are more likely to commit sexually motivated serial murder.
- *Revenge Killers*: Revenge killers methodically target and kill individuals in order to gain revenge. Jealousy is a frequent motive in this type of homicidal pattern.
- *Profit or Crime Killers*: These women kill for monetary gain, but do not fall within the classification of the Black Widow.

Kelleher and Kelleher (1998) note that "Team Killers" or women who kill with one or more partners, do so for a limited number of reasons. Additionally, their motives are often intermingled with those of their accomplice(s). According to Pozzulo et al. (2013), approximately 50% of female serial killers act as part of a team, whereas only 25% of males work with a partner. Hickey (2006) notes that 74% of female serial killers, as compared with only 26% of male serial killers, report that financial gain was the main impetus for their crimes.

In order to assist law enforcement with investigations and crime scene assessments, Kelleher and Kelleher (1998) identify three additional subcategories of female serial killers, who may kill with a partner or partners: those individuals whose sanity is in question, those killers whose motive is unexplained, and those whose crimes remain unsolved. Of those whose sanity is in question, the researchers describe a person whose kills appear to be random and without an immediately articulable motive. She will later be deemed legally insane. Additionally, this type of killer may be a woman whose murders are logical and planned, but it is subsequently discovered that the murders were the result of mental disorder.

INVESTIGATION STRATEGIES

Now that you have a firm grasp of the different types of homicide and the motives behind them, let's delve into how to effectively investigate them. Solving open homicide cases is important for a variety of reasons, including providing closure for the victims' families and friends and

decreasing fear and anxiety in the community. According to data compiled by the FBI, the clearance rate of homicides has steadily declined in
the past 50 years. In 1965, the average national clearance rate was 91%.
This dropped to 79% in 1976 and subsequently to 64% in 2002. Researchers
attribute this to multiple factors such as an increase in murders committed against stranger victims, witness intimidation, community reluctance
to assist law enforcement, gang violence, and an increase in the number
of verbal altercations that turn physically violent or fatal (Cronin, Toliver,
Murphy, Weger, & Spahr, 2007). Perhaps another incalculable factor is that
the justice system has advanced to the point where it now places an inor-
dinately greater emphasis on punishing the *guilty* party, rather than simply obtaining a conviction based on little to no solid evidence.

In order to combat this declining closure rate, police personnel must
utilize proven techniques and technologies, and avail themselves of the
relevant data. Research has shown that whether a homicide investigation
is solved is largely dependent upon three variables: law enforcement's
initial response, detectives' actions, and other/miscellaneous police
responses (Cronin et al., 2007).

Initial Response: The first officer to arrive should notify all relevant
parties (homicide unit, medical examiner, and crime lab). He or she
should immediately secure the scene to ensure that evidence is preserved,
and then attempt to locate potential witnesses. Because patrol officers are
often the first to arrive, they should be trained in how to avoid contami-
nating a crime scene and how to properly identify possible witnesses. In
order to make certain that the scene is processed quickly and correctly,
detectives should arrive within 30 minutes of notification (Cronin et al.,
2007).

Actions of Detectives: In order to solve a homicide, detectives must pay
close attention to detail. Research indicates that assigning three or four
detectives to a particular case, instead of only one or two, increases the
likelihood that the case will be closed. Additionally, taking detailed notes
of the crime scene is crucial, as is documenting (preferably via audio or
video recording) any interviews. Detectives should follow up on all information (i.e., potential leads) provided by witnesses and attend the autopsy
(Cronin et al., 2007).

When investigating the BTK serial homicide case, the Wichita Police
Department employed a strategy known as "practical homicide investigation." Using this method, individual detectives were assigned to each
of BTK's 10 victims. Therefore, each detective became intimately familiar
with victimology, witness information, crime scene analysis, evidence,

autopsy results, and so on, for each specific crime scene uncovered in the multiple-victim investigation (Geberth, 2010).

Other Police Actions: The third variable sums up miscellaneous steps that law enforcement can take to gather additional useful information. It includes checking police and FBI databases for criminal histories of suspects, checking serial numbers on any firearms/weapons recovered, gathering collateral information by interviewing not only witnesses, but friends, family members, and colleagues of the victim, obtaining information from confidential informants, interviewing the medical examiner (instead of just glancing through the report!), and asking the medical examiner to prepare a drawing (also called a body chart) of wound location(s), scars, tattoos, and other indicators of trauma on the victim's body (Cronin et al., 2007) (see Figure 5.2).

Not surprisingly, the FBI stresses the importance of identifying, collecting, analyzing, and processing information quickly, efficiently, and accurately. In order to do so, they utilize a fact-finding capsule that encompasses three central guidelines (Edwards, 2005):

- *Haste*: Quickly complete all tasks to learn facts and develop leads.
- *Specificity*: Meticulously examine evidence in order to determine facts and draw objective conclusions.

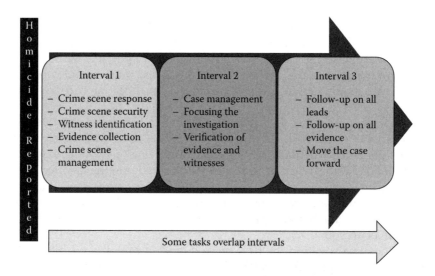

Figure 5.2 The "First 48." (From Carter, D. L., The "First 48." *Homicide process mapping: Best practices for increasing homicide clearances*, Bureau of U.S. Justice Assistance, U.S. Department of Justice, 2013, p. 33.)

- *Element of surprise*: Prevent interviewees from conferring with one another on their version(s) of the story and prevent potential suspects from colluding with one another.

A homicide investigation should also include a precise timeline documenting the whereabouts of the suspect(s) and victim(s) at the time of the murder and in the hours (and possibly days) leading up to the crime. Investigators should take care to utilize proper techniques when interrogating suspects and interviewing eyewitnesses. Psychological research indicates that the truthfulness of confessions as well as the degree of accuracy of eyewitness accounts can be strongly influenced by police procedures. In this way, psychological principles can help to shape effective and efficient investigative tactics. Problematic police procedures, how to avoid them, and information regarding empirically supported alternatives for eliciting useful information will be discussed in depth in Chapter 9.

In addition to reviewing social science literature on identification and lineup techniques, some departments are evaluating how crime analysis can aid in closing both single- and multiple-victim homicide cases. In some larger departments, crime analysts concentrate on performing research, which permits detectives to focus their efforts on conducting interviews and following up on leads. While more traditional forms of profiling and crime scene analysis will be discussed in Chapter 8, it is important to note that problem-oriented policing and the "scanning, analysis, response, and assessment" (SARA) model have proven extremely useful. The SARA Model approaches crime scenes as problems (or puzzles) to be solved through critical thinking and has enabled departments to identify patterns among homicides. Such links have led to more efficient investigations and homicide reduction strategies (Schmerler, Perkins, Phillips, Rhinehart, & Townsend, 2002). When we combine technologies, techniques, teamwork, and critical thinking skills, with an understanding of the psychological aspects of homicide, we increase the likelihood that cases will be closed and victims will get justice.

6

Sex Crimes

UNDERSTANDING SEX CRIMES: A PRACTICAL OVERVIEW

From 1996 until 2012, an unidentified man known only as the "Teardrop Rapist" terrorized Los Angeles, California. He struck almost exclusively in the early morning hours, targeting women and girls who were on their way to work or school—alone. He approached his victims and engaged them in conversation before threatening them at knifepoint. Once he had them physically under his control, the Teardrop Rapist forced his victims to accompany him to a secluded location where he sexually assaulted them (Goldstein, 2015).

According to statements ascribed to several victims, the attacker had a tattoo of a teardrop beneath his eye. Although his identity was never discovered, DNA in combination with signature rituals related to his offending behavior linked him to a total of 35 sexual assaults. The victims ranged significantly in age, with the youngest known victim being only 14 at the time of the crime (Goldstein, 2015).

Cases similar to that of the Teardrop Rapist often instill fear in the general public. In fact, sexual offenses, possibly more than any other type of crime, elicit an intense emotional response from the community, resulting in an undeniable stigma attached to these crimes and the individuals who commit them. Therefore, it is critical for law enforcement to be specifically educated about sexual offenses in order to protect the community and deliver justice to the victims. Officers who work sex crimes will need to recognize and overcome social stigma in order to bring these unique offenders to justice—or supervise them throughout their incarceration or community correctional sentences. As you read through this chapter, note how your own preconceived ideas about these offenders and their motivations are challenged, how public perception influences these crimes, and how social and cultural attitudes toward sexual behavior play a significant role.

WHAT IS SEXUAL OFFENDING?

Although statutory definitions vary by state, a *sexual offense* is generally considered to be the use of physical force or coercion to engage in sexual behavior with someone against his or her will or with someone who cannot legally consent to such acts. The U.S. Department of Justice (2015) defines *sexual assault* as "any type of sexual contact or behavior that occurs without the explicit consent of the recipient." Sexual activities including forced sexual intercourse, forcible sodomy, child molestation, incest, fondling, and attempted rape are included under this definition. It should be noted that *child molestation* is sexual contact between an adult and a child. It is criminalized because a child is not a sexual being and therefore cannot legally provide consent. The term "child" is defined on a state-by-state basis and typically refers to a person age 13 or under.

When discussing sexual assault, it is necessary to differentiate the meaning of the word *rape*. Although rape is a type of sexual assault, not all sexual assaults are acts of rape. Rape was previously defined as "unlawful sexual intercourse with a female, by force or without legal or factual consent" (U.S. Department of Justice, 1988). The *Uniform Crime Reports* (UCR) formerly distinguished between *forcible rape* or "the carnal knowledge of a female forcibly and against her will" (Federal Bureau of Investigation, 2005, p. 27) and *statutory rape*, which is engaging in sexual relations with a female who has not yet reached the age of legal consent.

As you can see, these definitions are limited and extremely antiquated. In order to more accurately reflect the assortment of sexual behaviors that falls within the purview of various states' rape or sexual assault statutes, as well as to create a gender-neutral conceptualization, the definition of *rape* has been revised to read: "The penetration, no matter how slight, of the vagina or anus with any body part or object, or oral penetration by a sex organ of another person, without the consent of the victim" (U.S. Department of Justice, 2012). The concept of *date rape,* or sexual assault that occurs within the parameters of a dating relationship, falls within the scope of this description. This broader characterization also encompasses offenses where the victim *could* not provide consent due to mental or physical impairment, intoxication, or unconsciousness.

Rape by fraud, deception, or impersonation occurs when a perpetrator engages in sexual relations with a *consenting* victim, but under fraudulent conditions. The logic is that had the fraudulent conditions not been present, consent would not have been obtained. For example, a therapist who has sex with his or her patient under the guise that it is part of the prescribed treatment is engaging in rape by deception (Bartol & Bartol, 2008). Currently, 27 states do not prosecute individuals who have sex through deception (Slomnicki, 2013). However, several states have proposed legislation to permit the prosecution of such offenders.

Additionally, there are numerous *noncontact sex offenses* such as lewd and lascivious conduct, indecent exposure (e.g., flashing), possession (or production) of child pornography, luring a minor for the purpose of sexual contact, and sex trafficking. Although there is no direct sexual contact involved, the motivation itself is sexual and therefore the preceding crimes are considered sexual offenses.

Nature and Scope of Sexual Violence

Sexual violence is a pervasive epidemic in the United States. Results from the National Violence Against Women Survey found that an estimated 302,100 women and 92,700 men are forcibly raped in the United States every year. Additionally, approximately one in six women and one in 33 men has been the victim of an attempted or completed sexual assault (Tjaden & Thoennes, 1998a). By the time they reach adulthood, one out of four females and one out of seven males will have been subjected to sexual abuse (Finkelhor, 1994). This data is mirrored in official statistics such as those compiled by the National Incidence Based Reporting System (NIBRS), which indicate that just over two-thirds (67%) of victims of reported sexual assaults are minors (under the age of 18) and half of those victims are under the age of 12 (Snyder, 2000).

Research illustrates that females are particularly vulnerable to sexual victimization. In fact, they are more than 6 times as likely as males to be the victims of sexual violence. According to a report published by the Bureau of Justice Statistics, nearly all forcible rapes (99%) are committed against females. Similarly, females comprise the majority of victims who are sexually assaulted with an object (87%) and subjected to forced sexual contact/molestation (82%). In contrast, the majority (54%) of victims of forcible sodomy are male (Snyder, 2000).

101

Additionally, statistics indicate that a male's risk of being sexually abused decreases as he enters adolescence, whereas a female's chances increase as she progresses from childhood to adolescence. The NIBRS data concludes that a female's risk reaches its height at approximately age 14, whereas a male is most likely to become the victim of sexual assault when he is age 4. A male's risk decreases dramatically (by a factor of 5) by the time he reaches age 17 (Snyder, 2000).

These statistics highlight an important issue—all of our information about sexual assault is based on data from crimes that have been reported to authorities. However, experts estimate that as many as 84% of victims do not report having been sexually assaulted (Kilpatrick, Edmunds, & Seymour, 1992) because they are ashamed, embarrassed, afraid, or consider it too personal to disclose (Catalano, 2005). Given these findings, sexual assault is likely the most underreported of all crimes.

Of those sexual offenders who are detected and subsequently arrested, approximately 95% are male (Federal Bureau of Investigation, 2005). Perhaps unsurprisingly, sex offenses committed by females are even less likely to come to the attention of law enforcement than those committed by male perpetrators. In recent years, public awareness about the commission of sex crimes by females has increased in large part due to cases involving high school teachers engaging in illicit sexual contact with male students. However, these cases do not adequately illustrate the scope of sexual abuse committed by women. According to the Center for Sex Offender Management (CSOM) (2007), women account for 1% of all adult arrests for forcible rape and 6% of those for other types of sex crimes. However, victimization surveys reveal that as many as 63% of female victims and up to 27% of male victims report having been sexually abused by a woman (Schwartz & Cellini, 1995).

As you read through this chapter, keep in mind that although anyone can perpetrate sexual violence, the majority of the research to date focuses on male sex offenders. Therefore, best practices or evidence-based technologies for treating, assessing, and managing female sex offenders do not exist at this time. Most of the current practices extrapolate from methods utilized with male offenders and seek to incorporate gender-responsiveness.

SEX OFFENSE LEGISLATION

Legislation surrounding sexual assault has undergone significant modifications, including several landmark rulings that have come to define public awareness about sex crimes. The following laws were enacted as a result of highly publicized (and markedly vicious) attacks committed by previously convicted sex offenders who had been released into the community. Although the requirements set forth by these laws apply to all individuals who have committed a sexual offense, readers should be mindful that not all sex offenders are violent.

The Jacob Wetterling Act

In October of 1989, 11-year-old Jacob Wetterling was abducted at gunpoint by a masked man near his home in St. Joseph, Minnesota. Despite an abundance of community assistance and support, young Jacob was never found. His kidnapping resulted in the establishment of Minnesota's Sex Offender Registration Act. Prior to this act, police personnel had no resources for identifying the whereabouts of convicted (and released) sex offenders in the community in order to assist in investigations of this sort. In 1994, Congress passed the Jacob Wetterling Crimes Against Children and Sex Offender Registration Act, which requires each state to establish a mandated sex offender registry to catalogue and track sexual offenders residing in the community (CSOM, 2001).

Megan's Law

In 1994, Jesse Timmendequas raped and murdered his 7-year-old neighbor Megan Kanka. He had twice been convicted of child molestation prior to moving into Megan's neighborhood in Hamilton, New Jersey. In the wake of Megan's murder, the Kanka family became strong proponents of community notification. They were outspoken about their belief that Megan's death would have been avoided had they known that Timmendequas was a sexual predator (CSOM, 2001).

The heinous murder of Megan Kanka resulted in mandatory *community notification*, which requires each state to release sex offender registration information to specific individuals as necessitated by public safety standards. The extent of notification varies depending upon the offender's risk of reoffense. It follows that if the risk of reoffense is low (referred to as Level or Tier 1), only law enforcement likely to encounter the individual are directly informed. Level or Tier 2 offenders are reported to relevant agencies such as schools, day care centers, domestic violence shelters, and so on. In many states, moderate risk offenders' information is also published on the Internet registry and made accessible to anyone actively searching the database. With regard to high-risk offenders, some community members (i.e., neighbors within a certain radius), in addition to police personnel and designated agencies, must be notified (Bartol & Bartol, 2008; CSOM, 2001).

Despite the vigorous advocacy of the Kanka family and impassioned public response, community notification does not necessarily serve to reduce sexual reoffending. Prentky (1996) argues that due to the relatively small radius of notification, offenders can reasonably continue to offend in nearby neighborhoods outside the range of notification. This information is supported by the results of Washington Institute for Public Policy's study, which found no statistically significant difference in recidivism rates between offenders subject to notification (19% rate of recidivism) and those who were not (22% rate of recidivism) over a 1 to 4 year follow-up period (Levenson, 2003).

The Pam Lychner Act

The Pam Lychner Act made further changes to sex offender registration by increasing registration requirements for repeat and violent offenders. Under this act, those offenders who pose the greatest risk to society are required to register wherever they go throughout the course of their entire lives. This piece of legislation is named for Pam Lychner who was a real estate agent in Houston, Texas. She was brutally attacked by a convicted sex offender who had been lying in wait for her at a vacant home she was showing (Bartol & Bartol, 2008).

It is important to note that while registration and notification work in tandem, they are different entities under the law. Registration refers to a system for monitoring and "keeping tabs" on sex offenders once they have been released from incarceration and are living in the community. Notification is the process of informing specific parties, as previously described, as to the whereabouts of these offenders. In many states, Internet databases play a key role in community notification.

Sexually Violent Predator Act

The wide array of behaviors that constitute sexual abuse has led to the logical conclusion that certain perpetrators are more dangerous than others due to their predatory nature and the likelihood that they will reoffend (Kendall & Cheung, 2004). The law addresses this point by differentiating a subtype of sex offender, known as a sexually violent predator

(SVP), who is subject to more stringent supervision. According to Lieb and Matson (1998), in many states, the term "sexual predator" applies to sexual "offenders who target strangers, have multiple victims, or who commit especially violent offenses" (p. 1). Washington State's Community Protection Act of 1990 defines a sexually violent predator as "any person who has been convicted of ... a sexually violent offense and who suffers from a mental abnormality or personality disorder which makes the person likely to engage in predatory acts of sexual violence" (Fitch, 1998, p. 237). This classification has informed public policy to enact (controversial) SVP statutes that seek to isolate those convicted sex offenders most likely to reoffend until such time as they no longer pose a threat to society (Carlsmith, Monahan, & Evans, 2007; Levenson, 2003).

SVP laws have led 17 states to pass sex offender civil commitment legislation (Jackson & Richards, 2007). Although such statutes have been rather widely implemented, a universal agreement has yet to be reached regarding their constitutionality. Those who oppose these laws have argued that they merely seek further retribution against individuals who have already been punished, while those in favor of them make the utilitarian argument that civilly committing sexually violent predators increases the well-being of society (Carlsmith et al., 2007).

Research indicates that the efficacy of SVP statutes is largely dependent upon the ability to assess risk accurately, identify those offenders most likely to recidivate, and determine whether sexually violent offenders have been adequately treated or sanctioned upon their release from prison (Kendall & Cheung, 2004).

RAPE MYTHS AND RAPE CULTURE

It is impossible to have a comprehensive discussion about sexual assault without first acknowledging and dispelling rape myths. *Rape myths* are false beliefs based on the traditional and outdated concept that masculinity requires men to sexually dominate women. Some of these beliefs serve to explain, excuse, and justify sexually based offenses as almost "natural" due to a "boys will be boys" mentality, while others outright deny the existence of sexual assault or place the blame on victims. Research reveals that many rapists endorse such distortions, and that subscribing to rape myths is correlated with misogynistic attitudes and hostility toward women (Forbes, Adams-Curtis, & White, 2004). Some common myths are detailed in Table 6.1.

105

Table 6.1   Common Rape Myths

Myth	Fact
Women who dress provocatively or act in certain ways are "asking for it."	No one asks to be sexually assaulted. The responsibility for committing the crime falls solely on the offender. Additionally, there is much variation among victims' styles of dress and behavioral patterns.
Date rape and spousal rape are not *real* rape.	No means no, regardless of the relationship between victim and offender.
Most rapes are committed by strangers.	The majority of rapes are perpetrated by someone known to the victim.
Rape is the result of men not being able to control their sexual urges. Therefore, once a man is aroused, he *can't* stop until he has sex.	A man *can* physically stop at any point during sexual activity. If he *chooses* not to and commits a sexual offense as a result, his crime is about power and control—not sexual attraction.
If someone initially agrees to have sex and then changes his or her mind, it is not considered rape if his or her partner keeps going.	Everyone has the right to say no to sexual activity *at any point*. It is their partner's responsibility to respect these boundaries.
Women secretly fantasize about/want to be dominated and raped.	While some women fantasize about rough sex, they are in control of their fantasies. No one wants to experience the trauma and terror associated with sexual assault. Rape is *not* just rough sex.
If the victim isn't severely injured, it isn't really rape.	Coercion, threats, and verbal pressure are tactics often used by assailants. It is *never* acceptable (or legal) to pressure someone into sexual activity. This is *always* a form of sexual assault.
Women make rape allegations as a means of getting revenge or overcoming guilt following a regrettable sexual encounter.	When a rape is reported, the victim must disclose details of the crime which can be humiliating. By and large, the victims that subject themselves to this difficult task are telling the truth.
Rape is a crime against women—men and boys cannot be sexually assaulted.	Anyone, regardless of age, race, gender, sexual preference, marital status, creed, or culture can be a victim of sexual assault.

As you can see, several of the myths fail to hold the offender accountable, and in most cases put the victim's behavior on trial instead. Such beliefs can be detrimental to victims, as they may begin to blame themselves and subsequently avoid seeking help.

An extreme example of the overwhelming damage caused by rape culture occurred in Steubenville, Ohio. In August of 2012, two high school football players publically sexually assaulted an intoxicated female student. The assault was captured on video and posted—with callous disregard for the victim—to social media outlets. Other students perpetuated the objectification and offending behavior by posting comments that made light of the assault and shamed the victim for having been drinking and "putting herself" in that situation. Although the perpetrators were brought to justice, much of the community sympathized with the offenders for having lost their promising futures, and appeared to blame the victim for *causing* this loss.

The Steubenville case highlights the all too frequent problem whereby the court of public opinion judges an offender's accountability based upon how the victim's behavior is viewed. In the Steubenville case, many people focused on the fact that the victim was intoxicated and therefore blamed her. Similarly, victims can be judged for their sexual behavior. In order to protect victims of sexual assault from being criticized, dismissed as unreliable, or worse yet, put on trial themselves, rape shield laws have been enacted. These rulings protect victims by excluding their sexual history, including their sexual reputation, from the courtroom.

CHARACTERISTICS OF SEXUAL OFFENDERS

Logic dictates that it would be helpful for both criminal justice professionals and the public to know which personality traits and demographic characteristics are common among sex offenders. Law enforcement's ability to recognize such qualities could assist them in narrowing suspect pools and closing sexual assault investigations. Additionally, having a specific personality profile to reference could make court proceedings involving sex crimes smoother and supervising sexual offenders in the community easier. Having access to this type of information would also inform the development of appropriate protective measures for society.

Many people believe that all sex offenders are easily identifiable because they fall into expected and stereotypical categories such as the child molester who lures children from the playground with promises of candy and puppies, or the masked man who rapes unsuspecting women at knifepoint in dark alleyways (CSOM, 2015). Do you think these stereotypes are accurate reflections of the broad spectrum of sexual offenders?

Despite efforts to discern a specific set of qualities to describe all individuals who engage in sexually abusive behavior, researchers have found that no single profile exists with which to define the "typical" sex offender. That is because sexual offenders are a heterogeneous population. With the exception of having committed a sex crime, it is often difficult to decipher what sets them apart not only from other types of criminals, but from the general public as well. As a group, sex offenders hail from a variety of backgrounds and demographics; they are more similar to the general population than they are different (CSOM, n.d.a.). To further examine the diversity among these individuals, see Table 6.2.

Table 6.2 Sex Offender Demographics

Trait	Description
Age	Juveniles as well as adults (ranging greatly in age) commit acts of sexual violence.
Race	Sexual offenders come from all racial backgrounds.
Gender	Although male sex offenders are more common, females also commit acts of sexual violence.
Socioeconomic Status	Some sex offenders have achieved high SES, while others are destitute.
Intellectual Functioning	Some sex offenders exhibit high intellectual ability, while others are of average intelligence. Still others have below average intellect and may be described as cognitively limited.
Mental Health	Mental health diagnoses are no more prevalent among the sex offender population than they are among the general population.
Sexual Preference	Sex offenders may be heterosexual, homosexual, bisexual, transsexual, or transgendered.

Source: CSOM, *Understanding sex offenders: An introductory curriculum*. Retrieved from: http://www.csom.org/train/etiology/3/3_1.htm, n.d.

As you can see, engaging in sexually abusive behavior is not limited to any particular demographic. You may be wondering what exactly these perpetrators *do* have in common with each other. Studies have established the existence of several issues that appear to be prevalent among a broad range of sexual offenders:

- *Deviant sexual arousal; deviant sexual interest/preference*: Sex offenders are aroused by things outside the realm of what is considered to be sexually appropriate. These include sexual contact with children/minors, forced sex, peeping/watching others undress, engaging in sexual acts in public, or inflicting or receiving pain during sex (Laws & O'Donohue, 1997).
- *Cognitive distortions*: There is a general consensus among experts that most sex offenders know that their actions are both illegal and harmful. Yet, they commit their crime(s) anyway. Their behavior is likely the result of having engaged in distorted thinking and/or having held pro-offending attitudes. They often tell themselves (and others) that their behavior wasn't that bad, that the victim initiated the sexual contact, or that the victim deserved it. Such statements seek to minimize or justify the offense and additionally give the offender "permission" to continue his or her abusive behavior (CSOM, n.d.a.).
- *Social, interpersonal, and intimacy deficits*: Social difficulties, such as communication deficits, isolation, and difficulty maintaining intimate relationships appear to be rather common among sex offenders (Bumby, 2000).
- *Lack of victim empathy*: Researchers previously held the notion that sexual offenders lack empathic concern for humanity. In other words, they are unable to put themselves in someone else's shoes emotionally speaking. However, more recent research indicates that sex offenders' lack of empathy is specific to their victim(s) (Bumby, 2000).
- *Poor coping skills*: Problems with self-regulation, specifically with regard to emotions and behavior, may be relevant to sexual violence. Many sex offenders lack prosocial coping techniques, which may be part of what leads them to engage in sexually abusive activity.
- *Abuse history*: Although having been victimized as a child does not *cause* someone to go on to become an abusive adult, many sex offenders have a history of emotional, physical, or sexual abuse.

109

TYPOLOGIES OF ADULT MALE RAPISTS

Similar to the broader population of sexual offenders, rapists' motivations vary widely. In order to assist investigators, psychologists, and other criminal justice personnel, several typologies of rapists have been developed, based largely upon research with male offenders (Pozzulo et al., 2013). Such typologies are useful in recognizing the variations among offenders, identifying crime patterns, understanding victim selection, and examining the motives underlying such crimes.

Groth, Burgess, and Holmstrom (1977) developed a widely utilized classification system that divides adult male rapists into four subtypes: (a) power reassurance, (b) power assertive, (c) anger retaliatory, and (d) anger excitation. *Power reassurance rapists* lack confidence especially with regard to their interactions with women. By forcing their victims to engage in sexual contact, they feel empowered; it is their way of proving their masculinity to themselves. While their crimes inflict unquestionable harm, these offenders do not intend/want to injure or degrade their victims, as evidenced by the minimal amount of force they use. Although power reassurance rapists are not typically acquainted with their victims, they often fantasize some sort of relationship with them. They are driven by this fantasy to the extent that they believe the sexual offense is consensual (Hazelwood & Burgess, 2001).

Unlike in the case of power reassurance rapists, fantasy does not play a vital role in the crimes committed by *power assertive rapists*. These individuals are not motivated by a lack of self-confidence, rather, they sexually offend as a means of exerting dominance over women; they believe that this is their right as men. These offenders experience a sense of male entitlement and routinely objectify females. They are responsible for a significant amount of acquaintance, date, and spousal rapes (Hazelwood & Burgess, 2001).

Attacks by *anger retaliatory rapists* are highly impulsive and motivated by rage. They seek revenge against their victims, who are often women, for real or perceived injustices committed against them by (other) females. Their attacks are violent and employ sex as the weapon with which to brutalize and degrade the victim(s). Although this typology of rapist is more physically vicious, they are less common than the previous two classifications discussed (Hazelwood & Burgess, 2001).

Anger excitation rapists comprise the fourth classification. These individuals are markedly sadistic. They derive pleasure from and achieve sexual arousal by causing their victims to suffer. Their assaults are overtly violent and may involve extreme brutality and bizarre forms of torture.

They live a rich fantasy life, which plays a major role in the excruciatingly detailed planning of their offenses. Under the most extreme circumstances, these offenders may commit sexual homicide or even mutilate their victims (Hazelwood & Burgess, 2001).

Hazelwood and Burgess (2001) also discuss a fifth type of sex offender—the highly impulsive *opportunistic rapist*. The individuals that fall into this category commit sexual assaults in order to achieve sexual gratification. They are likely the only type of rapist whose motivation is predominantly sexual. Their offenses are often committed as an afterthought to another crime. For example, they may enter a home with the intention of burglarizing it, however, upon finding an attractive female alone in the house, they take the opportunity to act upon a sudden sexual urge. A well-known example of an opportunistic assault is the Steubenville, Ohio case discussed earlier in this chapter. According to reports, the perpetrators did not attend the party for the purpose of committing an act of sexual violence, however, when the opportunity presented itself, they took advantage of it in order to achieve sexual gratification.

Knight and Prentky (1990) of the Massachusetts Treatment Center developed a similar classification system, wherein rapists were typed based upon five primary motives: opportunity, pervasive anger, sexual gratification, sadistic fantasy, and vindictiveness. Similarly, Groth (1979) outlined three subtypes of rapists based upon both their motivations and crime characteristics: anger rapist, power rapist, and sadistic rapist.

Cameron Hooker

One of the most highly publicized sadistic sexual assaults was that committed by Cameron Hooker. Growing up, Hooker was shunned by his peers due to his gangly appearance and inherent awkwardness. He was socially inept and lacked athletic prowess. As a result of the peer rejection that he suffered, Hooker sought solitary activities, such as collecting pornography. He became mainly interested in material focused on misogynistic acts involving bondage, domination, sadism, and masochism (BDSM) culture. He began to fantasize about torturing women, especially those that had ignored him (McGuire & Norton, 1988).

At the age of 19, Hooker met 15-year-old Janice. She boasted little self-confidence, having been mistreated by men for most of her life. Playing on her insecurities, Hooker refrained from initiating her into his fetishistic lifestyle until their dating relationship had been solidified. Once she

111

was fully under his control, Hooker made his fantasies—and expectations—known. Although she found the idea aberrant, Janice feared losing Hooker so much that she complied with his wishes. As the relationship progressed, so did Hooker's sadistic fantasies. He began introducing torture devices into his repertoire. Regardless of Janice's discomfort with Hooker's inclinations, the two were married in 1975 (Ramsland, n.d.).

Soon after their nuptials, the couple developed marital difficulties. Janice had grown tired of her husband's deviant interests and yearned to be a mother. Hooker, however, needed increasingly violent and sadistic activities in order to achieve sexual satisfaction. Therefore, the two came to an agreement. Hooker would father a child and in return Janice would help him abduct a sex slave with whom he could act out his fantasies (Ramsland, n.d.).

In 1976, Janice became pregnant with the couple's first child. That same year, Cameron and Janice Hooker kidnapped their first "slave." Their victim was Marie Spannhake, a hitchhiker. According to McGuire and Norton (1988), the Hookers drove her to their home, stripped her, and tied her to the ceiling. Spannhake screamed and cried, causing Hooker to deem her uncooperative; the crime ended in murder. Then, on May 19, 1977, the Hookers, while out with their infant daughter, abducted another hitchhiker. Her name was Colleen Stan and she would remain with them until 1984 (Ramsland, n.d.).

During the 7 years that Hooker held Stan hostage, he beat and molested her daily. He also used medieval torture devices to inflict physical pain on her as well as homemade contraptions to disorient her. He raped her repeatedly. Further into Stan's captivity, Hooker built a box shaped like a coffin in which he kept her for a period of approximately one month. He reportedly tested Stan's obedience by forcing her to point an unloaded gun down her own throat and pull the trigger (McGuire & Norton, 1988).

In addition to the intense physical and sexual abuse endured by Stan, one of the most striking aspects of this case was the psychological trauma. For instance, Hooker convinced her that he belonged to an underground organization of slave traders that would kill her and her family if she disobeyed him or attempted to escape. Confident that his control over Stan was firm, Hooker began stalking and photographing other women he planned to take as slaves. He then engaged Stan to build a dungeon for future conquests (Ramsland, n.d.; Towers, 2009).

Stan's imprisonment came to an end when Janice, having been influenced by her newly found religious convictions, became disturbed by the acts taking place in her home and reported them. Cameron Hooker was apprehended on November 18, 1984. When he was arrested, police found a collection of leather straps, handcuffs, and homemade torture devices in his home. Although he pleaded not guilty to a total of 16 felony charges including kidnapping, rape, and sodomy, Hooker was convicted at trial and is currently serving a 106-year custodial sentence (Ramsland, n.d.). As part of a program meant to reduce its prison population, the state of California granted Hooker an early parole hearing. However, his petition for release was denied and he will not become eligible for parole again until 2017 (Parry, 2015).

As you can see, sadism was the overriding factor throughout Cameron Hooker's offense history. However, his crimes also exhibited characteristics of other subtypes, illustrating that there is some crossover among the classifications. For example, Hooker's lack of self-confidence, lust for power, and use of fantasy overlap the power reassurance typology. His anger toward women combined with his desire for vengeance is indicative of the anger retaliatory subtype. However, Hooker clearly qualifies as an anger excitation/sadistic rapist, given his need to brutalize and torture his victims (including his own wife) in order to achieve sexual satisfaction. Fantasy played a key role in his offenses, from his obsession with pornography to his creation of torture devices, to the lies that he told Colleen Stan in order to control her. His crimes were premeditated and his behavior resulted in the ultimate act of physical aggression: homicide.

CLASSIFICATIONS OF CHILD MOLESTERS

As with rapists, typologies have been developed to better grasp the differing motivations and potential targets of child molesters. In order to understand sexual crimes against children, we must initially define a few important terms. The first is *pedophilia*, which is sexual attraction to children, usually prepubescent children. This is often differentiated from *hebephilia*, which is sexual attraction to and/or sexual contact with adolescents. Both of these are considered to be *paraphilias* or sexual disorders in which the afflicted individual is almost exclusively attracted to deviant stimuli. When discussing child molesters, we recognize that there are those that offend against children to whom they are not related (or *extra-familial child molesters*) and those that target children within their families, to whom they have ready access (*intra-familial child molesters*).

113

Using this information as well as data gleaned from research with incarcerated child molesters, Groth, Hobson, and Gary (1982) developed what is perhaps the most widely implemented classification of child molesters. It divides these offenders into two categories:

- *Fixated child molesters* have a fundamental sexual attraction to children. Most do not engage in age-appropriate sexual encounters; instead, they focus their energies on establishing relationships with vulnerable children. Fixated child molesters often target minor male victims and their pre-offense behavior includes premeditation and grooming. Because their primary sexual interests and preferences are deviant, they are considered to be at higher risk for reoffense.
- *Regressed child molesters* are motivated by an emotional void, rather than a deviant sexual desire. Most of them maintain "typical" sexual interests and engage in sexual contact with children as a means of coping with significant stressors. Their crimes are opportunistic, situational, and impulsive. Unlike fixated child molesters, regressed child molesters tend to target minor females with whom they are familiar. Victims often include children to whom they have access during times of stress such as family members.

FEMALE SEXUAL OFFENDERS

Like men, women who commit sexual offenses tend to have poor coping skills, intimacy deficits, cognitive distortions, and a lack of empathic concern for their victim(s) (Allen, 1991; Denov & Cortoni, 2006; Grayston & DeLuca, 1999; Mathews, Matthews, & Speltz, 1989; Nathan & Ward, 2001, 2002). Preliminary findings suggest that adult female sex offenders may also commonly exhibit the following: a history of childhood abuse, symptoms of mental illness, personality disorder, and/or substance abuse, a tendency to victimize children and adolescents, a propensity to offend against individuals known to them, and an increased likelihood to commit sexual offenses with a male partner. Females are also more likely than males to commit sexual abuse within the context of a caregiving relationship (CSOM, 2007).

While most research has focused on typologies of male offenders, Mathews et al. (1989) developed an influential framework with which to categorize women who sexually victimize others:

- *Male-coerced*: These women are passive and dependent and have suffered significant abuse. Because they fear abandonment, they are pressured by male partners to commit acts of sexual violence, usually targeting their own children.
- *Predisposed*: These offenders often act alone and victimize their own children, or other children in their families. They frequently present with abuse histories (incestuous victimization), psychological difficulties, and deviant sexual fantasies.
- *Teacher/lover*: Women in this category often struggle with age-appropriate relationships and believe that they have a romantic or sexual mentoring "relationship" with their adolescent victim. Therefore, they fail to view their behavior as "criminal."

RISK ASSESSMENT AND RECIDIVISM

Police, parole, probation, and correctional officers responsible for the apprehension, interrogation, and supervision of sex offenders often need to know which offenders should be considered high risk and most likely to engage in recidivistic behavior. Becoming familiar with risk factors can help officers spot warning signs during the course of an interview with an offender or determine whether a specific individual may benefit from treatment (Fernandez, Harris, Hanson, & Sparks, 2012).

There are three types of risk factors or variables with which we need to be concerned: static, dynamic, and risk management. *Static factors* are those things in an offender's life that do not change over time, such as criminal history. Such factors are important because the single best predictor of future behavior is past behavior. The following are examples of static variables that directly correlate with reoffense:

- Young age at onset of sexually offensive behavior
- Prior history of sexual violence
- Prior history of (nonsexual) violence (i.e., assault, attempted murder, battery, etc.)
- Prior imposition of sentencing for law-breaking behavior (not limited to sexual or violent offenses)
- Targeting male victims
- Having a victim who is either unrelated or unfamiliar (i.e., not a family member and/or not previously known to the offender)
- Demonstrated sexually deviant interest (i.e., attraction to children)

- Unmarried, with no history of appropriate long-term relationships
- A diagnosis of antisocial personality disorder (ASPD) or psychopathy

Unlike static variables, *dynamic risk factors* can change over time. Because they represent an offender's moods, attitudes, thoughts/beliefs, and interpretation of the world, they can improve with therapeutic intervention. The following dynamic (or changeable) variables tend to predict sexual reoffending:

- Intimacy deficits; problems in intimate relationships
- Hostility toward women
- Feelings of rejection and/or overall negative outlook
- Emotional identification with children
- Sexual preoccupation or deviant sexual preference
- Impulsivity or lifestyle instability (such as in the domains of employment, housing, substance use, etc.)
- Antisocial attitudes (i.e., attitudes that support criminal behavior)
- Noncompliance with parole/probation or court-mandated sex offense-specific therapy

Lastly, *risk management predictors* focus on the offender's current environment (or the environment to which the individual will be released once incarceration has ended). Such variables include stable housing, access to food, employment, appropriate familial support such as contact with family members who know the offender's situation and encourage compliance with supervision, and therapeutic support, including drug, alcohol, mental health, and offense-specific treatment as indicated. These factors are typically assessed with regard to risk of violent reoffense (rather than risk of sexual reoffense). However, the general premise holds true for sex offenders: the more supportive an individual's post-release environment, the more stable that person will become. Stability inherently lowers the risk of recidivism.

Triggers and Their Relationship to Sexual Offending

Now that you have an understanding of the various issues present in the lives of many sex offenders, and the risk factors that indicate a risk to reoffend, let's examine the behavioral chain that leads to sexual violence.

Research indicates that the pattern of a sex offense begins with *lifestyle risk factors* (Morin & Levenson, 2002). When individuals do not know how to get their emotional needs met in healthy or acceptable ways, they are more prone to engage in unhealthy or criminal behaviors. For example, persons struggling with poor self-esteem are more likely to stay in a dead-end job (because they do not believe that they can achieve more), remain in an unhealthy relationship (because they feel that they do not deserve better), isolate themselves, or resort to substance abuse to dull the emotional pain (known as self-medicating).

Triggers represent the next link in the offense chain. A trigger is anything that sparks the thought of offending and can be internal (feelings), external (situations or events), or a combination thereof. Oftentimes, an individual's unhealthy lifestyle may result in negative emotionality, such as feelings of anger, frustration, depression, hurt/rejection, or powerlessness. These feelings in turn lead to deviant desires and thoughts of offending.

An example of an external trigger would be a child walking down the street by herself. Seeing this could cause the would-be offender to become excited by the opportunity to commit a sexual assault. An external trigger may also result in an internal trigger. For example, a man experiencing feelings of inadequacy and whose sexual advances toward women have been rejected may find himself at risk if surrounded by attractive (or scantily clad) women at a local bar. This situation (external trigger) may drive him to feel resentment or anger (internal triggers). He may then begin to obsess about how unfair it is for women to flaunt their sexuality in front of him, but refuse his overtures. This resentment may lead him to think about forcing a woman to have sex with him (Morin & Levenson, 2002).

Fantasy is the next step in the pattern. As explained in Chapter 5, fantasy offers an escape from hurtful or harmful emotions. For sexual offenders, this is coupled with their pattern of deviant arousal (Morin & Levenson, 2002).

Once the potential offender has engaged in a deviant fantasy, the next step in the behavior chain is the development of a *plan of action*. In other words, it is at this point in the offense pattern that the individual makes the decision to control inappropriate urges and avoid (or cope with) triggers or to proceed with committing the offense.

An individual's decision to engage in sexual violence (the plan) gives way to a subsequent *high-risk situation*, such as coming into contact with a potential victim. The offender begins to lose control and engages in behaviors that can potentially give way to an actual offense. For example, an assailant who targets children may let a child sit on his lap, whereas an adult female-target rapist may make the decision to walk a drunken woman home after a party (Morin & Levenson, 2002). This *lapse*, or loss of control, provides the opportunity to offend. The final step in the chain is the *offense* itself.

INVESTIGATING SEX CRIMES

In order to thoroughly and successfully investigate a sex crime, police not only need to be trained in investigative strategies, but they also must be cognizant of certain characteristics specific to sexual assault. The first is that most (up to 80%) sexual offenses go unreported; therefore, the majority of sex offenders are undetected by law enforcement. This means that although a suspect may have never encountered the criminal justice system prior to the present investigation, he or she may well have committed undocumented and uncharged sex crimes. Additionally, many of these offenders may not present as stereotypically "criminal" due to a high degree of psychological sophistication (Archambault, Eisenga, Lisak, & Keenan, 2001). This is when it becomes especially critical for police to remember that *anyone* from the career criminal to the Wall Street trader to the teacher to the favorite relative can be a sex offender.

Investigators should additionally be mindful of the fact that the majority of assailants are acquainted with their victims. This preexisting relationship may lead some suspects to use "consent" as a defense. In other words, when confronted about their crime, they may shift the focus onto the victim's behavior and couch the attack in terms of victim regret, following a consensual sexual encounter. Such claims seek to minimize the offender's culpability, while undermining the victim's credibility. As this is a common tactic employed by offenders, investigators should *expect* to encounter suspects that refer to their victims as promiscuous, troubled, dishonest, unreliable, and so on (Archambault et al., 2001). Being aware of this will help police make informed decisions about employing various investigative strategies.

Prior to conducting an interrogation, police should review *all* pertinent background information. It is crucial that investigators are prepared when they commence the first interview for two reasons: First, being unprepared can result in the investigators tipping their hand so to speak, which serves only to provide the suspect with unparalleled insight into their case. Second, the likelihood is high that the suspect's cooperation will decrease with each subsequent police contact. Detectives should allow suspects to complete their statement, offering up as much information as possible, without interrupting them to address inconsistencies (Archambault et al., 2001; Johnson, 2012).

In the case of rape, police should determine whether the attack was a "blitz attack" committed by a stranger or a "confidence attack," which manipulates a preexisting relationship between the victim and offender and causes the victim to drop his or her guard. In the case of a confidence rape, investigators may choose to set up a pretext phone call. Although such tactics are not admissible in court in certain states, they can be highly impactful in those states where they can be entered into evidence. A pretext phone call, also referred to as a monitored call, occurs when police instruct the victim to phone the offender while they record the call. Although a confession is unlikely, such conversations can offer assistance, as the suspect may make incriminating statements useful to the ongoing investigation (Archambault et al., 2001). Despite the utility of this method, police should keep in mind that asking a victim to contact his or her assailant can result in further trauma to that victim.

Sex offenders, similar to the larger criminal population, are likely to exhibit personality disorders such as antisocial personality disorder, narcissistic personality disorder, and paranoid personality disorder. Interview and interrogation techniques, which will be described in Chapter 9, should be tailored to such deficits. However, sex crimes investigators specifically are sure to interview suspects who exhibit various paraphilias, such as sadism, pedophilia, exhibitionism, necrophilia, and voyeurism. Such paraphilic behaviors should be viewed as pervasive (Archambault et al., 2001).

Although it sounds obvious, an investigator responsible for interviewing sex offenders should be comfortable hearing about and discussing sexually deviant behavior. He or she should avoid using abrasive labels such as "rapist," "child molester," or "pervert" as these will ensure the suspect's lack of cooperation. Many sexual offenders experience shame and guilt attached to their offending behavior; they feel isolated from and rejected by society. Therefore, investigators should build rapport by demonstrating that they understand the offender's emotional experience and struggles. Without ever displaying doubt with regard to the victim's account of the crime, investigators can minimize the offense by not conferring moral judgment. A suspect who does not fear rejection from the detective is more likely to engage in open dialogue. The detective should also be prepared to call in an investigator of the opposite gender, as some suspects will relate better to men as opposed to women or vice versa (Archambault et al., 2001).

119

SEX OFFENDER MANAGEMENT

Post incarceration (or sometimes in lieu of it), most sexual offenders will be subject to community supervision, the purpose of which is to monitor/ ensure their compliance with the law and facilitate their rehabilitation. Because these offenders require specialized supervision approaches, they present unique challenges to the community correctional agencies (i.e., probation and parole) tasked with overseeing them.

Research supports the implementation of collaborative supervision models, which utilize a multidisciplinary approach where victim and community safety are of the utmost importance. One such paradigm, known as the Containment Model, combines the efforts of a parole or probation officer, a sex offense-specific treatment provider, and a polygraph examiner. Information is shared among all of the supervising professionals assigned to a particular offender's case in order to form a comprehensive management team (CSOM, 2002).

To illustrate the efficacy of this model, imagine an offender who, despite having been convicted, denies culpability for his or her commitment offense. Struggling with denial impedes the individual's ability to progress in treatment. Therefore, the sex offense-specific therapist may refer him or her for a polygraph, the results of which would be used to further the offender's therapy. Through active engagement in the treatment process, the offender will develop an understanding of his or her triggers and risk factors, which will in turn inform the officer's specialized supervision strategy. For instance, the officer might mandate special conditions reflective of the offender's needs, such as participation in substance abuse counseling or a no Internet usage policy. As you can see, shared knowledge helps to not only protect the community, but also to assist the offender in avoiding reoffense.

Polygraph

Three types of polygraphs, each targeting a different issue, are utilized during the course of sex offender management: instant offense (or disclosure), single or specific issue, and maintenance (CSOM, 2002). The individual in the previous example would have been referred for an instant offense polygraph. These are used when (convicted) offenders deny having committed their crime. A polygraph examination assists both the officer and treatment provider in breaking down barriers to denial. A specific issue polygraph is appropriate when the officer or treatment provider has reason to believe that the offender is engaging in an identifiable behavior that either puts him or her at risk for reoffense or violates the conditions of supervision. Lastly, a maintenance polygraph is a more generalized examination, used to ensure that an offender has remained in compliance with the requirements of parole/probation. Community supervision strategies relating to a broader array of offenders (i.e., nonsexual offenders) will be discussed in Chapter 13.

MOTIVATING CHANGE

As you can see, all parties responsible for any facet of sex offender management are striving not only to keep the community safe, but also to assist the offender. Research indicates that the most effective interventions (i.e., programs that reduce recidivism and aid offenders in developing prosocial life skills) target three specific issues: risk, needs, and responsivity. The "risk" principle refers to the fact that programming should be geared toward those offenders who have a higher risk of recidivism. Intensive supervision and highly focused intervention will benefit this population more than low-risk offenders, because high-risk individuals have an increased need to develop adaptive skills and coping mechanisms (Walters, Clark, Gingerich, & Meltzer, 2007).

"Needs" refers to those aspects of an offender's life that predict reoffense *and* can be changed, in other words, dynamic risks. Research conducted by Andrews and Bonta (2003) identifies six dynamic variables that are directly correlated with the commission of criminal behavior. Therefore, addressing them serves to reduce recidivism (Walters et al., 2007):

- Improving impulse control
- Increasing social supports
- Developing empathy (and other prosocial values)
- Abandoning antisocial peers in lieu of prosocial people, places, and activities
- Engaging in (substance abuse) treatment
- Reestablishing primary/healthy relationships

Targeting criminogenic needs with offenders who pose the highest risk of reoffense will result in the greatest benefit to both the offenders and the community.

Lastly, "responsivity" means that interventions should be tailored to the needs of the individual offender. They should take into account how

121

motivated the person is to change and what type of intervention would be best suited to the individual at any given point in time (Walters et al., 2007).

One such person-centered approach is motivational interviewing (MI), which will be discussed in detail in Chapter 13. MI is recommended for use with individuals who do not see the need to change their own negative thoughts, feelings, or behaviors—and by extension, their criminal lifestyle. This method is collaborative and meant to inspire not only behavioral change, but also the desire to create said change. Professionals employing it should be empathetic and supportive in order to foster an environment in which offenders feel safe admitting to their vulnerabilities. Becoming confrontational is often futile as it increases offenders' resistance.

In order to make marked change, offenders need to become invested in their own recovery. Those officers supervising them can promote this process by providing supportive assistance in evaluating problematic qualities. One way to get offenders onboard, so to speak, is to elicit dialogue about positive change by phrasing questions in an encouraging way. For example, asking, "What would you like to change about your current situation?" is much more effective than threatening, "If you don't change, I'm going to lock you up." MI aims to move the offender through a spectrum of emotional and cognitive responses that range from denial to acceptance to positive change. This evidence-based practice highlights the influence officers can have on offenders' recovery and, by extension, the community's safety.

SECONDARY TRAUMA IN LAW
ENFORCEMENT PROFESSIONALS

As interesting and important as working with the sex offender population can be, professionals in the field should be aware of the potential repercussions that it can have on them. They should regularly self-evaluate for *secondary trauma*, which is the sometimes extreme stress caused by exposure to traumatic events or by assisting traumatized individuals. As author Rachel Remen (1996) said, "The expectation that we can be immersed in suffering and loss daily and not be touched by it is as unrealistic as expecting to be able to walk through water without getting wet."

Police officers, detectives, and investigators who work to solve sex crimes are at risk for secondary trauma because they hear horrific stories from both victims and offenders. They may additionally be exposed to disturbing crime scenes and graphic crime scene photos. The risk of secondary trauma is also great for parole, probation, and correctional officers who supervise and help rehabilitate these offenders. These professionals are not only likely to become intimately familiar with the criminal history of offenders on their caseload, but they may also find themselves privy to information about an offender's deviant fantasies or own abusive past.

These unique stressors can be exacerbated by large caseloads, tight deadlines, and lack of downtime between cases. Additionally, the more severe and lengthy the violence or deviance one is exposed to, the more complex and intense his or her own stress can become.

In order to combat secondary trauma, professionals should be mindful of their own past experiences as well as any vulnerabilities. They should consider how these contextual factors could affect the amount of tension that they experience as a result of exposure to trauma. For example, an officer whose sister was a victim of a sexual predator may react more strongly to cases involving a similar modus operandi (MO). Law enforcement officers should also be self-aware should they experience symptoms of secondary trauma. Some of the more mild signs include chronic fatigue, headaches, sadness, emotional exhaustion, anxiety, mistrust/paranoia, decreased immunity (often resulting in physical ailments and absenteeism), and gastrointestinal problems. More severe symptoms can include migraines, ulcers, and even heart attacks or strokes.

As you can see, recognizing secondary trauma and how to combat it is equally as important as understanding how to investigate a sex crime or supervise an offender. Although it may sound like common sense, officers should maintain a healthy lifestyle (eating well, getting enough sleep, and exercising often). They should also emotionally invest in at least one friendship with a colleague in whom they are able to confide about work-related matters and how they affect them. Additionally, developing strong relationships with people outside of their professional circle is extremely valuable, as is pursuing non work-related hobbies, and knowing (and admitting) when it is time to take a vacation.

7

Domestic Violence

DOMESTIC ABUSE IN THE MEDIA

In 2009, singers Chris Brown and Rihanna made headlines when a verbal altercation turned physical. Multiple media outlets confirmed that on the night of the assault, the couple had an argument over a woman with whom Brown had previously been involved. As the dispute escalated, Brown repeatedly punched Rihanna in the face. He also bit her, choked her, and threatened to kill her. By the time police received a frantic call from a bystander, Rihanna's face was already bloody and visibly swollen.

Following the attack, Rihanna openly discussed battling a flood of conflicting emotions, chief among them her anger toward and continued affection for Brown. Approximately one month after the incident, Rihanna and Brown officially announced that they had reunited. Of her decision to return to her abuser, Rihanna said, "I decided it was more important for me to be happy. I wasn't going to let anybody's opinion get in the way of that … I'd rather just live my truth and take the backlash" (Bernard, 2013). She also openly expressed her desire to protect Brown from the court of public opinion, as fans had turned against him following photographic evidence of the assault.

Despite the couple's very public reunification, their rekindled relationship was brief. Rihanna ultimately recognized that she had the potential to influence young fans by making a healthy—and courageous—choice for herself: she left Chris Brown. This victim-directed split had a significant impact on the nation's understanding of the stigma surrounding domestic violence. This case highlights the fact that anyone—regardless

125

of wealth, talent, beauty, or popularity—can be a victim (or perpetrator) of intimate partner violence. It also reflects that domestic violence is cyclical in nature, and is the result of a combination of societal issues. The reasons why victims stay in (or return to) abusive relationships are complex and need to be recognized and addressed by both law enforcement and society as a whole (Bernard, 2013; Rodriguez, 2009).

OVERVIEW OF DOMESTIC VIOLENCE

As depicted in the opening vignette, domestic violence (DV) is a serious and pervasive issue that has far-reaching effects on the community. It not only impacts the victim and the perpetrator, but their friends and family as well. Abusive episodes additionally leave a lasting impression on children who witness them.

Motivations for as well as ramifications of DV are core concerns that law enforcement seeks to understand, manage, and prevent. Incidents of violence between intimate partners raise a plethora of questions such as: How often does DV occur? Who is at risk of becoming a victim (or a perpetrator)? What causes attitudes supportive of domestic abuse to develop? How can police successfully—and safely—intervene? How can law enforcement and the community aid victims of domestic abuse? In order to thoroughly discuss the answers to these questions, we must first operationalize the definition of DV.

DEFINITION

The U.S. Department of Justice's Office on Violence Against Women (2015) defines *domestic violence* as:

A pattern of abusive behavior in any relationship that is used by one partner to gain or maintain power and control over another intimate partner. Domestic violence can be physical, sexual, emotional, economic, or psychological actions or threats of actions that influence another person. This includes any behaviors that intimidate, manipulate, humiliate, isolate, frighten, terrorize, coerce, threaten, blame, hurt, injure, or wound someone.

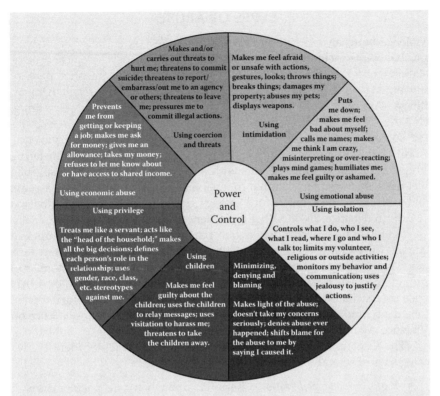

Figure 7.1 Power and control wheel. (Adapted from Domestic Abuse Intervention Programs [DAIP], Power and control wheel, 2011. Retrieved from: http://www.theduluthmodel.org/pdf/PowerandControl.pdf.)

The term domestic violence includes not only abusive behavior committed within the context of a dating or marital relationship, but also abuse between former spouses, individuals who have had or are expecting a child together, and current or former members of the same household (i.e., immediate family members such as parents, children, siblings, or roommates). For our purposes, we will mainly focus on violence between intimate partners.

In order to combat this epidemic, it is crucial for law enforcement to understand the dynamics of abuse. Figure 7.1 depicts the commonly referred to "Power and Control Wheel," which illustrates the various behaviors that take place within an abusive relationship.

TYPES OF ABUSE

Violence between intimate partners can manifest as an array of destructive behaviors including physical or sexual violence, psychological cruelty, stalking, or financial manipulation. *Physical abuse* is the intentional use of unwanted (and illegal) physical force that has the potential to result in injury, illness, disability, or death. Hitting, punching, slapping, kicking, pushing, choking, biting, burning, throwing things, using a weapon, or restraining someone against his or her will are examples of physical violence. Additionally, depriving a partner of medical care or forcibly administering drugs or alcohol to someone falls within the scope of physical abuse. Such incidents often result in criminal charges such as assault, aggravated assault, and even homicide (Centers for Disease Control, 2015; New Jersey Division of Criminal Justice, 2003a; Office on Violence Against Women, 2015).

Sexual abuse occurs when one partner engages in or attempts to engage in sexual contact without the explicit consent of the other partner. This includes occasions when the victimized partner is unable to provide consent because he or she is intoxicated, unconscious, or otherwise incapacitated. The broad label of sexual abuse includes marital rape, forced sex, and treating a partner in a sexually demeaning way (Office on Violence Against Women, 2015).

The Centers for Disease Control and Prevention (2015) identify five categories of sexual violence:

- *Rape (forcible penetration)*: Rape occurs when one partner uses physical force or threats of physical violence against the other partner in order to engage in any form of sexual penetration. Drug- and alcohol-facilitated sexual assaults are included in this category.
- *Forcing the victim to penetrate someone else*: This is when the victim is forced to penetrate the perpetrator or a third party.
- *Coerced sexual penetration*: This happens when the perpetrator pressures or intimidates the victim into submitting to sexual activity.
- *Unwanted sexual contact*: Unwanted sexual contact occurs when the offender purposely touches the victim without consent (or makes the victim touch him or her). Contact can be direct or through clothing.
- *Unwanted noncontact sexual abuse*: This final category is comprised of sexual experiences that do not involve physical contact and to which the victim has not consented. For example, a boyfriend

who takes nude photographs of his girlfriend and/or dissemi-nates such photographs without her explicit permission has com-mitted an act of noncontact sexual abuse.

Unlike physical and sexual violence, *psychological abuse* (also referred to as emotional or mental abuse) is not always obvious. It entails a pattern of behavior that seeks to undermine the victim's sense of safety or self-esteem or to inflict psychological trauma. Some such abusive behaviors are strictly verbal, for example, constant criticism, put-downs, and name call-ing, while others are subtler, and include intimidation and manipulation. Emotional abuse may take the form of humiliating the victim in public, disparaging his or her beliefs and values, belittling the victim's achieve-ments, or blaming the victim for things that are not his or her fault.

Psychological abuse can also encompass more aggressive behavior, such as making threats of self-harm, threatening to hurt the victim's friends or relatives, injuring pets, destroying property, or isolating the victim from his or her support system (i.e., friends and family). All forms of psychological abuse leave the victim with emotional scars and put him or her at risk for chronic stress, depression, anxiety, and posttraumatic stress disorder (PTSD) (Centers for Disease Control, 2015; Office on Violence Against Women, 2015).

Stalking is defined as "a pattern of repeated, unwanted, attention and contact that causes fear or concern for one's own safety or the safety of some-one else (e.g., family member or friend)"(Centers for Disease Control, 2015). Because of the intrinsic element of fear and resulting mental trauma, stalking behaviors are considered to be closely related to emotional abuse. Examples of stalking include repetitive unwanted communication such as phone calls, text messages, emails or social networking requests. More intrusive forms of stalking include leaving unwanted gifts for the victim, following him or her, showing up in places that the victim frequents, spying on the target, or break-ing into his or her home. A detailed discussion of stalking within the larger framework of threat assessment can be found in Chapter 12.

Another way that an abuser may attempt to control an intimate part-ner is via *economic abuse*. This occurs when one partner takes control of the couple's finances, thus forcing the other partner to be financially dependent on him or her. For instance, the perpetrator may control all spending/financial decisions, restrict the victim's access to funds, with-hold money, or prohibit the victim from maintaining employment (Office on Violence Against Women, 2015).

With the evolution of the digital age, abusers have learned to exploit various technologies in order to exert dominance over their victims and cause them emotional injury. ***Digital abuse*** is psychological violence that is perpetrated via the Internet or other form of technology. Abusive digital behavior includes using social media, text messaging, or email to bully, intimidate, threaten, harass, or stalk an intimate partner. Instances of digital abuse occur when one partner (National Domestic Violence Hotline, 1996):

- Tells the other who he or she can be friends with on social media
- Sends threatening emails, tweets, or Facebook messages to the other
- Uses social media to keep tabs on where the other partner goes and with whom
- Insists on having the other partner's email and social media passwords and/or cell phone access code
- Looks through the other partner's phone (text messages, incoming/outgoing call logs, etc.)
- Posts demeaning or embarrassing status updates about the other

Dating Violence

It is not always possible to know whether a relationship will involve domestic violence at the outset. Within the context of a dating relationship, physical, sexual, and emotional abuse are collectively referred to as ***dating violence***. Dating violence can take many forms including the following (Love Is Respect, 2014):

- *Isolation*: Controlling who the victim spends time with or using jealousy as a justification for engaging in controlling behavior
- *Peer pressure*: Using popularity or spreading/threatening to spread rumors as coercive tactics
- *Anger*: Putting the victim down, insulting him or her in front of other people, name-calling, or playing mind games
- *Sexual coercion*: Threatening, intimidating, manipulating, or coercing the victim into participating in unwanted sexual behavior; giving the victim alcohol or drugs so that he or she will comply with sexual activity
- *Intimidation*: Overtly or covertly causing the victim to feel afraid for his or her own safety or that of friends, family members, or pets
- *Minimizing, denying, blaming*: Blaming the victim for causing the abuse, or denying that the abuse occurred or is a problem

When handling cases involving possible occurrences of dating violence, police should be cognizant of the fact that such situations typically involve impressionable (and often hormonal) teenagers, who may not recognize their relationship as abusive. The following are warning signs that may signal dating abuse (Murray, 2009):

- The victim is often sad or frequently cries
- The victim feels an urgent need to respond immediately to calls or texts from the abuser
- The victim becomes secretive or stops engaging in activities he or she once enjoyed (i.e., team sports, etc.)
- The victim's academic performance deteriorates
- The victim stops socializing with friends or has fewer friends than he or she did prior to dating the abuser

Alternatively, some of the red flags that may indicate someone is (or is at risk for) committing acts of dating violence include (Murray, 2009):

- Extreme jealousy
- Volatile or explosive temper
- Failure to accept responsibility for his or her behavior
- History of assaultive behavior (e.g., fights, brawls, harming animals)
- Becoming too serious about the relationship too soon
- Insulting his or her partner's family or friends

DOMESTIC VIOLENCE BY THE NUMBERS

Every 9 seconds, a woman in the United States becomes a victim of domestic violence (Bachman & Saltzman, 1995). Every minute, nearly 20 people (men and women) are physically abused by an intimate partner, which totals more than 10 million victims of domestic abuse each year (Black et al., 2011). As a result, crisis hotlines across the country receive approximately 20,000 phone calls per day (NNEDV, 2013). Women aged 18–34 are at the greatest risk of being victimized by an intimate partner. With 25% of women experiencing nonfatal intimate partner violence over the course of their lives and 4 million women becoming victims of domestic abuse annually, the DV epidemic is one of the most challenging issues faced by law enforcement today (Safe Horizon, 2015).

Nonfatal Domestic Violence

Research conducted by Truman and Morgan (2014) highlights even more disturbing statistics. Their data, taken from the National Crime Victimization Survey, indicate that DV accounted for slightly more than one-fifth (21%) of all violent crime in the United States in the years 2003–2012. Of these offenses, 15% were committed by intimate partners, with the highest number of assaults being attributed to current or former boyfriends/girlfriends. Spouses committed the next highest number of assaults, followed by former spouses. An additional 4% of attacks were perpetrated by immediate family members, whereas only 2% were the result of violence between more distant relatives. Females were victimized at a much higher rate (76%) than males (24%), and the vast majority of incidents transpired in or in close proximity to the victim's home (77%) (Table 7.1).

In addition to identifying the relationship between victim and offender, the researchers were able to describe various characteristics of known assaults, including the extent of the injury incurred by the victim and whether the offender used a weapon. For example, weapons were used more often during violent acts committed by distant relatives (26%) than by intimate partners (19%) or immediate family members (19%). Firearms made up a smaller percentage of the weapons employed by intimate partners than did knives or other (miscellaneous) weapons, whereas weapon-involved acts of DV committed by distant relatives employed firearms just as often as knives, with each comprising 10% of such episodes (Truman & Morgan, 2014).

From 2003–2012, approximately 45% of domestic assaults resulted in injury to the victim. Violence between intimate partners accounted for 48% of this total, while violence perpetrated by immediate family members was responsible for 37%. Violence committed by intimate partners resulted in more serious injury to the victim than did attacks launched by relatives. The majority of domestic assaults were classified as simple assault (64%) versus serious violence (36%) such as aggravated or sexual assault (Truman & Morgan, 2014).

Domestic Violence Fatalities

As noted in Chapter 5, homicide is the most extreme form of violence, and has been named the seventh leading cause of premature death in women worldwide (Greenfield et al., 1998). When homicide is a sequel to family violence, it is especially distressing. Research indicates that domestic

Table 7.1 Violent Crime by Type of Crime and Victim-Offender Relationship, 2003–2012

Victim-Offender Relationship	All Violent Crime		Serious Violent Crime[a]		Simple Assault	
	Average Annual Number	Percent %	Average Annual Number	Percent %	Average Annual Number	Percent %
Total	6,623,500	100	2,194,070	100	4,429,430	100
Known	3,514,570	53.1	1,072,520	48.9	2,442,050	55.1
Domestic	1,411,330	21.3	501,220	22.8	910,110	20.5
Intimate partner[b]	967,710	14.6	343,760	15.7	623,950	14.1
Spouse	314,330	4.7	116,520	5.3	197,810	4.5
Ex-spouse	134,690	2.0	29,330	1.3	105,350	2.4
Boy/girlfriend	518,700	7.8	197,910	9.0	320,790	7.2
Immediate family	284,670	4.3	98,520	4.5	186,150	4.2
Parent	80,890	1.2	31,400	1.4	49,480	1.1
Child	97,490	1.5	32,820	1.5	64,680	1.5
Sibling	106,290	1.6	34,300	1.6	71,990	1.6
Other relative	158,950	2.4	58,940	2.7	100,010	2.3
Well-known/ casual acquaintance	2,103,240	31.8	571,300	26.0	1,531,940	34.6
Stranger	2,548,860	38.5	929,450	42.4	1,619,410	36.6
Unknown[c]	560,080	8.5	192,100	8.8	367,970	8.3

Source: Bureau of Justice Statistics, National Crime Victimization Survey, 2003–2012.
Note: Details may not sum to total due to rounding.
[a] Includes rape or sexual assault, robbery, and aggravated assault.
[b] Includes current or former spouses, boyfriends, and girlfriends.
[c] Includes unknown victim-offender relationships and unknown number of offenders.

homicides, specifically those committed by an intimate partner, account for nearly half (40%–50%) of all femicides in the United States. This means that more American women die at the hands of an intimate partner (i.e., spouse, lover, or ex-lover) than as a result of violence committed by an acquaintance or a stranger (Bachman & Saltzman, 1995; Bailey et al., 1997; Mercy & Saltzman, 1989).

According to data collected by the New York City Domestic Violence Fatality Review Committee (2015), 851 domestic fatalities involving 881 individual perpetrators were reported in the years ranging from 2002 through 2013. In 2013 alone, the NYPD responded to 284,660 DV calls, 62 of which resulted in homicide. To put this into perspective, those 62 cases accounted for 20% of (or one out of every five) homicides in New York City that year.

The statistics clearly outline the fact that both intimate partner violence and intimate partner homicide pose significant challenges to police. In order to best combat deaths resulting from domestic tragedies, law enforcement must develop an understanding of the risk factors that contribute to them. In more than two-thirds (67%–80%) of the murders studied by the NYC Fatality Review Committee (2015), physical abuse of the female partner by the male partner was a precipitating factor. This held true regardless of which partner was killed. Additional risks included whether the perpetrator had made threats involving the use of a weapon and had access to such a weapon. Whether the perpetrator's stepchild was present in the familial home was also a risk factor. Noteworthy situational elements included instances of stalking, forced sexual contact, physical abuse of the female partner during pregnancy, and occasions when the victim had left the abuser for someone else. Perhaps surprisingly, the strongest predictor of intimate partner femicide was the perpetrator's lack of employment.

CHARACTERISTICS OF VICTIMS AND BATTERERS

Principal research findings indicate that in order to recognize domestic violence in its various forms, the qualities frequently found among batterers must first be identified. Batterer typologies serve to inform criminal justice professionals about which individuals are more likely to engage in which types of abusive behaviors, thus allowing for the implementation of appropriate interventions (Costanzo & Krauss, 2012). It should be noted that although the subtypes reference men, females can also be abusers. By reviewing dimensions such as the severity of intimate partner violence, generality of violence, and psychopathology, Holtzworth-Munroe and Stuart (1994) were able to distinguish three identifiable subtypes of male batterers: family only, dysphoric-borderline, and generally violent/antisocial.

Violence committed by *family-only batterers* is limited to occurrences within the context of the family. These individuals typically do not exhibit violence toward nonfamily members. Additionally, they are the least likely to be sexually or emotionally abusive, or to have been involved in other violence-related legal matters. They exhibit little to no psychopathology (Holtzworth-Munroe & Stuart, 1994).

Similar to family-only batterers, *dysphoric-borderline abusers* mainly engage in violence toward family members. However, their abuse is typically more severe than that perpetrated by men in the family-only class. Dysphoric-borderline batterers are the most psychologically distressed of the three subtypes. These men experience extreme jealousy and maintain a pathological fear of abandonment, which in turn leads them to be suspicious of the motives of their partner's family and friends. As a result, they try to restrict their partner's activities and social contacts. These offenders present with borderline tendencies and may have a diagnosis of borderline personality disorder (Holtzworth-Monroe & Stuart, 1994). As you'll recall from Chapter 3, the hallmark features of BPD are emotional volatility and instability in interpersonal relationships.

The third cluster of batterers is that of *generally violent/antisocial abusers*. These men perpetrate the most severe abuse and engage in extrafamilial violence as well as DV. They are likely to have an extensive history of arrests for violent and/or drug-related offenses, and are also the most likely subtype to have a diagnosis of antisocial personality disorder or psychopathy. It is not uncommon for these individuals to engage in significant denial with respect to their offense(s) (Costanzo & Krauss, 2012; Holtzworth-Monroe & Stuart, 1994).

It is especially important for police to be mindful of the fact that *anyone* can be an abuser. Batterers are a heterogeneous group comprised of individuals that hail from a variety of backgrounds and walks of life. Battering is not limited to any particular culture, religion, or socioeconomic level. Moreover, to outsiders, many abusers appear to be upstanding citizens, as they display law-abiding behavior outside the home and do not have criminal records. They may even come across as kind or charming to people other than their partner (Corry, 1993). Despite the fact that batterers are relatively diverse as a group, there are a number of general characteristics common among them.

These men often (AARDVARC, 2011):

- Exhibit poor self-image
- Are overly jealous
- Are controlling

135

Research has shown that as a group, batterers tend to exhibit certain personality characteristics and/or deficits (AARDVARC, 2011):
• Poor self-image • Rush to establish relationships • Maintain unrealistic expectations • Believe in gender stereotypes • Poor communication skills • Maladaptive coping responses (including alcohol abuse) • Hypersensitivity • Personality disorder
Other qualities tend to cluster together and relate to batterer typologies (Holtzworth-Munroe & Stuart, 1994; Saunders, 1992):
• Domineering • Narcissistic
• Impulsive • Emotionally dependent • Overly jealous • Controlling • Emotionally reactive
• Antisocial • Violent • Brutal and/or sadistic

Figure 7.2 Characteristics of batterers. (From AARDVARC, Abusers, batterers, DV offenders. Retrieved from: http://www.aardvarc.org/dv/batterer.shtml, 2011; Holtzworth-Munroe, A., & Stuart, G. L., *Psychological Bulletin, 116*(3), 476–497, 1994; Saunders, D. G., *American Journal of Orthopsychiatry, 62*, 264–275, 1992.)

- Use isolation as a tactic
- Hold stereotypically masculine views
- Have communication deficits
- Lack prosocial coping mechanisms
- Fail to take responsibility for their actions (and blame others!)
- Are hypersensitive
- Rush into relationships

To better understand these experiences in terms of concrete warning signs, review Figure 7.2.

BATTERED WOMAN SYNDROME

In addition to classifying the characteristics of batterers, efforts have been made to understand the commonalities among victims. According to

Walker (1979), there is a collection of traits exhibited at least in part by the majority of female victims. These include attitudes supportive of traditional gender roles (i.e., men should be dominant and women submissive), low self-esteem, and a propensity for holding themselves accountable for their partner's abusive behavior. Because battered women frequently believe that their actions provoke the abuse, they often experience feelings of shame and may try to hide the abuse from others. This in turn may lead to social isolation, which can result in increased dependency on the abusive partner. Subsequently, these women eventually feel that they have few if any options for achieving independence, and thus their ability to walk away from the relationship diminishes (Costanzo & Krauss, 2012). Although research has primarily focused on female victims of domestic abuse, it is important to note that like battering, victimization is not gender specific.

The Ibn-Tamas Murder

Beverly and Yusef Ibn-Tamas were married in 1972. In the years that followed, their union was marred by frequent bouts of physical abuse separated by fleeting intervals of peace. Various accounts describe Dr. Yusef Ibn-Tamas as having been exceptionally violent toward his wife, beating her with his fists as well as with other objects. On one occasion, he pinned her to the floor and pressed his knee into her neck until she lost consciousness.

On February 23, 1976, another one of the couple's arguments turned violent. Dr. Ibn-Tamas punched his wife repeatedly and demanded that she move out of the marital residence. When she refused, he threatened to kill her. At the time, Mrs. Ibn-Tamas was pregnant and feared not only for her own safety, but for that of her unborn child.

Mrs. Ibn-Tamas ran down the stairs and into a room where she knew her husband stored a firearm. She grabbed the gun, crouched, and hid, waiting for Dr. Ibn-Tamas to continue his assault. When he entered the room, she shot him once in the head, killing him. As a result, Beverly Ibn-Tamas was charged with murder. She was found guilty of murder in the second degree—without the jury ever hearing any testimony about the couple's history of domestic violence.

Mrs. Ibn-Tamas appealed the verdict, but a subsequent hearing determined that she could not present evidence of psychological trauma stemming from abuse (i.e., battered woman syndrome) in her defense (*Ibn-Tamas v. United States*, 1979). *Battered woman syndrome* or **BWS** is a set of symptoms experienced by a victim in response to continued physical and/or psychological abuse by an intimate partner. (In order to avoid gender specification and acknowledge that anyone can be victimized, this is now widely referred to as battered person syndrome or battered spouse syndrome.) Experts close to the case speculated that Mrs. Ibn-Tamas experienced several of the syndrome's hallmark features, including learned helplessness, poor self-image, and impaired functionality.

Learned helplessness refers to the victim's feeling of powerlessness after having been exposed to traumatic or abusive situations over which he or she had no control. Eventually, the victim comes to believe that he or she has no agency in the world and therefore cannot change the abusive situation. The victim often loses his or her sense of safety and security and sees few alternatives to remaining in the relationship (Walker, 1984a,b).

The victim's self-image is damaged when he or she begins to believe the abuser's negative, hostile, and/or degrading comments. The victim begins to devalue him or herself and may come to feel worthless or essentially unlovable.

Impaired functionality includes the victim's inability to engage in deliberate, planned behavior. A victim suffering from battered spouse syndrome typically experiences fear, terror, anger, and anxiety in response to the abuser. Because DV is cyclical, a battered person becomes conditioned to view his or her partner as an imminent threat *at all times*—even when he or she is not in the midst of an abusive episode. Despite temporary reprieves, the victim knows that it is only a matter of time before his or her partner becomes abusive or violent again. As a result, the victim exhibits *hypervigilance*, or an intensified awareness of potential indicators of danger. The victim may interpret verbal and nonverbal cues as threatening even when others do not; he or she may also make a preemptive strike in order to ward off impending violence.

With regard to the Ibn-Tamas case, it can be argued that the consistent abuse perpetrated against Mrs. Ibn-Tamas by her husband primed her to take anticipatory action. In her mind, she was shooting him before he had the opportunity to kill her—as he had threatened. According to research by Walker (1979), many battered women believe that their husbands will make good on threats of homicide—even after they leave the relationship. This notion is supported by the fact that a significant number of victims are murdered by their abusers *after* they leave the home or end the relationship (Costanzo & Krauss, 2012).

CYCLE OF VIOLENCE

As mentioned previously, there is a general pattern or cycle that intimate partner violence tends to follow. This sequence may take place all in one day or be drawn out over the course of several weeks or even months. The length of time that the progression takes varies in every relationship. Moreover, the cycle is meant to describe DV in general terms and therefore does not reflect the dynamics of every abusive relationship; it is not applicable to those relationships where victims report a constant state of violent abuse with minimal periods of relief. Often, the severity of the abuse escalates over time and therefore the periods of acute violence become incrementally larger.

The "Cycle of Violence" is comprised of three phases of behavior and relational dynamics common to many (violently) abusive relationships (Walker, 1979):

- *Tension building phase*: Much like the title indicates, this is the time when the victim feels tension building within the relationship. He or she responds to incidents of emotional abuse by acquiescing or attempting to please the abuser. The victim may additionally feel as though he or she is "walking on eggshells" in order to avoid a violent outburst by the batterer. Eventually the emotional friction combusts and physical violence ensues.
- *Battering or explosion phase*: This is the occurrence of violence—most often physical or sexual. Physical abuse is typically triggered by either an external stimulus or an internal event (such as a change in the emotional state of the abuser). It is not caused by the victim's behavior, meaning that it is unpredictable and not something that the victim can control.
- *Honeymoon phase*: During the third phase, the abuser expresses remorse and attempts to make amends. The batterer is likely to appear contrite and to even apologize. It is not unusual for an abuser at this juncture to minimize the severity of the abuse or to blame the victim. The abusive partner also appears loving, concerned, and may shower the victim with gifts, attention, and romantic gestures. Promises are made to the victim that the abuse will end. The peaceful calm and romantic interludes found during this phase provide relief from the anxiety, hostility, and brutality that built up during the previous two phases. Oftentimes, this convinces the victim that there is no longer a valid need to end the relationship (see Figure 7.3).

139

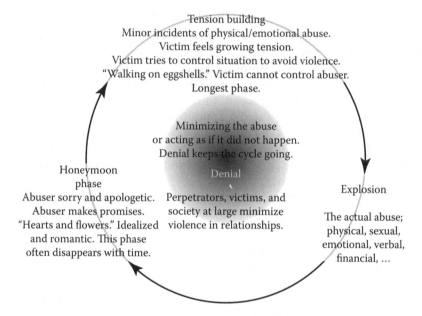

Tension building
Minor incidents of physical/emotional abuse.
Victim feels growing tension.
Victim tries to control situation to avoid violence.
"Walking on eggshells." Victim cannot control abuser.
Longest phase.

Minimizing the abuse
or acting as if it did not happen.
Denial keeps the cycle going.

Denial

Honeymoon
phase
Abuser sorry and apologetic.
Abuser makes promises.
"Hearts and flowers." Idealized
and romantic. This phase
often disappears with time.

Perpetrators, victims, and
society at large minimize
violence in relationships.

Explosion

The actual abuse;
physical, sexual,
emotional, verbal,
financial, ...

Figure 7.3 Cycle of violence. (From Domestic Violence Solutions for Santa Barbara County, The cycle of violence, http://www.dvsolutions.org/info/cycle. aspx, 2015.)

WHY DO VICTIMS STAY?

Given the damage caused by domestic violence, it is frequently difficult for people—including police—to understand why victims stay in or return to abusive relationships. The general public assumes that the best course of action for any victim is unequivocally to leave the abuser. While this may seem logical, there is a plethora of reasons why victims stay. Although these reasons are numerous and complex, we will seek to address and demystify the most widespread victim-specific, as well as socially and culturally based factors.

Many victims are aware of the increased risk to their safety if they try to leave the relationship. Abusers often fear abandonment and hence go to great lengths to prevent their victims from leaving. In the face of possible desertion, it is not uncommon for abusers to threaten violence or even murder as a way to coerce the victim into staying. If a victim does leave, the abuser is more likely to carry out such violence, as threats of separation or actual separation initiated by the victim have been deemed to be precipitating events to domestic homicide (NCADV, 2014).

In addition to fearing for their own safety, many victims often anticipate that the abuser will carry out threats to harm or even kill children, pets, or other family members. A 2007 analysis of DV fatalities indicated that in 20% of cases studied, the murder victim was not the DV victim, but rather a friend, relative, police officer, bystander, or other intervening individual (Rothman, Hathaway, Stidsen, & de Vries, 2007).

The victim may also be afraid that the batterer will file for custody of the couple's children, or may feel unable to be a single parent. He or she may have been isolated from family and friends and, as a result, may not have a support network that can provide assistance with regard to shelter, money, and so on. The victim may fear being homeless and may have no means with which to support him or herself. The victim may also be concerned about becoming destitute, due to the belief that the abuser will terminate his or her access to shared finances. Finally, because the violence within these relationships is often inconsistent, meaning that there are good times and bad times, the victim may truly harbor romantic feelings for the abuser. The victim may feel that the batterer fulfills his or her needs at times and therefore has mixed feelings about ending the relationship (NCADV, 2014).

When speaking with someone who has suffered intimate partner violence, police should keep in mind that the victim is the best (and only) expert on his or her particular case. The victim alone knows how violent the abuser could become. If a victim says that he or she cannot safely leave the relationship at any given time, believe it!

In addition to the hindrances pertaining to individual victims' situations, society in general creates barriers that diminish victims' ability to escape abuse. For instance, some victims fear losing custody of their children or forfeiting joint/marital assets if they "desert" the relationship. Additionally, religious and cultural values may support male-dominated households, or may strictly forbid divorce, causing victims to feel trapped in unhealthy relationships. Some spiritual organizations focus solely on salvaging marriages rather than saving victims from a life of violence. Moreover, the historically pervasive myth that a woman's worth is based upon her relationship status is extremely damaging to female victims of domestic abuse (NCADV, 2014).

The criminal justice system also plays a significant role in whether victims feel that they have realistic options. For example, when prosecutors are reluctant to take DV cases to court or encourage batterers to plead guilty to lesser charges, victims often feel unsupported. Similarly, when authorities treat domestic violence as a "family dispute" rather than a crime, minimize the abuse, or fail to believe a victim's account of events, they are causing harm. Even sometimes despite law enforcement's best efforts, the system itself still fails victims. To illustrate, the issuance of a restraining order does not necessarily protect against future violence; it is not bulletproof (NCADV, 2014).

PERCEPTIONS OF DOMESTIC VIOLENCE

Stigma

As you've already learned, stigma and societal norms influence a victim's response to domestic abuse. The Intimate Partner Violence (IPV) Stigmatization Model highlights the negative impact of anticipated stigma, cultural stigma, and stigma internalization on a victim's ability to seek help. *Anticipated stigma* refers to a victim's apprehension about the potential repercussions that could result from others learning of the abuse. For instance, the victim may worry that he or she will be judged, rejected, or lose the support of family and friends. *Cultural stigma* comprises culture-specific beliefs that discredit and minimize the experience of all victims. *Stigma internalization* is a construct whereby a victim begins to believe negative stereotypes about victims of intimate partner violence—and apply them to him or herself (Overstreet & Quinn, 2013).

Cultural Implications

In order to successfully resolve a DV incident, law enforcement must be cognizant of the influence of cultural beliefs and perspectives. For instance, although beating one's wife is illegal in the United States, some patriarchal societies uphold ideals of male dominance and rigid gender roles. Therefore, police may encounter some individuals whose culture does not consider wife beating to be a criminal act, but rather a husband's innate right. Police must be mindful of these variances and address the parameters of acceptable and legal behavior with cultural competence.

Interviews conducted in Ghana by Fischbach and Herbert (1997) illustrate that most villagers support a husband's right to physically discipline his wife. Similarly, many Japanese people view wife battering as an appropriate and tolerable behavior (Magnier, 2002). In some Islamic regions, it is socially acceptable for women to be brutalized by not only their husbands, but by other male relatives as well (Douki, Nacef, Belhadj, Bouasker, & Ghachem, 2003). In other cultures, victims will not acknowledge the extent to which domestic abuse occurs due to shame, fear of not being believed, or fear of reprisal.

Due to the entrenchment of these cultural mores, many victims do not view intimate partner violence as a criminal act, rather, they accept it as a customary part of a relationship. Female victims who were raised with such beliefs may present as uncooperative to law enforcement because they fear the abuser or believe that it is their duty to honor his demands. The common thread in these scenarios is secrecy; it ensures that the abuse will be kept private and treated as a family matter, which serves to undermine the victim's autonomy and value to the culture and society as a whole.

Culturally and socially perpetuated DV myths also have consequences that transgress generations. Consider, for example, little boys who witness their mothers being abused; they are more likely to grow up to abuse their own partners. Similarly, little girls who witness violence in their home are more likely to come to regard abuse as an acceptable relationship dynamic, and therefore endure violence from partners later in life.

POLICE RESPONSE TO DOMESTIC VIOLENCE

In 1976, the International Association of Chiefs of Police (IACP) issued a directive stating, "Wife abuse should not be considered a victimless crime" (Browne, 1987, p. 168). Since then, protocols regarding police response to DV incidents have consistently evolved. In the wake of largely ineffective methods of intervention, the federal government has sought to establish a strategic approach to domestic violence that acknowledges both the severity and complexity of these crimes, while holding offenders accountable and providing victims with access to appropriate services.

This was achieved with the enactment of the Violence Against Women Act (VAWA). The 1994 rendition of this landmark piece of legislation stipulated that all police departments uphold *mandatory arrest*. In other words, when indications of physical abuse were present, police were *required* to arrest the abuser at the scene.

While it may seem logical, this policy has significant pitfalls, such as increasing the risk of violence and victim fatality. It would appear that arresting the abuser would ensure the victim's safety. However, as previously mentioned, emotional, financial, and sociocultural concerns can weigh heavily on victims, and if they know that calling the police will result in the batterer's arrest, it may deter them from seeking help.

In addition to the distress experienced by the victim, mandatory arrest procedures also raise concerns for police. Mandatory arrest is a nondiscretionary policy; in other words, it eliminates law enforcement's ability to use their own judgment and/or tailor their responses on a case-by-case basis. This means that mandatory arrest procedures increase the incidence of dual arrest. To illustrate this point, consider instances of bidirectional violence in which the victims defend themselves against physically abusive partners. Under mandatory arrest, such victims may be charged with assault (Hirschel, 2008; Saunders, 1995).

In light of the aforementioned issues, the 2005 reauthorization of VAWA shifted its support away from mandatory arrest in lieu of pro-arrest policies. *Pro-arrest statutes* strongly encourage law enforcement to place batterers under arrest, but leave the ultimate decision to the individual officers. Research has proven that arrest—with the informed discretion of trained officers—is the preferred method for dealing with DV. In fact, law enforcement's decision to arrest the abuser has been more effective in reducing recidivism than interventions such as talking with the couple or separating the victim from the offender (Sherman & Berk, 1984).

In addition to implementing an appropriate arrest strategy, police responding to domestic disturbances are tasked with securing and carefully documenting the scene, protecting the victim, and ensuring the safety of themselves and fellow officers. See Table 7.2 for a comprehensive checklist of points to be addressed, reviewed, and reported by officers. The sections that follow will discuss various psychological considerations that must be addressed in order to safely and securely execute these functions.

De-Escalating DV Calls

DV calls are some of the most dangerous and potentially deadly calls to which officers respond. In fact, police personnel nationwide report that such calls pose a serious threat to officers. This increased risk level is predicated on numerous factors.

When approaching a domestic dispute, officers should be keenly aware that both the victim and the perpetrator are often highly emotional. Increased emotionality, such as acute fear, anger, or desperation on the part of either party, may manifest as impulsive aggression and/or violence. In addition to the affective state of the couple, friends, relatives, or neighbors of either involved person may attempt to intervene. Some of

Table 7.2 Officer Checklist

Prior to arriving on the scene, officers should note:
- How the call was received (i.e., whether the victim sought help, or someone else such as a neighbor contacted authorities)
- The nature of the altercation (based on facts gathered by the dispatcher)

Upon arriving at the scene, officers should:
- Identify the relationship between victim and offender
- Verify whether an active/valid order of protection is in place
- Determine whether there is a history of threats, assault, and so on
- Document physical injuries incurred by both parties
- Inquire as to whether strangulation/choking occurred
- Document the emotional state of both victim and offender
- Document any sexual violence reported by the victim—and take steps to activate SART/SANE response as appropriate
- Articulate use of force, threats, coercion, and fear experienced by victim
- Diagram the scene for the report

Officers should be aware of and address the following legal implications:
- Whether the perpetrator is prohibited from possessing a firearm due to a previous DV conviction, order of protection, or other felony offense
- If bidirectional violence occurred, did officers conduct a thorough assessment to determine whether one party acted in self-defense? If so, did police utilize appropriate discretion with regard to arrest provisions?

After the situation has been de-escalated and there is no immediate threat of harm, officers should:
- Assist the victim with safety planning
- Provide the victim with information about obtaining an order of protection/restraining order
- Provide the victim with referrals to social services

Source: Adapted from the International Association of Chiefs of Police, National law enforcement leadership initiative on violence against women. Retrieved from: http://dnn9ciwm8.azurewebsites.net/Portals/0/documents/pdfs/ResponsetoDomesticViolenceChecklist.pdf, n.d.a.

these individuals may view police efforts as an interference or even as a threat to their loved one; they may therefore present as hostile toward responding officers. Many people incorrectly view DV as a personal or family matter and therefore do not appreciate law enforcement's involvement. Additionally, weapons may be on the scene and/or may have been used in the assault. When we add to those elements the fact that alcohol and/or drugs are frequently involved in these scenarios, officers should consider these calls to be highly volatile.

145

A frightening example of how quickly officers can be ambushed during these calls was illustrated by the ordeal endured by Officer Jarred Slocum of the El Cajon Police Department. Officer Slocum was shot when he and his rookie partner responded to a domestic abuse call. The gunman, identified as Kevin Collier, had murdered his infant daughter and mother-in-law before setting their house on fire. Neighbors called 9-1-1 and later reported that Collier's violence was likely triggered by his wife's decision to file for divorce. Reports also indicated that Collier purposely targeted the officers once they arrived on the scene. Luckily, Officer Slocum survived, having suffered a bullet wound to his left temple, a cracked skull, and multiple severed arteries (Shroder, 2012).

As you can see, the scene of a domestic altercation is fraught with peril for well-meaning police. A careless mistake could cost an officer or fellow first responder his or her life. Law enforcement should be aware of the following critical tactics used to survive these scenes (Garner, 2005):

- *Always work with a partner*: Officers should never respond to DV complaints alone. Remember, multiple individuals—any of whom can turn on an officer at any time—are involved in these situations. Always work in teams.
- *Be alert and look for red flags*: Not only are DV incidents unpredictable, but officers are usually entering the home of a potentially violent abuser. In other words, the perpetrator has the home field advantage. Responders should be alert to signs such as an offender whose hands are not visible (i.e., in his or her pockets), presence of or allusions to weapons, alcohol, and emotional outbursts. If these occur, police should slow down and reassess their approach.
- *Take your time*: When on the scene of a domestic assault, do not rush! As mentioned in Chapter 3, speaking or moving slowly can have a calming effect on a suspect—especially one who is emotional (or suffers from emotional disturbance). Likewise, if the first officer on the scene has determined that arrest is the appropriate avenue to pursue, he or she should wait until backup arrives, as an arrest may incite an explosive reaction.
- *Be alert to actual AND potential weapons*: When approaching the scene, officers should not only be vigilant regarding the presence of firearms and knives, but also any object that could possibly be used as a weapon. For instance, a pot of boiling water on the

stove could be launched at an officer in an attempt to inflict severe burns, or a responder could be fatally beaten with an iron, a hammer, a piece of firewood, etc.

- *Be aware of ALL potential threats/attackers*: Due to the phenomenon of learned helplessness among other barriers to independence, victims frequently do not believe that they can survive without the batterer. Therefore, they may not want that person arrested—and may (violently) defend him or her. Officers may find that they intervene in order to help the victim but end up being attacked by him or her. A close eye should be kept on the victim's movements as well as on those of the abuser and any intervening bystanders.

Interviewing and Safety Planning

Although in-depth interviewing procedures will be examined in Chapter 9, the following section identifies a general approach for interviewing persons involved in domestic assaults. First and foremost, the attitude of police personnel should reflect the gravity of the situation by conveying to all concerned parties that DV is a *criminal* offense. As soon as it can be done safely, officers should institute a policy of sight and sound separation meaning that the victim and perpetrator can neither see nor hear one another while being interviewed. This method serves to increase the victim's level of comfort and decreases the possibility of intimidation by the perpetrator, thus resulting in a greater likelihood that the victim will cooperate with police. When separating the couple, officers should seek a neutral and stable location in which to interview each individual. Police should never speak with the suspect *or* the victim in their kitchen or garage, as these two locales store the majority of household objects most likely to be used as weapons (New Jersey Division of Criminal Justice, 2003b).

In addition to establishing an environment in which the victim feels safe disclosing details of the assault, officers should be attentive to the victim's reluctance to discuss intimate details of his or her relationship—especially when those details will likely result in a criminal complaint against his or her partner. While police should seek specific information from their interaction with the victim, they should take care to avoid asking inappropriate or ill-timed questions, as these can elicit fear, embarrassment, or confusion (New Jersey Division of Criminal Justice, 2003b). For example, officers should avoid phrasing questions in ways that appear to blame or intimidate the victim, or minimize the abuse. Rhetorical questions such as "Are you okay?" should also be avoided.

Victims are accustomed to being asked this question. Therefore, it is likely to induce the conditioned response of "I'm fine" rather than drawing out useful information (New Jersey Division of Criminal Justice, 2003b).

Officers are faced with a delicate balancing act—trying to control factors that impair the victim's capacity to feel safe and secure, and helping him or her to overcome feelings of helplessness, guilt, shame, and isolation, in order to move forward. One way of being sensitive to this emotional turmoil is to acknowledge that this may be the first time the victim has sought help, or that someone else (like a neighbor) may have called the police—against the victim's wishes. It is important for officers to acknowledge and normalize the victim's experience. Responders should immediately reassure the victim and emphasize that he or she is not to blame for the abuse. Police should let the victim know that he or she is safe while in their company and should not take it personally (or exhibit frustration) if the victim is reluctant to cooperate with their investigation.

Regardless of whether the victim chooses to remain in the relationship, prepares to end it, or actively leaves the abuser, police should not consider their duties complete until after they have assisted the victim in the development of a safety plan. A *safety plan* is an actionable plan that prepares the victim in the event of another physically violent or emotionally abusive episode. It includes ways to keep the victim, as well as any children or pets, safe. Because victims often describe an influx of emotions during a domestic crisis, they are sometimes too overwhelmed to think clearly. Therefore, the safety plan should also include information about where the victim can go, emergency contacts, important articles to be packed (i.e., medication, ID, birth certificate, etc.), and how to obtain money. See Table 7.3 for a sample safety plan.

With regard to speaking with the suspect, officers should be alert to the use of manipulative language. They should be prepared to implement de-escalation and calming techniques. The batterer may present as antagonistic and angry that strangers have "intruded" into a family affair. In other cases, the perpetrator may be conciliatory or engage in denial and/or victim blaming (New Jersey Division of Criminal Justice, 2003b).

PREVENTATIVE PROGRAMS

In addition to a strategic and sympathetic police response, preventative and supplementary support programs are in place to cope with DV at the community level. The majority of these programs are collaborations

Table 7.3 Safety Planning

SAFETY IN THE HOME

In the midst of an altercation, avoid the kitchen (which has knives).

Keep a "go bag" in the event that you need to escape quickly. Necessities, including a passport, birth certificate, ID, cash, keys, and medication, should be kept in this bag. It should be in a safe place *outside* the home where the batterer will not find it.

During a conflict, flee to a room with a (locking) door and call 9-1-1.

Arrange a code with children, family, friends, and neighbors to alert them to call the police. This can be a code word or a visual signal such as flickering the porch lights.

GETTING HELP

Protect your privacy. If you dial a hotline number, dial something else, such as a 1-800 number or the local takeout restaurant immediately afterward. This is to prevent the abuser from using a callback code.

When searching for information about DV resources online, *do not* use your own computer. If you have previously used your home computer, erase your Internet history.

AFTER YOU'VE LEFT...

Change any predictable habits. For example, take a different route to work, go to a different grocery store, etc. Vary your routine.

Change your phone number and block the abuser's number so that he or she cannot call or text you. Also block him or her from social media accounts.

Alert your job that the abuser should not be permitted on the premises and to phone police should he or she show up. Do the same with your child's school. If possible, have someone escort you to your car at the end of the workday.

Get a PO Box rather than publicly listing a new home address.

MAKING TECHNOLOGY SAFE

Create a new email address and password. Be discriminating about to whom you provide it. Choose a password that the abuser will not guess. You may wish to change passwords/pins to all accounts including online banking, voicemail, and so on.

Use a safe cell phone. Family or shared cell plans result in billing records that are accessible to everyone listed on the account. This means that the abuser may have access to who you're calling and whether you're seeking help.

(Continued)

149

Table 7.3 (Continued) Safety Planning

To prevent the abuser from using one of any multiple apps to track your location, turn your cell phone's GPS off! Should you choose to stay in a DV shelter for a short time, the staff will likely require that you turn your phone and its GPS off as a safety precaution.

Consider disabling all social media accounts. However, if you do choose to remain active on social media, avoid "checking in" or posting updates about your location.

Source: Adapted from Sudbury-Wayland-Lincoln Domestic Violence Roundtable, *Safety planning.* Retrieved from: domesticviolenceroundtable.org, 2008.

Note: This table is meant to provide an overview of the key advice officers should present to victims with regard to safety planning. It includes safety measures that can be implemented at various stages of the relationship—even before the victim has decided to leave the batterer.

between law enforcement and mental health and/or social justice agencies.

One such example is the New York City Housing Authority's Domestic Violence Response Team (NYCHA DVRT). This program is part of the Mayor's Office to Combat Domestic Violence, and its objective is to provide crisis response in cases of intimate partner violence. The NYCHA DVRT also pilots outreach efforts to raise community awareness about the impact of DV, and refers affected individuals to appropriate social services. This program is currently active throughout 15 of New York City's public housing developments (New York City Domestic Violence Fatality Review Committee, 2015).

Many police departments across the United States have chosen to forge partnerships with DV service agencies and mental health facilities in order to implement a similar DVRT model. In these cooperatives, individuals from the community are trained and certified by mental health professionals in order to appropriately provide crisis intervention to victims of domestic violence. Community volunteers then respond to the police department when a DV call occurs and provide the victim with emotional support, crisis intervention, and important information regarding safety planning, restraining orders, and referrals for (long and short-term) supportive counseling. Another socially progressive approach to the DV epidemic is the creation of Family Justice Centers (FJCs), which offer comprehensive multidisciplinary services for survivors of intimate partner/family violence, elder abuse, and sex trafficking in a single location.

150

The FJCs are housed in various district attorney's (or prosecutor's) offices across the country, where they utilize specially trained police officers (Domestic Violence Prevention Officers or DVPOs) as well as staff from other community agencies to offer on-site counseling, legal assistance, immigration help, financial advice, and so on. The FJCs provide free and confidential services in a safe, secure, and nurturing environment (New York City Domestic Violence Fatality Review Committee, 2015).

Additionally, there are community programs that take a preventative approach to domestic abuse. These programs inform teenagers, young adults, parents, and educators about the dynamics and dangers of dating violence and cyber abuse. They also offer interactive workshops facilitated by peer educators who help to begin the discussion about these difficult (and uncomfortable) topics (New York City Domestic Violence Fatality Review Committee, 2015).

DV is a crime unlike any other. It causes people to feel unsafe in their own homes—and frightened within the context of their intimate and familial relationships. It is a global epidemic with various social and cultural interpretations and implications. Well-informed and well-trained law enforcement personnel are needed to combat it with compassion and fortitude.

Part III

Forensic, Police, and Investigative Work

8

Behavioral Profiling

INTRODUCTION

There is some debate as to whether offender profiling is a reasonable topic to discuss within the context of forensic psychology. While many students are attracted to careers in the fields of criminal justice, criminology, and forensic psychology because of their desire to become expert profilers akin to those depicted in Hollywood, some mental health clinicians make the argument that profiling does not fall within the purview of forensic psychology. One of the main reasons for this is that the vast majority of careers involving profiling are in law enforcement (i.e., federal agent, investigator, detective, crime lab technician, etc.), and not social science. For our purposes, we will introduce the various methods of profiling, discuss their utility, and explain the psychological principles upon which they are based (Fulero & Wrightsman, 2009).

Fact Versus Fiction

In order to acquire a thorough grasp of profiling as an investigative tool, we must first separate fact from fiction. In film and on TV, profiling is portrayed as a sensational—and almost mystical—craft. Take *The Silence of the Lambs,* for instance. FBI Cadet Clarice Starling (Jodie Foster) is called upon to conduct a round of interviews with forensic psychiatrist and serial killer Hannibal Lecter (Anthony Hopkins). Before she has even completed her field training, Starling builds a rapport with Lecter in an attempt to glean insight from him to assist her in accurately profiling and anticipating the moves of another serial murderer—Buffalo Bill. While the film highlights the importance of forensic evidence, profiling is treated as a dramatic and dangerous game of cat and mouse. Starling must outwit and out-manipulate the psychopathic Lecter in order to entice him to divulge virtually clairvoyant information about Buffalo Bill.

In reality, *profiling* (also known as criminal or offender profiling) can be defined as the creation of a psychological, behavioral, demographic, or geographical sketch of the type of person likely to have committed a specific crime or crimes. It is an educated attempt to assemble logical information about a certain variety of criminal in order to bring an unknown subject (UNSUB) to justice. According to Woodsworth and Porter (1999), a profiler is someone "who examines evidence from the crime scene, victims, and witnesses in an attempt to construct an accurate psychological (usually concerning psychopathology, personality, and behavior) and demographic description of the individual who committed the crime" (p. 241).

WHY SHOULD WE PROFILE?

Law enforcement's ability to prevent, detect, and solve crimes is essential to the well-being of society. Therefore, the implementation of profiling as an investigative tool serves to help detectives narrow their pool of suspects while addressing law enforcement's key goal of containing crime. Profiling, however, is not applicable to every crime. Because it draws inferences from patterns, its framework is frequently applied to multiple and/or serial offenses such as various forms of homicide, including serial (sexual) murder, sniper attacks, and bizarre lust and mutilation murders. Research indicates that profiling has proven to be an essential tool for homicide investigators, especially when one or more of the "typical" motives for murder (discussed in Chapter 5) are not clearly present (Douglas & Burgess, 1986; Douglas, Burgess, Burgess, & Ressler, 1992). Additionally, other offenses such as sadistic sexual assaults, serial rape, occult crimes, child sexual abuse, serial arson, bank robberies, and terroristic or obscene written threats are suitable for profiling (Geberth, 1983). Research reveals that behavioral profiling techniques are most effective when the UNSUB's offense/behavioral pattern has been symptomatic of psychopathology (Holmes & Holmes, 2000).

The "Mad Bomber"

Offender profiling dates back to the 1950s when psychiatrist Dr. James Brussel developed a frighteningly accurate profile of George Metesky, the

"Mad Bomber." At the time of his arrest, Metesky had been terrorizing New York City for over 16 years by planting homemade explosive devices in public places around the city. In November of 1940, the first bomb was found—undetonated—outside the Consolidated Edison electric company's headquarters with a note stating, "Con Edison crooks—this is for you" (Cochran, 1999). The note gave investigators pause. Why would the perpetrator have attached an important communication to a bomb? Had it gone off, the note would have been obliterated. Could this act have been indicative of emotional disturbance? Or had the bomber never intended for the device to explode?

Less than a year later, another unexploded bomb was found in the neighborhood of Con Edison. After examining both devices, police gathered that one perpetrator was responsible and that he or she had extreme antipathy toward the electric company giant. That estimation was confirmed when the individual claiming to be responsible for setting the bombs contacted police directly promising not to make any further bomb threats during the war (World War II) on account of his patriotism. The Mad Bomber kept his word (Ewing & McCann, 2006).

Then, in 1950, after the war, a third unexploded device was found in Grand Central Station. Although similar in composition to the previous two, this one demonstrated a higher level of sophistication. Authorities feared that although no one had yet been hurt, it was only a matter of time. Their fears were justified as less than a month later, a similar bomb exploded in a public phone booth located in Grand Central Terminal. Although the blast only resulted in property damage, it appeared as though the bomber was not giving up; he subsequently mailed a bomb directly to Con Ed and planted another in an upholstered seat cushion in a movie theater (Ewing & McCann, 2006).

Metesky continued his assault by sending threatening communications to various newspapers promising more bombings until he had not only achieved revenge against Con Ed, but had been acknowledged as an important figure by city officials. The frequency of the attacks increased and places such as Radio City Music Hall were targeted. People were being severely injured. Police knew that they were dealing with a serial bomber—and they sought the expertise of Dr. Brussel.

After reviewing the case, Dr. Brussel developed a profile, which was published in newspapers across New York (Bixby, 1995):

Single man, between 40 and 50. A lone wolf. Introverted. Unsocial, but not anti-social. Skilled mechanic. Immigrant, or first-generation

American. Neat with tools. Cunning. Egotistical of mechanical skill. Contemptuous of other people. Disinterested in women. Resentful of criticism of his work, but probably conceals resentment. Expert in civil or military ordinance. Religious, probably a Roman Catholic. Present or former employee of Consolidated Edison. Possible motive: discharge or reprimand. Resentment kept growing. Probably a case of progressive paranoia. (p. A6)

The profile also noted that the bomber, although single, would likely be residing with a sibling. In chilling detail, Brussel went on to inform police, "When you find him, chances are he'll be wearing a double-breasted suit. Buttoned" (Brussel, 1968, p. 47). George Metesky was eventually arrested based upon details that he provided throughout his communications with the media. He was a 54-year-old former employee of Con Edison who had been injured on the job. He was single and living with his two older sisters. When he was apprehended, Metesky was dressed in a bathrobe. He requested to change prior to accompanying the arresting officers to police headquarters; they agreed. When he reemerged from his room, Metesky was clad in a blue double-breasted suit—and it was buttoned (Costanzo & Krauss, 2012).

AN ART, NOT A SCIENCE

At first glance, profiling may seem like the perfect solution to crime fighting—one that affords officers a near-telepathic understanding of an offender. However, profiles are not always as accurate as the one developed by Dr. Brussel. In fact, two profilers will not necessarily draw the same conclusions about the same case (Bekerian & Jackson, 1997; Stevens, 1997) because profiling is more of an art than it is a scientific approach to investigation.

DC Sniper Case

Let's review the DC Sniper case from Chapter 5. As you'll recall, the Washington, DC metropolitan area endured a 3-week-long sniper attack in the fall of 2002. The shootings claimed the lives of 10 people and injured another three. Various criminology experts took to the media to discuss their theory of the crime. Several of the profilers concluded that the sniper did not have any children and was local to the DC area. Military experts asserted that the UNSUB lacked a military background. Former FBI agent and media commentator, Candice DeLong, projected that the killer was employed as a firefighter or construction worker. James Alan Fox, Professor of Criminology at Northeastern University, noted that the average age of a sniper is 26, with 91% of such offenders being under the age of 40. Most work alone as opposed to with a partner and the majority (55%) are Caucasian (Gettleman, 2002, p. A-23). Reports also noted that police should be on the lookout for a white minivan or box truck as the perpetrator's vehicle.

On October 24, 2002, police arrested John Allen Muhammad, age 41, and Lee Boyd Malvo (aka John Lee Malvo), age 17, in association with the shootings. The offenders were apprehended in a 1990 Chevy Caprice; it was blue. Their arrests highlighted key facets of the initial profile that were glaringly incorrect. First, and perhaps most obviously, there were two snipers, rather than a lone shooter. Additionally, Muhammad had four children. He was a Gulf War veteran with over a decade of military experience before he became an unemployed drifter. The most interesting feature of the case was that both Muhammad and Malvo were African American, a fact that was predicted by almost no expert. As (former) Agent DeLong stated following the arrest, "A Black sniper? That was the last thing I was thinking" (Gettleman, 2002, p. A-23). For a side-by-side comparison of the profiling predictions versus the facts learned following closure of the case, see Table 8.1.

Stereotypes

There were a number of simplistic stereotypes and flawed assumptions woven into the DC Sniper profile. When profiling a case, investigators must guard against allowing common stereotypes present in society's collective unconscious to influence their determinations. For example, if

Table 8.1 DC Sniper Profile Outcome

Original Profile	Actual Case Findings
Single male in his mid-20s (approx. age 26); under age 40	Team killers: Muhammad, age 41; Malvo, age 17
UNSUB is Caucasian	Both men are African American
UNSUB does not have children	Muhammad has four children
UNSUB drives a white minivan or box truck	Suspects arrested in a 1990 blue Chevy Caprice
UNSUB has no military background	Muhammad is a Gulf War Veteran
UNSUB is a firefighter or construction worker	Muhammad was unemployed at the time of arrest

asked to characterize the type of person most likely to be an assassin, most people would describe a lonely man suffering from severe psychopathology, acting out threats of violence against a single target upon whom he is laser focused. In reality, however, the Secret Service determined that of the 83 people who killed or attempted to kill U.S. political figures or foreign politicians in the past several decades, less than 50% exhibited signs of mental illness. Moreover, many of these offenders shifted their attention from one target to another, focusing more on the act of killing than on the identity of their victim(s). Additionally, none of the 83 offenders studied made direct threats to the intended victim or to law enforcement prior to the commission of their offense(s) (Dedman, 1998).

Other crimes that carry misleading connotations are bank robbery, embezzlement, and homicide (Fulero & Wrightsman, 2009). For example, a common misconception is that bank robbers are clever, debonair, and highly skilled. This image of them has been depicted in a plethora of films and TV shows, such as Court TV's *Masterminds*. In reality, however, research concludes that most convicted bank robbers are young, impulsive, and either under the influence of drugs, or experiencing a personal crisis at the time of their crime (Associated Press, 1986).

Similarly, many people view embezzlers as long-term trusted employees approaching retirement. These criminals are believed to have spent the majority of their working lives loyally employed by one company. However, a survey of such felons (both male and female) indicates that the "typical" embezzler is a 26-year-old female. She is married, holds a high school diploma, and earns minimum wage. At the time of her crime, she is employed in an entry-level position, which she has likely held for less than 1 year. She most frequently cites marital or family difficulties as her motivation.

Lastly, it is a widely held belief that murderers are the products of broken homes (Ressler & Shachtman, 1992). However, after conducting interviews with 36 convicted killers, Ressler, Burgess, and Douglas (1988) concluded that more than half were raised in an intact family (i.e., both mother and father residing with the child).

With regard to the DC Sniper case, you can see how stereotypical assumptions, such as that all snipers are loners or single white males in their 20s, may have misguided the investigation. When profiles are too strictly adhered to, it can cause rigidity in police work. In other words, it is unproductive for law enforcement to focus on the profile to the exclusion of other suspects and/or theories of the crime.

Consider for example, the fact that roadblocks and SWAT teams were looking to apprehend a sniper in a white minivan or box truck. How many times do you think Muhammad and Malvo may have escaped officers' attention because they were driving a blue Chevy Caprice? As criminologist Jack Levin stated, "I wouldn't be surprised if the suspects just passed right by" (Gettleman, 2002, p. A-23). Furthermore, how many additional victims do you think were (or could have been) targeted while police focused on an incorrect or incomplete profile? How do you think the inaccuracies in the DC Sniper profile impacted the public's confidence in profiling and in the police in general?

The Boston Strangler

From June 1962 through January 1964, the city of Boston was crippled by the work of a serial killer. Thirteen women were strangled to death. The first victims were older, ranging in age from 55 to 75, while the latter ones were younger, mainly in their 20s. The crime scenes revealed hate and chaos—and echoed enough commonalities to warrant the use of criminal profiling.

The final victim in the string of brutal murders was 19-year-old Mary Sullivan. This scene was particularly gruesome. When she was found, Sullivan's nude body lay on her bed, with a broom handle inserted into her vagina. Both of her breasts were exposed and someone—presumably the killer—had ejaculated on her face. Next to her left foot was a card that read "Happy New Year" (Frank, 1966; Holmes & Holmes, 1996).

A team of experts was assembled in order to develop a profile of the "Boston Strangler," as the killer was dubbed. The team included a psychiatrist with expertise in the area of sexual offenses, an anthropologist, a gynecologist, and Dr. James Brussel of "Mad Bomber" fame (Frank, 1966). The team's majority opinion suggested that the two types of strangulation scenes were the result of two perpetrators working in tandem. They asserted that the older women were murdered by a man who had been raised by a domineering and seductive mother. This killer harbored unspeakable hatred toward her, and as a result of not having been able to express it, took his anger out on other (older) women. The profilers predicted that this offender lived alone and would be able to engage in normal relationships once he had psychologically overcome his issues with his mother. The committee proposed that the second killer was a homosexual man acquainted with the younger victims (Holmes & Holmes, 2002). However, Dr. Brussel offered a dissenting opinion which posited that one killer was responsible for the totality of the murders (Frank, 1966).

Albert DeSalvo was initially arrested on burglary charges; he subsequently confessed to all of the Boston Strangler murders. DeSalvo was married and residing with his wife at the time of the crimes. Reports indicated that he had an insatiable sexual appetite, at times demanding sex from his wife upwards of five times per day. He was ultimately sentenced to life in prison where he was stabbed to death by a fellow inmate. DeSalvo displayed no signs of the predictions outlined in the profile—no uncontrollable rage toward his mother, no lack of sexual potency, and no Oedipus complex (Frank, 1966; Holmes & Holmes, 2002).

THE EFFICACY OF PROFILING: EXAMINING THE RESEARCH

The DC Sniper and Boston Strangler cases clearly illustrate the dangers of relying solely on profiling to solve a crime. In fact, you may be wondering why we should use this technique at all! How effective is profiling, really?

While it is easy to assume that profiling's only utility is solving crime, research has found other uses for it. For example, a study conducted in Great Britain concluded that although profiling resulted in the identification and/or apprehension of the perpetrator in only 2.7% of the cases reviewed, police commonly found other associated benefits. These included expanding their insight into the case or the UNSUB (61%), supporting their own suppositions (52%), and informing interview and interrogation strategies (5%) (Gudjonsson & Copson, 1997).

While the hypotheses generated by profiling can be invaluable to an investigation, they should not be considered absolute. Police should avoid fixating on the profile to the exclusion of other possibilities. Since a profile may be misguided, making such a myopic error may result in arresting the wrong person(s) simply because they appear to fit the profile (Fulero & Wrightsman, 2009).

Pinizzotto and Finkel (1990) set out to assess the efficacy of profiling and to establish whether the process used by professional profilers results in a significantly better outcome than that used by their less experienced counterparts. The researchers arranged a controlled experiment in which they provided the same material to 28 subjects. Each person was presented with two actual cases—one homicide and one sexual offense. Materials for the murder case included several crime scene photos, information about the victim, and autopsy, toxicology, and police reports. With regard to the sex crime, participants received a detailed victim statement, reports from the first responding officer as well as detectives on the scene, and victimology information.

The subjects were divided into five groups:

- Group A: Experts/Teachers (n = 4)—This group comprised experts who had taught profiling to other law enforcement officials at the FBI Academy in Quantico, Virginia. Each group member was an FBI agent with a minimum of 4 years of profiling experience.
- Group B: Profilers (n = 6)—This group was composed of investigators from various police agencies who had received specific training in personality profiling via an extensive program offered by the FBI. These individuals each had 7 to 15 years of investigative experience and between 1 and 6 years of profiling experience.
- Group C: Detectives (n = 6)—These subjects were seasoned investigators, none of whom had received specific training in profiling.
- Group D: Psychologists (n = 6)—These participants were clinical psychologists without expertise in profiling or criminal investigation. (This group did not include forensic psychologists.)
- Group E: Students (n = 6)—The last group consisted of undergraduate students who had not studied profiling or criminal investigation.

After the cases were presented, all of the subjects were asked to craft a profile of each UNSUB based on 15 specific questions posed by the researchers. In both cases, the professional profilers (Groups A and B) developed more elaborate and detailed profiles than did the individuals in the nonprofiler groups. Overall, the professional profilers made more accurate predictions than did the detectives, psychologists, or students. However, the vast majority of these differences were attributed to the sex offense case. When profiling the homicide, on the other hand, students averaged 6.5 correct predictions (out of 15), whereas the profilers only averaged 5.3. This was deemed a statistically insignificant difference by the researchers. Why do you think the profilers fared better in making predictions about the sex crime and sexual offender than they did about the homicide and unidentified killer?

In their conclusion, Pinizzotto and Finkel (1990) stipulated that the profilers did not appear to process the information differently than the other participants. They therefore determined that through their experience, the profilers had learned or developed a profound ability to extract details which enhanced their predictive accuracy.

A similar study was undertaken by Kocsis, Irwin, Hayes, and Nunn (2000), in which various cases were presented to professional profilers (n = 5), police officers (n = 35), psychologists (n = 30), college students (n = 31), and "psychics" (n = 20). As in the Pinizzotto study, Kocsis et al. (2000) established that the professional profilers were more adept at developing a profile. The Kocsis research also found that the psychologists were more successful in terms of creating an accurate profile than were police or psychics. These studies embody the notion that profiling is not a scientific formulation, but rather a set of evaluative and intuitive skills meant to inform investigations.

INDUCTIVE VERSUS DEDUCTIVE REASONING

Throughout the remainder of this chapter, we will discuss various techniques for developing a profile. As we do so, keep in mind two styles of problem-solving: inductive and deductive. Consider the merits of each and how they pertain to offender profiling.

When applied to profiling, *inductive reasoning* assumes that if different crimes perpetrated by different people share similar qualities, then the offenders must also share similar characteristics (i.e., personality traits). A profile resulting from inductive methodologies seeks to identify common characteristics among offenders, such as consistencies in their personality constellations, backgrounds, and behaviors. For example, inductive reasoning led to the conclusion that serial killers such as Ted Bundy and Jeffrey Dahmer viewed their victims as objects upon which to act out their sadistic sexual fantasies (Fulero & Wrightsman, 2009). This approach is considered to be generalist in nature as these profiles are based upon information gleaned mainly from past crimes and previously identified offenders. An inductive profile might answer questions such as "Are all rapists similar?" or "Do all murderers share common personality traits?" Additionally, descriptive profiles drawn from research with known offenders can serve to dispel criminological myths. Murphy and Peters (1992) highlight this fact in their statement, "There is a good deal of clinical lore that a history of being sexually victimized is predominant in the backgrounds of sex offenders" (p. 33).

Deductive reasoning, on the other hand, formulates an in-depth analysis of a crime based upon evidence found at that specific crime scene. It requires the scrutinization of police and forensic reports, victimology, and other crime scene-specific evidence. From this information, the profiler develops an impression of an unknown offender.

Deductive logic is based upon the premise that physical evidence is a strong indicator of nonphysical (emotional, psychological, behavioral) evidence and that criminal behavior is inextricably linked to an offender's rich fantasy life. Deductive profiling also makes the assumption that the more the profiler knows about the victim, the more conclusions he or she can draw about the offender—both physically and emotionally. Therefore, profiles created from this approach reflect physical as well as psychological evidence and allow profilers to "interpret" the crime scene with regard to the offender's (deviant) fantasy (Holmes & Holmes, 2002).

What can we infer from details such as where the victim's body was found, in what position it was found, whether the crime scene was in disarray, or whether a weapon was present? Holmes and Holmes (2002) provide an excellent example of the importance of crime scene-specific assessment with their discussion of the murder of an older Caucasian woman, found beaten to death in her own home. On the night of the murder, the victim had gone out with friends. When she returned, the killer was already inside her house. The victim proceeded to undress in her bedroom—without bothering to turn on the light, thus giving the killer the opportunity to attack her from behind. She was hit forcefully in the head and subsequently bludgeoned to death.

The crime scene revealed that the perpetrator had been present in the victim's home for a length of time prior to the killing. An uncorked bottle of wine belonging to the victim was found in the hallway, but according to collateral information, the victim was a tidy housekeeper who would not have left an open container of alcohol out. Additionally, the victim stored her wine in a cabinet, rather than in more obvious places such as a wine rack or the refrigerator. Speculation was made that perhaps the killer knew that the victim was out for the evening and that he or she would have to wait for her (Holmes & Holmes, 2002). Consider not only the killer's level of familiarity with the victim's home to know that she kept her wine in the cupboard, but also his or her level of comfort to drink a partial bottle of her wine while waiting.

When crime scene technicians entered the bedroom where the victim's body was found, they came across multiple framed photographs of the victim's nieces and nephews that had been laid facedown. From the blood spatter, it appeared that the killer had done this prior to attacking the victim. If we apply both inductive and deductive reasoning, a picture of the UNSUB emerges. Employing information gathered from other cases involving same-aged females, we can assume that because there was

165

no evidence of sexual assault, the killer was probably a friend or relative of the deceased. Bearing in mind the facedown picture frames found at the scene, deductive logic supports our inductive conclusion that the victim was acquainted with her killer (Holmes & Holmes, 2002). Preferably, investigators should recognize the potential benefits of both inductive and deductive reasoning, and utilize a combination of the two when creating a psychological profile.

THE APPLICATION OF PROFILING

Profiling techniques have been used to distinguish specific characteristics about known individuals whose behavior needs to be understood by authorities. For example, the U.S. Office of Strategic Services (OSS) created profiles of controversial and powerful world leaders whose actions had wide-reaching effects. During World War II, psychiatrist Walter Langer (1972) developed a profile of Adolf Hitler in order to describe his motivations, diagnose his mental illness, and predict his potential reaction(s) to defeat.

Langer's (1972) analysis viewed Hitler's war crimes from a psychodynamic stance—as a response to his inability to maintain intimate and/or personal relationships in the face of adversity due to his lack of trust in humanity. Basing his summations partly upon Hitler's relationship with his parents, Langer concluded that Hitler viewed himself as all-powerful and invincible, and considered his rule over Germany a way to prove himself to his deceased mother. The profile projected that rather than flee or cower, he would opt to lead his troops into one final battle. If defeat seemed imminent, Langer predicted that Hitler would commit suicide. As we now know, a multitude of reports were released stating that Adolf Hitler and his wife Eva Braun took their own lives in 1945.

A similar profile was developed of Saddam Hussein during the Gulf War. Post (1991) determined: "there is no evidence that he (Hussein) is suffering from a psychotic disorder. He is not impulsive, only acts after judicious consideration, and can be extremely patient; indeed he uses time as a weapon" (p. 283). Post described Hussein as possessing "... absence of conscience, unconstrained aggression, and a paranoid outlook" (p. 285). He predicted that Saddam Hussein would "stop at nothing" if cornered by enemies and left without options.

In addition to identifying important characteristics of political and military figures, profiling has also been implemented in hostage situations in order to provide police with in-depth information about the hostage taker's background, personality, and psychological disposition. Such profiles also offer guidance regarding how the offender might react to police intervention, so that law enforcement can ultimately de-escalate and resolve the situation without casualties.

In 1993, a hostage crisis erupted at the Mount Carmel Compound in Waco, Texas. David Koresh, the leader of the Branch Davidian cult, was barricaded inside, and police had received reports that children were being abused on the premises. Following a 51-day-siege, veteran FBI agents made the recommendation to take the compound by force—based largely upon a profile of Koresh that they had developed. However, the end result was a disaster. An estimated 24 cult members were shot as the compound burst into flames and a total of 86 people were trapped inside (Verhovek, 1993). Clearly, this tragedy raised significant doubt as to the accuracy of the profile of Koresh.

CRIME SCENE ANALYSIS

As you can see, the rubric of profiling includes various approaches to the analysis of criminal behavior. In addition to extracting identifiable characteristics of known individuals, profiling has been successfully used to aid in the investigation of serial crimes, particularly those that involve a sexual component such as serial rape and serial sexual homicide. In this section, we will discuss the FBI's approach to evaluating behavioral patterns in order to profile violent serial offenses.

The process of developing a criminal profile by analyzing a crime scene dates back to the 1970s. At that time, the Behavioral Science Unit (BSU) of the FBI was using this technique to assist other law enforcement agencies in resolving serial crimes (Homant & Kennedy, 1998). Investigators at the BSU (which later became part of the National Center for the Analysis of Violent Crime or NCAVC, and which houses the Behavioral Analysis Unit or BAU) developed a deductive criminal profile-generating process. This method, referred to as *Crime Scene Analysis*, involves the evaluation of evidence found at the crime scene in order to extrapolate psychological and/or physical attributes of the unknown offender. With this information, investigators can narrow down the pool of suspects, focusing on individuals whose traits match those outlined by the profile. Additionally, a determination can be made regarding crime linkage—or whether behavioral patterns at a given crime scene are related to patterns present at other scenes (Ressler & Shachtman, 1992).

167

Crime Scene Analysis seeks to assess criminal behavior and offender characteristics in part by identifying an UNSUB's MO (modus operandi) and signature. *MO* refers to how an offender actually goes about committing a crime or series of crimes; in other words, it refers to his or her standard operating procedure. This protocol evolves over time as the perpetrator gains criminal competence in order to reduce his or her risk of being apprehended. For example, a first-time burglar may break a window to gain entry into a home that he or she has targeted. However, realizing that breaking glass creates noise, which may lead to unwanted attention and subsequent arrest, he or she may refine this process and begin using glass-cutting tools or disabling alarm systems and picking locks (Douglas & Munn, 1992).

Unlike the MO, the *signature* never changes. Its presence signifies the fulfillment (emotional and/or sexual) of the offender's fantasy—and is not required for successful completion of the criminal act. To illustrate this point, Douglas and Olshaker (1998) cite a bank robber that forced his victims to undress in his presence. He then posed them in sexually degrading positions while he photographed them. Not only did this not assist the perpetrator in completing the robbery, it actually hindered him by slowing him down. This behavior put him at greater risk of being apprehended because he remained at the scene of the crime longer than necessary in order to pose and photograph the victims. Because this was something that the offender was compelled to do for his own sense of unique satisfaction, it is classified as a signature (see Figure 8.1).

Crime Scene Analysis involves six procedural stages, which help investigators to generate hypotheses about how the crime occurred, why it occurred, the type of person that committed it, and how to best apprehend the offender. As you read through the next section, you'll notice that the first five stages, (1) profiling inputs, (2) decision-process models, (3) crime assessment, (4) criminal profile, and (5) investigation, tend to overlap and culminate in the sixth stage: apprehension (Douglas, Ressler, Burgess, & Hartman, 1986).

Profiling Inputs

In the initial stage of the profile-generating process, investigators obtain and review extensive case materials. In order to build a thorough and accurate profile, such resources should include a comprehensive summary of the crime, a detailed description of the crime scene, and information specific to the locale where the offense occurred, such as weather

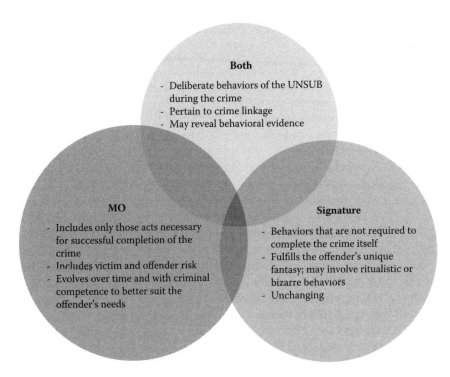

Both
- Deliberate behaviors of the UNSUB during the crime
- Pertain to crime linkage
- May reveal behavioral evidence

MO
- Includes only those acts necessary for successful completion of the crime
- Includes victim and offender risk
- Evolves over time and with criminal competence to better suit the offender's needs

Signature
- Behaviors that are not required to complete the crime itself
- Fulfills the offender's unique fantasy; may involve ritualistic or bizarre behaviors
- Unchanging

Figure 8.1   MO versus signature.

conditions and political and social climate. Additionally, profilers should gather information pertaining to victimology, such as the victim's living situation, employment history, diagnosed medical and psychological conditions, personality, reputation, criminal history, and so on. Forensic documentation such as the autopsy and accompanying toxicology reports should also be obtained. The medical examiner's assessment should express findings about time and cause of death, whether a weapon was used (and if so what type), the sequence in which wounds were administered, and if possible, a diagram of the wounds. If available, crime scene photos and sketches illustrating scale and relevant distances should be evaluated. While it is crucial for profilers to carefully examine evidence germane to the crime, they should not be given a list of potential suspects as this may erroneously influence the profile (Douglas et al., 1986).

Decision-Process Models

The data collected and analyzed in the previous stage can reveal significant information about the behaviors, motivations, and characteristics of the perpetrator. Therefore, in the decision-process models phase of the profiling process, investigators arrange the information into meaningful patterns across seven decision points: homicide classification, motive, victim risk, offender risk, potential for escalation/serial offending, temporal factors, and location.

Homicide Classification
As you'll recall from Chapter 5, homicides are classified based upon the number of victims (single or multiple), number of separate homicidal events or occurrences, number of crime scene locations, and whether the killer engaged in a cooling off period between murders. As the label indicates, a single-victim homicide involves one victim who is murdered during the course of one homicidal event at a specific location. Conversely, multiple-victim murders, which are more typical fare for profilers, may be classified as spree killings, mass murders, or serial murders.

A multiple-victim homicide is classified as a *spree killing* when three or more individuals are killed in at least two separate locations by the same perpetrator(s) without a cooling off period separating the murders (Bartol & Bartol, 2008). *Mass murder* involves the killing of three or more victims during the course of one incident at a single location. Again, there is no cooling off period. In contrast, a series of homicides is classified as *serial murder* when three or more victims are killed by the same offender(s), during separate events, and there is a cooling off period between the murders. The cooling off period may be brief and last only a day or two or it may be prolonged, sometimes in excess of several years. It is this cooling off period that separates serial killers from other multiple murderers (Bartol & Bartol, 2008; Douglas et al., 1986).

Motive
Douglas et al. (1986) denote three separate motivations for murder: criminal enterprise, emotional/selfish/cause-specific, and sexual. If a killer's motive is classified as criminal enterprise, it means that the primary motivation was financial. For instance, he or she may have been involved in criminal business dealings that resulted in murder, despite not having had any personal malice toward the victim. This category includes contract killings, gang murders, and political hits.

Emotional disturbance, selfish, and cause-specific murders include such offenses as mercy killings, familial or domestic violence resulting in homicide (i.e., spousal murder, matricide, patricide, infanticide, etc.) and murder as a form of self-defense. Homicides committed by mentally disordered individuals as a result of symptomatic paranoia or psychosis are also included. Additionally, some assassinations and fanatical killings, such as those perpetrated by Jim Jones, Charles Manson, and the Ku Klux Klan, fall within the category of emotional intent. They can then be further categorized as religiously motivated, cult, and fanatical, respectively (Douglas et al., 1986).

Lastly, we need to consider that an offender may have sexual motives for committing homicide. Sexually motivated killings are those murders that occur so that the killer can engage in sexual contact or achieve sexual gratification through activities such as dismemberment, evisceration, mutilation, etc. These acts have a specific sexual meaning to the killer (Douglas et al., 1986).

Victim Risk
Victim risk is significant in that it provides insight into the type of victim that the perpetrator targeted. The level of risk is determined by factors such as the victim's age, occupation, lifestyle, location, physical stature, and ability to resist an attacker. Low-risk victims are those whose lifestyles do not make them vulnerable or lead them to being victimized. Because of its importance, the concept of victim risk is revisited throughout the profiling process (Douglas et al., 1986).

Offender Risk
Similarly, we can assess the amount of risk that the offender took in attacking a particular victim. Combined with victim risk, this paints an overarching picture of the offender's brashness. For example, kidnapping a victim in broad daylight from a city street is high risk for the UNSUB and makes certain suppositions about his or her emotional state. For instance, one might assume that the offender may have been under extreme stress, excited by the commission of his or her crimes, or believed that he or she would not get caught (Douglas et al., 1986).

Potential for Escalation/Serial Offending
Via analysis of the UNSUB's behavioral patterns, profilers determine the sequence in which events occurred during the crime. From this information, they deduce whether the offender's behavior is likely to escalate

(i.e., from peeping to molestation to sexual assault to sexual homicide). Additionally, they are tasked with determining whether patterns intrinsic to the crime indicate that the perpetrator is likely to offend in serial fashion (Douglas et al., 1986).

Temporal Factors
It is important for profilers to consider multiple timing factors, such as the length of time that it took the perpetrator to kill the victim, commit any additional acts with the body (such as sexual acts, dismemberment, etc.), and dispose of the body. Investigators should also pay close attention to the time of day (or night) that the crime was committed as it may provide clues about the victim/offender risk as well as the offender's lifestyle or occupation (Douglas et al., 1986).

Location
Temporal elements are closely linked with location factors. For example, a killer who intends to spend time with the victim either before or after killing him or her would need to select a location that would ensure privacy for an extended period of time. Additional location-related information, such as where the perpetrator initially approached or abducted the victim, where the crime took place, and where the body was found, provide further information about the offender (Douglas et al., 1986). For example, if the victim was snatched from outside his or her office in the city, but the body was later found several miles outside the city, it might indicate that the killer had access to a personal vehicle.

Crime Assessment

The third stage is crime assessment, which requires investigators to establish the actions of both the victim and offender in order to reconstruct the sequence of events. To do this, profilers must make determinations about the antecedent (or trigger), method of attack, cause of death, post-offense behavior, and body disposal.

Antecedent refers to what occurred before the murder, or in other words, the circumstances that set the perpetrator's criminal behavior in motion. This may be an emotionally devastating event such as the death of a loved one, a divorce, or the loss of a much-needed job. This is often referred to as a *trigger* or *stressor*.

When we examine the cause of death, we are seeking to determine the underlying disease, injury, or violent circumstance that directly resulted in the victim's demise. When we evaluate the method of attack, however, we are in essence trying to answer the question: "What tactic was used to con, abduct, or physically overcome this person?"

Body disposal refers to what the killer did with the victim's remains. It encompasses whether the victim's body was discarded at the scene of the crime, buried, left out in the open, moved to a secondary location, hidden, burned, dismembered, etc. The broader category of post-offense behavior in general seeks to predict how the UNSUB is likely to react after the crime has been completed. This includes whether he or she will return to the burial site to "visit" the victim(s), whether the UNSUB will inject him or herself into the investigation, and whether the perpetrator will keep abreast of news coverage on the case and eventually reach out to the media or law enforcement. Most facets of the UNSUB's behavior at the crime scene can be described by applying the widely implemented organized-disorganized typology of criminal behavior.

Organized-Disorganized Typology

As the name suggests, the *organized-disorganized* model categorizes an UNSUB's behavior as either organized or disorganized based upon characteristics of the crime scene (see Table 8.2). An organized scene suggests planning and control on the part of the offender whereas a disorganized crime scene appears unplanned and reflects a lack of control in addition to elements of impulsivity, disorder, chaos, and possible psychosis.

What do you think an organized crime scene says about an offender's fundamental qualities? What does it imply about his or her relationship to the victim? Organized offenders are methodical, so they are more likely to engage in careful victim selection than their disorganized counterparts. Additionally, an organized UNSUB—especially one who is not a first-time offender—is more likely to stage a crime scene in order to mislead the police (Douglas et al., 1986) (see Figure 8.2).

At this point in the profile-generating process, detectives integrate the organized-disorganized typology with their evaluation of the crime scene dynamics. They piece together elements including cause of death, crime scene location, positioning of the body, location of the wounds, choice of weapon, and so on to reveal behavioral patterns and personality characteristics unique to the offender (Ressler et al., 1986). Consider the following vignette:

> A 42-year-old female is found dead on her kitchen floor. The autopsy indicates that the cause of death was multiple stab wounds to the head, neck, and face. The victim was stabbed a total of 17 times; eight of these

Table 8.2   Organized Versus Disorganized Typology

Crime Scene Characteristics

Organized	Disorganized
Planned, controlled	Impulsive, chaotic
Victim is manipulated with conversation prior to the crime	Little to no conversation with victim
Violence/aggression toward victim prior to death	Sexual acts committed postmortem
Restraints used to make victim submissive	No restraints used; violence to victim is sudden
Weapon brought to the scene	Weapon improvised at the scene
Body hidden or disposed of	Body left in view
Body transported to secondary location	Body left at crime scene; possibly repositioned

Offender Characteristics

Organized	Disorganized
Average to above-average intelligence	Below-average intelligence
High birth order, possibly first born	Low birth order
Charismatic; socially integrated	Socially inept and immature
Sexually competent	Sexually incompetent; seldom dates
Triggered by stressful event(s)	Minimal situational stress
Married and/or lives with a partner	Lives alone
Geographically mobile	Lives and/or works near crime scene(s)
Controlled emotions during the crime(s)	Experiences anxiety during the crime(s)
Skilled worker	Unskilled laborer

> Note: Staging should not be confused with undoing. Staging is an offender's purposeful misrepresentation of criminal activity in order to mislead police and escape apprehension. For example, a homicide scene may be staged to look like a suicide. Undoing, however, is an offender's remorseful way of psychologically reversing the effects of his or her crime. When undoing, he or she may redress the victim, apply makeup, pose the victim in bed as if he or she is sleeping, etc. For the offender, this serves to symbolically undo the harm he or she has caused the victim.

Figure 8.2   Staging.

174

wounds were delivered post-mortem. Forensic analysis reveals that the weapon was a carving knife taken from the victim's own collection. There were no signs of forced entry.

Although this description is very brief, it provides us with significant insight into the behavioral characteristics and motivations of the offender. The first impression of this crime is that of an emotionally charged and impulsive murder. Because the UNSUB did not bring his or her own weapon to the crime scene, but rather took a knife from the victim's home, we can assume that the killing was unplanned. Additionally, the crime scene was not staged—this is clearly a vicious homicide. Therefore, we are most likely dealing with a disorganized killer.

Now, let's review the cause of death. Brutal facial injuries typically indicate a perpetrator who is well acquainted with his or her victim, as this is not only a personal way to kill someone, but also a substantial sign of rage. Additionally, there were multiple stab wounds, some of which were delivered *after* the victim was already dead. We refer to this as *over-kill*, because more effort was exerted than was necessary to kill the victim. Overkill is also a strong indicator of extreme anger. These behavioral clues, along with the lack of forced entry, point to a killer who was known to the victim.

As you can see, the organized-disorganized dichotomy is a fundamental feature of crime assessment. This typology is based on the trait theory of personality, which posits that (internal) personality traits determine (external) behavior. Because such traits are presumed to be stable and unchanging, they are thought to result in consistent patterns of behavior over time and across varying situations (Alison, Bennell, Mokros, & Ormerod, 2002; Mischel, 1968). Within the context of profiling a criminal offender, this means that a perpetrator's personality traits remain constant throughout both his or her criminal and noncriminal activities. For instance, an organized offender would exhibit planning and control at crime scenes as well as organized characteristics such as intelligence, social proficiency, and charisma in noncriminal endeavors (Alison et al., 2002; Homant & Kennedy, 1998).

While the trait model has been useful in profiling certain crimes, some researchers believe that situational factors impact behavior more heavily than do personality characteristics (Cervone & Shoda, 1999). What does this mean with regard to profiling? Fluid situational components, such as a highly resistant victim, an unplanned interruption during the crime, or a hard day at work, may result in behavioral inconsistencies across an offender's crimes, making it difficult to profile him or her accurately (Bennell & Canter, 2002; Bennell & Jones, 2005). Therefore, profilers should remain cognizant of the fact that not every offender will fall squarely into either the organized or disorganized category, as these can be too general. It is more likely that a specific crime scene or UNSUB will display some crossover between organized and disorganized features. In fact, the FBI has now refined this model to account for those offenders who exhibit a combination of both organized and disorganized characteristics (Douglas et al., 1992).

The Profile

During the profiling stage, investigators create a description of the type of person they believe committed the crime under investigation. This description should include detailed demographic information, as well as an outline of the offender's beliefs, values, criminal history, and psychological status. The profile may also include recommendations for how to apprehend the UNSUB safely, and may additionally predict the offender's expected response to law enforcement (Douglas et al., 1986).

A typical profile should include the following information about the UNSUB:

- Race, sex, age (differentiating between chronological and emotional age as appropriate)
- Marital/relationship status
- Living arrangements
- Occupation/employment status
- Psychological diagnoses, history of past treatment, prognosis
- Beliefs and values (including extremist views)
- Past criminal history, including similar/related offenses and pattern of escalation
- Expected reactions to law enforcement, including whether he or she will become violent, commit suicide by cop, or inject him or herself into the investigation

Investigation

Once the profile has been drafted, a report is disseminated to the agency overseeing the case, advising detectives of investigative recommendations. Additionally, suspects matching the profile criteria are evaluated.

176

The profile is deemed successful if it results in the identification and apprehension of a suspect, especially one who subsequently offers a confession. If new evidence is obtained, the profile is reexamined and new conclusions may be drawn (Douglas et al., 1986).

Apprehension

Apprehension is the final step in the profile-generating process, and logically follows from the closely related investigation stage. Based upon the behavioral evidence gathered about the UNSUB, investigators are advised as to the safest way to arrest the suspect. The profile also recommends interview strategies (Douglas et al., 1986), which we will cover in detail in the next chapter.

GEOGRAPHIC PROFILING

We've discussed how commonalities among crime scenes, behavioral evidence, and personality traits can assist law enforcement in narrowing their pool of suspects. Now, let's turn our attention toward geographic analysis and how understanding an offender's mobility as well as the geography of the crime scenes can assist with crime linkage, suspect/tip prioritization, DMV searches, and surveillance.

Geographic profiling (GP) is a nontraditional profiling method that systematically plots serial offense locations in order to discern the spatial range of criminal activity, including the location of the offender's home, and likely areas of reoffense (Canter & Larkin, 1993; Rossmo, 2000). This method is based on the assumption that the offender operates from a fixed residence. Its use therefore results in the calculation of both a home range as well as a criminal range. The *home range* represents the offender's spatial knowledge of his or her environment, which includes his or her home. The *criminal range* represents the distance that the offender is willing to travel in order to perpetrate the crimes (i.e., abduct, assault, or kill victims and dispose of their bodies). Geographic profiling seeks to reconcile the difference between these two ranges (Canter & Larkin, 1993).

The development of these ranges led to the proposal of two hypothetical GP models. In the *commuter model*, the offender is highly geographically mobile and travels a considerable distance from home to commit his or her crimes. The criminal range is therefore not limited by the parameters of the home range. Conversely, the *marauder model* typifies a pattern

177

in which the offender's home acts as a base from which he or she moves out in all directions to commit his or her offenses (Canter & Larkin, 1993). This movement pattern is referred to as *domocentric* (Kocsis, Cooksey, Irwin, & Allen, 2002).

When applying geographic profiling to an investigation, it is important to consider several elements, such as the suitability of its use. It is necessary for the offender to have a fixed place of residence to implement this method (Rossmo, 2000). GP will not work with a transient offender. As with other forms of profiling, verifying and identifying case information is crucial. Additionally, all locations instrumental to the investigation should be clearly plotted on a map of the overall area.

A key component in the development of such profiles is circle measurement (Canter & Larkin, 1993; Kocsis & Irwin, 1997; Kocsis et al., 2002). The basic principles of circle measurement are applicable to all serial offenses in varying degrees. Although GP was originally developed to be an effective tool for solving crimes such as serial murder, rape, and arson, it is now also being used to assist in cases of serial bombings, burglary, and child abduction (Guerette, 2002). Profilers should plot a diametric circle using the locations of the two furthest offenses. The space within this circle has a high probability of encompassing the offender's residence. However, plotting the two furthest offenses assumes that all offenses have been committed and detected (Canter & Larkin, 1993; Kocsis & Irwin, 1997).

Distance chronology should also be evaluated as some offenders commit their initial crimes closer to home and then travel further away as they gain confidence, or vice versa. Travel clusters may emerge as areas surrounding the offender's place of employment or other comfort zones may serve as additional home bases from which he or she is operating (Brantingham & Brantingham, 1981; Rossmo, 1995). When mapping the offender's movements, profilers should take environmental considerations, such as the terrain and climate, into account. Additionally, adjustments and interpretations are made, as with other types of profiling. GP serves to help detectives geographically focus their investigation.

The Yorkshire Ripper case in England was one of the first in history to implement the use of geographic profiling (Canter, 2003). Following several years of brutal murders without an arrest, an advisory team was appointed to reassess the investigative strategy. After careful review, the team hypothesized that the offender was local. To support their assertion, they developed a geographic profile (Kind, 1987) in which they plotted the UNSUB's 17 known murders. From that, they calculated the central point, which was near Bradford, where most of the murders had occurred. When Peter Sutcliffe, the confessed Yorkshire Ripper, was apprehended, it was discovered that he resided in a district of Bradford (Canter, 2003). This is just one of many cases that successfully used a form of profiling to better focus the investigation.

9

Eliciting Useful Information

INTRODUCTION

On July 19, 1996, 14-year-old Crystal Champagne left her apartment in Jefferson Parish, Louisiana to run a local errand; she never returned home. Within hours, her cousin Damon Thibodeaux, along with several neighbors, had formed a search party to look for her. Meanwhile, police began an investigation into Crystal's disappearance and interviewed everyone who had seen the teenager in the hours just before she vanished—including Thibodeaux. In fact, while detectives were speaking with him, patrol officers made a gruesome discovery. Crystal's body was found partially nude and she had been strangled to death (Innocence Project, 2016).

The missing person's case had become a murder investigation. A homicide detective took over the interview with Thibodeaux, who was cooperative and reported that he had no information regarding his cousin's death. In order to assist police, he even agreed to take a polygraph examination, which investigators later told him he had failed. Following nearly nine hours of intense interrogation, Damon Thibodeaux provided an incriminating statement. He told investigators that he had forcibly raped Crystal before beating and ultimately killing her (Innocence Project, 2016).

For authorities, it was case closed. However, there were several inconsistencies between Thibodeaux's account of the events leading up to the murder and the facts of the case. For instance, there was no semen present in or on the victim's body. Additionally, Thibodeaux claimed to have used a white or gray speaker wire as the ligature, but Crystal had been strangled with a red electrical cord. Despite these discrepancies, Thibodeaux was arrested and charged with rape and murder. Only then was he permitted to eat and sleep, after which he immediately recanted his confession in its entirety (Innocence Project, 2016).

THE SIGNIFICANCE OF A CONFESSION

A confession is perhaps the most damaging piece of evidence that can be presented at trial (Kassin, 1997). Consider the words of Supreme Court Justice William Brennan: "No other class of evidence is so profoundly prejudicial ... Triers of fact accord confessions such heavy weight in their determinations that the introduction of a confession makes the other aspects of a trial in court superfluous" (*Colorado v. Connelly*, 1986, p. 182).

For a multitude of potentially obvious reasons, police tend to favor confessions over other types of evidence. First, confessions save the criminal justice system both time and money. Suspects who confess typically accept a plea bargain, thereby waiving their right to a trial, which entails less cost for the court. Second, offenders who confess their guilt frequently tell investigators where to find key pieces of evidence (e.g., the murder weapon, the victim's remains, etc.). This means that other evidence becomes less critical and police can streamline or even bypass tedious and time-consuming tasks, such as locating and interviewing potential witnesses. Third, and perhaps most importantly, juries typically opt to convict defendants who have confessed (Leo, 2008).

If you had been a member of the jury in the Thibodeaux case, how would you have found the defendant—guilty or not guilty? How much would his confession have influenced you? What consideration would you have given to the fact that he later recanted his statement? As you can probably imagine, listening to someone openly admit to having committed a heinous crime carries emotional weight with a jury. Most people, including jurors, tend to believe in the veracity of a confession. Because of the power of this particular type of evidence, the court needs to consider not only the confession itself, but also the circumstances under which it was obtained.

Let's take a look at the outcome of Damon Thibodeaux's case. Based almost exclusively on his confession, Thibodeaux was found guilty and sentenced to death. He spent 16 years in prison, 15 of which were on Death Row, before he was exonerated based on post-conviction DNA evidence. DNA analysis revealed that blood found on the murder weapon contained male DNA—and did not belong to Thibodeaux. Additionally, there was nothing to indicate that Crystal had been sexually assaulted. The forensic examination concluded that there was no physical evidence linking Thibodeaux to the murder of his cousin (Innocence Project, 2016).

To further support Thibodeaux's innocence, eyewitnesses who had reported seeing him near the location where the body was found admitted that they had seen his picture in the news and knew that he was a suspect prior to giving their statements. Additionally, they claimed to have seen him near the crime scene a day *after* the body was found, when Thibodeaux was already in police custody. During the exoneration proceedings, an expert witness described Thibodeaux's false confession as the tragic result of extreme exhaustion (from his lengthy overnight participation in the search party followed by relentless interrogation), combined with psychological vulnerability and extreme fear of execution (Innocence Project, 2016).

INTERROGATION

Contrary to widely held stereotypes, police have two main goals when questioning suspects: obtaining information to further their investigation and eliciting a confession. Police training manuals describe interrogation as "not simply a means of inducing an admission of guilt" (O'Hara & O'Hara, 1980, p. 111), but rather a methodology for learning the location of physical evidence, identifying accomplices, or linking a particular individual to other criminal acts. However, once someone has been identified as a suspect, the objective of the interrogation becomes obtaining a confession (Costanzo & Krauss, 2012).

Understandably, guilty suspects typically want to avoid incriminating themselves. Therefore, law enforcement has developed various interrogation techniques in order to combat such resistance. Police receive specialized training in tactics such as how to elicit a confession from obstinate suspects. Research indicates that between 39% and 48% of interrogations result in the suspect offering a full confession. An additional 13% to 16% of suspects make self-incriminating statements or provide partial admissions of guilt (Moston, Stephenson, & Williamson, 1992). Police report that they are able to extract incriminating statements from approximately 68% of the suspects that they interrogate (Kassin et al., 2007).

While these statistics highlight the ability of modern interrogation methods to induce full or partial admissions of guilt, they do not document whether the confessing suspects are guilty or innocent, as Damon

183

Thibodeaux was. Some interrogation procedures are too narrowly focused on eliciting a confession—to the exclusion of acquiring useful (i.e., truthful) information. In this chapter, you will learn the distinction between interview and interrogation techniques, and how to strategically apply them. You will also discover how to extract the most accurate information from eyewitnesses. As you read, consider how improper use of certain methodologies could lead to injustices such as provoking a false confession, which could then result in a wrongful conviction.

The History of Interrogation

Interrogation procedures have evolved considerably since their initial inception in part due to laws regulating use of force by police. Such techniques have become increasingly sophisticated over time, progressing from overt physical violence to covert physical tactics, and finally to psychological coercion sans physical force (Leo, 2008).

Prior to 1930, blatant physical abuse was used to elicit confessions. Police would commonly beat suspects with their fists or other objects. Officers would additionally inflict cigarette burns on or administer electric shocks to uncooperative subjects. Females in custody were often dragged or pulled by their hair, while males would have their testicles pulled or twisted. These savage techniques began to change in 1931 with the publication of the *Report on Lawlessness in Law Enforcement*, which publicized the pervasive issue of police brutality against suspects in custody (Costanzo & Krauss, 2012).

THE REID TECHNIQUE

While occurrences of physical abuse still arise within the confines of interrogation, most modern investigators rely solely on psychological tactics in order to obtain confessions. One such methodology is the *Reid Technique*. Developed by John E. Reid, this widely used practice is based upon underlying psychological principles.

The Reid Technique is arguably best known for its directives regarding interrogation. However, in its totality, it is a three-part crime-solving procedure, which encompasses investigation, interview, and interrogation. The investigation begins with factual analysis, which involves the collection and evaluation of case-specific evidence, such as victimology information and a list of potential suspects. At this juncture, the direction of the investigation is determined (Jayne & Buckley, 2014).

During the second phase, investigators interview potential suspects, using a structured interview format known as a Behavior Analysis Interview. This nonaccusatory approach is meant to prompt the subject to disclose detailed information while in a controlled environment. The questions are designed to provide the investigator with insight into the subject's verbal and nonverbal behaviors, which are then interpreted as being indicative of truthfulness or deception. If the investigator determines that the interviewee has not been forthright during this exchange, then he or she moves on to the next part of the process: the accusatory interrogation (Jayne & Buckley, 2014).

Understanding Deception

Before we discuss the specific steps involved in the Reid Technique interrogation, it is important to first understand two fundamental concepts related to deception. First is the idea that deception is predicated upon people's desire to avoid adverse consequences, such as serving a prison sentence, paying a fine, being fired from a job, or even experiencing negative emotions (i.e., embarrassment or shame). The second notion is that people who have committed a crime have also justified it to themselves. For a clearer picture of this concept, think back to our discussion of sexual offenses in Chapter 6. Rapists justify their offenses by supporting rape myths and engaging in victim blaming. Similarly, embezzlers convince themselves that the company owes them more money because their dedicated service has been underpaid and underappreciated. A related concept is the idea of "victim mentality" in which offenders feel that they are the victim of an unfair justice system. Despite having committed a crime, they believe that their situation is unique and therefore calls for special consideration (Jayne & Buckley, 2014). As you read the following section, consider how the Reid Technique addresses these principles and works to resolve them. An overview of the steps involved in this interrogation procedure can be found in Table 9.1.

The Accusatory Interrogation

Establishing an environment conducive to obtaining truthful information and/or a confession is of paramount importance during an investigation. Before beginning the accusatory portion of the interrogation, The Reid

Table 9.1   The Reid Technique

Interrogative Step	Description
Establish rapport	Provide a formal introduction that places you (the investigator) in a higher status position than the suspect.
Obtain pedigree	Attain basic information about the suspect, which serves as a baseline for truth.
Ask why the suspect believes he or she is being questioned	A good guess is indicative of a willingness to be truthful, whereas a bizarre guess may mean the suspect is going to be deceptive.
Direct positive confrontation	Make an accusatory statement about the suspect's involvement in the crime in question.
Development of plausible themes	Offer moral (not legal) justifications for the crime.
Interrupt/overpower suspect's denial	Shut down the suspect's attempts to deny his or her culpability or involvement.
Keep the suspect mentally and emotionally present	Engage the suspect in active thought that encourages him or her to tell the truth.
Apply compassionate approach	Approach the suspect with understanding.
Prompt an initial admission of guilt	Showing empathic concern and understanding makes the suspect feel more comfortable, thus making giving an incriminating statement easier.
Development of incriminating statement into a confession	Continue the interview, guiding the suspect to develop the brief admission into a full-fledged confession.
Written confession	Obtain a detailed written confession from the suspect, to be used in court.

Source: Jayne, B. C., & Buckley, J. P., The Reid Technique, Reid.com website. Retrieved from: https://www.reid.com/educational_info/canada.html, 2014.

Technique dictates that the investigator should establish a basic rapport with the suspect. One way to do this is to engage in small talk. Ask the suspect about his or her day, comment on the weather, and so on, and he or she is likely to lower his or her defenses ever so slightly.

Next, it is crucial for the detective to formally introduce him or herself using an official title (i.e., "Detective Smith"), while consistently referring to the suspect by his or her first name. The investigator may also choose to physically position him or herself above the suspect by standing or leaning against a piece of furniture, while the suspect remains seated in a chair.

This tactic serves to subconsciously place the officer in a position of authority over the suspect. Then the investigator obtains pedigree information from the suspect, such as his or her full name, date of birth, home address, etc. While it may seem trivial, this is an important piece of the puzzle, as the investigator already has this information. Therefore, the suspect's answers to these basic questions help to establish a baseline for truthfulness. The interrogator should follow up with an open-ended question such as "Do you know why I'm here talking with you?" Realistic speculation on the part of the suspect may be indicative of a willingness to tell the truth, whereas a bizarre guess is potentially suggestive of deception.

Step One of the accusatory interrogation process is referred to as "direct positive confrontation." This means that the investigator tells the suspect in no uncertain terms that his or her guilt is clearly indicated in relation to the crime in question. This declaration should be definitive—entirely unmarred by tenuousness. It is important to understand that this may not necessarily be a truthful assertion; it is a tactic. By overstating his or her certainty about the suspect's guilt, the investigator hopes to persuade the subject to abandon a position of innocence (Jayne & Buckley, 2014).

Immediately following direct positive confrontation, the interrogator offers a transitional statement. For example, he or she might say, "While there is no doubt that you committed this crime, what I really need to do is determine the circumstances that led up to it." Such a statement seeks to provide a context for the interrogation—one other than simply inducing a confession. It also circumvents the question of whether or not the suspect is guilty and/or whether law enforcement has sufficient evidence to proceed. Additionally, guilty individuals who shift the responsibility for their offense onto other people, or view their crime as the result of circumstances beyond their control, may desire the opportunity to explain. The transitional statement provides a segue for the investigator's demeanor to shift from accusatory to empathetic or understanding, which is crucial during the second step of the process (Jayne & Buckley, 2014).

Step Two is the development of realistic themes. This procedure seeks to emotionally and psychologically minimize the offender's guilty intentions, while being careful not to provide a legal defense for any criminal actions. In other words, the investigator attempts to show the suspect that he or she views the crime and/or the motivation for the offense as reasonably understandable. This phase of the interrogation is based on the aforementioned idea that suspects have already justified their behavior in their own minds; the theme simply reinforces that already present justification.

For example, there are some appropriate themes that could offer moral or psychological excuses for the commission of a burglary. Perhaps the suspect needed the money in order to feed his or her family, or perhaps the offender was being bled dry by an ex-spouse. Maybe the burglar believed that the wealthy family he or she stole from could afford it, and therefore the crime wasn't really causing any significant harm (Jayne & Buckley, 2014).

The investigator delivers the theme as a monologue. For instance (Jayne & Buckley, 2014):

> Jim, I think you acted out of desperation because of your financial situation. I don't think you are a common criminal who enjoys doing things like this. I think you tried hard to keep up with your utility bills, rent, and car payments but kept falling further and further behind. Because you are conscientious and want to pay your bills on time, you saw this as your only chance to catch up financially.

You'll notice how the investigator emphasizes the offender's *understandable* feelings of desperation. He or she might even make a statement that further offers an ethical exemption, such as "You acted out of desperation. If you were really dishonest, you would have taken more or robbed a bank. You did what you felt pressured to do in that moment."

According to Jayne and Buckley (2014), the rationalizations implied during the course of theme development are grounded in the idea that most criminals engage in cognitive distortions. They fail to accept responsibility for their role in the events leading up to their crimes and further justify, minimize, excuse, or deny deviant motivations for said offenses. Let's take a look at an example of how an interrogation might sound without the use of a theme. As you read through it, consider how someone who has not acknowledged the reasons underlying his or her crime might react (Jayne & Buckley, 2014):

> John, you're the lowest form of sexual deviant I have ever encountered. When a man has to resort to forcing a woman to have sex with him it tells me that he's got serious psychological problems. A person who would pick on a helpless woman has no conscience. Even animals who live in the wild don't rape other animals to show their superiority. You really are a disgusting example of the human race and I hope they put you away for a long time.

As you can see, this example does not provide a moral justification for the sexual assault. While the passage may highlight how the investigator *actually* feels about sex offenders, approaching a suspect in this manner can have disastrous consequences. Such a confrontation is likely to exacerbate the shame that the offender may already be feeling. Because anger is a secondary emotion in that it is the product of an underlying negative feeling, the offender may subsequently become angry; he may in turn be more resistant to the idea of cooperating with the investigation.

Steps Three and Four of the interrogation process are closely related, as both address declarations of denial made by the suspect during the theme development phase. In step three, the interrogator unfailingly interrupts the suspect each time he or she utters a statement of denial (Inbau, Reid, Buckley, & Jayne, 2004). This tactic is based upon the principle that every time a suspect endorses denial, he or she becomes more committed to the position of innocence. Eventually, the suspect feels that admitting any involvement in the offense will cause him or her to lose face, and therefore strongly rejects the idea of offering a truthful confession (Jayne & Buckley, 2014).

Similarly, in step four, the interrogator verbally overpowers the suspect's attempts to deny the crime, thus causing him or her to silently withdraw. The investigator accomplishes this by continually steering the discussion back to the theme and denying the suspect's requests to interject. Should the suspect have the opportunity to voice disagreement, the investigator either shifts focus to a different theme or cuts him or her off with a closed-ended statement such as "We are well past that—we already know that you're guilty" (Jayne & Buckley, 2014).

When suspects become discouraged that their attempts to convince investigators of their innocence have been unsuccessful, they are more likely to psychologically withdraw and focus on the potential consequences of the crime. Therefore, during *Step Five* the detective ensures that the suspect remains mentally and emotionally present for the remainder of the interrogation. Investigators achieve this by physically positioning themselves closer to the suspect, thus reducing the psychological distance between them. Investigators may also choose to ask hypothetical questions intended to engage the suspect in active thought. If done correctly, investigators will notice the suspect's demeanor changing. For example, the individual's body language may become less defensive (e.g., uncrossing arms or legs), his or her posture may become more relaxed, and he or she may focus on the floor, thus avoiding eye contact. At this point, the suspect may consider telling the truth (Jayne & Buckley, 2014).

In *Step Six*, the interrogator approaches the suspect with understanding and compassion. He or she summarizes the varying thematic concepts and presents one or two central ideas. The investigator again encourages the suspect to tell the truth by appealing to his or her sense of morality. This paves the way for *Step Seven*, the purpose of which is to prompt an initial admission of guilt (Inbau et al., 2004).

In this phase, the investigator presents the suspect with two options—usually a negative one and a more ethically or socially acceptable one—regarding significant aspects of the crime. These choices offer the suspect face-saving alternatives to admitting to morally reprehensible behavior. It is important to note that the alternatives provided not only play on the suspect's sense of victimization, but are also meant to result in an admission of wrongdoing regardless of which choice is selected. For example, the investigator might ask: "Have you assaulted many people before or was this only your first time?" "Did you waste all the money you stole on drugs or did you use it to pay your bills?" "Was this your idea or did someone else talk you into it?" A guilty suspect who does not want to be viewed as evil or malicious would likely choose the more acceptable option in such a scenario. The alternative questions presented by the investigator should speak strictly to the offender's sense of decency. They should not address the actual consequences of the offense, make threats, or offer promises of leniency (Jayne & Buckley, 2014).

It may take an investigator several hours to advance through the first seven steps of the process. While not all suspects will offer an admission when confronted with the alternative question, a general guideline is that if a suspect does not confess within the first 4 hours of interrogation, he or she may not succumb to the Reid Technique. Instead of further pursuing an interrogation that has not yielded helpful results, the investigator should terminate it and shift his or her focus to gathering evidence. However, when a suspect does accept the face-saving alternative, the interrogator should be mindful of the fact that such an admission does not have any legal standing. He or she should therefore proceed to *Step Eight*, during which the investigator works to develop the admission into an oral confession. Rather than using a confrontational or persuasive approach, the investigator resumes use of a patient question and answer format. In *Step Nine*, the suspect writes out the confession, which is an admissible piece of evidence. For this documentation to have any substantial utility at trial, the suspect must accept personal responsibility for having committed the crime in question (Jayne & Buckley, 2014).

Criticisms of The Reid Technique

Those investigators using the Reid Technique report that it guards against eliciting false confessions by making interrogators aware of how innocent suspects respond to it in contrast to their guilty counterparts. However, critics believe that due to the potentially extreme manipulation involved, even innocent people can be compelled, pressured, or coerced into confessing. Additionally, this procedure teaches investigators to assume that each suspect is blameworthy and to view nonverbal cues as indicative of such guilt. It does not account for the fact that stress-induced responses (such as twitching, blinking, and sweating) may be exacerbated by mental illness or the use of psychotropic medication. According to Redlich (2004), regardless of their guilt or innocence, subjects with mental illness are more likely to confess when questioned under manipulative conditions than are nonmentally disordered individuals. Despite the Reid Technique having initially been designed to guard against inducing false confessions, coercion of this nature can certainly drive innocent suspects to proffer false admissions of guilt.

FALSE CONFESSIONS

People tend to assume that all confessions are reliable and therefore denote a suspect's involvement in criminal activity. After all, why would someone admit to something he or she didn't do? In reality, a significant percentage of all confessions are later *recanted*, meaning that the suspect asserts that the confession or other incriminating statement was untruthful. While some confessions are retracted because guilty suspects fear consequences, others are recanted because the suspects are actually innocent.

There are a variety of reasons why people falsely confess. Some suspects do so to avoid further interrogation, while others offer incriminating statements as a means of gaining notoriety. Still others come to believe that they are guilty, when in fact they are not.

Saul Kassin (1997; Kassin & Kiechel, 1996) developed a paradigm to test the theory that certain interrogation techniques can convince people of their culpability despite their actual innocence. Each student-participant involved in the experiment was paired with a confederate. The subjects were told that they were participating in a reaction time task that would involve typing on a keyboard. Before beginning, they were instructed to

191

avoid pressing the ALT key, as hitting it would cause the program to crash and all data to be lost. At a certain point during the experiment, the computer crashed and the researcher accused the participants of having hit the ALT button (Kassin & Kiechel, 1996).

Initially, each and every subject denied having struck the key. However, in half of the cases, the confederate team member then confirmed that he or she had seen the student-participant hit the ALT key, a procedural element intended to simulate the presentation of fabricated (incriminating) evidence by police. The participants in the experimental condition were then offered the opportunity to sign a written confession; each of them agreed to do so (Fulero & Wrightsman, 2009).

Upon exiting the experiment, the subjects were approached by a confederate posing as a student-participant who asked what had happened. Two-thirds of the participants reported that they had mistakenly hit the wrong button. They offered responses that underscored their accountability, such as "I hit the wrong key and crashed the computer." The fact that they did *not* say things like, "He said I hit the forbidden key" or "They told me I hit the wrong key, but I didn't," illustrates the potential for certain interrogation tactics not only to illicit compliance, but to initiate internalization. In other words, subjects (or suspects) may internalize the statements made by interrogators and as a result, come to believe that they are guilty of something that they did not do. It is also of note that a portion of the participants in the Kassin study went on to confabulate details to explain how they mistakenly hit the ALT key (Fulero & Wrightsman, 2009).

What do these results mean in terms of the criminal justice system? Following the analysis of 205 cases of confirmed wrongful conviction, Rattner (1998; Huff, Ratner, & Sagarin, 1996) determined that 8% were the result of coerced false confessions. False confessions were even more common among high-profile and highly publicized cases involving major crimes (Fulero & Wrightsman, 2009). In the sections that follow, we will discuss three types of false confessions as identified by Kassin and Wrightsman (1985; Wrightsman & Kassin, 1993): voluntary false confessions, coerced-compliant confessions, and coerced-internalized confessions.

Voluntary False Confessions

Voluntary false confessions are not coerced, provoked, or elicited; they are offered willingly and for a plethora of reasons. In some cases, the old adage, "There's no such thing as bad press," is true in that the catalyst for the confession is the individual's desire for fame of any sort. Such a confession may be indicative of psychosis.

Another reason that people volunteer such admissions is that they experience generalized guilt for other, often unrelated, offenses. Still others are motivated to falsely confess to a lesser crime than that which they actually committed, in order to avoid more serious consequences. For example, if a suspect killed someone, but is *only* being questioned in relation to a burglary, he might confess to breaking and entering in the hope that police will not focus on him during the murder investigation. Voluntary false confessions can also be driven by the desire to protect someone else. For instance, a mother may falsely confess to a crime that she believes her son or daughter actually committed.

Throughout history, highly publicized crimes have repeatedly prompted people to come forward and falsely confess or even boast about their culpability. For example, when the Lindbergh baby was kidnapped in 1932, over 200 people confessed to the crime (Note, 1953). More recently, John Mark Karr made headlines when he confessed to having murdered 6-year-old beauty queen Jon Benet Ramsey. Karr told police that he loved Jon Benet and that he had been with her when she died. He classified her death as an accident and went so far as to warn, "The DNA might not match, but you can't trust the test" (McClish, 2006). Karr even attempted to discredit his alibi witness (his ex-wife) by stating that she was merely trying to protect him.

Karr's confession was largely viewed as the result of his infatuation with Jon Benet in combination with his pathological need for attention—a need so intense that it took priority over the potential consequences of confessing to murder. According to Gary Harris, the appointed spokes-person for the Karr family, John Mark Karr had been "obsessed with this case for a long time." Harris further described Karr as "… a dreamer. The kind of guy who wants to be famous" (Fulero & Wrightsman, 2009).

Coerced-Compliant Confessions

Coerced-compliant confessions are those in which a suspect offers a false confession despite knowing that he or she is innocent. The impetus for such statements is often the suspect's desire to escape further inter-rogation, gain a promised benefit such as a plea bargain, or avoid threats of physical harm including the death penalty. Coerced-compliant confes-sions typically occur when a suspect is pressured, intimidated, or other-wise coerced by law enforcement to submit by offering a confession.

The Central Park Five

An example of such a situation occurred during the headline-making Central Park Jogger case. On the night of April 19, 1989, 28-year-old Trisha Meili was raped and savagely beaten while jogging in New York City's Central Park. When she was found, Meili was naked, bound, gagged, and covered in blood; she was near death. Following the attack, she remained in a coma for 12 days. When Meili regained consciousness, she had no memory of the assault—or her assailant(s).

Various accounts of the incident estimated that the attack on Meili took place at approximately 9:15 pm. On that same night, there were also reports of "wilding" by gangs of teenagers in the park. *Wilding* is a term used to describe a violent rampage perpetrated by gang members against strangers in a public place. In other words, while Meili was being assaulted, dozens of teens were beating, kicking, punching, and robbing multiple victims at random during acts of deliberate and indiscriminate violence.

When police responded to Central Park—and before they were aware of the offenses committed against Meili—they arrested a group of teenagers, including Raymond Santana (14), Kevin Richardson (14), Yusef Salaam (15), Antron McCray (15), and Kory Wise (16). These boys later became known as the Central Park Five. While in custody, several of the juveniles offered statements in reference to the assault on Meili. Their assertions ranged from denying their involvement, to pointing fingers at one another, to admitting that they had been accomplices in her rape. Under questioning, each of the suspects ultimately admitted to having played an integral role in Meili's assault, such as restraining her or molesting her. However, each suspect accused one of the other five of having been the actual rapist.

In the weeks following the attack, the suspects recanted their confessions claiming that they had been coerced and misled by police. One of the boys alleged that prior to confessing, detectives had told him that they had found his fingerprints at the scene of the crime. In reality, however, police lacked physical evidence implicating him. In fact, DNA taken from the crime scene did not match any of the Central Park Five, but rather indicated an unidentified male. Despite this, the prosecution moved forward with the confessions as key evidence. At trial, each of the juveniles was convicted and sentenced to between 5 and 15 years in prison.

Then, in 2002, while serving a life sentence for other crimes, convicted murderer and serial rapist Matias Reyes confessed to having been the sole perpetrator in the attack on the Central Park jogger. He provided a detailed description of the assault and his story was corroborated by DNA evidence. The convictions of the Central Park Five were subsequently vacated—after they had collectively served more than 30 years in prison.

Coerced-Internalized Confessions

The third type of false confession is appropriately termed *coerced-internalized*. These are confessions made by innocent suspects because they have come to believe (i.e., have internalized) the notion that they are guilty. You may be wondering how anyone could be persuaded to think that they had committed a heinous crime when in fact they had not. The answer lies in the intensity of police interrogation. Undue stress of this nature can result in heightened suggestibility on the part of the suspect. Foster (1969) describes this phenomenon as a state in which "truth and falsehood become hopelessly confused in the suspect's mind" (p. 690–691). Gudjonsson (1992) opines: "After confessing for instrumental gain, the persistent questioning continues and the accused becomes increasingly confused and puzzled by the interrogator's apparent confidence in the accused's guilt" (p. 273).

The Paul Ingram Case
Consider the case of Paul Ingram. By all accounts, Ingram was a well-respected pillar of his community. He was a husband, father of five, and state deputy sheriff. He even spent a significant amount of time visiting local schools to warn children about the dangers of drug use (Wright, 1994).

Then, in the summer of 1988 all of that changed when Ingram's 22-year-old daughter Ericka alleged that her father had sexually abused her on multiple occasions when she was a child. Ericka initially disclosed the alleged assaults at a church camp where she was working as a counselor at the time. When she later spoke to police, her account grew significantly in depth, detail, and extremity.

Following Ericka's claims, Ingram's other daughter Julie provided a graphic account of her father's alleged abuse against her. Having been accused of ongoing sexual abuse, raping his own daughters, orchestrating the gang rape of one of his daughters, forcibly removing a near-term fetus from one of his daughter's wombs, and leading satanic rituals that included the slaughtering of babies, Ingram was ultimately charged with multiple felonies (Wright, 1994). He was subsequently arrested and jailed for a period of 5 months, during which he was interrogated 23 times.

Despite being a sheriff's officer, Ingram lacked experience with inter-rogations (Ofshe & Watters, 1994). When he was first questioned, he denied having committed or participated in the commission of any of the crimes reported by his daughters. A forensic psychologist working on the case then informed him that it is not uncommon for sex offenders to repress memories of their crimes due to the heinous nature of their behavior. Even Ingram's pastor encouraged him to accept responsibility, as he believed that children would not make up such stories, and therefore the allega-tions had merit. Police additionally confronted Ingram with a barrage of leading questions and coercive tactics, such as having him visualize vivid and disturbing scenes involving gang rape and cult sacrifices.

Ingram's initial response of "I didn't do it" began to be replaced by "I don't remember doing it" (Ofshe & Watters, 1994, p. 167) and "If this did happen, we need to take care of it" (Wright, 1994, pp. 6–7). Under fur-ther questioning, Ingram reported (Ofshe & Watters, 1994):

> I really believe the allegations did occur and that I did violate them and abuse them and probably for a long period of time. I've repressed it, probably very successfully from myself, and now I'm trying to bring it all out. I know from what they're saying that the incidents had to occur, that I had to have done these things ... my girls know me. They wouldn't lie about something like this. (p. 167)

Despite this statement, Ingram still maintained that he had no recol-lection of any of the offenses. Later, however, in response to the sugges-tive guidance of detectives, Ingram reported that he was able to visualize various elements of the abuse. As a result, he offered a confession wherein he confabulated details of the crimes, such as admitting to having had sex with each of his daughters on numerous occasions (dating back to when they were 5 years old) and having impregnated one of his daughters when she was 15. Ingram additionally "recalled" having witnessed numerous cult rituals, including people in robes kneeling around a fire and cutting out the heart of a live cat (Fulero & Wrightsman, 2009).

Social psychologist Richard Ofshe (1992) became a pivotal expert in the case. After interviewing Ingram, he concluded that the interrogation process—which included hypnosis—had "brainwashed" him into believ-ing that he had committed the alleged offenses. To test his theory, Ofshe suggested to Ingram that he had forced one of his sons to have sex with one of his daughters while he watched. Such an allegation had never been made against Ingram. After repeated questioning riddled with sugges-tive statements, Ingram reported that he could "remember" the incident.

Ingram then wrote a lengthy account of the incestuous activity, replete with excessive detail; this further supported Ofshe's position. Therefore, Ofshe reported that he had serious doubts as to Ingram's guilt and viewed him as a highly suggestible person with an alarming desire to please authority figures (Wright, 1994).

Despite Ofshe's suppositions and an utter lack of physical evidence, Ingram pleaded guilty to six counts of rape in the third degree. As a result, he was sentenced to 20 years in prison, with parole eligibility after serving 12 years. Ingram later came to believe in his innocence, and thus his attorneys filed an appeal to withdraw his guilty plea. His final appeal was denied by the Washington State Supreme Court in 1992 and Ingram remained incarcerated until his scheduled release in 2003 (Fulero & Wrightsman, 2009).

THE LEGAL LIMITS OF INTERROGATION

It is evident that interrogations induce intense emotional stress, which can undermine a suspect's ability to think clearly and make rational decisions. Although police are trained to conduct themselves professionally and are cautioned to employ established interrogation protocols, it remains commonplace for detectives to exert considerable pressure on the accused. This begs the questions: Where do we, as a society, draw the line? What limitations are placed on law enforcement's latitude within the confines of the interrogation room?

Police are legally authorized to use various forms of psychological manipulation. One common example is referred to as *trickery*, whereby police mislead or lie to suspects. Trickery often takes the form of a *knowledge bluff*, meaning that an interrogator tells the suspect that incriminating evidence has been found linking him or her to the crime, when in fact, it has not. For example, the suspect may be told that his or her fingerprints were found at the crime scene or that an eyewitness identified him or her. Investigators often combine a knowledge bluff with the use of *baiting questions*. Although these are not directly accusatory, they often indicate to the suspect that there is evidence, which signifies his or her guilt (Fulero & Wrightsman, 2009).

Two more prevalent methods are minimization and maximization. *Minimization* is a softer approach in which the investigator downplays the suspect's malicious intent or the severity of the offense itself. This is often accomplished when the interrogator offers sympathy, moral (not

197

legal) justification, and/or face-saving rationalizations for the crime. Conversely, *maximization* is the use of "scare tactics" intended to intimidate and unnerve the suspect so that he or she confesses (Kassin & McNall, 1991). Maximization may involve overemphasizing or exaggerating the gravity of the crime or the extent of the charges.

Minimization and maximization are often used in tandem during the course of a method widely known as *good cop–bad cop*. In this setup, two interrogators join together to speak with the suspect. The "good" cop focuses on rapport building by initially expressing understanding and sympathy for the suspect while the "bad" cop expresses his or her belief that the suspect is undoubtedly guilty and deserving of severe punishment. The bad cop may also display anger toward the suspect for lying (i.e., denying culpability). As the interrogation progresses, the good cop may change his or her demeanor to reflect disappointment in the suspect for his or her continued denial. Often, the intimidating anger exhibited by the bad cop combined with the perceived intent of the good cop to help the suspect achieve a favorable resolution results in a confession (Cialdini, 2008; Skolnick & Fyfe, 1993). For a comprehensive list of legal interrogation tactics, see Table 9.2.

The primary goal of the aforementioned interrogation formats (including the Reid Technique) is to elicit a confession. This is accomplished by convincing the suspect that offering an admission is in his or her own best interest while minimizing the suspect's perceived consequences of telling the truth. While manipulation of this sort is permissible, investigators cannot make explicit promises of leniency in exchange for a confession. In other words, law enforcement may not promise the suspect that he or she will receive a plea bargain, a shorter sentence, or escape the death penalty

Table 9.2   Legality of Interrogation Techniques

Legal	Illegal
Trickery	Threats (even implicit) of physical harm
Knowledge bluff	Physical abuse/torture
Presentation of false evidence	Deprivation of food, water, or sleep
Baiting questions	Prolonged isolation
Rapport building: Good cop–bad cop	Promises of leniency
Minimization	Failure to Mirandize
Maximization	Denial of legal counsel

upon confessing. Only the prosecutor has the power to offer plea bargains and other such legally binding agreements.

Additionally, police may not subject a suspect to physical abuse, which includes withholding food, water, and sleep. The case of 15-year-old Brenton Butler is a prime example of the perils of problematic police interrogation procedures. Butler was charged with having shot and killed a female tourist in front of her husband in Jacksonville, Florida. Upon being apprehended by police, Butler was identified as the shooter by the victim's husband during a highly suggestive identification procedure known as a show-up. Police then interrogated Butler without his parents present and without the benefit of counsel for a period of 9 hours.

During the course of the interrogation, detectives physically assaulted the minor suspect. Butler later reported that the investigators had punched him, threatened to shoot him, and threatened him with death by electric chair. Defense counsel corroborated Butler's claims by presenting photographic evidence of bruising to the boy's face. Ultimately, Butler was intimidated into signing a confession prepared by one of the detectives, which outlined a timeline of events leading up to the murder. Butler was acquitted at trial and two other suspects were later identified; one of them pleaded guilty to second degree murder, while the other was convicted at trial of first degree murder (Jeanneau, Le Goff, Poncet, & de Lestrade, 2001).

INTERROGATION VERSUS INTERVIEWING

As noted earlier in this chapter, once police have honed in on someone as a suspect, their objective becomes eliciting a confession. It therefore follows that contemporary interrogation techniques are intended to persuade guilty suspects to confess (Ofshe & Leo, 1997). This is accomplished by causing suspects to view their conviction as predetermined and then convincing them that an admission will improve their current situation or future prospects. As you can see, interrogation techniques—even those that are legally acceptable—can be innately suggestive and coercive. But what happens in the case of a particularly vulnerable suspect?

According to Levin (2012), individuals afflicted with mental illness, including psychosis, anxiety, depression, and substance addiction or withdrawal, are particularly susceptible to police influence. Persons with cognitive deficits and memory problems are also considered vulnerable. Levin notes that a survey conducted by Peter Dell, MD and summarized at the October 2012 meeting of the American Academy of Psychiatry and the

Law, found that police categorize questioning in one of two ways: "interviews" during which the subject is presumed innocent and "interrogations," which imply that the police believe the person to be guilty. With regard to interrogation techniques and police attitudes toward individuals with mental illness, Dell reported: "With one exception, there were no significant differences between the interrogation techniques they used with persons with mental illness and those without mental illness." Dell found that when dealing with mentally ill suspects, police less frequently presented (or claimed to be in possession of) false evidence.

American Academy of Psychiatry and the Law panelist Veronica Hinton, PhD noted that in Canada, unlike in the United States, officers use structured interviewing in their investigations. This process is focused on fact finding and eliciting important information about the crime, rather than confronting a suspect or manipulating an individual into offering a (false) confession. This method is based upon the ideals of fairness, forthrightness, and accountability.

Clearly, there is a need for the focus of interrogations to shift from obtaining a confession to eliciting useful information—especially when a vulnerable subject is involved (Levin, 2012).

Interview Techniques

Unlike confession-focused interrogations, interviews are nonaccusatory question-and-answer exchanges with suspects, witnesses, or victims. They can be viewed as goal-oriented conversations, the purpose of which is to gather information. In addition to implementing a non-confrontational approach, investigators remain objective and professional. Interviews should additionally be devoid of threats, intimidation, and coercion. The following are basic guidelines for conducting a successful interview (Sattler, 1998):

- *Review all relevant background information beforehand*: In order for an interview to be an effective fact-gathering tool, it must be thorough. By availing themselves of all information germane to a given case, investigators can prepare questions targeting the specific information that they seek (AICPA, n.d.). When interviewers are ill-prepared, they may fail to ask critical questions.
- *Use an appropriate combination of open and closed-ended questions*: Open-ended questions ask for broad or general information and are typically preferable, as they allow the interviewee to freely

share his or her thoughts. According to Sattler (1998), open-ended questions give the interviewer insight into the interviewee's priorities and frame of reference while allowing the subject to talk through ideas. This in turn reveals facts about the interviewee and his or her emotions. Open-ended responses also highlight the interviewee's level of articulation and depth of knowledge on the topic being discussed. At the other end of the spectrum are closed-ended questions, which target specific information and are often designed to be answered "yes" or "no." They are ideal when only brief explanations or answers are necessary. Interviewers should be aware that closed-ended questions more readily allow the interviewee to provide false information. That is, an interviewee may answer "yes" to a bipolar question in order to deceive the interviewer or even to please the interviewer by providing the "right" answer.

- *Listen*: Do not cut off the interviewee. Because open-ended questions are conversational in nature, a subject's answers may become tangential and therefore be more difficult for the interviewer to control. However, the interviewer should strive to make the interview person-oriented by remaining receptive to all information offered (Sattler, 1998).
- *Check your understanding*: Interviewers should utilize reflective listening techniques in order to ensure that they have correctly understood the subject's statements. One way for investigators to accomplish this is by paraphrasing their understanding of what the subject has told them. For example, "What I'm hearing you say is that you recognized the assailant as your friend Joe. Is that correct?"
- *Fully and accurately document the interview*: Video and audio recording is crucial as it maintains the purity of the interview by recording not only the subject's answers, but also the associated questions. This way, should confusion or disagreements arise, there is an accurate record of events.
- *Be mindful of body language*: Facial expressions and body postures are critical nonverbal elements that affect the climate of the interview. For instance, an inviting smile is likely to be perceived positively and make the interviewee feel more comfortable. Similarly, maintaining eye contact is often interpreted as a sign of attentiveness. It should be noted, however, that eye contact is considered disrespectful in certain cultures, so interviewers

should be mindful. Positive postures include those oriented toward encouraging interpersonal interaction, such as leaning in or squarely facing the subject (Sattler, 1998).

In addition to ways that the interviewer can set the tone, other elements such as the interviewee's cognitive capacity, attitudes, feelings, or mood can also significantly impact the tenor of the interview. Sociocultural factors such as the interviewee's socioeconomic status, customs, and perception of social taboos, can strongly influence the dynamics of the interview, as can the length of the interview itself and the level of psychological stress experienced by the subject. Even the physical atmosphere, such as the room temperature and the amount and type of distractions, can have a substantial impact (Sattler, 1998).

EYEWITNESSES IDENTIFICATION

A discussion about obtaining credible information during the course of an investigation would not be complete without addressing eyewitness identification. Eyewitness testimony is extremely powerful when presented in a court of law. Imagine that you have been selected to serve as a juror in a murder trial. You are uncertain as to whether the defendant committed the crime when a witness takes the stand, points to the defendant, and says with utter certainty that she saw him shoot the victim at point blank range. Consider the evidentiary value of this statement. How might it impact your decision during the deliberation process?

The presumption of innocence diminishes in the face of an eyewitness account such that errors in eyewitness identification are the most frequent cause of wrongful conviction (Wells, 1993). The U.S. Department of Justice examined the first 28 cases of exoneration based on post-conviction DNA evidence (Connors, Lundregan, Miller, & McEwan, 1996). Their findings were disturbing: 24 out of 28 were the result of mistaken eyewitness identification. In some cases, multiple eyewitnesses had incorrectly identified an innocent person as the perpetrator. A subsequent study, which analyzed 40 cases of wrongful conviction, determined that 36 (or 90%) involved an incorrect identification by an eyewitness (Wells et al., 1998). Similar research conducted by Scheck, Neufeld, and Dwyer (2000, as cited in Fulero & Wrightsman, 2009) found that eyewitness error was involved in 84% of the over 100 wrongful convictions analyzed. As you can see, it is crucial for investigators to minimize the possibility of an incorrect identification—and that is where forensic psychology steps in to assist police.

Memory and Eyewitness Testimony

An eyewitness description or identification of a suspect involves numerous psychological components. The witness's memory, level of suggestibility, self-confidence, desire to conform, desire to please authorities, and reasoning ability all play key roles (Fulero & Wrightsman, 2009). As you probably already know, memory is not like a video that can be rewound and played back to display an exact depiction of a particular event (Loftus, 1979). In fact, each time that a memory is retrieved, it may be different; certain parts may be embellished, while others may be minimized. Still other details may be confabulated to fill gaps where the specifics can't be recalled. Such memory fallibilities are common and occur in everyday life. For example, you may remember that you ate a chicken sandwich for lunch yesterday, when in reality you had turkey. That seems like a rather insignificant mistake. However, remembering whether a criminal was right-handed or left-handed could be critical to a police investigation (Pozzulo, Bennell, & Forth, 2013).

Eyewitness memory can be divided into two categories: recall and recognition memory. *Recall memory* refers to the retrieval of information from the past. When applied to eyewitness memory, it is the recounting of details of a previously witnessed person or event. For example, describing what the culprit was wearing at the time of the crime is a recall task (Pozzulo et al., 2013). In contrast, *recognition memory* is the ability to recognize previously encountered people or objects. Therefore, when an eyewitness determines whether the person he or she is viewing in the police lineup is the same person that committed the crime in question, recognition memory is being utilized.

According to Wells (1995), there is also a significant differentiation between "memory testimony" and "memory." *Memory testimony* is similar to recall memory in that it is a witness's statement regarding what he or she recalls about a previous incident. It is beneficial for such statements to be the product of the witness's memory—and the witness's memory alone. However, these recollections can be tainted by external influences—including some police identification procedures.

203

System and Estimator Variables

Logic dictates that there are variables over which law enforcement has no control, and that can influence a witness's ability to make an accurate identification. These are known as *estimator variables* (Wells & Luftus, 2002). Examples include environmental dynamics such as the time of day that the crime occurred, the distance that the witness was from the incident or the perpetrator, and the length of time that the witness was in the presence of the offender. Additionally, factors such as the witness's eyesight, mental state, or emotional reaction to the crime (i.e., stress, trauma) can impact identification precision.

On the other hand, *system variables* are procedural elements that police can regulate in order to avoid preventable errors in eyewitness identification. These include the way in which witnesses are questioned, the construction of the lineup or photo array, and the presence or absence of recording practices. Both system and estimator variables can impact the depth of detail reported by witnesses, the type of information reported (e.g., details about the offender versus the environment), and the accuracy of said information (Pozzulo et al., 2013). The distinction between system and estimator variables is an important one because although police cannot guard against poor lighting conditions or a witness's brief exposure to a crime, investigators can strive to improve practices that are known to lead to further inaccuracies (Fulero & Wrightsman, 2009).

Interviewing Eyewitnesses

One problematic police practice is the use of improper interviewing techniques. According to Fisher, Geiselman, and Raymond (1987), police officers unwittingly stifle their ability to obtain complete and accurate information when they interrupt eyewitnesses who are in the midst of offering an open-ended recall report. Such an interruption can actually limit the amount of detail retained in the witness's conscious memory. Additionally, when officers ask closed-ended, short, or specific questions, they are more likely to receive short answers, possibly devoid of important detail, in response. Another issue is that police may fail to pose relevant questions. The line of questioning should be consistent with the information being provided by the witness at the time. Therefore, it follows that if the witness is describing the assailant's physical stature, detectives should refrain from asking about the perpetrator's voice at the same time (Fisher & Price-Roush, as cited in Fisher et al., 1987).

Police should also avoid asking leading questions. Research has demonstrated that the phrasing of a question can alter a witness's recall report. In a study conducted by Loftus and Palmer (1974), participants were shown a video of a car accident. After viewing the video, the subjects were asked, "About how fast were the cars going when they hit each other?" The word "hit" was subsequently replaced with one of the following words: smashed, collided, bumped, or contacted. Changing this critical word impacted respondents' reports about the speed of the cars involved in the accident. Perhaps unsurprisingly, the word "smashed" was correlated with the highest speeds reported by participants, whereas the words "bumped" and "contacted" were associated with slower speeds. One week after viewing the video, the participants were questioned again. This time, they were asked whether they had seen any broken glass on the video. Those subjects who had been asked about the rate of speed when the cars "smashed" into one another were the most likely to report having seen broken glass—even though there was none in the video.

Similarly, the introduction of inaccurate information during questioning can alter a witness's recollection of an event. When presented with erroneous details, a witness may incorporate that information into his or her recollection and incorrectly report the inaccurate details later (Loftus, Altman, & Geballe, 1975). For example, if a witness saw three people fleeing from the scene of a bank robbery, but the investigator questions him or her about the *four* suspects involved, the witness may later report that there were four suspects when in reality he or she only saw three. In addition to guarding against proffering misinformation, officers should avoid asking the same question several times. Repeating a question gives the impression that the officer is seeking a specific answer from the witness (Fisher, 1995).

Detectives should also pay attention to environmental considerations. Witnesses should not be interviewed amidst chaotic conditions such as when they are traumatized, injured, or distracted. Witnesses should also not be questioned in the presence of other witnesses, as this can unduly influence accuracy. When witnesses are afforded the opportunity to confer with one another, each witness's narrative has the potential to become contaminated. Research indicates that the majority (71%) of those witnesses privy to a co-witness's report, end up agreeing on an incorrect version of events or otherwise incorporating (false) elements from their co-witness's statement into their own report (Gabbert, Memon, & Allan, 2003). For a list of tactics used to improve the accuracy of information elicited from eyewitnesses, see Table 9.3.

Table 9.3   Improving the Accuracy of Eyewitness Accounts

Technique	Description
Slow down the rate of questioning	Allow witnesses the time to consider each question without interrupting them. They may need a moment to recall past events.
Conduct a cognitive interview	Re-create the sensory environment experienced by the witness at the time of the crime. In other words, ask questions about what he or she saw, smelled, heard, tasted, or touched. This technique allows many witnesses to recall details that they were unable to remember separately.
Do not "interrogate" witnesses	Be mindful not to use a coercive, threatening approach that might otherwise be used with suspects.
Ask witness-centered questions	Avoid a standardized checklist of questions and be sensitive to the witness's unique perspective.
Do not draw premature conclusions	Be mindful of biases and preconceptions; do not disclose these to the witness as it might affect his or her statement.

Source: Fisher, R. P., *Psychology, Public Policy, and Law, 1*, 732–764, 1995.

Identification Procedures: Lineups, Show-ups, and Photo Arrays

In addition to avoiding inadequate questioning protocols, officers should abandon suggestive visual identification techniques. Witnesses are sometimes shown a group of possible suspects and asked to identify the perpetrator. This procedure is known as a *lineup*. Police often include the suspect and other individuals who are known to be innocent, called *foils*. Lindsay, Martin, and Webber (1994) note that in order for a lineup to be considered fair, the suspect should not stand out from the foils. While the foils need not resemble one another, each person in the lineup should match the witness's initial description of the suspect. For example, if the witness described the offender as an African-American male, with close-cropped hair and a moustache, the foils should meet these criteria. If the only man with a moustache in the entire lineup is the suspect, that becomes highly suggestive.

On TV and in movies, you will often see a lineup conducted in such a way that the witness simultaneously views multiple individuals. However, this process can cause the witness to compare the subjects to one another rather than to his or her recollection of the offender. Therefore, a *sequential lineup* is preferred. In a sequential lineup, the witness views one individual at a time. He or she determines whether that person is the culprit based upon his or her memory of the offender at the crime scene.

Officers should also be cognizant of their language when speaking with a witness during a lineup. Police should never imply that the offender is definitely in the lineup with statements such as "Which one is the man that attacked you?" Instead, they should ask, "Do you see the person that attacked you?" Officers should also avoid encouraging a loose threshold for recognition with phrases such as "Does anyone look familiar?" Looking or seeming familiar is not the same thing as being identified as the perpetrator. Furthermore, witnesses should never be pressured to identify someone in the lineup—the fact is that the culprit may not be present! Lastly, police should never say "right" or "good job" after the witness has made his or her selection. This implies that the witness chose the correct person—the suspect whom police believe to be guilty (Ellison & Buckhout, 1981).

An alternative to conducting a formal lineup is to arrange a *photo array*. Assembling a photo spread, which includes the suspect as well as foils who are similar in appearance to the witness's report, is typically easier than holding a live lineup. One reason is that when involved in a lineup, a suspect is afforded the right to counsel, which can delay the process. That same privilege is not extended to individuals whose likenesses appear in a photo array. Photo arrays should follow the same guidelines as lineups, including the use of sequential presentation of the images (Fulero & Wrightsman, 2009).

A third procedure, known as a *show-up*, is sometimes used for identification purposes. In this practice, police show a singular suspect to the witness and ask whether he or she is the criminal. Such a prejudicial procedure led to the misidentification of Father Bernard T. Pagano, a Catholic priest, as an armed robber (Fulero & Wrightsman, 2009).

Following several similar armed robberies in and around Wilmington, Delaware, the state police employed the assistance of eyewitnesses in order to develop a composite sketch of the perpetrator. Circulation of the drawing prompted an influx of anonymous tips pointing to Father Pagano, who was affiliated with a nearby parish (Ellison & Buckhout, 1981). In order to confirm whether Pagano was in fact the perpetrator, police put him under surveillance. They then brought two eyewitnesses to his health club, so that they could get a good look at him. Investigators subsequently conducted two photo arrays. In the first, they used a 10-year-old photo of Pagano. The pictures of the foils differed from him in several important respects, including age, hairstyle, and clothing. In the second procedure, police placed a recent photo of Pagano (age 53) alongside pictures of multiple foils for comparison; none of the foils were more than 32 years old. Additionally, Pagano's clothing was different, and his profile picture faced to the left, while all of the foils faced to the right in their photos. When Father Pagano was brought to trial, a guilty verdict seemed likely until the actual robber, Ronald Clouser, came forward and confessed. Clouser bore a striking resemblance to Father Pagano (Fulero & Wrightsman, 2009).

In summary, the techniques used by police have a considerable impact on the veracity of the information collected during the course of an investigation, which in turn plays a major role in whether justice is served.

10

Working with Victims

INTRODUCTION

Imagine that you have been tasked with responding to a sexual assault call. Upon your arrival, the 22-year-old female victim reports having awoken to find an unknown male climbing through her bedroom window. Following a brief physical altercation, the perpetrator pinned her to the floor, held a knife to her throat, and forcibly raped her. The victim has several fresh cuts and bruises consistent with a violent sexual assault; she is crying and appears visibly traumatized.

What feelings does this scene evoke? As the responding officer, you would likely have empathic concern for the victim accompanied by a desire to apprehend the perpetrator. Perhaps you would be disgusted by the offender's actions or feel uncomfortable with having to interview a victim of sexual assault. All of these are common responses frequently experienced by law enforcement.

Conversely, it is unlikely that you would feel sympathy for or identify with the assailant in this instance, as the opening vignette depicts a highly vulnerable (i.e., sleeping) victim who appears credible and a frighteningly violent offender whose behavior was unprovoked. However, in scenarios where the labels "victim" and "perpetrator" are ambiguous to any degree, the situation can become difficult to navigate.

For example, in May of 2015, a federal lawsuit was filed in response to allegations that seven correctional officers at Rikers Island had sexually assaulted female inmates over the course of a 2-year period. According to reports, two of the prisoners were being held in pretrial custody when they were allegedly "repeatedly raped and sexually abused" by an officer who threatened retribution if they reported him. One of the victims reported that she had been molested by one correctional officer (CO) while other officers watched, and another victim claimed to have been impregnated by a guard (Dienst, 2015).

How does your initial response to the victims in this vignette differ from your reaction toward the victim in the opening passage? Does the fact that these women are inmates affect your perspective? Or how you would respond to the case? Do you find yourself questioning the reliability of the female prisoners? Do you wonder whether they fabricated the allegations in order to fulfill a self-serving agenda, such as gaining revenge against strict officers?

Law enforcement officials are sworn to "protect and serve." Therefore, there is an expectation that they will solve crimes, apprehend dangerous suspects, and work to prevent violence in the community. However, this critical phrase also refers to society's need for police to relate to and support victims as they occur in various contexts. In this chapter, we will focus on the response of criminal justice professionals to adult crime victims. You will learn about common responses to traumatic victimization, techniques for overcoming victim resistance, and the impact of officers' preconceptions on their assessment of and assistance to victims. In Chapter 11, empirically supported methods for working with child victims will be addressed.

POLICE PERCEPTIONS: DOMESTIC AND SEXUAL VIOLENCE

Research reveals that officers' personal biases and perspectives about domestic violence are critical to the outcome of such cases (Logan, Shannon, & Walker, 2006). While law enforcement has the ability to protect victims and diffuse DV incidents, negative police attitudes can impact not only the way that a case is handled, but also the victim's immediate and future help-seeking behaviors (Logan et al., 2006). Studies suggest that officers' complex feelings regarding DV influence the demeanor with which they approach victims as well as offenders. While some officers view domestic abuse as a criminal infraction, others minimize it by classifying it as an interpersonal or family issue that should be dealt with privately.

As discussed in Chapter 7, learned helplessness is a victim's feeling of powerlessness following a traumatic or abusive situation over which he or she had no control. When police fail to be sensitive to a victim's situation, it increases the likelihood that he or she will experience learned helplessness. A victim of DV who is seeking assistance from law enforcement is actively making strides toward regaining control. However, if police do not take the victim's complaint seriously or if they fail to believe the victim, it reinforces the idea that he or she has no means with which to change the current situation or to protect him or herself; the victim is left feeling helpless and often hopeless.

One of the central elements common among cases of DV is that the victim often remains in or returns to the abusive relationship. You will recall from Chapter 7 that the general public frequently assumes that a victim's best course of action is to extricate him or herself from the toxic relationship. Numerous victims consciously choose to stay in the relationship because they fear that the batterer will carry out threats of extreme violence if they leave, while others love the perpetrator and desperately hope that the abuse will stop. Additionally, it is not uncommon for victims to feel as though their allegations will not be believed, especially if the abuser is well respected within the community (Los Angeles Police Department, 2016).

It is sometimes difficult for people, including police officers, to fully grasp the impact of these complex dynamics. Therefore, officers must be mindful of their own perceptions and avoid making victim-blaming assumptions such as "If it were really that bad, she would just leave," or "She brought this on herself." Attitudes such as these can cause victims to experience toxic shame, while undermining their sense of safety, self-assuredness, and hope.

Sexual assault cases are similar in that victims are often explicitly or implicitly blamed not only by the offender, but by society. This serves to transform an already horrifying attack into a source of deep shame. When police hold negative attitudes toward victims of sexual violence, it is destructive; it strongly impacts the resolution of the case, as well as the victim's ability to begin the healing process (Lonsway & Archambault, 2016). As you read the following vignette, consider how societal bias toward sexual violence can result in unjust outcomes. How do you think law enforcement can begin to effect change? (See Table 10.1.)

In 2004, Sara Reedy informed police that the convenience store just outside of Pittsburgh, Pennsylvania, where she worked had been robbed at gunpoint. According to statements ascribed to Reedy, the perpetrator then proceeded to sexually assault her, threatening to shoot her if she did not comply with his demands. When police responded, one of the

Table 10.1 Societal Bias Toward Domestic and Sexual Assault Survivors

Domestic Violence Victims	Sexual Assault Victims
"If it were really that bad, she would just leave."	"She was dressed provocatively."
"He's such a nice guy—he can't be an abuser."	"She knew what she was getting herself into."
"Why doesn't she just leave? What's wrong with her?"	"She was drunk."
"She must be weak."	"She's promiscuous."
"If she doesn't leave him, she's asking for it."	"If it was really rape, she would have fought back."
"She initiated the assault."	"She didn't say anything about it right away—she's probably just looking for attention."

first questions asked of Reedy was whether she used illegal drugs. She was further questioned about where the money from the robbery was. The responding officer arrested Reedy and charged her with three misdemeanors: theft, receipt of stolen property, and filing a false report; she spent 5 days in jail (Lonsway & Archambault, 2016).

Reedy indicated that not only did the nurses in the emergency room not believe her, but she was also unable to utilize services afforded to victims of crime because her report had been classified as a false allegation. Police personnel did not investigate Reedy's sexual assault claim and additionally failed to link it with a similar attack committed shortly thereafter. More than a year following Reedy's ordeal, the man responsible for having assaulted her was arrested. He confessed to a total of 12 sexual assaults, 10 of which he had committed *after* he attacked Reedy. Therefore, 10 sexual assaults might have been prevented had the professionals involved in responding to Reedy's case reacted appropriately—by believing the victim (Lonsway & Archambault, 2016). In December of 2012, Reedy was awarded a $1.5 million settlement as a result of law enforcement's mishandling of her case (Walters, 2012).

In a set of similar circumstances, the judicial system responded inappropriately to another sexual assault survivor by blaming her. According to various news outlets, a judge in Southern California stated that a rape victim in one of his cases "didn't put up a fight" and that a woman's body would not permit unwanted (i.e., forced or coerced) sexual intercourse. The judge was quoted as saying (Associated Press, 2012a):

> I'm not a gynecologist, but I can tell you something: if someone doesn't want to have sexual intercourse, the body shuts down. The body will not permit that to happen unless a lot of damage is inflicted, and we heard nothing about that in this case.

Equally as disturbing, the judge was a former sex crimes prosecutor. Thankfully, the California Commission on Judicial Performance sought to mitigate the damage inflicted on this victim, as well as society, by publicly admonishing the judge for breaching judicial ethics. The events of the crime were described as follows: "a man who threatened to mutilate the face and genitals of his ex-girlfriend with a heated screwdriver, beat her with a metal baton and made other violent threats before committing rape, forced oral copulation, and other crimes" (Associated Press, 2012b).

Sadly, the victim-blaming attitudes exhibited by police, healthcare workers, and the judge in the two previous cases, are not unique to these individuals. Rather, they are reflective of larger distortions that permeate society, causing damage to victims (Lonsway & Archambault, 2016) and allowing offenders to not be held fully accountable for their actions. It is the responsibility of law enforcement officials to be supportive of crime victims, and thereby be instrumental in each victim's healing process. If you had responded to either of the aforementioned cases, what would you have done differently?

MARGINALIZED VICTIMS

It is a logical assumption that police should respond to all crime victims in a compassionate and professional manner. However, stereotypical views about who qualifies as a *legitimate* victim can significantly impact officers' responses. There is an erroneous perception in society that there are two types of victims: innocent individuals who were harmed through no fault of their own, and people whose behavior precipitated the violence perpetrated against them. Recall the introductory story about the female inmates who were sexually abused while incarcerated on Rikers Island. Does someone's prior criminal activity make him or her any less of a victim? As you read through the next few sections, consider how law enforcement might be inclined to respond to victims in each scenario.

Justice-Involved Victims

There is a substantial overlap between victims and offenders in the criminal justice system. Offenders are more likely to be victimized than their nonoffending counterparts, and similarly victims are more likely to commit offenses than are nonvictims (Entorf, 2013). Criminological perspectives seek to explain this relationship as a result of sociodemographic similarities among victims and offenders (Gottfredson, 1984), a subculture of violence (Singer, 1981), and the presence of poor self-control (Gottfredson & Hirschi, 1990) and anger among these individuals (Kubrin & Weitzer, 2003; Jacobs & Wright, 2010).

Early research suggests that lifestyle risks relevant to both victims and offenders result in negative reciprocity between the two groups. In other words, when victims and offenders reside in the same neighborhood and assume similar habits, both groups are more likely to participate in the same routine situations and engage in the same risky behaviors, thus making them more prone to *either* victimize or be victimized. This idea is particularly relevant to minors lacking adult supervision (Osgood, Wilson, O'Malley, Bachman, & Johnston, 1996).

Moreover, there is a correlation between the victim-offender continuum and poor self-control. Many crimes are the culmination of thrill-seeking behavior combined with a failure to consider the consequences of said actions. Offenders often behave impulsively, exhibiting little control over their desires/fantasies and presenting with poor self-regulation. Therefore, individuals who participate in situations over which they have minimal control or who fail to exert self-control as appropriate are more likely to become either victims or offenders (Gottfredson & Hirschi, 1990).

Of course, the correspondence between victimization and offending does not mean that all victims are in some way responsible for crimes committed against them or that they should have foreseen the potential risk. Regardless of the biological, psychological, or sociological rationale, the link between criminality and victimization simply means that police will undoubtedly encounter offenders, such as inmates, prostitutes, gang members, and drug dealers, who have themselves been victimized.

Prison Rape Elimination Act

The victimization of offenders—especially incarcerated individuals—is such a widespread phenomenon, that Congress passed the Prison Rape Elimination Act (PREA) in 2003. The statute is meant to "provide for the analysis of the incidence and effects of prison rape in Federal, State, and local institutions and to provide information, resources, recommendations and funding to protect individuals from prison rape" (PREA, 2003).

Substance Users

Controlled dangerous substance (CDS) charges comprise a significantly large portion of arrests. Therefore, it is reasonable for law enforcement to regard individuals found to be in possession of or under the influence of illicit drugs as criminals. However, this label does not consider the relationship between prior victimization and self-medication or subsequent addiction. Research supports the conclusion that girls who have been subjected to physical or sexual abuse are twice as likely to smoke, drink, and/or use drugs as are girls who have not been abused. Similarly, women who have experienced sexual abuse during childhood are more than 3 times as likely to be alcohol dependent and 2.5 times as likely to be afflicted with drug dependency as are women who were not abused (National Center on Addiction and Substance Abuse at Columbia University, 2003).

Research also reveals that the association between physical/sexual abuse and addiction is not gender specific. According to the 1995 National Survey of Adolescents (NSA), 34% of boys aged 12 to 17 who survived sexually based assaults became dependent on or otherwise abused substances at some point in their lives. Comparatively, 9% of nonvictimized boys went on to abuse alcohol or drugs. The lifetime rate of substance dependence was approximately 5 times higher (27.5%) for girls who had been sexually abused than for those who had not (5%). The NSA's findings also highlight the trauma of witnessing violence, as 17% of boys and nearly 18% of girls subjected to this experience reported lifetime dependence on drugs or alcohol as compared with 4% and 3%, respectively (National Institute of Justice, 2003). These statistics clearly indicate that people often use drugs or alcohol as a means with which to "escape" past trauma.

Now that you have an understanding of the causal link between victimization and drug or alcohol use, let's take a closer look at the cyclical pattern of substance abuse and offending. According to a recent study, 40% of minors (aged 12–17) who reported using marijuana at least 300 days per year, also engaged in serious fighting at work or school (Substance Abuse Mental Health Services Administration, 2004). In 2002, the victims of 1 million violent offenses perceived the offender to be under the influence at the time of the crime (Bureau of Justice Statistics, n.d.). Similarly, in approximately two out of every five sexual assaults and one out of every four robberies committed against college students, the perpetrator was perceived by the victim to be under the influence of drugs or alcohol (Bureau of Justice Statistics, 2003).

Repeat Victims

It is not uncommon for the same individual to be victimized multiple times. In fact, one of the most robust predictors of future victimization is past victimization (Kilpatrick & Acierno, 2003). The increased risk, which follows the initial transgression, is inherent to a variety of offenses including racially based violence, domestic assault, and white collar crime (Johnson & Bowers, 2004). Therefore, it follows that 4% of victims suffer approximately 44% of all assaults (Farrell & Pease, 1993). Additionally, the risk for experiencing a new assault over the course of a 2-year period is 2 times higher for women with a history of one prior assault, 4 times higher for women with two previous assaults, and 10 times higher for women with three or more prior victimizations than it is for women who have never experienced physical, domestic, or sexual violence (Kilpatrick & Saunders, 1997).

Victims of domestic violence are more likely to experience future occurrences of abuse than are victims of any other type of offense (Starmer, 2011). On average, women are subjected to 35 domestic assaults before making the decision to report the batterer to law enforcement (Yearnshaw, 1997, as cited in Starmer, 2011). According to a survey conducted by Lloyd, Farrell, and Pease (1994), 43% of domestic assaults that occurred over a 25-month period involved only approximately 7% of the 1450 households studied.

This means that it is not unusual for police to be called to the same house multiple times to de-escalate a domestic incident. The same holds true for repeat victims of sexual violence. Research reveals that women who experienced sexual abuse as children are 2 to 3 times more likely to be sexually victimized later in life (Arata, 2002), and in general, victims of childhood sexual abuse are 3 to 5 times more likely to experience adult victimization than childhood victims of any other type of crime (Maker, Kemmelmeier, & Peterson, 2001). Thus, it is imperative for police to avoid stereotypical thoughts such as "She asked for it by staying with him," "She's lying," or "She plays the victim to get attention."

Trafficking Victims

Human trafficking involves forcing people to perform work or engage in commercial sex against their will. Trafficking victims can be subdivided into three categories: children under the age of 18 who have been brought into the commercial sex trade, adults engendered into commercial sex by means of force, fraud, or coercion, and children and adults induced to provide labor by means of force, fraud, or coercion (National Human Trafficking Resource Center, 2007).

Although human trafficking traverses all demographics, some circumstances and vulnerabilities can make specific individuals more susceptible to this type of victimization. For example, youth who have run away from home or are homeless are particularly at risk; in fact, research has found that more than half (56%) of prostituted women were previously runaways. Traffickers also often recognize and exploit prior abuses suffered by survivors of DV, sexual assault, war/military conflict, or social discrimination, and actively target people with a history of such trauma. In some cases, these victims have come to normalize the experience of violence, while in others, the victims experience toxic shame and feelings of diminished self-worth associated with their prior victimization, thus making it more likely that they will fall victim to trafficking (National Human Trafficking Resource Center, 2007).

Right now, you may be saying to yourself that trafficking victims, marginalized as they may be by society, are clearly victims who should evoke the sympathy and care of police personnel. However, their situation is often compounded by the fact that many victims of human trafficking do not readily seek help, nor do they self-identify as victims when approached by police (National Human Trafficking Resource Center, 2007). For some, this lack of disclosure is the result of self-blame, while for others it is self-preservation; it is not unusual for victims to have previously been arrested for crimes such as prostitution associated with trafficking and to therefore maintain a distrust of law enforcement. Additionally, many victims have been explicitly instructed by their traffickers on how to behave if confronted by police.

Still other victims engage in sexually intimate relationships with their traffickers, which can result in significant psychological trauma and cause them to exhibit symptoms of Stockholm syndrome, or capture-bonding. When experiencing Stockholm syndrome, victims (hostages) present with positive feelings toward and attachment to their captors, which can take the form of vehemently defending these perpetrator(s) or otherwise trying to protect them from police (McGough, 2016). Similarly, some victims, despite their traumatization, may come to believe that they deserve what is happening to them and therefore have difficulty finding a way out (Farrell, McDevitt, & Fahy, 2008). This creates a unique challenge for law enforcement because in most nontrafficking investigations, there is a cooperating victim who is invested in the resolution of the case and the apprehension of the offender.

According to the National Institute of Justice, recognizing trafficking victims as such is one of the most difficult tasks faced by law enforcement. Properly differentiating between individuals willingly engaging in illegal prostitution and those being forced into the commercial sex industry is made more complex by the fact that human trafficking is inherently covert. While traffickers are careful to conceal their victims from police, consumers of trafficked services, such as "johns," are also engaging in unlawful behavior, and are therefore motivated to be equally discreet (Farrell et al., 2012). Such surreptitiousness necessitates a proactive approach from law enforcement. Unfortunately, however, experts have found that when these victims do come to the attention of police, it is either during the course of another, sometimes unrelated investigation, or via means of a tip (Farrell et al., 2008). Both modes of identification are insufficient as they are merely reactive in nature.

Often, detectives in units such as vice and others likely to encounter trafficking receive special training with regard to victim identification. However, patrol officers and other first responders rarely receive similar instruction. Even in cases where patrol officers do accurately identify a victim, it is rare for the jurisdiction to have formal channels in order to ensure that the case is handled by specialized personnel (McGough, 2016).

Psychologically Disordered Victims

As a result of the deinstitutionalization of people with mental illness, most individuals with severe psychopathology now reside in the community, which puts them at significant risk for becoming crime victims. According to Cotton (2004), mentally disordered persons are more likely to come into contact with law enforcement (as both perpetrators and victims of crime) than are other individuals. Additionally, they are more apt to seek help from police and are considered more susceptible to victimization than individuals not afflicted with mental illness.

Studies suggest that persons with psychiatric disorders who are not taking psychotropic medication(s), are 2.7 times more likely than the general population to fall victim to violence (e.g., physical assault, rape, mugging) (Hiday, Swartz, Swanson, Borum, & Wagner, 1999). In a study conducted by Friedman and Harrison (1984), during which the researchers interviewed 20 women who had previously been hospitalized for schizophrenia but were no longer symptomatic, 10 of the women reported having been raped once, while five reported having been sexually assaulted on more than one occasion during adulthood. In a similar study, researchers questioned 64 women with schizophrenia and 26 women with bipolar disorder with regard to their abuse histories. They found that 22% of those diagnosed with schizophrenia and 15% of those with bipolar disorder had been sexually assaulted during their adult lives, while only 8% of the general population report similar abuse (Darves-Bornoz, Lemperiere, Degiovanni, & Galliard 1995). Findings support the belief that schizophrenia is a risk factor for violent victimization (Gearon et al., 2003).

The amplified probability of victimization also holds true for mentally disordered adult males. According to a study conducted by Padgett and Struening (1992), psychosis puts homeless men at a significantly higher risk of being robbed, beaten, threatened with a weapon, or otherwise injured, as compared with nonpsychotic homeless men. Additionally, a study of individuals who had experienced psychiatric hospitalization found that 35% of those who were residing with their family had suffered severe victimization at the hands of a family member. "Severe" abuse was defined as "hitting, punching, choking, beating up, and threatening with or using a knife or gun." The majority of patients also reported having behaved aggressively toward family members (Cascardi, Mueser, DeGiralomo, & Murrin, 1996). Silver, Arseneault, Langley, Caspi, and Moffitt (2005) sought to explain the propensity for individuals with mental illness to be victimized: "To the extent that a mental disorder undermines a person's capacity to engage in alert self-protection, or leads a person to appear as if he or she would be ineffective at self-defense, people with mental disorders may be attractive targets to those motivated to engage in violent assault."

In addition to being prone to victimization, mentally ill persons may also contend with law enforcement's sometimes negative perceptions of psychiatric illness. Recall our discussion in Chapter 3 about commonly held myths surrounding psychological disorders. For example, it is widely (and incorrectly) believed that individuals with mental illness *often* engage in violence or unpredictable behavior, thus promoting the notion that "mentally ill" is synonymous with "violent." Additionally, persons suffering from psychological disorders are so frequently funneled through the justice system due to a lack of inpatient treatment facilities and funding, that police become used to arresting these individuals, typically following a display of belligerence or disrespect toward officers.

Endorsing the aforementioned myths or other antiquated ideas such as that mental illness is the result of character flaws or weakness (U.S. Department of Health and Human Services, n.d.a.) can impact how police respond to mentally disordered persons reporting victimization. Consider how you might feel if tasked with taking a statement from a victim with active symptoms of psychological disturbance or a history of psychiatric hospitalization. How would you approach him or her? How might your interaction with him or her differ from an interaction with a nonmentally disordered victim?

You may notice that the individual's narrative is tangential or otherwise difficult to follow, or that he or she is a poor historian. You may experience frustration if the victim's delusions or affect interfere with his or her ability to clearly identify the details of the crime. Do you think that the presence of mental illness makes the victim less credible? What about less honest? Do you think that you would minimize the victim's experience, even subconsciously, or write off his or her report as "the product of a delusion?" These are the attitudes that law enforcement must guard against when interfacing with a victim who presents with a mental disease or defect.

OVERCOMING VICTIM RELUCTANCE

In this chapter, you have learned about the unique challenges presented to law enforcement with regard to responding effectively to various types of victims. One of the most frustrating and perhaps incomprehensible scenarios faced by investigators occurs when a victim does not appear to be cooperating with police or is not invested in the resolution of his or her own case. Victims may be reluctant, or appear to be reluctant, for a variety of reasons.

Recanting

In instances of domestic and sexual violence, the victim and perpetrator may have close ties to one another and may even reside in the same household. Such intimate relationships can complicate the investigation and prosecution of these cases as victims may be reluctant to help the justice system punish someone close to them. This hesitation can lead victims to recant previous statements or otherwise hinder law enforcement's efforts.

Recanting occurs when a victim changes or withdraws his or her accusation. This is a particularly prevalent phenomenon among cases of domestic violence and sexual assault between acquaintances (i.e., interfamilial molestation, incest, spousal rape, and date rape). Although victims may recant at any point throughout the investigative or adjudicative process, they most often do so at the outset of the investigation in an attempt to have charges against the attacker dropped (Thomson Reuters, 2016).

There are multiple reasons why victims recant. As previously mentioned, a victim's personal relationship with his or her assailant often underscores the decision to retract an accusation. A victim may also be faced with external pressure from family or friends or be financially dependent on the attacker. In some instances, a victim may experience guilt, as many offenders minimize their behavior and engage in significant victim blaming. Additionally, fear of retribution has also been identified as a key factor underlying recantations (Thomson Reuters, 2016).

Understanding Inconsistencies in Victims' Statements

It is not unusual for a victim's story to change as he or she repeatedly tells it to police, prosecutors, doctors, etc. In fact, many victims experience confusion or difficulty remembering events surrounding their assault. According to Martin (as cited in Purposefully Scarred, 2015), the brain's response to trauma accounts for discrepancies in a victim's story because brain activity changes during a trauma as a measure of self-protection. This causes the victim to enter either "fight, flight, or freeze" mode. Fight refers to an active defense response such as engaging in a physical altercation, while flight is the victim's instinctual reaction to run away. Freeze, or "tonic immobility," is the victim's involuntary inability to either fight or flee. *Tonic immobility* is defined as "self-paralysis or as the inability to move even when not forcibly restrained" (Gigler, 2015).

The "freeze" response to extreme stress is especially prevalent among victims of sexual assault. It serves to explain why many of these survivors report having felt as though they were unable to escape from their assailant, even when no weapon was present. As a result of this shift in brain activity, victims often experience difficulty providing a linear chronology of events related to their assault. Moreover, because this is a relatively new area of research, police and even the friends and family members of victims tend to assume that the victim is lying or engaging in attention-seeking behavior if his or her story changes. In actuality, however, such discrepancies often represent data that was temporarily "lost" or suppressed during the course of the trauma. Law enforcement should be mindful that when a victim attempts to retrieve such information, it is unlikely to be expressed in a clear, concise, or linear manner. Such inconsistencies in a victim's narrative are not indicative of untruthfulness, but rather further evidence that he or she has, in fact, endured a trauma (Purposefully Scarred, 2016).

False Versus Unsubstantiated Allegations

As you know, sexual assault is one of, if not the most underreported crime, with only approximately 32% of all rapes coming to the attention of law enforcement (U.S. Department of Justice, 2013). Of those allegations, 90%–98% are true, meaning that the rate of false report is between 2% and 10% (Lisak, Gardinier, Nicksa, & Cote, 2010).

In order to understand a false rape allegation, we must first define it. A report of sexual assault should be deemed false or fraudulent if, after a thorough investigation, it is established that no such offense took place (IACP, 2005). In other words, when investigators obtain significant evidence (such as physical evidence or statements from credible witnesses), which contradicts the victim's account by indicating that an assault did not occur, it is labeled as a false report (Kelly, Lovett, & Regan, 2005; Lea, Lanvers, & Shaw, 2003).

According to the New York City Alliance Against Sexual Assault (2012), individuals who falsely report having been sexually victimized typically do so for one of three reasons. They are either psychologically disordered, using the claim for self-protection (against an abusive husband, father, etc.), or purposely maligning against the accused.

The Federal Bureau of Investigation (FBI 1997, 2004) and the International Association of Chiefs of Police (2005) have set forth guidelines to differentiate false allegations from those that are unsubstantiated. An unsubstantiated claim occurs when an investigation fails to prove that a sexual offense took place. For example, the victim may decide not to cooperate with investigators or there may be insufficient evidence to proceed with prosecution. Cases in which the victim was highly intoxicated at the time of the crime or in which the offense was not reported until significantly after it occurred, present investigative challenges that may result in an unfounded case. It is important to remember that none of these circumstances by themselves constitute a false allegation (FBI, 1997, 2004; IACP, 2005). Remember that not having enough evidence to prove that a crime occurred is not the same as having evidence which proves that an assault did *not* take place.

TECHNIQUES FOR INTERACTING WITH VICTIMS

A victim's traumatic response depends upon the level of personal violation he or she experienced during the crime. Often, violent crimes such as sexual assault cause the victim to suffer a deeper sense of intimate violation than do nonviolent crimes, such as theft. However, each victim's reaction differs depending upon his or her mental and physical state (i.e., physical illness, emotional and situational stressors) at the time of the offense.

The primary injuries incurred by crime victims can be divided into three categories: physical, financial, and emotional. Physical injuries include cuts, bruises, and broken bones which occur during the commission of the offense. Similarly, depression, fatigue, anxiety, anger, irritability, hypervigilance, and other symptoms associated with acute stress or posttraumatic stress disorder (PTSD) are classified as emotional injuries. Financial loss or hardship resulting from theft or destruction of property are considered financial injuries (National Center for Victims of Crime, 2012).

If a victim does not receive appropriate intervention, he or she may experience a secondary injury. In fact, many victims report feeling "revictimized" by their dealings with the criminal justice system. Consider the experience of survivors of sexual assault. After having endured the offense itself, they are asked to discuss personal and often embarrassing details of the crime with police, prosecutors, and medical personnel. Once the perpetrator is apprehended, they may be called to testify against their attacker in court. The same can be said about victims of trafficking and domestic abuse. For example, it is crucial to provide the requisite support to a victim of human trafficking, as it is often the victim alone who is able to describe the coercion and control that is innate to the crime of trafficking—and central to making a case against the perpetrator (Office for Victims of Crime, n.d.a.). Because of the sensitive nature of such cases, it is important for law enforcement to implement appropriate interview techniques in order to guard against causing further psychic injury to the victim.

223

Victim-Centered Investigations

Law enforcement agencies recognize the importance of victims with regard to thoroughly investigating and successfully prosecuting offenders. Therefore, the Office for Victims of Crime (n.d.b.) recommends that police implement a victim-centered approach in order to make the investigative process less distressing for victims. Such investigations respect the dignity of victims while empowering them to tell their story in a meaningful way. To that end, law enforcement should:

- Recognize the crucial role of the victim in the investigation and subsequent prosecution.
- Ensure the protection of the victim's rights.
- Provide linkage to appropriate social services in order to support the victim throughout the investigation and assist him or her in the healing process (Figure 10.1).

Similarly, the Department of Justice's Office on Violence Against Women and the International Association of Chiefs of Police (n.d.b.) have recognized the need to better equip law enforcement to understand the

---

Crime Victims' Rights Act

Under 18 U.S.C. 3771a., victims of crime in the United States, are entitled to the following rights and protections:

1. To be protected from the offender who harmed them
2. To be notified in a timely manner of the accused's court dates and parole hearings, and to be made aware should the accused be released to the community or escape confinement
3. To not be excluded from public court proceedings relevant to the offense committed against him or her, unless the victim's presence/exposure to other people's testimony would taint the accuracy or admissibility of his or her own testimony
4. To provide a victim impact statement, or otherwise give feedback regarding the offender's plea, sentence, or conditional release
5. To confer with the U.S. Attorney's Office (i.e., the prosecution) about the case
6. To receive swift restitution
7. To justice proceedings without an unreasonable delay
8. To be treated with dignity, respect, and compassion by the criminal justice system

Figure 10.1 Crime victims' bill of rights. (From the Office of the United States Attorneys, Crime Victims' Rights Act. 18 U.S.C. 3771, U.S. Department of Justice, Washington, DC, 2014.)

neurobiological impact of the trauma associated with sexual assault. Investigators should develop an understanding of the societal and psychological complexities of sex crimes, such as how their own actions and reactions can impact a victim, the influence of rape myths/rape culture, and the importance of focusing on offender behavior rather than explicitly or implicitly blaming the victim. Police should also remember that victims often reveal details of the assault piece by piece over a period of time. Therefore, they should work to build rapport with the victim and to create an environment conducive to such divulgence.

Trauma-Informed Interviewing

One way to assist a victim with his or her disclosure is to implement trauma-informed interviewing practices. Such interviews are nonthreatening and non-confrontational. They seek to minimize further trauma to the victim, while maximizing the amount of useful information obtained. They also reduce contamination to the victim's memory recall, thus maintaining investigative integrity (Office for Victims of Crime, n.d.a.).

The victim should be afforded some control over the interview scenario, such as where to sit and when to take a break. Interviewers should also adopt the ideology that the victim's reality is the interviewer's reality. In order to accomplish this, the interviewer should avoid confronting the victim about distortions or inconsistencies in his or her story. For example, if the victim reports that the assailant threatened to harm him if he disclosed the crime to police, investigators should validate that fear and work to build the victim's trust. It is not uncommon for an investigator to need to interview a victim several times before the individual feels comfortable disclosing details of an offense such as sexual assault or human trafficking.

Investigators should use a conversational tone and avoid interrogating the victim. Open-ended questions are best. Also, because trauma can cause a victim to experience memory loss and emotional reactivity, difficulty providing a linear narrative should not be interpreted as evasiveness. Rather, interviewers should relieve the victim's stress about his or her memory by asking questions such as "What else happened?" rather than "What happened next?" Framing questions in the proper manner allows police to initially focus on crucial elements of the crime while the victim begins the healing process. A timeline can be established during subsequent interviews (Office for Victims of Crime, n.d.a.).

Additionally, police must maintain cultural awareness when conducting an interview in order to avoid alienating the victim by deviating from his or her sociocultural norms in a manner that may be interpreted as offensive or inappropriate. Culture can influence attitudes toward gender, the discussion of certain topics with "outsiders" such as police, and even narrative style (circular vs. linear). Therefore, it is recommended that police acquire the assistance of a service provider well-versed in the intricasies of the victim's culture, prior to such an interview (Office for Victims of Crime, n.d.a.).

Interviewing Victims with Developmental and Intellectual Disabilities

Special considerations should be made when interviewing crime victims with developmental or intellectual disabilities. As is common among individuals who have endured trauma, these victims may have difficulty providing a chronological account of the offense. Additionally, because they may process information differently, they may have difficulty comprehending questions asked during the interview. Moreover, individuals with disabilities are sometimes more likely to try to please the investigator by providing the "right" answer to each question (U.S. Department of Justice, 2011).

To combat this and to ensure the soundness of the interview, investigators should directly tell the victim that they are pleased with his or her truthful participation in the process. Interviewers should also utilize clear, plain language as a victim with a cognitive disability may not say that he or she does not understand a particular question. Interviewers should be patient, calm, and respectful, and should allow the interviewee to talk at his or her own pace. Additionally, interviewers should watch for signs of stress, such as withdrawal, distraction, leg swinging, humming, rocking, etc. In such instances, it may be appropriate to terminate the interview for the time being and reconvene at a later date, or to request the assistance of a facilitator who specializes in the individual's disability (U.S. Department of Justice, 2011).

Start by Believing

A crucial element of appropriately interviewing a victim is validating his or her experience. The "Start by Believing" campaign was begun to improve the responses of justice professionals to victims of sexual assault. The campaign seeks to provide support and empowerment at the time of the victim's initial disclosure, by encouraging police and other personnel to begin the investigative/legal process by believing that the victim is being truthful. In turn, this significant measure of support works to prevent secondary emotional injury. It also facilitates healing by allowing the victim to be instrumental in the pursuit of justice. The Start by Believing campaign recognizes the unique ability of law enforcement to change the antiquated notions that inflict pain and hardship upon victims (EVAWI, n.d.).

VICTIM SUPPORT UNITS

In addition to making victims feel heard and supported during the interview process, police should provide them with referrals to agencies that offer victim assistance. Such services are available at the federal, state, county, and city level and include: crisis intervention, counseling groups, assistance in obtaining a court order such as a restraining order, safety planning, referrals to shelters, court accompaniment, assistance in applying for monetary reimbursement for crime-related medical expenses, and reclaiming stolen property. Specially trained social workers, advocates, and even volunteers are available to assess the needs of individual victims and advocate on their behalf with law enforcement and court personnel. Although it may seem as though police and victim advocates have different responsibilities, (i.e., to investigate and to help the victim regain control, respectively), they are both working toward the same goal. It is in the best interest of the victim, the case, and the community, for obtaining justice to be an integral part of the victim's recovery process. Therefore, police should strive to work in tandem with victims' service agencies for the betterment of the victim and society.

11

Working with Minors

INTRODUCTION

In August of 1993, the body of 4-year-old Derrick Robie was uncovered in a secluded wooded section of a small upstate New York town. The crime scene reflected inconceivable brutality. Derrick had been strangled and beaten to death with rocks. The killer had also poured red Kool Aid into his wounds. The little boy was then sodomized with a tree branch before his body was posed for investigators to find.

Police in Savona, New York, feared that Derrick had fallen victim to a recidivistic predator, and began their search for a violent adult with a penchant for harming young children. However, the investigation took an abrupt turn when 13-year-old Eric Smith walked into the police station of his own accord and asked whether he could be of help in solving the homicide. Investigator John Hibsch described Smith as follows: "very upbeat, very happy. He likes the fact that he's being talked to" (Leund, 2004).

Smith initially denied having seen Derrick on the morning of the murder, but quickly changed his story; Smith placed himself at the crime scene and accurately described Derrick's clothing on the morning of his disappearance. When investigators asked Smith where he had last seen Derrick, his demeanor changed drastically. According to Hibsch, Smith became emotional. "His voice started cracking. He put his head down. He brings his fists up and his fists were vibrating a little bit and he goes, 'You think I killed him, don't you?'" (Leund, 2004).

Following this outburst, Smith requested to take a break from the intense conversation with investigators, at which time his father brought him a glass of Kool Aid. When the discussion with the detectives resumed, Smith purposefully dumped the Kool Aid on the ground, thus signaling to investigators that he had potentially been triggered by its presence. Police began to suspect that Eric Smith had witnessed something traumatic and that they would need to help him confront that in order to close the case. Similarly, Smith's family believed that he had information about the crime but had been threatened not to disclose it (Leund, 2004).

In the days following the murder, Smith began to inquire about the investigation. Specifically, he asked what would happen if the perpetrator were a child and exactly how conclusive DNA would be. Then, approximately one week following the death of Derrick Robie, Eric Smith confessed to the killing (Leund, 2004).

Smith was subsequently arrested and charged with murder in the first degree—as an adult. During the trial, the jury heard testimony that as a toddler, Smith was prone to temper tantrums and fits of rage, with which his parents did not appear equipped to help him. Smith additionally had speech problems and developmental delays, which caused him to be held back in school. The red-haired, freckle-faced adolescent with low-set ears had endured relentless bullying from his peers (Leund, 2004).

Dr. Stephen Herman, the defense psychiatrist, diagnosed Smith with intermittent explosive disorder (IED), which he described as episodes of "deadly rage and anger" after which Smith "... may appear to be normal." However, forensic mental health experts for the prosecution disagreed with Herman's findings. They discounted the possibility of IED due to the rarity of the disorder. Following significant medical testing, they determined that Smith's brain function and hormone levels were within the normal range and therefore not indicative of violent predilection (Leund, 2004).

The prosecution drew one conclusion: that Eric Smith had chosen to commit murder—and that he had enjoyed it. Smith reportedly characterized his crime as a loss of control. However, the prosecution argued that the crime reflected premeditation and that Smith was fully cognizant of the wrongfulness of his actions as evidenced by the fact that he had admitted luring young Derrick into the woods (Leund, 2004).

The jury agreed that Smith's emotional issues did not excuse his crime; on August 16, 1994, Eric Smith was convicted of the lesser included charge of second degree murder. The court handed down the maximum penalty that a minor could receive for homicide: 9 years to life in prison (Dale, Riley, & Charleston, 2010). By the end of the trial, Smith still had not adequately addressed the question of *why* he killed Derrick Robie.

During a 2014 parole hearing, however, Smith offered a brief explanation regarding his motivation. He described his actions as having been a horrific and unhealthy coping response to poor self-esteem. Years of bullying had resulted in rage, which he took out on a nonthreatening target: Derrick Robie. Smith admitted to the parole board that at the time, killing the little boy felt good "because instead of me being hurt, I was hurting someone else" (Leung, 2004). Since his incarceration, Smith has been denied parole on numerous occasions.

CHILD PSYCHOPATHY

The case of Eric Smith raises the question, "Can a child be a psychopath?" As we discussed in Chapter 4, psychopathy is a cluster of interpersonal, affective, and behavioral characteristics, the hallmark features of which include: remorselessness, shallow affect, grandiosity, irresponsibility, impulsivity, and antisocial behavior. Psychopaths lack conscience and engage in risky behaviors in order to further their own agendas.

According to Pardini and Loeber (2007), the interpersonal and affective elements central to adult psychopathy have also been recognized in minors. However, labeling a child as a psychopath suggests not only that he or she is not amenable to treatment, but also that his or her personality deficits and negativistic behavioral traits are pervasive and thus indicative of recidivistic criminal behavior. Such a label can be condemning. It is therefore often shied away from, as is the detrimental diagnosis of conduct disorder in favor of the milder diagnostic label of oppositional defiance.

Many experts believe that there is ample research to support the existence of psychopathy in children (Salekin, 2016). Findings have repeatedly revealed that childhood psychopathy is associated with characteristics such as fearlessness, thrill seeking, risk-taking, aggression, and serious rule and/or law violations. Genetic transmission of such traits has also been indicated. Through various studies, a specific profile has emerged of the neurocognitive and temperamental composition of child psychopathy (Aasscher et al., 2011; Blair et al., 2006; Viding, Blair, Moffitt, & Plomin, 2005). The traits that comprise this construct are divided into three dimensions: callous-unemotional (CU), grandiose-manipulative (GM), and daring-impulsive (DI) (Salekin, 2016). Of these, only the CU dimension, now referred to as limited prosocial emotion (LPE), is included in the DSM-5 (American Psychiatric Association, 2013). LPE consists of the following

231

symptoms: remorselessness, callous lack of empathy, superficial affect, and lack of concern about performance in school and within other contexts.

Measuring Psychopathy in Juveniles

One of the scales used to assess psychopathic tendencies in children is the 20-question Antisocial Process Screening Device or APSD. The items on the APSD address the CU factor, which is reflective of emotional insensitivity and disregard for or lack of concern for others, as well as the DI, or impulsive/conduct problems (I/CP) factor, which is representative of impulsivity, grandiosity, and a propensity for deviant behavior. Children who score highly on only the I/CP factor tend to exhibit below-average intelligence, reactive aggression, and heightened emotionality when triggered. In contrast, subjects with high scores on both the I/CP and CU factors demonstrate average to above average intellect, low anxiety, minimal reactivity to stressful events, and an attraction to risky activities. These children also fail to learn from punishment and engage in more persistent violent behavior over time (Frick & Marsee, 2006).

Another measure of psychopathy in minors is the Hare Psychopathy Checklist-Youth Version (PCL-YV). Comprised of a 20-item rating scale, the PCL-YV is for use with both male and female offenders aged 12–18. Adapted from the Hare Psychopathy Checklist-Revised (PCL-R), which is for use with adults, the PCL-YV similarly measures interpersonal, affective, and behavioral characteristics relevant to psychopathy. The PCL-YV is scored using multisource data drawn from a semi-structured interview and collateral information (Hare, n.d.). Although some of the items are modified from the PCL-R in order to focus more on peer, family, and school adjustment, the PCL-YV makes the assumption that psychopathy is manifested in adolescents in much the same way as it is in adults (MacArthur Foundation, 2016). For a complete list of the items found on this measure, see Table 11.1.

Immaturity and Psychopathy: The Research

It is impossible to discuss the idea of child psychopathy without addressing the impact of immaturity as well as that of social and emotional development on the persistence of psychopathic traits over the lifespan. Research conducted by the MacArthur Foundation (2016) compared the stability of PCL scores over time in both adults (n = 120) and juveniles (n = 200). Each participant was assessed using the appropriate PCL format on four separate occasions: baseline, 1 month later, 1 year later, and 2 years

Table 11.1   PCL-YV Items

Interpersonal Factors	Affective Factors
Impression management	Lack of remorse
Grandiose sense of self	Shallow affect
Pathological lying	Lack of empathy
Manipulation for personal gain	Failure to accept responsibility
Lifestyle/Behavioral Factors	**Antisocial Factors**
Stimulation seeking	Poor anger control
Parasitic lifestyle	Early behavioral problems
Lack of goals	Juvenile delinquency
Impulsivity	Serious violations of conditional release
Irresponsibility	Criminal versatility
Unclassified Factors	
Impersonal sexual behavior	
Unstable interpersonal relationships	

Source: Cauffman, E., & Skeem, J., The juvenile psychopath: Is there such a thing as an adolescent superpredator? Retrieved from: http://www.adjj.org/downloads/7893Microsoft%20PowerPoint%20-%20Juvenile%20Psychopathy.pdf, n.d.

later. The researchers also paid close attention to three specific developmental characteristics: responsibility, perspective, and self-control.

Preliminary findings suggest that the PCL scores of juveniles decline more over time than do those of adults. One implication of this data is that the decrease in adolescents' scores is linked to their increasing level of maturity. In contrast to the stability of psychopathy, immaturity is something that is outgrown. Therefore, an inverse association between the two suggests that developmental immaturity may result in inflated PCL scores. Further research concludes that increases in psychosocial maturity features (e.g., consideration for others, self-control, etc.) are correlated with decreases in PCL-YV scores (MacArthur Foundation, 2016).

CRIMINAL RESPONSIBILITY AND CHILDREN

In our society, for someone to be held legally responsible for his or her criminal acts, two elements must be present: *mens rea* and *actus rea*. **Mens** *rea* ("a guilty mind") refers to an offender's intent at the time of the offense. *Actus rea* ("a guilty act") refers to the illegality or wrongfulness of the crime itself. When children commit egregious offenses such as murder, the justice system must determine to what extent they should be held criminally responsible.

The U.S. Common Law defines murder as "the killing of a human being by another human being with malice aforethought." Whether the offender acted with "malice" is determined by retroactively evaluating his or her state of mind. Criteria for "malice" are met if the individual possessed any one of the following four mental states at the time of the offense (Mauro, 2010):

- The intent to kill another person
- The intention to inflict serious bodily harm upon another person
- Reckless disregard for human life
- The intent to commit another felony, the commission or attempted commission of which resulted in the death of a human being

The question surrounding juvenile culpability is predicated on the pretense that children are unable to understand the seriousness of their behavior. Stated simply, children do not fully grasp the wrongfulness or consequences of their actions. However, the statute does not codify an exemption for children. In fact, there is disagreement among legal professionals regarding the age at which children reach the requisite level of maturity and understanding in order to be held criminally responsible. Therefore, this issue has been addressed at the state level.

In most states, a judicial waiver can remove a case from juvenile jurisdiction to adult court, thus denying a minor who has committed an extreme act of brutality the protections of the family court system. Each state has set its own lower age limit, with most states refusing to try a youth under the age of 17 as an adult. In other states, however, the minimum age to be tried as an adult is as young as 13 (Table 11.2).

The question of criminal responsibility was raised in the case of Jordan Brown, who at age 11 was accused of having shot his pregnant stepmother to death as she slept. During the course of the investigation, police discovered that Brown had made statements about wanting to kill his stepmother (Mauro, 2010), thus implying premeditation or "malice aforethought." Similarly, 10-year-old Mary Bell murdered two boys, aged 3 and 4, in England in 1968. According to an article by Shirley Lynn (as cited in Mauro, 2010), psychiatrists testified at the trial that Bell was a psychopath. Dr. Robert Orton was quoted as saying, "I think that this girl must be regarded as suffering from psychopathic personality," as

Table 11.2   Lower Age Limits for Juveniles to Be Transferred to Adult Jurisdiction: Stats by State

Minimum Age	States
None specified	Alaska, Arizona, Colorado, Delaware, Florida, Georgia, Hawaii, Idaho, Indiana, Maine, Maryland, Nebraska, Nevada, Oklahoma, Oregon, Pennsylvania, Rhode Island, South Carolina, South Dakota, Tennessee, Washington, Washington, DC, West Virginia
Age 10	Vermont, Wisconsin
Age 12	Kansas, Missouri, Montana
Age 13	Illinois, Mississippi, New Hampshire, New York, North Carolina, Wyoming
Age 14	Alabama, Arkansas, California, Connecticut, Iowa, Kentucky, Louisiana, Massachusetts, Michigan, Minnesota, New Jersey, North Dakota, Ohio, Texas, Utah, Virginia
Age 15	New Mexico

Source: Office of Juvenile Justice and Delinquency Prevention, Statistical briefing book: Juveniles tried as adults. Minimum transfer age specified in statute, 2014. Retrieved from: http://www.ojjdp.gov/ojstatbb/structure_process/qa04105.asp?qaDate=2014&text=, 2015.

expressed by an acute "lack of feeling quality to other humans" and "a liability to act on impulse without forethought." As a result of the psychological findings, Mary Bell was not found guilty of murder, but rather convicted of "Manslaughter because of Diminished Responsibility" (Mauro, 2010). In other words, the court determined that although she had committed a crime, psychopathy had impaired her psychological functioning resulting in her diminished capacity.

The crimes committed by Mary Bell and Jordan Brown are especially disturbing because they do not appear to be the result of young age, but rather a cold and calculated disregard for others. As a society, we tend toward the assumption that immaturity—and not absence of conscience—is the cause of violent behavior perpetrated by children. But at what point do we draw the line between developmental immaturity and psychological disturbance? Table 11.3 outlines psychological defenses (i.e., insanity and diminished capcity) as well as the guilty but mentally ill verdict. As you review it, consider each item's applicability to the cases of Mary Bell and Jordan Brown; would you have judged their culpability

Table 11.3 Differentiating among Psychological Defenses and Verdicts

Defense/ Verdict	Description	Relevant Statutes/ Considerations
Not guilty by reason of insanity (NGRI)	• A defendant may enter a plea of not guilty by reason of insanity. • NGRI is an affirmative (or complete) defense. • It seeks to fully excuse the defendant from criminal responsibility for his or her crime due to *relevant* psychological circumstances. • If successful, an NGRI defense results in a not guilty verdict (and psychiatric hospitalization).	• The definition of legal insanity varies by jurisdiction. • Following the Insanity Defense Reform Act, insanity was codified as follows (U.S.C. §17): • At the time of the crime, the defendant, as a result of mental disease or defect, either did not know the nature and quality of his actions or was unable to appreciate the wrongfulness of his conduct. • An NGRI defense is applicable when mental illness directly impacted the defendant's mental state at the time of the offense.

Diminished Capacity (DC)	• A defendant may use a DC defense to mitigate his or her culpability.
	• These are partial defenses that utilize psychological evidence.
	• The purpose of a DC defense is to show the court that at the time of the crime, the defendant's mental state or relevant psychological disorder interfered with his or her ability to form the requisite *mens rea* (intent) to commit the crime with which he or she was charged.
	• If successful, a DC defense results in a conviction to a lesser crime.
		• Common Valid DC Defenses:
		  • PTSD
		  • Battered woman syndrome (BWS)
		  • Rape trauma syndrome (RTS)
		• Unsuccessful or Invalid DC Defenses:
		  • Pathological gambling syndrome
		  • Amnesia
		  • Dissociative identity disorder (DID)

Guilty But Mentally Ill (GBMI)	• A verdict, not a defense. • The defendant is held responsible, while his or her mental illness is acknowledged.	

differently had they been over the age of 18 at the time of their respective offenses?

JUVENILE SEX OFFENDERS

Serious juvenile offending is not limited to homicide. In fact, juveniles perpetrate a significant percentage of the sexual offenses committed against adult women as well as children. Current statistics estimate that minors are responsible for one-fifth of all rapes and one-half of child molestation offenses annually (Barbaree, Hudson, & Seto, 1993; Becker, Harris, & Sales, 1993; Sickmund, Snyder, & Poe-Yamagata, 1997). The vast majority of juvenile sexual aggression is committed by adolescent males aged 13–17 (Davis & Leitenberg, 1987; Sickmund et al., 1997). However, research indicates that prepubescent children and minor females also engage in sexually abusive acts.

The onset of sexually offensive behavior in youth is associated with experiential factors as well as developmental deficits. For example, a history of physical and/or sexual abuse has been found in 40%–80% of juvenile sexual offenders (JSOs) (Hunter & Becker, 1998; Kahn & Chambers, 1991). The age at which the child was first abused, the frequency of the abuse, and the perceptions of familial responsiveness to the abuse, are all factors relevant to whether the victimized child will go on to abuse others (Center for Sex Offender Management, 2010).

Child maltreatment in any form (e.g., neglect, physical or emotional abuse, sexual victimization, etc.) may prove to be a substantial predictor of sexually offensive behavior in minors. The repercussions of having been subjected to abuse in any sphere include effects related to both post-traumatic stress disorder (PTSD) and modeling (Freeman-Longo, 1986; Gil & Johnson, 1992). Indications of PTSD have been observed in minors, specifically females and children aged 13 and younger, who exhibit disordered sexual behavior. Such symptoms include intrusive memories of past trauma and increased levels of anger and irritability. Youth who have either experienced or witnessed sexual abuse may model this behavior and thus perpetrate aggressive and/or inappropriate sexual behavior in their interactions with others (Center for Sex Offender Management, 2010).

While evidence suggests that exposure to aggressive or violent role models is a clear risk factor for abusive sexual behavior in minors, research regarding other considerations such as substance abuse and viewing pornography is not conclusive. Studies reveal that boys who witness domestic violence at home are more likely than girls to externalize this experience

237

by engaging in interpersonal aggression as a response to psychological conflict (Stagg, Wills, & Howell, 1989). Similarly, exposure to domestic or familial violence increases not only the likelihood that an adolescent will perpetrate sexually offensive behavior, but it also increases the probable severity of the psychosexual disturbance (Fagan & Wexler, 1988; Smith, 1988). Additionally, direct exposure to other forms of severe violence, such as gang killings or drive-by shootings in the community may increase the likelihood of future violent and antisocial behavior (Johnson-Reid, 1998).

While there are strong implications of the association between alcohol use and generalized violence, the link between substance abuse and sexual offending is not clearly established. Data regarding estimates of the prevalence and scope of drug abuse in juvenile sex offenders varies greatly (Lightfoot & Barbaree, 1993). Similarly, the impact of pornography on future sexual offending in adolescent males is controversial. Although further research is needed and sexually abusive behavior in minors is a complex phenomenon, which encompasses risks beyond substance abuse and exposure to pornography, research has found that sexually abusive youth were exposed to pornography at a younger age and viewed "harder core" pornographic material than did their status offending and violent (nonsexual) offending counterparts (Ford & Linney, 1995).

Most juvenile sex offenders share common traits, including learning disabilities, impulsivity, and conduct disorders. However, there are palpable distinctions between the characteristics exhibited by youth who offend against children and those who are aggressive toward their peers or adults. Tables 11.4 and 11.5 discuss the general qualities of JSOs and

Table 11.4 Common Characteristics among JSOs

Most JSOs are adolescents aged 13–17	30%–60% either have a learning disability or experience academic difficulties
The majority of JSOs are male	20%–50% have suffered physical abuse
They lack impulse control and exhibit poor judgment	40%–80% have been sexually abused
Most (up to 80%) have a diagnosable mental illness	

Source: Center for Sex Offender Management, Understanding juvenile sexual offending behavior: Emerging research, treatment approaches and management practices. Retrieved from: http://www.csom.org/pubs/juv-brf10.html, 2010.

Table 11.5 Comparing Two Subgroups of JSOs

Characteristics	JSOs Who Offend Against Children	JSOs Who Offend Against Adults or Peers
Victims	• Nearly 50% assault at least one male victim • Victimize mainly female children • Often offend against child relatives (i.e., siblings)	• Target mainly females • Offend against mostly strangers or acquaintances (as opposed to relatives)
Offense features	• Crimes of opportunity • Child victims are groomed or otherwise manipulated	• Offenses are more likely to be committed in conjunction with other criminal acts • Offenses more frequently occur in public places
Social/ criminal history	• Poor self-esteem • Socially incompetent • Lack requisite interpersonal skills	• More likely to have committed prior nonsexual offenses • Criminal versatility as evidenced by general delinquency and symptoms of conduct disorder
Behavioral patterns	• May display signs and symptoms of depression • Minors with personality and/or psychosexual disturbance are more likely to experience aggression and engage in violent behavior	• Higher levels of violence and aggression • More likely to use weapons and/or inflict physical injury upon their victims

Source: Center for Sex Offender Management, Understanding juvenile sexual offending behavior: Emerging research, treatment approaches and management practices. Retrieved from: http://www.csom.org/pubs/juvbrf10.html, 2010.

those of each aforementioned subgroup, respectively. While reviewing these images, it is important to remember that while sexual aggression may emerge in childhood, there is no clinical evidence to suggest that most sexually abusive minors will go on to become adult sex offenders. In fact, longitudinal studies suggest that aggressive sexual behavior in childhood rarely continues into adulthood (Loeber & Stouthamer-Lober, 1998).

239

JSOs Who Offend Against Children

Preliminary conceptualizations of juvenile sex offenders were based largely upon what was known about adult child molesters, specifically adult pedophiles. However, early logic overestimated the applicability of deviant sexual preferences to juvenile sex crimes. Current research suggests a diversity of motivations that underscore abusive sexual behavior in youths. For example, some JSOs appear to be primarily motivated by sexual curiosity, while others have a history of engaging in behaviors that violate the rights of others. A number of such offenders also present with severe psychological disorders. Moreover, some of the sexually offensive behavior perpetrated by minors can be classified as compulsive, but more often than not, it is reflective of impulsivity or poor judgment (Becker, 1998; Center for Sex Offender Management, 1999; Chaffin, 2005; Hunter, Figueredo, Malamuth, & Becker, 2003).

In addition to differences in motivation, contemporary clinical implications denote significant disparities in behavior and prognosis between juvenile and adult sexual offenders. For example, the offensive or otherwise inappropriate sexual behaviors that result in a youth coming to the attention of social service professionals or law enforcement include wide-ranging behaviors such as sharing pornography with younger children, fondling children, touching or grabbing same-aged minors in a sexual manner, date rape, gang rape, or performing sexual acts (i.e., oral, vaginal, or anal sex) with a much younger child. Offenses may involve a single instance, a few isolated occurrences, or multiple events with multiple victims.

The RNR Method

The assessment of juveniles who have engaged in sexually offensive behavior is paramount to informing correctional placement, appropriate legal action, and treatment planning (Prescott, 2007). Properly identifying and evaluating a JSO's specific deficits and relevant risk factors can help to shape decisions regarding the modality of sex offense-specific treatment, the appropriateness of family reunification in cases of sibling incest, and whether residential or foster placement is necessary.

With regard to the treatment of JSOs both in the community and in custodial placement, Andrews and Bonta (2006) delineate three critical domains for treatment providers to evaluate and therapeutically target: risk, needs, and responsivity (RNR). As discussed in Chapter 6, the *risk* principle stresses the proper allocation of clinical resources. In other words, the most intensive treatment interventions should be focused on the highest risk offenders. *Needs* refers to the idea that treatment should focus on those factors related to recidivism (i.e., criminogenic needs). Noncriminogenic needs should only be addressed within the context of offense-specific treatment insofar as they facilitate engagement in said therapy. Lastly, *responsivity* means that treatment is not one size fits all. Rather, treatment should be tailored to the cognitive capacity, learning style, personality traits, cultural characteristics, and socioeconomic status unique to each individual offender. The efficacy of the RNR approach is empirically supported.

While the RNR model specifically sets guidelines for clinicians providing sex offender treatment, law enforcement personnel can also benefit from understanding and applying these concepts. For example, parole and probation officers who supervise JSOs in the community would do well to allocate the majority of their time and effort to those offenders who present with the highest risk to recidivate. Similarly, supervision targets should be directed by the offender's specific risk factors and criminogenic needs, and an officer's supervision style should take into account the juvenile's level of understanding and emotional maturity. Officers should remain cognizant that each offender's response to parole or probation is dependent upon his or her own unique blend of biopsychosocial characteristics.

Registration of JSOs

There is much debate among criminal justice professionals about whether the registration of juvenile sex offenders is more helpful to society than it is harmful to these minors. Prior to the enactment of the Adam Walsh Child Protection and Safety Act in 2006, only those JSOs adjudicated as adults were subject to community notification under the federal Wetterling Act (discussed in Chapter 6).

The Adam Walsh Act (2006) seeks "to protect children from sexual exploitation and violent crime, to prevent child abuse and child pornography, to promote Internet safety, and to honor the memory of Adam Walsh and other child crime victims." In its Declaration of Purpose, the act establishes nationwide registration requirements for sex offenders in response to "vicious attacks" perpetrated against numerous victims. One such case outlined in the statute is that of 8-year-old Amie Zyla, who was sexually assaulted by a juvenile offender in Wisconsin in 1996. The act now stipulates that all JSOs aged 14 and above, whose offenses were comparable or more severe than aggravated sexual abuse, must register (Center for Sex Offender Management, n.d.b.).

The registration of juveniles adjudicated delinquent for sexually-based offenses requires a specialized approach. For example, in some states, information regarding the conviction of JSOs is only accessible by the court system in an effort to limit the dissemination of information about minors to the general public. Many states additionally offer some flexibility with regard to how long juveniles must remain on the registry and whether they can petition the court for removal after a significant amount of time has lapsed since the commission of their crime. This allows the court to exercise discretion in considering the individual's offense history, risk level, and progress in offense-specific treatment.

Similarly, 20 states have instituted age limits at which juveniles no longer need to register. Such laws designate an age (typically between 18 and 21) at which offenders who have emerged into adulthood are relieved from the registration mandate. The following states subscribe to such practices: Alabama, Arkansas, Arizona, Colorado, Idaho, Illinois, Indiana, Minnesota, Mississippi, Ohio, Oklahoma, Oregon, Nevada, New Jersey, North Carolina, Rhode Island, South Carolina, South Dakota, Texas, and Washington (Matson & Lieb, 1997; Szymanski, 2003). Currently, six states have adopted lower age limits that define the youngest age at which a

Table 11.6   Registration Age Limits for JSOs

State	Lower Age Limit	Special Considerations
North Carolina	11	Juveniles must also be found by the court to pose a danger to the community.
Indiana	14	The court must determine by "clear and convincing evidence" that these juveniles are likely to recidivate.
Ohio	14	All JSOs 14 and above must comply with registration laws.
Idaho	14	All JSOs 14 and above must comply with registration laws.
Oklahoma	14	All JSOs 14 and above must comply with registration laws.
South Dakota	15	The juvenile must have been aged 15 at the time of the crime.

Source: Center for Sex Offender Management (2012a,b).

242

juvenile can be required to comply with registration. See Table 11.6 for a complete listing.

CHILD VICTIMS

In addition to encountering the criminal justice system as offenders, minors also come into contact with law enforcement as victims. Crimes against children run the gamut of behaviors, ranging from neglect and emotional abuse to physical violence, sexual assault, and murder. When a child is victimized, the trauma disrupts the trajectory of healthy psychological and physiological development. Child victims often experience adjustment difficulties, as they must learn to adapt to the complexities of each developmental stage within the framework of their past trauma.

Characteristics of Child Victims

Similar to adult victims, children who have suffered abuse in any sphere may suffer both physical and psychological trauma. Child abuse has been linked to problems with cognitive development, psychosocial adjustment, and emotional integration. For example, child victims of sexual abuse as compared with nonvictimized children have been shown to internalize their struggles (e.g., depression, social withdrawal, fearfulness) as well as to externalize problems by exhibiting aggression and acting out sexually (Inderbitzen-Pisaruk, Shawchuck, & Tamara, 1992). Additionally, survivors of child sexual abuse (CSA) may experience long-term psychological consequences. According to Coid et al. (2003), women with a history of CSA are 5 times more likely to be diagnosed with PTSD as adults than are nonvictims. Additionally, research indicates that survivors are at an increased risk of depression (Saunders, Kilpatrick, Hanson, Resnick, & Walker, 1999), suicide (Stratham et al., 1998), alcohol abuse (Galaif, Stein, Newcomb, & Bernstein, 2001), and relational difficulties, such as trouble developing and maintaining close relationships. Moreover, experiencing extreme abuse has been associated with symptoms of borderline personality disorder (i.e., instability in interpersonal relationships, parasuicidal behaviors, impulsivity as exhibited by unsafe sexual practices, and substance abuse) (Warner & Wilkins, 2004).

Similarly, studies indicate that physical and emotional child abuse and neglect have negative long-term repercussions. Physically, these children are at an increased risk of developing chronic health conditions including cardiovascular disease, poor lung function, liver disease, hypertension, diabetes, asthma, malnutrition, and obesity (Felitti & Anda, 2009; Widom, Czaja, Bentley, & Johnson, 2012). Children who have suffered a head injury (traumatic brain injury) as a result of physical abuse may incur damage to the neck or spinal cord; these children may subsequently suffer from impaired brain development.

As a result of disrupted brain maturation, children may have diminished cognitive capacity, manifesting as language deficiencies and limited academic ability. In addition, such abuse is connected with psychological disorders (Tarullo, 2012). Children whose neurodevelopment has been stifled by maltreatment may develop persistent fearfulness in addition to adaptive qualities, which although helpful during abusive instances, are counterproductive in the absence of threatened or actual harm. Such responses include hypervigilance, anxiety, and impulsive behavior (Perry, 2012).

As in cases of sexual abuse, children who have suffered physical abuse are more prone to depression, anxiety, suicidal ideation, and emotional dysregulation than are their nonvictimized counterparts (Felitti & Anda, 2009; Mesman-Morre & DeLillo, 2010). Parental neglect is often associated with the development of antisocial personality characteristics, attachment disorders, aggression, inappropriate modeling of adult behaviors, and the exhibition of affection toward relative strangers (Perry, 2012).

Additionally, there is a significant correlation between abuse during childhood and juvenile delinquency. Children who have experienced physical abuse or neglect are 9 times more likely than non-child victims to engage in criminal behavior (Gold, Wolan Sullivan, & Lewis, 2011). These children are also more likely to smoke cigarettes, abuse alcohol, or use illicit drugs (Felitti & Anda, 2009).

As you can see, the correlation between childhood maltreatment and later difficulties is substantial. Given the vulnerability of child victims and the developmental impact of such abuse, early intervention is critical, although far too rare. Therefore, it is imperative that police implement tactics that can mitigate the long-term effects of trauma on these children.

SUGGESTIBILITY

In addition to being vulnerable to victimization, children are also highly suggestible, which has significant implications with regard to psycholegal issues. Research indicates that young children (aged 3–4) are particularly susceptible to suggestion. Additionally, children aged between 3 and 12 are overwhelmingly vulnerable to post-event misinformation, which can distort memory. However, studies reveal that when misleading information is provided by another child as opposed to an adult authority figure, the effects of suggestibility are reduced, thus indicating that the impact of suggestion on children is partially informed by a desire to conform with the expectations, wishes, or implied demands of adults (Ceci, Ross, & Toglia, 1987).

Child Abuse Hysteria

One tragic illustration of such suggestibility is the child abuse hysteria of the 1980s and early 1990s. During this time, numerous accusations were made against day care providers regarding the commission of extreme acts of child abuse, including satanic ritualistic abuse. Moral panic swept across the United States and other countries including Canada, New Zealand, Brazil, and European nations as allegations continued to surface.

Kern County
The Kern County child abuse scandal was the first prominent case of its kind. In 1982, Debbie and Alvin McCuan of Kern County, California, were alleged to have committed acts of ritualistic sexual abuse against their own children. Their accuser was a relative who was reportedly suffering from psychosis at the time. Police interviewed the children repeatedly until disclosures of parental sexual abuse were elicited. The children also later accused friends of their parents of having participated in the abusive behaviors. As a result, the McCuans as well as their codefendants were sentenced to 240 years in prison; their convictions were later overturned.

Fells Acres Day Care
In a 1984 incident that paralleled the Kern County case, a 5-year-old boy reported that Gerald Amirault, an employee of the Fells Acres Day Care Center, had molested him. Authorities subsequently launched an intensive investigation, which included the questioning of other children at Fells Acres. Several of them reported having been subjected to an array of abuse, including having been raped by a robot and a clown in a secret room at the day care facility. Additional claims were made that the children had been tied to a tree and forced to drink urine. One young girl accused Amirault of having anally penetrated her with a large knife, from which she sustained no injuries. Although law enforcement's interview techniques were later called into question for being overly

245

coercive, and despite a lack of physical evidence, Massachusetts Attorney General Martha Coakley, stated: "the children testified to being photographed and molested by acts that included penetration by objects ... the implication ... that the children's allegations of abuse were tainted by improper interviewing is groundless and not true" (Hardoon, 1995). The Commonwealth proceeded with the prosecution and Amirault was ultimately convicted of having sexually assaulted nine children. Following his 1986 trial, Amirault was sentenced to 8–20 years in prison; he was released in 2004 after serving 18 years.

FALSE ACCUSATIONS, MISREPRESENTATIONS, AND MEMORY

Both the Kern County and Fells Acres cases relied heavily upon testimony from children, which poses the following questions: how reliable are such reports by children and how malleable are children's memories when exposed to misinformation or coercion? In other words, how vulnerable are said memories to distortion and under what conditions are children's memories most likely to be contaminated? Several circumstances occur throughout the criminal justice system, such as repetitive interviews peppered with leading questions or accusatory inferences by law enforcement and social services, as well as cross-examination by attorneys, which may promote distortion of episodic memory in children. When a child offers a misrepresentation, it is most often the result of one of the following: suggestion by authority, pseudomemories/unintentional cognitive distortion, or intentional prevarication.

Encoding, Retention, and Retrieval

Errors in memory accuracy can result from issues during the encoding phase, retention period, or retrieval phase of memory processing. According to Yarmey and Kent (1980), there is a developmental continuum, which influences the type of information that is likely to be encoded at different ages across the lifespan. An individual's ability to ignore extraneous information and focus on relevant details, such as a suspect's physical appearance, increases with age. Young children exhibit little selectivity, meaning that they encode all "incoming information without discrimination." Teenagers and young adults, however, have moderate central focusing proficiency, while older adults possess acute central focusing capabilities.

With regard to memory retention potential in children, research reveals that memories become more easily influenced, and thus contaminated, as time progresses. This is especially true if the information was not clearly encoded initially (Johnson & Howell, 1993).

As with encoding, developmental differences account for the disparity between the memory retrieval ability of children and that of adults. Temporal concepts do not resonate with children until the approximate age of 10, and therefore young children exhibit difficulty dating events or recalling the proper sequence of a series of events. When using free recall without prompting, children are able to recall much less information than adults. However, children perform comparably to adults on tasks dependent upon recognition (Johnson & Howell, 1993).

Memory Distortion

Children are susceptible to memory distortion from a multitude of sources, including interference, fantasy, and stress. *Interference* refers to a phenomenon wherein old information and new information conflict or otherwise interfere with one another, thus affecting long-term memory. Interference can be classified as either retroactive or proactive. *Retroactive interference* is defined as the loss of previously learned information due to its being confused with new (similar) information. A prominent example of this occurs when a child has difficulty recalling the actual events surrounding allegations of having endured child abuse or having witnessed a crime in the face of leading questions and/or other misinformation. In other words, a child may "lose" his or her memory of *not* having been abused and replace it with a new "memory" (a "pseudomemory") of victimization created by suggestive interview techniques (Johnson & Howell, 1993).

Proactive interference, on the other hand, is difficulty learning (or encoding) new information due to preexisting information. For example, someone who speaks English may have a hard time learning French or Spanish if he or she attempts to assign English syntax and grammar to the new language. With this form of interference, recall can be influenced by preconceptions that were perhaps initially acquired in order to give context to an experience. Additionally, children's interpretations of events are expressed in terms of their achieved level of developmental understanding. Therefore, because children lack a framework with

247

which to conceptualize sexual events, child sexual abuse may not register as either sexual or abusive until the child victim matures (Johnson & Howell, 1993).

With regard to fantasy and its impact on memory, research indicates that the vague conclusion that children are always less able than adults to differentiate fantasy from reality is overly simplistic. While young children tend to experience difficulty discriminating between activities that they have actually performed and those that they have imagined themselves carrying out, this is not necessarily indicative of an inability to differentiate between actions they have witnessed and those they have imagined. Applying this distinction to child abuse investigations is critical.

Stress has also been shown to have a significant effect on the veracity of children's memories. Research reveals that the responses of children who have been exposed to extreme stress during the course of custodial disputes and parental divorce, have implications for the criminal justice system. According to Terr (1986), in cases in which one parent has attempted to indoctrinate the child by repeating a false story of abuse committed by the other parent, the child often comes to believe the fictitious and maligning story. This error is further complicated by the fact that the child is often dependent upon the parent who has created the false accusation for basic physical needs such as food, clothing, and shelter, as well as emotional fulfillment needs such as approval. However, *actual* abuse also causes a child to experience intense stress, which can result in perceptual and cognitive errors, contradictions, fantasies, elaborations, or recanted statements. Therefore, such inconsistencies are not necessarily an indication of untruthfulness.

In summary, misrepresentations, inaccuracies, and false accusations by children result from one of the following: undue influence, suggestion, or bias exhibited by authority figures; interference with memory processes leading to the creation of "pseudomemories;" or intentional prevarication often influenced by adults seeking to use the child as a pawn in gaining vengeance against the accused (Lipian, Mills, & Brantman, 2004). Despite the potential for misinformation, every report of child abuse or neglect must be taken seriously and investigated thoroughly by both law enforcement and social service professionals. According to statistics compiled by the U.S. Department of Health and Human Services' National Center on Child Abuse and Neglect, an estimated 3 million reports of child abuse or neglect were received by authorities in 2001. Of those allegations, investigations substantiated nearly one-third, meaning that approximately 1 million children were determined to be victims (U.S. Department of Health and Human Services, 2003 in Lipian et al., 2004). Similarly, 135,573 investigations into reports of child abuse and neglect were undertaken in Canada in 1998 (Public Health Agency of Canada, 2004). Of these, 45% were substantiated, 22% were suspected, and 33% were unsubstantiated.

FORENSIC INTERVIEWING

As you know, the victimization of children inflicts not only physical and emotional trauma, but also disrupts the healthy achievement of developmental milestones. Unavoidably, when child victims or witnesses come to the attention of authorities, they are thrust into very "adult" dealings with the criminal justice system. To mitigate the stress of this, justice professionals should approach children in an age-appropriate fashion. This begins with giving consideration to the physical space in which interviews occur.

Arranging a Child-Friendly Interview Space

First and foremost, interviews with children should take place in an environment, such as a Child Advocacy Center (CAC), that is safe, secure, and comfortable, and thus conducive to sensitive disclosures. A CAC is a neutral and child-friendly place that affords access to a multidisciplinary team consisting of law enforcement and child protection workers. CACs are most often the preferred venue for interaction with child victims and minor witnesses to violent crime, as they cater to the comfort level of children. For example, they may be decorated with vivid colors and "happy" artwork, be stocked with children's toys, or outfitted with child-sized furniture. Forensic interviews, case meetings (involving nonoffending family members), trial preparation, targeted mental health treatment, and medical evaluations take place at CACs across the country. Additionally, nonoffending family members can participate in trauma-focused and integrative psychotherapy sessions as well as receive crisis intervention.

The Office for Victims of Crime (n.d.c.) has set forth the following developmentally informed guidelines with regard to creating comfortable interview scenarios for minors of varying ages:

- The interviewer/investigator should take the time to establish rapport with the child; child victims and witnesses should trust the person with whom they are speaking.
- Preschool aged children (ages 2–6) should be interviewed at home unless of course child abuse occurred there. In the event that a home interview is inappropriate or otherwise impossible, the child should be interviewed somewhere very familiar and with a trusted (nonoffending) adult nearby.
- Elementary school children (ages 6–10) are often reluctant to reveal critical information in the presence of a parent if they believe that such a disclosure could cause them or their parent(s) to "get in trouble." Therefore, a parent or other trusted adult should be situated close by (e.g., in the next room), but not in the interview room itself.
- Preteens and preadolescents (ages 10–12 for girls and ages 12–14 for boys) are peer-oriented and seek to avoid parental scrutiny. Therefore, the interviewee may be most comfortable with a friend nearby.
- Adolescents (ages 13–17) often fear betraying (or "ratting out") peers. Therefore, interviewing them at school or in the presence of peers should be avoided.

Interviewing Techniques

A *forensic interview* refers to a structured conversation with a child, the purpose of which is to obtain information about a particular event or series of events, which has been brought to the attention of the court system. Both victims and witnesses can be the subject of forensic interviews.

Certain basic considerations must be taken into account when interviewing a child. For instance, investigators may find that it is more difficult to interview a child than it is to interview an adult due to the child's developmental limitations, such as minimal linguistic or conceptual capabilities. As previously mentioned, although a child may have experienced or witnessed maltreatment, he or she may not yet have developed the sociocultural framework necessary to intellectualize the context of the situation as abusive. Additionally, children may experience emotions as somatic symptoms. Commonly among young children, anxiety is expressed as a stomachache. Therefore, when conducting an interview with a child, it is important to be mindful of his or her chronological (and emotional) age, level of cognitive development, manner of expression, and the presence (and extent) of psychological disturbance (Sattler, 1998).

Although specific goals of the initial interview will vary depending upon the referral question, the child's age, and his or her communication skills, Sattler (1998), outlines the following general goals for forensic interviews:

- To gauge the child's understanding of why he or she is being interviewed and how he or she feels about it.
- To develop an understanding of the child's perception of the situation that led to the interview. When the interviewee is the alleged victim of abuse or maltreatment, this often refers to the scenario which led to the allegations.
- To determine relevant antecedent events and consequential outcomes.
- To gather information regarding the severity, frequency, duration, and pervasiveness of the alleged issue(s) or maltreatment. While such information should be collected from victims, it is important to ask witnesses to discuss the dimensions of their awareness as well.
- To gain an understanding of the child's perceptions of the key players in the situation (i.e., offending versus nonoffending family members, peers, teachers, etc.).
- To evaluate the child's strengths and resilience, as well as his or her willingness to proceed with the indicated treatment and/or assessment protocols.

When conducting a legally defensible forensic interview regarding child abuse or maltreatment, a plethora of details must be kept in mind. First and foremost, it is important to consider how the alleged abuse became known to authorities. In other words, who initially reported the concern? Did the child victim disclose the abuse to a teacher or other trusted adult? Did he or she tell a friend? If so, was that friend sworn to secrecy? Or was the abuse suspected by a mandated reporter such as a physician, teacher, or psychologist? The interviewer should also determine whether anyone familiar with the allegation (e.g., a parent or a social worker) discussed it with the child and if so, what specifically was said. Consideration must be given to whether the child's narrative was possibly influenced.

Forensic interviews pertaining to allegations of child abuse (i.e., physical, sexual, or other forms of maltreatment), typically target one or more of the following objectives (Burgess, Groth, Holmstrom, & Sgroi, 1978; MacFarlane & Krebs, 1986; Vizard & Tranter, 1988):

- To discern whether or not abuse took place.
- To evaluate the child's overall functioning capacity with regard to trauma as a result of maltreatment. When interviewing a minor victim, it is important to estimate his or her functioning prior to the alleged incident (Sattler, 1998).
- To assess the family's relational dynamics, relationship to the child victim, and reaction to the abuse. This is especially relevant in cases of known or substantiated child abuse.
- To make appropriate recommendations for requisite intervention, including how to protect the child and assist in his or her recovery.

General Guidelines

Asking questions is an effective way to assist children in remembering and talking about themselves or events that they have endured or witnessed. However, asking developmentally inappropriate questions or exhibiting judgment may inhibit the interviewer's ability to obtain forthright and/or detailed information. In addition to phrasing questions properly, questions should be devoid of inappropriate intonation (which may influence or lead a child). Interviewers should also be sure to make statements of acknowledgment and acceptance, such as "Mmhm," "Oh," or "I see."

Phases of the Interview

Now that you have a general understanding of how to approach forensic interviews, we will discuss the four specific phases of child abuse and maltreatment interviews. The initial phase is known as the *rapport* phase. It is during this time that the interviewer focuses on developing a positive and trusting relationship with the (often) fragile minor. Interviewers should keep in mind that initiating a trusting rapport with a child who has been abused may be especially difficult because he or she may have been harmed by a trusted adult whom he or she trusted; the exploitation of that confidence is difficult to overcome. Interviewers should introduce themselves, reassure the child that they speak with children often, and explain why they are documenting the interview (i.e., videotaping or taking notes). A simple statement such as "This will help me to remember what you tell me today" can accomplish this task.

The interviewer should then proceed to let the child know that he or she wants to understand and help the child. The interviewer should expressly tell the child that it is ok to disclose something, even if he or she promised to keep it secret. This is because abusers often make their victims promise not to tell anyone what happened or frame the abuse as "our little secret." Additionally, interviewers should explain that they are looking to understand the truth (i.e., everything that the child can remember) and that if they repeat a question, the child need not change or revise his or her answer. This exchange might look something like this (Sattler, 1998):

Interviewer: Sometimes I get mixed up and don't understand what you said. I need your help if I don't understand. If I do say the wrong thing, will you please tell me? Just say "That's not right" or "You made a mistake." Okay?

Interviewer: I may ask you some questions more than one time. Sometimes I forget that I already asked you that question. You don't have to change your answer, just tell me what you remember the best you can.

Following the rapport phase is the *free narrative account and non-leading question* phase. In this segment, the child is encouraged to tell the interviewer what happened. The child should not be interrupted. If clarification is needed, primarily open-ended questions should be utilized. This is the time for the interviewer to ask about those events which preceded and followed the abuse. At no point in time, should the interviewer employ coercive tactics or imply that he or she is seeking a specific answer.

The third phase is the *closed questioning* phase. If the child discloses all of the necessary information during the non-leading question phase of the process, this portion may be skipped. However, if the interviewer has specific questions about the abuse or maltreatment, he or she can ask during this part of the interview. Lamb, Sternberg, and Esplin (1995) suggest beginning with a focused question that refers to a specific topic or event, followed by an open-ended question. For example, if the interviewer suspects that sexual abuse took place in the offender's bedroom, he or she might ask, "Did anything happen in the bedroom?" followed by, "Tell me everything you remember about what happened there." However, interviewers should avoid phrasing the question as "Did Joe come into your room at night?" If the child has not mentioned "Joe," this question becomes unduly influential and serves to contaminate the child's memory (Sattler, 1998). During the course of focused or non-leading questioning, the existence of key evidence may be disclosed. Should the child report for example, that there were items/objects used during the abuse, a search warrant should be obtained.

The final phase is the *closing* phase. During this, the investigator summarizes what he or she has learned about the case, using language appropriate to the child's developmental level of comprehension. This is a form of reflective listening, and affords the child the opportunity to make spontaneous corrections to previous statements. While some children may recant or deny earlier statements, others may report that they are confused by what happened or believe it was their fault. Although such declarations should be evaluated carefully, interviewers should not immediately accept them at face value (Walker, Bonner, & Kaufman, 1988). During the fourth phase of the interview, it is critical to try to relieve the child's distress. He or she should be complimented for being cooperative throughout the process. The door should be left open should the child want to talk with the interviewer again. For instance, the interviewer might provide the child with his or her business card and tell the child to call if he or she would like to speak further. The child and nonoffending family members should then be kept informed of progress throughout the investigation (Sattler, 1998).

As you can see, responding to both juvenile offenders as well as to children who have either been victimized or have witnessed a traumatic event requires a unique skill set. Law enforcement should receive specialized training as well as continuing education in this arena, as even the best of intentions when combined with ineffectual techniques will not yield results. In order to ensure investigative integrity, it is crucial for police to utilize the aforementioned best practices, which seek to minimize the likelihood that a child's narrative is incomplete, contaminated, or otherwise incorrect.

12

Threat Assessment

OVERVIEW

In 2001, a high school student in New Bedford, Massachusetts, informed a teacher that she had overheard some of her classmates talking about bombing the school and shooting people as they evacuated; the scene sounded eerily similar to that which had occurred just 2 years earlier in Columbine, Colorado. Upon learning of the possible threat, police launched an investigation, which turned up bomb-making materials, instructions for constructing an explosive device, and weapons. Three teenagers were arrested in connection with the plot and subsequently charged with conspiracy to commit murder, conspiracy to commit assault and battery, and possession of ammunition. As a result, a potential massacre was averted.

Law enforcement officials credited the swift de-escalation of the situation to having adopted techniques set forth by the U.S. Secret Service in response to previous large-scale assaults. One such protocol was to encourage students to report threats of violence made by fellow classmates, as assailants often discuss their plans prior to fulfilling them. According to Melissa Randazzo, PhD, the former chief research psychologist for the Secret Service (as cited in Miller, 2014), the New Bedford case is the first known instance of threat assessment research informing a practical police response in order to successfully impede a potentially deadly attack.

Threat assessment is a procedure wherein the amount of risk posed by actual or perceived threats is evaluated. During this process, precursors to violence are identified and appropriate tactical responses and psychologically based interventions are recommended. Threat assessment principles are predicated on the notion that targeted violence is preventable if law enforcement and community officials are aware of the warning signs.

Threat assessment studies review the histories of individuals who have previously engaged in violent behavior in order to develop an understanding of the etiology and trajectory of targeted violence. Critical research conducted by the U.S. Secret Service indicates that, "targeted violence is the end result of an understandable and often discernible process of thinking and behavior" (Fein & Vossekuil, 2000). In other words, targeted attacks do not "just happen" nor do people simply "snap." Rather, such acts are the culmination of stressors, negative emotionality, and cognitive distortions.

Threat assessment differs from the forensic psychological task of violence risk assessment in that evaluating risk places an individual's likelihood to engage in future (and often recidivistic) violence on a continuum from low to high. While threat assessment encompasses the determination of whether a particular threat is credible, its focus is on intervening when someone is troubled and thus disrupting his or her path toward committing intentional or predatory violence (Meloy & Hoffmann, 2013). Threat assessment is about preventing brutality, not predicting it. According to Cornell and Sheras (2006), "We don't intervene because we predict someone is dangerous, we want to intervene because they're troubled or there's conflict … Prevention becomes a bonus or a secondary gain from dealing with the underlying issue."

The threat assessment process is comprised of three steps (Miller, 2014):

- *Identification*: This refers to identifying a potential threat.
- *Assessment*: This involves gathering pertinent information from a multitude of sources (e.g., security professionals, school counselors, supervisors, peers, social media, etc.) and making a determination about whether the subject poses a realistic threat. Investigators ascertain the suspect's current situation, how he or she has responded to adversity in the past, his or her likely motivation, and whether he or she has a specific target and the means with which to carry out an attack.
- *Management*: When the assessment indicates a manageable underlying issue, such as bullying, anxiety, or depression, it is dealt with by trained mental health professionals (Figure 12.1).

- The suspect's motivation.

- What, if anything, the subject communicated about his or her intent.

- The individual's interest in weapons and/or mass murder.

- Criminal history, especially stalking or harassment.

- Whether the person is capable of planning and carrying out an attack.

- History of mental illness, specifically paranoia or psychosis.

- Whether people close to the suspect are concerned about his or her behavior or the potential for him or her to act on the threat.

- Recent loss, feelings of desperation, or suicidal intent.

Figure 12.1   Threat assessment investigations: Central considerations. (From the National Threat Assessment Center, *Attacks on Federal Government 2001–2013: Threat assessment considerations,* U.S. Secret Service, Department of Homeland Security, Washington, DC, 2015.)

Types of Threats

A *threat* is defined as "an expression of intent to do harm or act out violently against someone or something. A threat can be spoken, written, or symbolic—for example, motioning with one's hands as if to shoot another person" (O'Toole, 2000). Threats can be subcategorized into the following four classifications: direct, indirect, veiled, or conditional (O'Toole, 2000).

- *Direct threats* expressly state that violence *will* occur. Such statements are made in an explicit and straightforward manner, and identify a specific act to be perpetrated against an identifiable target. Direct threats are made using unambiguous language such as "I am going to burn down my ex-girlfriend's house" or "I am going to put a bomb in the school cafeteria" (O'Toole, 2000).
- *Indirect threats*, unlike direct threats, are vague and ambiguous. Aspects of the intended harm, such as the specific plan, target, or motivation are often concealed. Indirect threats imply that

257

violence *could* occur and are delivered with equivocal statements such as "I could kill everyone in the theatre if I wanted to"
(O'Toole, 2000).
- *Veiled threats* refer to strong implications that violence may occur.
  However, they lack context (O'Toole, 2000). An example of such
  a statement might be "I would be better off without you around
  anymore." In such cases, the intended victim must often interpret
  the threat's meaning.
- *Conditional threats* are expressed as ultimatums. They threaten to
  take violent action if certain demands are not met. For example,
  "If you don't pay $1 million, I will kill your daughter." These are
  often seen in cases of extortion, kidnapping, and hostage taking
  (O'Toole, 2000).

Threats of harm are relevant to a multitude of scenarios and criminal activity, including stalking, school shootings, terrorism, politically
motivated violence, and hostage crises. In general, the more direct a given
threat is, the more serious the risk it poses. All high-level threats, and
some lower-level threats, require an immediate and appropriate response
from law enforcement. As you read through this chapter, make note of
the array of considerations law enforcement agents must take into account
when evaluating or de-escalating a threat.

MENTAL HEALTH AND MOTIVE

Operational considerations for threat assessment focus largely on: (1) identifying a continuum of problematic behaviors engaged in by the subject;
(2) understanding the connection between mental health and motivation;
and (3) evaluating the impact of environmental, emotional, or psychological triggers within the context of the suspect's decision-making capabilities. Concerning behaviors may occur over time and range from causing
minimal worry to eliciting extreme fear. Such actions include (National
Threat Assessment Center, 2015):

- Sudden behavioral changes, typically related to interpersonal
  or occupational functioning, including dropping out of school,
  declining job performance, mood lability, and drastic changes in
  physical appearance.
- Interpersonal difficulties, such as withdrawing from social cir-
  cles, or experiencing increased personal conflict.

- Making final gestures, such as giving away belongings or getting one's affairs in order.
- Stalking, harassing, making threatening or abusive communications, conducting extensive research (online or otherwise) about a specific person or persons, invading someone's privacy, or perpetrating blackmail, vandalism, or violence.
- Making disturbing communications involving grievances, threats, or veiled references to engaging in harmful behaviors, exhibiting extreme ideological or delusional beliefs, or expressing depression or feelings of hopelessness (Figure 12.2).

It is critical for law enforcement to explore the presence of mental illness in a suspect. A study conducted by the National Threat Assessment Center (2015) suggests that more than 50% of individuals who have carried out threats of violence were experiencing active symptoms of psychological disorder at the time of their offense. Additionally, the motivations of just fewer than 25% of those offenders were influenced in some way by psychiatric indicators. Research also reflects that a significant number of offenders were multisymptomatic, with the most common symptoms being paranoia, depression/despondence, and delusional thinking. However, other symptoms such as suicidal ideation, disorganized thinking/behavior, hallucinations, and mania were also represented.

In September of 2013, Aaron Alexis shot and killed 12 people at the Washington Navy Yard in Washington, DC. One month prior to the attack, police responded to Alexis' hotel room in Newport, RI; he asserted that he was being followed. Alexis reported that he had changed hotels twice in order to escape the voices that he was hearing and had placed a microphone on the ceiling of his hotel room in order to record them. Alexis had additionally disassembled the bed, as he believed that someone was hiding underneath it and sending vibrations into his body from a microwave machine. Following the deadly attack on the Washington Navy Yard, authorities discovered three words etched into Alexis' shotgun: "My ELF weapon!" Officials determined that the incident had resulted from Alexis' delusional belief that he was under attack and was being barraged with extremely low frequency (ELF) waves. This case highlights the importance of asking someone who is expressing paranoia what steps he or she feels are necessary to protect him or herself; such information can significantly inform the threat assessment process.

Figure 12.2 Paranoia and threat assessment. (From the National Threat Assessment Center, *Attacks on Federal Government 2001–2013: Threat assessment considerations*, U.S. Secret Service, Department of Homeland Security, Washington, DC, 2015.)

Impact of Psychiatric Symptoms on Motivation

Recognizing symptoms is of little assistance to police without an under-standing of the potential influence of those symptoms. Therefore, the vignettes that follow describe the correlation between symptoms of psychological distress and targeted violence.

- *Paranoid delusions*: In 2006, George Curran took nine hostages at the Phoenix-based National Labor Relations Board (NLRB). At that time, he reportedly subscribed to several paranoid beliefs surrounding the termination of his wife's employment from the federal government. Although he had filed complaints with the NLRB, he believed that the officials with whom he had spoken were "imposters" (Ariz, 2006) and that a specific group of individuals with undue influence over the government was preventing his wife's case from being investigated. As his delusion progressed, Curran came to believe that some of his family members, who were government employees, were complicit in the conspiracy. As a result, he feared that his phone had been tapped and that he was being followed. Records indicate that all hostages were released unharmed following a lengthy standoff (National Threat Assessment Center, 2015).
- *Depression*: In 2001, Robert Pickett opened fire on the White House. He suffered from a history of depression, which included multiple suicide attempts. Although Pickett survived the incident, the investigation uncovered a suicide note in his car. He had fired shots toward the White House in an attempt to commit "suicide by cop," wherein a perpetrator knowingly enters into a situation in which he or she forces law enforcement to shoot him or her or otherwise resort to using deadly force (National Threat Assessment Center, 2015).

It is important to understand that since most police personnel are *not* trained mental health professionals, the purpose of exploring a suspect's psychological symptoms is not to make a psychiatric diagnosis. Rather, officials should seek to obtain information about what symptoms the individual is experiencing, how they may impact the person's behavior, and whether the symptoms may influence his or her decision to fulfill the threat and carry out an actual attack (National Threat Assessment Center, 2015).

OFFENDER PROFILES

As you learned in Chapter 8, making psychologically sound inferences about potential offenders can assist law enforcement in their efforts to prevent and contain violence. To that end, the National Threat Assessment Center (2015) conducted an assessment of known offenders (n = 39) who followed through with threats of violence against either federal facilities or public officials. The following information was compiled in order to provide law enforcement with the requisite tools with which to identify such individuals *before* they carry out a threat:

- *Demographic information*: The vast majority of offenders were men (87%) over the age of 30 (72%). Their educational backgrounds ranged from those who never received a high school diploma to those who had been awarded doctoral degrees.
- *Drug history*: More than one-third of the individuals studied had a history of alcohol and/or drug abuse. The substances abused included alcohol, prescription medications, marijuana, cocaine, methamphetamines, and hallucinogens, with marijuana and cocaine being the most commonly used illicit drugs.
- *Criminal history*: More than half (62%) of the perpetrators had a criminal/arrest history beyond traffic violations. Of these, all but two had at least one nonviolent offense on his or her record and one-third (n = 13) had arrests for violent crimes. Five (13%) had sex offense-related charges and an additional six offenders (15%) had engaged in criminal activity with which they had never been charged. For example, Bruce Ivins, who sent anthrax-laced letters to two U.S. Senators in 2001, had previously sent mail contaminated with anthrax to various media outlets. He had also committed burglary and vandalism prior to the 2001 attacks.
- *Violence against others*: Perhaps unsurprisingly, more than half (51%) of the known offenders had previously engaged in violent behavior such as assault, assault with a deadly weapon, domestic violence, or murder. An additional four individuals had exhibited aggressive or intimidating behavior that had come to the attention of law enforcement officials.
- *Concerning behaviors*: With the exception of one offender, all of the known perpetrators in the study had engaged in concerning behaviors prior to their offense. These acts included *concerning communications* (unrelated to their targets), such as extreme ideological or

261

sociopolitical beliefs, or delusional thinking, and *noticeable behavioral changes* related to occupational, interpersonal, physical, or social functioning. It should be noted that individuals who manifested significant behavioral changes were more likely to commit a serious (i.e., deadly or injurious) attack than were those people who did not experience such changes. Additionally, one half of the perpetrators had strained relationships or other *interpersonal difficulties*, while one-fifth engaged in *"final act" behaviors* such as writing wills, giving away belongings, rehoming pets, breaking leases, posting goodbye messages to social media, or setting fire to their own homes. Moreover, approximately two-thirds of the offenders had previously sparked concern in others (i.e., family members, colleagues, friends, mental health workers, police personnel, etc.) about the *risk they posed to themselves or others*. Nearly half (49%) of those studied showed evidence of *fixation* (defined as a persistent and obsessive interest in or preoccupation with something or someone), while one-fifth had previously engaged in stalking or otherwise harassing behavior. As previously discussed, 50% of the offenders had significant mental health histories.

In addition to the profile that emerges from this data, precipitating factors were identified in the time period leading up to 92% of the offenders' attacks. Family and/or marital issues such as divorce or the death of a loved one were significant triggers. Problems at work or school, justice involvement or legal struggles, acute illness, and substantial instability such as loss of housing were also cited as stressors (National Threat Assessment Center, 2015).

Research reveals that individuals who have experienced significant stress in more than one life domain are more likely to perpetrate a violent attack. For instance, Aaron Alexis, who opened fire on the Washington Navy Yard in 2013, had a history of conflict in interpersonal relationships, multiple arrests, disciplinary actions while enlisted in the U.S. Navy, repeated school drop outs, financial hardship, eviction, and degenerative illness (National Threat Assessment Center, 2015).

STALKING

As you've just learned, stalking is classified as a "concerning behavior" that often precedes violent attacks. However, stalking in and of itself is a target of the threat assessment work conducted by law enforcement.

Although it is legally defined by state statute, *stalking* is generally considered to be "a course of conduct directed at a specific person that involves repeated (two or more occasions) visual or physical proximity, nonconsensual communication, or verbal, written, or implied threats, or a combination thereof, that would cause a reasonable person to fear" (Tjaden & Thoennes, 1998b). In other words, stalking is a pattern of alarming and intrusive behavior, which targets a specific individual and continues despite the victim's desire for it to cease. The harassing and disturbing actions of or communications from the stalker often cause the victim to experience fear, emotional distress, intimidation, and/or anxiety. Victims often report feeling as though they are being "hunted."

Stalking behaviors may include any or all of the following (Office of Violence Against Women, 2016; Sexual Assault Prevention and Awareness Center, 2016; Stalking Resource Center, 2012):

- Following the victim or showing up where he or she is or is expected to be (e.g., home, work, school, social gatherings, etc.)
- Sending unwanted gifts, cards, emails, text messages, or social media requests
- Watching the victim via the use of hidden cameras
- Using GPS or apps with GPS capability to "keep tabs" on the victim's whereabouts
- Driving by the victim's home or place of employment
- Posting personal information about the victim on social media or otherwise spreading rumors (typically intended to defame the victim)
- Obtaining personal information about the victim via public records, going through the victim's garbage, conducting Internet searches, contacting the victim's family and/or friends, etc.
- Approaching or confronting the victim either publicly or privately
- Entering the victim's residence or lurking on his or her property without invitation or express permission
- Damaging the victim's home or property
- Making verbal or written threats

Cyberstalking

As you can see, technological advances have transformed the Internet and various electronic devices (e.g., GPS, spyware, cameras, tracking apps, etc.) into popular tools for stalkers. *Cyberstalking* refers to the use of technology to harass or engage in unsolicited and unrelenting contact with the victim. Cyberstalkers may inundate their victims with obscene, offensive, hateful, or threatening emails. Additionally, some such perpetrators even assume their victim's identity in social media forums.

Due to the accessibility of the Internet and society's urge to share personal life details with an impersonal audience, the web offers stalkers unprecedented access to their targets' private information. Take a moment to review your profile on any social media site. Does it give your full name or your hometown? How about your phone number, email address, school, or place of employment? Perhaps you have "checked in" to some of your favorite or frequent hangouts. If you're like most people, you've also probably posted pictures of friends and family members. Now, look at your settings. How much of this information is public (in that it can be viewed by anyone)? How much can be viewed by people with whom you share a contact?

Cyberstalkers often use these personal details in order to further terrorize their victims in real life. For those offenders who find in-person confrontation difficult, cyberstalking provides them with a remote, yet intrusive alternative (Department of Justice, 1999; National Institute of Justice, 2007).

Stalking Stats

Stalking may be more common than you think. According to statistics gathered by the CDC's National Intimate Partner and Sexual Violence Survey, one out of six women and one in 19 men are stalked at some point during their lives (Black et al., 2011) and as many as 7.5 million people are stalked in the United States each year. Individuals between the ages of 18 and 24 experience the highest rate of stalking of any age group. Additionally, 46% of victims receive a minimum of one unwanted contact from their stalker per week, and 11% of victims have been stalked for a period of 5 years or more (Stalking Resource Center, 2012).

Who Can Be a Stalker?

While stalking is a gender-neutral offense in that anyone can be a victim or a perpetrator, research reveals that most stalkers are male and that the majority of all stalking cases (75%–80%) involve men stalking women (Sexual Assault Prevention and Awareness Center, 2016). In over 85% of cases, there is an identifiable relationship between the stalker and his or her victim. In fact, approximately two-thirds of female victims and nearly half of male victims are terrorized by a current or former intimate partner. An additional 25% of female victims and 32% of male victims are stalked by an acquaintance. Cases where no relationship exists between the victim and the offender comprise only 20% of all stalking offenses (Stalking Resource Center, 2012).

Domestic Violence and Stalking

Similar to domestic and sexual violence, stalking is a crime about power and control. It is often used as a device by abusers to control their victims by instilling unrelenting fear in them. Therefore, it logically follows that stalking is strongly correlated with both physical and sexual violence. In fact, according to Tjaden and Thoennes (1998b), over 80% of women who are stalked by a current or former intimate partner are also physically assaulted by that person. Similarly, 31% of these women are sexually assaulted by that individual.

Stalkers often engage in behaviors that are intended to court their victims. For example, they may send flowers, notes, or other unwanted gifts in an effort to prove their love. However, in the face of rejection by their intended target, stalkers typically turn to intimidation tactics as their thinking changes from "If I can prove my love, you will love me" to "I will make you love me." Such inappropriate conduct often takes the form of jealous intrusions into the life of the victim. When these actions inevitably push the victim further away, the stalker's mindset often changes to "If I can't have you, no one can," and his (or her) behavior becomes aggressive and threatening (Sexual Assault Prevention and Awareness Center, 2016).

We need to differentiate between two types of intimate partner stalkers and their respective motivations: those who have or previously had a close relationship with the victim such as a spouse, and those without a close connection. The more extensive the relationship is or was between the stalker and the victim, the more likely it is that the stalker is attempting to gain or regain power and control in the relationship. However, when the relationship between the two can only be described as casual or fleeting, such as a brief dating relationship, it is more likely that the offender is delusional or otherwise psychologically disordered (Office for the Prevention of Domestic Violence, 2016).

265

Although no instance of stalking is predictable, special concern is warranted when the stalker is identified as a current or former paramour. Such perpetrators already possess intimate knowledge of the victim and his or her daily routine. Perhaps more frighteningly, they are also likely to be aware of the victim's deepest fears or phobias, which can be exploited, thus increasing the victim's experienced level of fear (Office for the Prevention of Domestic Violence, 2016).

Studies indicate that when an intimate partner is the stalker, the risk of victim fatality increases; this is especially true if the stalker has access to weapons (Office for the Prevention of Domestic Violence, 2016). Think back to our discussion on domestic homicide in Chapter 7 and consider the connection between intimate partner violence, stalking, and femicide. Research reveals that an overwhelming 76% of victims of intimate partner femicide were stalked by their attacker prior to their deaths. Moreover, 89% of femicide victims who were physically abused by their partner, were also stalked by the offender in the 12 months preceding the murder. Sadly, more than half of these victims made the stalking known to law enforcement before they were killed (Stalking Resource Center, 2012).

Assessing Stalking Threats

When stalking is reported to law enforcement, officers must take it seriously. Research reveals that police are more likely to charge stalking suspects with misdemeanor offenses such as harassment or violating a restraining order than they are to file felony stalking charges (Tjaden & Thoennes, 2001). Additionally, findings suggest that the majority of stalking victims fail to recognize or classify the perpetrator's behavior as "stalking" when communicating with authorities. Therefore, it is incumbent upon police to be well-versed in the vast array of potential stalking behaviors and to understand the risks associated with them.

When tasked with assessing threats in this arena, investigators must consider the risk posed to the victim. Such risk can be classified into three separate areas of concern (Mullen et al., 2006):

- *The likelihood that the stalking will continue or reoccur.* Stalking that has persisted for more than 2 weeks is likely to continue for several months. Such persistence is common among cases of workplace stalking or professionals who are pursued by former patients or clients (Fine, 1997; Pathé, Mullen, & Purcell, 2003; Schell & Lanteigne, 2000; Orion, 1997). On the other hand, offenders who pursue their victim for a period of years are frequently suffering from an erotomanic delusion and therefore desperately seeking intimacy with their target.

- *The impact on the victim's psychological, emotional, and social presence.* It stands to reason that the longer the stalking lasts, the greater the disruption to the victim's life, and possibly the more distress he or she experiences. The negative effect of stalking on victims encompasses responses of intense fear and anxiety, withdrawal from social activities, and suicidal ideation.

- *The potential for escalation to physical assault, sexual violence, or homicide.* Between one-tenth and one-third of all stalking victims are physically attacked (Monahan et al., 2001; Rosenfeld & Harmon, 2002) and up to 40% are directly threatened (Purcell, Pathé, & Mullen, 2002; Hall, 1998; Pathé & Mullen, 1997). With the exception of public figures that are targeted, explicit threats increase the probability of violence (Meloy, Davis, & Lovette, 2001). Such threats can be categorized as either instrumental or reactive. ***Instrumental threats*** are intended to manipulate or intimidate the victim, while ***reactive threats*** signal affective dysregulation or an emotional outburst (Meloy, 2001). Additionally, many stalking behaviors, such as surveillance or following the target, make implicit threats of violence (Kropp, Hart, & Lyon, 2002). Although most stalkers do not violently act upon these threats, all threats should be viewed as serious.

SCHOOL-BASED VIOLENCE

School-based violence is defined as aggression or violence that occurs on school property. Such incidents include verbal and physical abuse, bullying, and school shootings. In the wake of multiple instances of headline-grabbing and deadly school violence, many school districts have either developed or are in the process of developing comprehensive threat assessment protocols. Such practices focus not only on threats of physical brutality (e.g., shootings, bombings, etc.), but also seek to address bullying and other forms of student conflict in an effort to avoid further escalation.

What Is Bullying?

According to the U.S. Department of Health and Human Services (n.d.b.):

Bullying is unwanted, aggressive behavior among school-aged children that involves a real or perceived power imbalance. The behavior is repeated, or has the potential to be repeated, over time. Bullying includes actions such as making threats, spreading rumors, attacking someone physically or verbally, and excluding someone from a group on purpose.

There are four types of bullying: *verbal bullying*, such as name calling, taunting, or threatening; *physical bullying*, which includes hitting, punching, kicking, or tripping; *social bullying*, which entails excluding someone from group activities, or spreading rumors about him or her; and *cyberbullying*, which much like cyberstalking, involves the use of technology to harass or intimidate someone. Cyberbullying can take the form of sending mean or disturbing text messages or emails, spreading rumors via email or social media, posting embarrassing photos or messages, and setting up fake social media profiles. While in-person bullying often occurs during school hours, technology allows cyberbullies to contact their targets at any time, day or night. These victims often have no way to escape the intrusive electronic communications. Additionally, victims of cyberbullying are also typically victims of other types of bullying (U.S. Department of Health and Human Services, n.d.b.).

Effects of Bullying

The consequences of bullying are numerous and far-reaching. Children who are victimized may experience psychological effects such as depression, anxiety, loneliness, loss of interest in activities they once enjoyed, and suicidal ideation. It is not uncommon for victims to notice changes in sleeping or eating patterns. Victims may also suffer from somatic complaints and experience decreased academic achievement (U.S. Department of Health and Human Services, n.d.b.).

Relationship Between Bullying and Deadly Violence

The connection between bullying and the commission of serious, overt, and potentially fatal violence may seem somewhat counterintuitive at first. Research indicates that it is not the bullies, but rather their victims who may pose the gravest threat because some individuals who are bullied employ extreme brutality as a means of retaliation. While only a small number of victims do this, records reveal that in 12 of the 15 (80%) school shooting cases studied in the 1990s, the shooter(s) had previously been bullied (U.S. Department of Health and Human Services, n.d.b.).

Children and teens that are bullied are more likely to bring a weapon to school than are their nonvictimized counterparts. In fact, approximately 200,000 victims of bullying bring weapons to school each year (Pediatric Academy Societies, 2014). According to researcher Andrew Adesman, MD, FAAP, "Victims of bullying who have been threatened, engaged in a fight, injured, or had property stolen or damaged are much more likely to carry a gun or knife to school" (Pediatric Academy Societies, 2014). In recent years, society has sadly been forced to bear witness to school violence committed by children, adolescents, and young adults on an ever-increasing basis. As you read the following case examples, consider the impact of social rejection and mental health on the perpetrators.

Columbine
On April 20, 1999, Eric Harris, 18, and Dylan Klebold, 17, carried out one of the deadliest school shootings in history at Columbine High School in Littleton, Colorado. On the morning of the attack, the pair set two propane bombs in the school's cafeteria, with the expectation of killing hundreds of students and teachers. However, when the bombs failed to detonate, Harris and Klebold entered the school with semi-automatic weapons. In the minutes that followed, they killed 13 people and injured another 20. They then fatally shot themselves.

Two months prior to the massacre, Klebold submitted a writing assignment to one of his teachers; it was wrought with intense violence and described brutal mass murders in graphic detail. At the time, it was unclear as to whether this was an outlet for negative emotions, an expression of fantasy, or something more serious.

Additionally, the teens kept a journal leading up to the attack, which served to illuminate their perceived torment at the hands of their peers. The entries vacillated from depressive and isolative content focused on social rejection to grandiose plans of killing. They delineated violent fantasies and even anticipated society's response to their actions. For example, in one entry, Harris wrote, "Don't blame my family. They had no clue and there is nothing they could have done" (Johnson, 2006). The writings demonstrate that although the actions of Klebold and Harris may have been predicated on feelings of rejection and emptiness, their attack was not impulsive. Rather, it was calculated and extravagantly detailed.

Virginia Tech

Another brutal school shooting occurred on April 16, 2007, at Virginia Polytechnic Institute and State University in Blacksburg, Virginia. Twenty-three-year-old Seung-Hui Cho began his rampage early that spring morning, killing students and faculty members in a campus dormitory before proceeding to a classroom building. In total, he murdered 32 people and injured countless others before taking his own life.

In the time that elapsed between the two sets of localized attacks, Cho mailed a video diary, known as his manifesto, to NBC News. In it, he spoke tangentially about how having been bullied and rejected had made his attack inevitable. Cho further characterized himself as an avenger for and defender of the weak. His video clips were also infused with references to Harris and Klebold's attack on Columbine High School.

In the aftermath of the shooting, experts began to dissect Cho's psychological history, looking for behavioral and psychiatric clues. Relevant and prior to the shooting, Cho exhibited troubling behavior. A previously sullen and aloof high school student, he had progressed into a quiet loner in his college years. An English major, Cho expressed himself vividly through dark and grotesque writings. Additionally, he had twice been accused of stalking female students and had made a comment indicative of suicidal intent, which resulted in a court-mandated psychiatric assessment. In the weeks prior to the killings, Cho purchased several firearms. Evidence secured during the course of the investigation suggests that like Klebold and Harris, Cho had been planning his attacks for quite some time (Biography.com Editors, 2016d). To better understand the chronicity of events, review Table 12.1.

As an adolescent, Cho had been treated for selective mutism, a diagnosis that was later revisited by experts as the disorder lacks a correlative relationship to violence (McGrath as cited in James, 2007). Selective mutism is often likened to extreme shyness, and can be best understood as a manifestation of anxiety. Research presented at the 2007 APA conference clarified that it is "cynical shyness" as opposed to extreme shyness, social anxiety, or selective mutism, which is common among school shooters (Carducci as cited in James, 2007).

However, Cho's silence may have been symptomatic of larger problems. In combination with social phobia or ineptitude, attention deficit, marijuana abuse, and/or depression, Cho's selective mutism was likely indicative of more severe psychiatric conditions (Eth, as cited in James, 2007). Additionally, Cho experienced paranoid thinking and exhibited odd behavior, which may have resulted from a personality disorder or emerging schizophrenia spectrum disorder.

Table 12.1   VTECH Shooting Timeline

December 13, 2005
- Cho undergoes a psychological evaluation after having been court ordered to seek outpatient psychiatric care for making suicidal remarks.

February 9, 2007
- Cho obtains a P-22 pistol from an out-of-state dealer.

March 2007
- Cho purchases another firearm, this time a 9mm Glock; he obtains 50 rounds of ammunition.

April 16, 2007
7:15 AM
- Police receive a 9-1-1 call notifying them that there are two gunshot victims at a dormitory on the Virginia Tech Campus.

9:01 AM
- Cho mails his manifesto to NBC News.

9:26 AM
- Virginia Tech officials send out an email alert to notify students of the shooting in the dorm.

9:45 AM
- Several 9-1-1 calls report the second round of shootings in a classroom building; 32 students and faculty members are dead.

9:50 AM
- The university issues a second email alert cautioning students to "stay put" due to an active shooter scenario.

10:16 AM
- Emergency cancellation of all classes.

10:53 AM
- Students are notified that the gunman is in police custody.

April 17, 2007
- Campus police confirm the identity of the shooter: Seung-Hui Cho.

April 18, 2007
- NBC reports receipt of Cho's videotape manifesto.
- Classes at Virginia Tech resume.

Source: CNN, Virginia Tech shootings fast facts. Retrieved from: http://www.cnn.com/2013/10/31/us/virginia-tech-shootings-fast-facts/2016.

Sandy Hook

Another highly publicized and disturbing school shooting occurred on December 14, 2012. That morning, 20-year-old Adam Lanza murdered his mother in his family's home in Newtown, Connecticut. He then proceeded to Sandy Hook Elementary School, where he had once been a student. Dressed in combat fatigues and armed with multiple weapons, he opened fire, killing a total of 26 people.

Like Klebold, Harris, and Cho, Lanza killed himself at the scene. Although his motivations were not immediately apparent, a thorough investigation determined that there was evidence of early preoccupation with violence, which was not properly addressed by school officials and possibly overlooked by Lanza's parents (Eagan et al., 2014). In fact, Lanza participated in an online community for mass murder "enthusiasts"(Stanglin & Bello, 2014). Additionally, it appeared that he had experienced social, emotional, familial, and educational challenges, for which he was not provided adequate support or intervention. The Sandy Hook massacre highlights the need for more thorough mental health screenings and for parents, school staff, healthcare providers, and law enforcement to work together to appropriately respond to threats or alarming behavior in order to prevent violence.

ASSESSING THREAT IN CASES OF SCHOOL SHOOTINGS AND BOMBINGS

As you now know, the violent trajectory of a perpetrator of school violence is evolutionary in that it develops over time and there are warning signs along the way. Therefore, the FBI developed a four-prong approach to describe the personality characteristics, behaviors, and family, school, and social dynamics common among individuals who engage in school violence, as well as to environments that foster such offenses. This model is an effective tool for evaluating individuals who have made threats and to determine the likelihood that they will act on those threats.

The first prong consists of personality traits and behaviors. Assessors should consider how the student copes with conflict and disappointment, expresses anger, frustration, and other negative emotions, and responds to authority. Attention should be paid to whether the student exhibits empathic concern for his or her fellow classmates or dehumanizes them. Similarly, authorities should question whether the student regards his or her peers positively or contemptuously. School shooters often exhibit

272

resentment, vindictiveness, and an extreme sense of entitlement. Lack of resilience is also a trait relevant to school shootings (O'Toole, 2000). School counselors and police should determine whether the individual in question displays an ability to "bounce back" after setbacks, failures, or criticisms.

Another key element of the personality composition present in many school shooters is known as "leakage." Leakage occurs when the student intentionally or unintentionally expresses emotions, thoughts, fantasies, or attitudes, which often take the shape of threats or innuendos. These may be expressed as written stories, poems, or video diaries, as in the case of Cho, journal entries, as seen in the Columbine case, or other mediums such as drawings, tattoos, or songs, reflective of a rich and violent fantasy life. Themes may involve murder, suicide, dismemberment, prejudice, hatred, weapons, or bloodshed (O'Toole, 2000).

School shooters often also exhibit a lack of trust, present as manipulative, have difficulty regulating their anger, and externalize blame. Their arrogance and self-aggrandizing attitude serves to mask their poor self-image. Additionally, they often have a pathological need for attention—whether positive or negative (O'Toole, 2000).

The second piece of the puzzle is family dynamics. In order to better understand the circumstances and stressors present in a potential school shooter's life, it is wise to evaluate family interactions. What behavioral patterns, beliefs, customs, and values exist and how are they viewed by both the suspect and his or her parents/guardians? How might they impact the student's decision as to whether or not to carry out the threat (O'Toole, 2000)?

Families of school shooters often lack intimacy, and the offenders frequently have access to weapons. Additionally, the parents of school shooters have often failed to acknowledge their child's pathology. Relationships between school shooters and their caregivers are often turbulent (O'Toole, 2000).

Third, school dynamics play a key role. These are patterns, some of which may be obvious and others subtle, which draw the road map for acknowledgment, prestige, and approval from both school authorities and other students. Consider whether the school and those running it have exhibited tolerance for disrespectful behavior. A code of silence, inflexible culture, and inequitable discipline all contribute to an environment that is poised for violence. Additionally, school shooters often feel detached from the school's social strata (O'Toole, 2000). Police should be cautious when interviewing teachers about this domain, as it is sometimes difficult for people to objectively evaluate negative value systems at their place of employment—especially if they feel as though their job contributes to such negativity.

Lastly, social dynamics refer to patterns of thinking and behavior, belief systems, traditions, and customs that exist in the extended community in which the student resides. These include lifestyle choices, activities, entertainment, and attitudes toward and exposure to drugs, alcohol, and weapons. Additionally, adolescents are peer-focused, which means that if the suspect is a teenager, his or her choice of friends will often provide valuable insight into his or her attitudes, sense of identity, and even the viability of the threats that he or she has made (O'Toole, 2000).

The presence of one or two of the aforementioned features should not be considered in isolation, meaning that assessors should look for a constellation of negative traits and situational components when considering risk. Additionally, police and other professionals should be mindful that several of these characteristics may pertain to individuals who are experiencing depression or other psychiatric conditions. However, if a student who has made a threat appears to have significant problems in most or all of the four dimensions, and the threat is categorized as medium to high risk, urgent action should be taken (O'Toole, 2000). Additionally, immediate intervention is appropriate for some lower-level threats as well.

TERRORISM

Law enforcement is called upon to assess not only threats of school-based violence, but of terrorist activity as well. We define *terrorism* as the use of violence or intimidation to further specific agendas, such as extremist religious ideologies or political aims. More specifically, terrorist groups often seek to accomplish one of the following goals:

- Instill fear
- Weaken the (military) capabilities of a government that they oppose or that stands in opposition to their ideals
- Financially damage an enemy government by discouraging trade, tourism, or other economic support
- Undermine official efforts to protect citizens by creating doubt about a specific government's forthrightness and/or power to protect its people
- Obtain money and/or weapons to further terrorist activities

- Achieve vengeance
- Obtain recognition for their cause
- Influence government decisions
- Free political prisoners or prisoners of war (POWs)

Terrorism may be classified as either international or domestic. *International terrorism* consists of violent or life-threatening acts, which aim to intimidate civilians, influence government policies by employing intimidation or coercion, or affect government conduct through the use of extreme violence, such as mass murder, catastrophic destruction, assassination, or kidnapping. These crimes either occur primarily outside the United States or transcend national boundaries. *Domestic terrorism* on the other hand, involves the same or similar acts within U.S. jurisdiction. In cases of domestic terrorism, acts that are directly or indirectly linked to the attack itself such as planning, training, raising funds, and so on, also occur on American soil (18 U.S.C. § 2331).

With regard to the September 11, 2001 attacks on the World Trade Center, the plane hijackers were foreign nationals who subscribed to Al Qaeda, a terrorist organization centralized in the Middle East. The perpetrators conducted the majority of their planning and training efforts overseas. Although the attacks themselves occurred in New York City, they crossed national borders. Therefore, this was an act of international terrorism.

Terrorist activity can be further classified based upon the mode of attack. For instance, terrorism may take the shape of person-to-person violence, such as is perpetrated by Islamic State of Iraq and Syria (ISIS); nuclear terrorism, which involves the use of weapons of mass destruction; bioterrorism, which uses biological agents (e.g., anthrax) as weapons; cyberterrorism, which perpetrates attacks virtually; or ecoterrorism, which seeks to (violently) destroy or financially cripple businesses that pose a threat to the environment.

Psychology of Terrorism

Understanding the psychological underpinnings of terrorism and the relevance of group dynamics is a particularly difficult task. What makes someone decide to join a terrorist movement in the first place? Research reveals that while terrorists do not present with severe psychopathology per se, they do tend to share common distorted beliefs and negative emotions. For example, terrorists often feel angry and marginalized by society.

They believe that their current political affiliation or involvement does not afford them the leverage with which to effect change. Additionally, the majority of people who are open to terrorist recruitment and/or radicalization tend to identify with victims of the perceived injustice that they oppose, and believe that violently aggressing against a governing body does not constitute wrongful behavior. Furthermore, these individuals typically have close ties to people who are sympathetic to a terrorist cause; they believe that joining a terrorist movement will provide them with both social and psychological rewards, including adventure, camaraderie, and purpose (DeAngelis, 2009).

According to *terror management theory*, developed by Pyszczynski, Greenberg, and Solomon (1997), people cling to cultural and religious values as a way of protecting themselves from a subconscious fear of death. Throughout various studies, the researchers presented subliminal reminders of mortality to people in the United States, Iran, and Israel. After the subjects were reminded of their fragility, in-group identity among all three participant groups was enhanced, and the subjects were primed to condone violence against the out-group. For instance, the Americans were more likely to support the use of military warfare against Islamic extremists, even when that would mean the killing of innocent civilians. The Iranian participants were more apt to advocate suicide bombings in order to target Westerners, and the Israeli subjects similarly supported violence against Palestine (DeAngelis, 2009; Pyszczynski, Solomon, & Greenberg, 2003).

A conversation about the psychological dynamics of terrorism must also address the impact of a *collectivist mentality*. This communally focused mindset dictates that the social whole is of greater value than any single person. Through its lens, individuals are viewed as disposable and those who subscribe to its premise are willing to sacrifice themselves for the group's larger cause. Individuals who have achieved little personal success are more likely to be lured by the sense of security and greater meaning associated with collectivist terror groups. Also related is the notion that terrorism can be understood as reactive aggression to the fear of cultural extinction (i.e., that radical movements and the fundamentalist way of life are under attack and may be annihilated) (DeAngelis, 2009).

Responding to Ideologically Motivated Threats

Terrorist threats—especially international ones—primarily come to the attention of the intelligence community and federal law enforcement. However, assessing such threats is most effective when joint investigations are conducted. It is crucial for terrorism task force agents to initiate and maintain close contact with local law enforcement in order to evaluate a suspect's past behavior. Agents should query whether the individual has a history of violence, has begun outwardly supporting extremist or radical viewpoints, or has engaged in other concerning behaviors. Additionally, investigators should interview the suspect while remaining mindful that if the individual has in fact been indoctrinated, he or she will be willing to sacrifice him or herself for the cause. Additionally, collateral interviews should be conducted with family, friends, and colleagues in order to corroborate the threat potential (Department of Homeland Security, 2015a).

Throughout the course of these interviews, investigators should examine the role of stressors in the suspect's life. Current and past stressors should be identified; consideration should be given to problems affecting career, finances, relationships, or health. Additionally, contacts with the criminal justice system should be reviewed. Once the stressors themselves have been detected, the suspect's perception of these event(s) should be explored. In other words, agents should draw conclusions about the effect of these stressful situations on the suspect's mindset as well as on his or her behavior. Evaluating whether the individual has acted violently in response to extreme stress in the past may lend critical insight into his or her risk of future violence. Additionally, law enforcement should assess the suspect's access to social support and other emotional or psychological assistance. What are the suspect's options for managing stress? Does he or she have prosocial coping mechanisms or does he or she feel that there are no other options and therefore, there is nothing left to lose? (Department of Homeland Security, 2015b).

As is the case with school shooters, understanding a terror suspect's perception of negative events and his or her response to them is important when evaluating a potential threat. Responses to stress are highly subjective experiences, which are influenced by emotionality, psychological health, cultural identity, access to social supports, schemas, attitudes, beliefs, and biases. Remember, the best indicator of future behavior is past behavior.

HOSTAGE NEGOTIATION

Another important application of threat assessment involves evaluating the danger inherent to hostage crises. These assessments seek to inform law enforcement's critical response by providing predictive insight into the hostage taker's motivation/intent, his or her likely response to police, and the risk of fatality to the victim(s). In certain cases, force may be indicated, while in others, negotiation may offer a more peaceful resolution.

In 1994, a Kansas City man held his stepson hostage at gunpoint inside the family home. The hostage taker's estranged wife was able to escape the house following a lengthy standoff with law enforcement. Then, as police breached the house, the perpetrator barricaded himself and the hostage in a bedroom. After several hours, officers saw the opportunity to overpower and disarm the offender. However, as they did so, the teenage hostage ran from the room. Upon seeing an individual running frantically toward police, an officer shot him, fearing for his own life (Alm, 1994). This scenario highlights the importance of matching resolution and de-escalation techniques with the perpetrator's motivation and the potential for deadly harm.

Types of Hostage Takers

All hostage situations are different in large part because of the variety among hostage takers. These offenders can be classified into four categories: political activists/terrorists, criminals, individuals suffering from psychological disturbance, and prisoners (Fulero & Wrightsman, 2009). As previously discussed in this chapter, the terrorist acts perpetrated by political and religious extremists are motivated by an array of aims; hostage taking by such terrorists is no different. Specifically, taking hostages supports political terrorists' desire to demonstrate the government's inability to protect its people, causes widespread fear, generates publicity, and creates leverage with which to demand the release of POWs. You will recall the complete commitment to the collectivist mentality that is prevalent among terrorists; they have extensively planned their actions, and are willing to die for their cause. Therefore, they are the most difficult type of hostage taker with which to negotiate (Maher, 1977).

According to Maher (1977), mentally ill hostage takers pose the greatest threat, as their crimes stem from their own delusional or paranoid perceptions of the world. These thoughts are often unknown to or not well understood by law enforcement. While studies reveal that 50% of hostage takers may suffer from mental illness (Borum & Strentz, 1992; Grubb, 2010), early research suggests that criminals who take hostages during the commission of a crime are the most common of the four subtypes (Hassel, 1975 as cited in Fuselier, 1988). For example, a bank robber who takes a teller hostage in order to facilitate his or her escape would fit into this cat-egory. Prisoner hostage takers, on the other hand, are inmates who take hostages as a tactic to try and gain leverage (Fulero & Wrightsman, 2009). They often demand improved correctional conditions, better treatment, or additional privileges while incarcerated.

Police Response to Hostage Crises

A successful resolution to a hostage crisis is one in which there is no loss of life. According to Miller (2007), containment and negotiation tactics result in an astounding 95% success rate, meaning that in all but 5% of such incidents, there are no fatalities of hostages, police personnel, or hos-tage takers. While there is a potentially imminent threat of violence or death for the duration of a hostage crisis, experts pinpoint three particu-larly volatile points during such an event. The first is during the initial 15 to 45 minutes of the crisis, as this often generates confusion and panic among all parties involved. Second is the surrender of the hostage taker, as he or she may be highly emotional or ambivalent about turning him or herself over to police. Moreover, this part of the process requires a highly coordinated effort by crisis team members. Third, when force is used in order to rescue the hostages, it carries with it the greatest risk of casualty. This is likely due in part to the fact that when police proceed with tacti-cal measures, it is because negotiation has failed and one or more hos-tages have already been killed or injured, and the hostage taker's violence is escalating. Additionally, should a firefight ensue, the risk of crossfire raises the threat of violence against not only the hostages, but the officers as well (Miller, 2007).

Approximately 30%–58% of law enforcement agencies have estab-lished crisis intervention teams, which are responsible for addressing hostage situations (Bartol & Bartol, 2012). These teams consist of a team leader who is in charge of organizing efforts and making decisions about tactical deployment, a primary negotiator, as well as one or more second-ary negotiators. Hostage crises can range in duration from several hours to several days. Therefore, the primary negotiator is likely to require a break. Also, if there is a language barrier or communication deficit, the secondary negotiator may be of assistance. There is also a designated intelligence officer, whose job it is to gather information about the suspect, such as past criminal behavior and mental health history. A communica-tion officer facilitates regular and consistent communication among team members and a press officer provides an accurate overview to the media without compromising the operation. Additionally, a skilled tactical team is on hand for forcible response. Tactical measures, such as using sniper fire against the offender, gassing the building, using flash-bangs, or gaining forced entry are all implemented with the utmost discretion and are limited to cases in which serious injury or death to the hostages is imminent (Miller, 2007). As you can see, all members of the team should be well-versed in the psychological aspects of crisis response.

Psychological Strategies for De-Escalating Threats

Once the crime scene has been secured, it is important to establish contact with the hostage taker as soon as possible. Because face-to-face contact presents the most risk of harm, telephone communication is preferred. As referenced in Chapter 9, establishing rapport is of paramount importance. The negotiator should address the hostage taker respectfully and speak calmly and slowly, keeping in mind that his or her tone of voice and rate of speech can serve to either agitate or calm the perpetrator. Negotiators should use vocabulary relevant to the offender's level of language comprehension so that he or she does not feel as though authorities are talking down to him or her. The primary focus of any negotiation is about what the hostage taker can do from this point forward to avoid loss of life. To that end, the subject's criminal behavior should be minimized and emphasis should be placed on what he or she can do to improve the situation. For instance, in the case of a bank robber who took hostages as a means or preventing his or her own capture, a negotiator might say, "Right now, this is only attempted robbery. No one has been hurt," or if someone has been hurt, "No one else needs to get hurt" (Miller, 2007).

When assessing the risk of violence in a hostage situation, police should consider the fact that close to 80% of hostage crises are relationship-driven, meaning that there is a preexisting relationship between the hostage taker and the hostage(s). Such crimes are typically precipitated by perceived injustices within the relationship, other relationship difficulties, or resentment (Van Hasselt et al., 2005). These scenarios most often occur as a form of family or workplace violence and present a higher risk of serious injury or death for the victim(s) due to the fact that such hostages usually have either personal meaning to the offender or are symbolic targets. Additionally, such hostage takers are more likely to be suffering from significant mental health symptoms, such as florid psychosis. They are also more likely to be agitated, physically or emotionally exhausted, intoxicated, suicidal, or homicidal. Therefore, negotiation techniques should encompass suicide and/or homicide intervention (Miller, 2007).

When faced with a hostage taker who has mental illness, and is specifically experiencing delusions, it may seem logical to tell the individual that his or her beliefs are unrealistic or wrong and to focus on resolving the situation at hand. However, in order to establish a rapport and advance toward the goal of rescuing the hostage(s), officers must make the offender feel heard. Challenging the hostage taker's delusional beliefs too early will likely result in an inability to establish rapport. For example, imagine that you are responding to a man who is holding hostages on the subway because he believes that they are government operatives who have been sent to kill him. Telling him that he is wrong, paranoid, or ill serves to undermine one of his core beliefs. Instead, remember that the delusions, hallucinations, or paranoid cognitions of an offender who has a psychotic disorder, are in fact, very real to that person. To understand his or her intent, work to understand the impact and presentation of his or her illness (Ainsworth, 2002).

Special Considerations for Police

During hostage crises, teamwork and sustained focus are essential. Negotiations must be monitored consistently to determine progress or impending violence and thus require quick and psychologically sound decisions. When gathering intelligence about a suspect in order to infer potential risk of violence, many of the same issues are relevant as are with school shootings and other types of threats. For those aspiring to be an integral part of a crisis team, be prepared for years of training and learning to understand the psychology of hostage taking. Additionally, significant "on the job" training is required in order for responders to adapt to these chaotic environments where the risk of personal injury is ever present.

13

Reentry

WHAT IS REENTRY?

Reentry is an offender's transition from incarceration to the community. In 2011, studies show that, 1,885 inmates were released from state or federal custody each day (Carson & Sobel, 2012). By the end of that year, nearly 5 million offenders were being supervised in the community (Maruschak & Parks, 2012). The success of reentry exerts a profound effect upon the safety of society. Therefore, developing insight into the obstacles faced by former offenders and their relationship to recidivism is a critical activity for law enforcement.

The Challenges of Reentry

Reentry is a complicated and often challenging process for offenders as well as for their families, friends, and communities. Former inmates are likely to have difficulty securing employment due to a lack of education or job-related skills and often face limited housing options. Additionally, establishing or re-establishing connections with family can be arduous. Perhaps unsurprisingly, reentrants are likely to struggle with substance abuse and mental health issues (National Institute of Justice, 2015).

Berson (2013) describes such challenges as "collateral consequences." Criminal convictions, whether relating to misdemeanors or felonies, result in a host of sanctions and disqualifications for offenders. These in turn place an unforeseen burden on these individuals when they try to reenter society and live productive, crime-free lives. The impact of collateral

283

consequences often extends beyond the point at which a former offender has been rehabilitated and may last indefinitely.

To better understand how collateral consequences apply, consider how incarceration interrupts many offenders' educational or professional aspirations. When someone is remanded to custody, any higher education, job training, or promotion-eligible employment in which he or she is involved is put on hold for the duration of his or her imprisonment. However, being released from jail or prison does not necessarily ensure a return to business as usual. In fact, once someone has been convicted, employment opportunities diminish for a multitude of reasons.

First, certain industries require that employees be able to pass a background check. Second, individuals with certain types of offense histories are barred from obtaining employment in specific fields. For instance, community supervision conditions preclude paroled sex offenders from working in settings such as schools or with vulnerable populations (e.g., children, victims of domestic or sexual violence, older adults). Third, former felons may be denied access to government programs and miscellaneous benefits, including student loans. This means that they may be ill equipped for the fraction of employment opportunities available to them. Those offenders who do secure employment typically find work in low-skill jobs and make a significantly lower wage than they did prior to incarceration. As you can see, these difficulties are cyclical and particularly disheartening, given that social service providers cite lack of employment as the most crucial obstacle to successful reentry (Urban Institute, 2008).

Due to the employment barriers faced by ex-offenders, providing for a family is often difficult. Thus, the children of released prisoners are directly affected. Former inmates are frequently forced to rely upon family members for financial support. Additionally, they often have highly unstable housing situations, especially in the first year following incarceration. For example, a survey of released inmates in Cleveland, Ohio, reveals that nearly 70% of them had more than one residence in their first year back in the community (Urban Institute, 2008).

Due to the far-reaching effects of the aforementioned difficulties faced by reentrants, the Federal Bureau of Prisons (BOP) begins release preparations on an inmate's first day of his or her custodial sentence. In order to pave the way for a successful transition, prisoners at BOP facilities have access to vocational training, educational courses, and workshops focused on skills such as resume writing, job searching, and job retention.

RECIDIVISM AND REENTRY

Statistically, reentrants are considered at high risk for being rearrested. Across the United States, 68% of state and federal prisoners who were released in 1994 were subsequently arrested again. Additionally, over 50% returned to prison within their first 3 years in the community. An overwhelming 83% of prisoners analyzed in a Cleveland-based study reported at least one prior conviction, while many had lengthy arrest histories with multiple convictions. Interestingly, the vast majority of released offenders are rearrested for committing (technical) violations of parole (VOPs), rather than perpetrating new crimes (The Urban Institute, 2008).

Predictors of Recidivism

According to Andrews, Bonta, and Wormith (2006), the four most robust predictors of recidivistic behavior are the presence of a criminal history, antisocial personality features (poor self-management, anger, stimulation seeking, etc.), a pattern of antisocial thinking (attitudes supportive of criminal behavior, perception of neutral stimuli as malevolent or threatening), and an antisocial peer group. Additionally, substance abuse, minimal engagement in prosocial leisure activities, unstable employment, and family problems are considered moderate risk factors. Some theorists posit that clinical variables associated with mental illness (e.g., diagnosis and treatment history) are also directly related to criminal behavior. However, a meta-analysis conducted by Bonta, Law, and Hanson (1998) found that such factors did not clearly predict the commission of a new general and/or violent offense. Similarly, Douglas, Guy, and Hart (2009) found no statistically significant correlation between psychosis and violence in a sample of forensic psychiatric patients, and Phillips and colleagues characterized untreated mental illness as at best a weak predictor of recidivism among offenders (Phillips et al., 2005). Therefore, while psychological disturbance might be the most obvious difficulty in an offender's life, it appears to relate weakly to reoffense or revocation of conditional release (Skeem, Winter, Kennealy, Louden, & Tatar 2014).

So why then are offenders with mental illness overrepresented in the criminal justice system? Why do they get caught in the "revolving prison door?" While there may not be a direct causal link between psychiatric conditions and criminality, Skeem and Peterson (2012) theorize that prodromal symptoms of mental illness may cause people to gravitate toward environments that promote antisocial thinking and behavior and thus encourage

285

the development of general risk factors for criminal activity. Therefore it follows that the strongest predictors of violent reoffense in individuals with mental illness are also relevant to individuals without psychiatric disturbance. Such risk factors include antisocial personality characteristics, juvenile delinquency, criminal versatility, and age of onset of criminal behavior (Bonta et al., 1998; Hall, Miraglia, Lee, Chard-Wierschem, & Sawyer, 2012). Additionally, antisocial cognition is as common among offenders with psychological disorders as it is among their nondisordered counterparts (Morgan, Fisher, Dunn, Mandracchia, & Murray, 2010; Wolff, Morgan, Shi, Huening, & Fisher, 2011). It should be noted, however, that offenders with a dual diagnosis of a major psychiatric condition such as bipolar disorder, major depression, or schizophrenia as well as a substance abuse disorder have a significantly higher risk of parole revocation due to a technical violation or new offense in the 12 months following their release than do individuals with *either* a diagnosis of mental illness or substance abuse. These findings highlight the need to better understand the relationship between dual diagnoses and specific social and behavioral factors that forecast failure of conditional release (Baillargeon et al., 2010).

If mental illness occurs in parallel to criminality, traditional psychiatric treatment will be insufficient for achieving successful reentry. For instance, compliance with an antipsychotic medication regime may inhibit an offender with delusions from making a preemptive strike against a perceived persecutor. However, psychotropic medication is unlikely to dissuade him or her from picking fights with individuals whom he or she believes have treated him or her with disrespect (Skeem et al., 2014). The takeaway message for law enforcement as well as for clinical practitioners is that the efficacy of reentry programs that target the most and the strongest criminogenic needs, far surpasses that of programs which address only noncriminogenic disturbances in the offenders' lives (Lowencamp, Latessa, & Smith, 2006).

Contextual Factors

Research suggests that the neighborhood to which a released prisoner returns has a significant impact on both recidivism and employment outcomes. In an analysis of inmates released from Michigan state penitentiaries, those individuals who returned to more disadvantaged neighborhoods were more likely to abscond from parole, commit a technical violation, and have poorer labor outcomes. However, returning to a more affluent community was associated with an overall lower risk of rearrest, absconding, and returning to prison on a technical VOP. Additionally, reentrants to the wealthier neighborhoods enjoyed more positive employment outcomes with higher rates of employment and better wages. While the question of what constitutes a "risky" environment for a reentrant is complex, it is important to note the relationship between neighborhoods and employment outcomes, as being gainfully employed substantially reduces the risk of recidivism (National Institute of Justice, 2015).

PAROLE

Reentrants can be divided into two categories: those whose sentences expired (maxed out) in prison and are therefore not subject to community supervision, and those who will be mandated to such supervision. When an inmate serves out his or her full sentence minus jail credit, he or she is released directly into the community. However, many inmates fulfill a portion of their sentences in prison and then serve out the remainder under parole supervision.

Parole is a form of "conditional release" in that if an offender violates it by failing to meet his or her supervision conditions, he or she will be remanded back into custody to serve out the duration of the sentence. *Discretionary parole* exists in jurisdictions in which the parole board has the ultimate authority to determine parole eligibility either statutorily or administratively. *Mandatory parole*, on the other hand, occurs when sentencing statutes determine that an inmate will be conditionally released after serving a specific portion of his or her sentence (Bureau of Justice Statistics, 2016). These requisite percentages are codified on a jurisdictional basis.

Divisions of parole are often subdivided into specialized units including (Marion County, 2015; New Jersey State Parole Board, 2007; Texas Department of Criminal Justice, 2016):

- *Electronic monitoring (or global positioning system, GPS)*: The officers assigned to this unit supervise individuals ordered to wear electronic tracking devices.
- *Sex offender management*: These parole officers (POs) are tasked with supervising perpetrators who have committed sex crimes ranging from public indecency to forcible rape.
- *Fugitive apprehension*: Those serving in this unit investigate individuals who have absconded from parole and carry out missions to recapture them.

- *Gang violence*: These POs supervise known gang members and work to prevent gang recruitment.
- *Mental health*: These specialized caseloads require consistent contact between officers and mental health professionals in order to rehabilitate offenders with severe and persistent mental illness (SPMI).
- *Family/DV*: These units focus on domestic violence cases and often make referrals to batterer intervention programs.

As you can see, the aforementioned units require that officers receive highly specialized training and be well-versed in not only the psychological underpinnings of various types of offenses, but also the emotional and psychological impact of reentry.

Eligibility

Determining an inmate's eligibility for parole typically begins by calculating his or her parole eligibility date or PED. In many states, this occurs after the person has served a specific percentage (i.e., one-third) of his or her sentence, provided that the court did not order a period of parole ineligibility. However, unless the release is mandatory, an offender is not guaranteed to be paroled; instead, his or her appropriateness to reside in the community will be assessed by the governing board. If an inmate has failed to become invested in or has been uncooperative with his or her own rehabilitation, or if there is a reasonable expectation that he or she will violate the conditions of supervision, the request for parole will likely be denied (New Jersey State Parole Board, 2007).

EVIDENCE-BASED PRACTICES FOR SUPERVISION

Officers who supervise offenders in the community are responsible for not only enforcing the law, but also assisting individuals with successful reentry. To that end, evidence-based practices (EBPs) have been established, a hallmark of which is the use of risk-needs assessments. Such evaluations determine offenders' criminogenic needs and the likelihood of their success upon release; they therefore influence release decisions and inform supervision strategies (National Conference of State Legislatures, 2016).

Such assessments specifically address reentrants' criminal histories, educational or vocational needs, addiction/dependency difficulties, psychological vulnerabilities, the presence or absence of antisocial schema, association with an antisocial peer group, impulsivity, and other criminal risk factors (Hooley, 2010). They assist officers in the development of individualized case plans with relevant supervision targets and conditions (New Jersey State Parole, 2007). Additionally, they are essential to determining the appropriate intensity for supervision based on the individual's risk to reoffend or otherwise commit a violation. Moreover, such evaluations result in referrals to appropriate programming, such as offense-specific treatment or addiction counseling.

As you can see, EBP requires a collaborative effort from officers, mental health practitioners, and other support professionals. It also encompasses several components, which are meant to work in tandem with the risk-needs assessment (Hooley, 2010):

- *Individual motivators*: It is important to determine what specifically motivates an individual offender. For example, perhaps he or she wants to return home/be successfully discharged from supervision in order to be a positive parental role model. The earlier that intrinsic or extrinsic motivation is determined, the better.
- *Appropriate interventions*: Requiring offenders to attend programs that do not target their specific needs is futile. Reentrants should only be mandated to programs that speak to their individualized needs (e.g., drug counseling, job skills, mental health treatment, offense-specific therapy, etc.). Enrolling them in programs that do not target interventions that resonate with their specific issue(s) can create frustration and resistance.
- *Cognitive restructuring*: This literally refers to rewiring an offender's brain to think differently. The vast majority of individuals in prison or on parole have developed negative thought processes and maladaptive coping responses. They are more likely to interpret events negatively and therefore respond with hostility or violence. Trained practitioners using a cognitive behavioral approach can assist this population with identifying and changing negative thoughts, which in turn changes the associated negative emotion and resulting illegal or harmful behavioral response. For a list of typical types of cognitive distortions experienced by the forensic population, see Figure 13.1.
- *Positive reinforcement*: Most inmates (and subsequently parolees) have become accustomed to two things: being admonished

289

- Black and white thinking: This is all-or-nothing thinking. For example, if an offender's wife leaves him, he sees himself as a total failure or completely unlovable.

- Personalization: This occurs when individuals hold themselves responsible for and assume guilt for negative events, which they did not in fact cause.

- Generalization: A single negative situation is viewed as a pervasive pattern. People who subscribe to this distortion will often use phrases such as "you always" or "you never" in the midst of a confrontation. An exaggerated form of this is assigning negative and emotionally damaging labels to others or to one's self based upon a singular event.

- Minimization: Offenders often diminish the severity or harmfulness of their behavior as a way to assuage guilt. For instance, a sex offender might reason that his or her offense wasn't that bad because he or she didn't physically injure the victim or threaten him or her with a weapon.

- Justification: Justification provides an excuse for criminal behavior, such as "I attacked him because he provoked me," or "I embezzled because the company wasn't paying me enough for all of my effort."

- Catastrophizing: This entails the magnification or over-exaggeration of the importance of negative events. If something goes wrong, people holding this distortion, are likely to view it as "the end of the world."

- Emotional logic: With emotional reasoning, people allow their negative feelings to affect how they perceive the world.

- Drawing conclusions: This is the anticipation of a negative outcome or the interpretation of neutral acts as negative, without any factual basis.

Figure 13.1 Cognitive distortions.

and having sanctions imposed upon them. Some of them have rarely ever received positive feedback for appropriate behavior. Therefore, incorporating positive reinforcement in the form of verbal recognition can serve to enhance their self-image and create an inherent desire to be successful.

- *Ongoing support*: Once a prisoner has been released to the community, ongoing social support is of paramount importance. It can be difficult for reentrants to avoid former friends and associates, especially if they were deeply entrenched in gang culture. Therefore, it is incumbent upon community correctional

professionals to ensure that these individuals reside in a prosocial environment and to provide them with access to therapeutic
support.

THE IMPACT OF JUSTICE INVOLVEMENT

When considering the effects of reentry on a former inmate, we must first
consider the nature of institutionalization and its psychological influence.
While it is a misconception that incarceration inevitably leads to mental illness, acclimating to the prison environment is a difficult feat that
requires the acquisition of survival skills, which outside of a correctional
facility, are dysfunctional. Such adaptations are considered a typical (as
opposed to pathological) response to the unnatural conditions of prison.
However, they become destructive when they are internalized or long
lasting (Haney, 2001).

On the first day of their custodial sentence, prisoners are confronted
with the rigidity of life behind bars, as well as the overwhelming lack
of privacy and deprivation of liberty. Therefore, it is not uncommon for
offenders to eventually become dependent upon the institutional structure. Because the limits set within a penal facility are so clear and continu-
ous, and infractions are associated with regulated penalties, some inmates
may begin to rely strictly upon external controls. When this imposed set
of limitations is withdrawn, highly institutionalized individuals may find
that they no longer know how to impose self-control or refrain from illegal, harmful, or self-destructive behaviors (Haney, 2001).

Furthermore, because prison is an innately dangerous environment,
inmates quickly become hypervigilant and begin to approach others
with a sense of distrust. Inmates often put up a tough and/or threatening façade so that they will not become targets of violence. According to
McCorkle (1992), "unless an inmate can convincingly project an image
that conveys the potential for violence, he is likely to be dominated and
exploited throughout the duration of his sentence."

Creating and managing such an image requires the ability to anticipate others' reactions to various behaviors. The imposition of this high-
stakes form of self-monitoring, results in carefully planned and measured
emotional responses, and subsequent emotional overcontrol. Maintaining
the "prison mask" can lead inmates to develop flat affect and psychological distancing, both of which impede their ability to establish healthy,
enduring, and fulfilling social relationships (Haney, 2001). Therefore, the

likelihood that they will reap the protective benefits of a strong social support network upon release is decreased.

Perhaps unsurprisingly, many offenders find the degradation of prison to be deeply stigmatizing and damaging to their sense of self-worth. For some, incarceration is so painful and disturbing that they experience posttraumatic stress responses once released. According to Masten and Garmezy (1985), historical and background risk factors (as outlined in Table 13.1) in combination with early childhood trauma increase the likelihood that some individuals will engage in criminality. Then, once incarcerated, they find the unwanted proximity to violence, possibility of physical or sexual assault, lack of respect, and lack of consideration for their well-being to be unfortunately familiar and reminiscent of childhood. The presence of these factors in combination with the harsh nature

Table 13.1   Risk Factors

Early-Life Risks	Ongoing Risks	Immediate Triggers
Abuse (emotional, physical, or sexual)	Negative emotionality/ anger	Negative emotionality (anger, anxiety, depression)
Inability to communicate feelings or to assert oneself	Substance abuse	Lack of empathy
Peer rejection	Poor self-image	Poor self-esteem
Exposure to violence	High-risk and/or violent peer group	Isolation, social skills deficits, social anxiety
Cognitive or learning deficit(s)	Marital discord or other relationship difficulties	Cognitive distortions
Family issues (alcoholism, marital discord, divorce, domestic violence)	Violent or abusive fantasies	Over-controlled emotional responses
Neglect by either parent	Antisocial schema	Extreme stress
Difficulty forming appropriate attachments	Lack of prosocial interests and/or coping mechanisms	External scenarios: serious illness, death of a loved one, end of a marriage, termination of employment, etc.
	Boredom	Boredom

and punitive tactics employed by correctional facilities equates to "re-traumatization" for many offenders (Haney, 2001).

While few people are unaffected by correctional confinement, the extent, severity, and longevity of consequences are directly correlated with the harshness, dangerousness, and psychological difficulties associated with the specific prison environment. A multitude of ex-offenders continue to experience the aforementioned difficulties with social interaction once paroled. Compounding this issue, they may feel as though their family and friends have either moved on without them or no longer know/understand them. This feeling of isolation can be seriously damaging and increase an offender's risk of reoffense.

Many parolees also return to habitual drug and/or alcohol use after their release to the community. Such behaviors are often the offender's way of self-medicating. While diagnosable psychiatric conditions are treated with either psychotropic medication and/or therapy within the prison environment, once released, many offenders lack immediate access to mental health services. Therefore, they may stop taking their medication altogether or have a gap in treatment.

COMMUNITY REENTRY PROGRAMS

As you will recall from Chapter 6, criminal risk indicators fall into three categories: static, dynamic, and risk management. These factors denote not only an offender's statistical probability to recidivate, but also the things with which he or she needs help in order to live a good, safe, law-abiding life. Therefore, community correctional officers are encouraged to avail themselves of the variety of community programs available to assist the individuals on their caseloads with reentry.

Residential Reentry Centers

Perhaps better known as "halfway houses," residential reentry centers (RRCs) provide assistance to individuals who are approaching their release date. Within the confines of a secure and structured environment, offenders begin to engage in authorized community-based activities. They are held accountable for the duration of their stay via the use of random headcounts at the facility. They are only permitted to leave when an outside activity, such as a job interview, counseling, or work, has been preapproved. Upon their return, inmates may be required to undergo a random drug and alcohol screening (Bureau of Prisons, n.d.).

RRCs provide programming to assist inmates with rebuilding their ties to the community in order to reduce their risk of recidivism. Skills training, which targets emotional and financial stability, is offered. For example, RRC staff will help offenders develop interview skills, write resumes, and provide linkage to potential employers. RRCs also help inmates to locate and secure appropriate housing to which they can be released. In addition to receiving drug counseling, inmates are afforded access to medical and mental health treatment so that they can transfer to the community with the requisite supply of prescription medication (Bureau of Prisons, n.d.).

Assessment Centers

Similar in concept to RRCs, assessment centers provide a "step-down" process for inmates who have achieved full-minimum status. These secure facilities are located in various states across the United States. Unlike at halfway houses, residents at assessment centers are not permitted to leave the premises under any circumstances. Despite this restriction, residents wear their street clothes and move freely about the facility. Residents are thoroughly evaluated while residing at assessment centers and compre-hensive plans targeting their needs are established. Residents also receive an orientation to offense-specific treatment in preparation for transition to a halfway house. As assessment centers partner with federal, state, and local law enforcement, such programs are viewed as a step closer to com-munity reintegration, while also being one (mis)step away from returning to prison (Community Education Centers, Inc., 2016).

PRACTICAL CONSIDERATIONS FOR OFFICERS

The two main objectives of most correctional (and community correc-tional) agencies are facilitating rehabilitation and ensuring compliance with the law and prescribed supervision conditions by holding offenders accountable. As you might guess, these two goals are often at odds with one another (Walters, Clark, Gingerich, & Meltzer, 2007). Historically, two differing approaches have been utilized to change offender behavior: deterrence strategies and constructional strategies. *Deterrence strategies* focus on punitive measures, such as incarceration, fines, GPS monitoring, and additional supervision conditions, in order to discourage reoffense. *Constructional strategies,* on the other hand, seek to reduce undesirable behavior by creating opportunities for positive interactions and prosocial skills development (McGuire, 2002).

Not all of the tactics employed by the criminal justice system are equally successful with regard to reducing reoffense. Research reveals that punishment-oriented programs lack the intended positive outcome; in fact, those programs devoid of a treatment component can actually increase recidivism (Gendreau, Goggin, Cullen, & Paparozzi, 2002; Gendreau, Little, & Goggin, 1996; Taxman, 1999). More recent information speaks to the need for parole and probation officers to suspend confrontational approaches and to develop a collaborative relationship with offenders while holding them accountable (Clark, 2006).

Motivational Interviewing

As we know, methods that fall under the umbrella of EBP have a measurable outcome (i.e., reduced rate of reoffense, increased community safety, etc.), which is substantiated by scientific evidence (Andrews & Bonta, 2003; Miller, Zweben, & Johnson, 2005). As you read in Chapter 6, effective interventions are comprised of three principles: risk, needs, and responsivity. Specific responsivity means that interventions are tailored to the individual needs of a particular offender and should consider the following (Taxman, Shepardson, & Byrne, 2004):

- The offender's readiness to change
- His or her possible motivation to change
- The style of interaction that would be most effective with him or her

This is where motivational interviewing can be a significant asset for law enforcement. *Motivational interviewing (MI)* is a change-focused approach for fulfilling specific responsivity needs by suggesting a style of communication that is more likely to engage the offender and motivate behavioral change. An individual's responsivity needs are directly correlated with his or her own motivation for creating change.

Previously, correctional officers held the belief that motivation was a characteristic that an offender either had or lacked, and until an individual was ready to change his or her behavior, there was little assistance that could be offered by law enforcement. Per this viewpoint, POs were agents of the law who would enforce conditions; they were not active participants in the change process for their supervisees (Walters et al., 2007). Furthermore, POs formerly viewed motivation through the lens of compliance. In other words, when an offender did as he or she was directed, it was assumed that the individual was motivated to change. However, new evidence shows that compliance does not necessarily equate to a desire to change.

For instance, consider two offenders who have been mandated to attend anger management classes. The first one agrees to participate in order to avoid jail time, while the second person feels that the course has something important to offer him. He is concerned that his inability to control his rage will result in the loss of his marriage or his job (Walters et al., 2007); he is internally motivated to use the program as a vehicle for change. Therefore, the second offender is more likely to change his behavior, while the first offender is more likely to comply without experiencing a core change. The MI process meets each offender where he or she is at and tailors the process of change to his or her potential motivating factors and communication style. MI is comprised of six stages that represent an offender's journey of change (Walters et al., 2007):

- *Precontemplation*: During this initial stage, an offender does not recognize the need to change or has decided that his or her current (unacceptable) behavior is most beneficial. To combat these beliefs, officers should develop a rapport and increase the individual's awareness of the problem behavior and the need to change it.
- *Contemplation*: At this point in the process, the offender realizes that there *may* be a problem, but experiences mixed emotions with regard to exacting change. Officers should acknowledge the offender's ambivalence and highlight the discrepancies between his or her current (antisocial) behavior and his or her values or future goals.
- *Preparation*: In this phase, the offender is getting ready to change, but is figuring out how to go about it. He or she may begin asking questions or developing a plan. Officers should help the individual build self-confidence and offer options and advice, while resisting the urge to push him or her.
- *Action*: During this stage, the offender is actively making changes. Law enforcement should help offenders to establish realistic goals and monitor their progress.

- *Maintenance*: At this juncture, the offender has already made changes and needs to focus on maintaining them over time, even in the face of challenges. Officers should provide support and encouragement and should assist reentrants in managing their triggers.
- *Relapse*: When making significant life changes, falling back into old patterns of behavior is always a possibility. When someone relapses, his or her supervising officer should address the negative behavior without shaming the person. An honest conversation should address where the individual went off track, and he or she should be encouraged to try again.

Motivational interviewing is effective because it focuses on the specific goals most important to an individual offender. It additionally forges a collaborative bond between the officer and the reentrant; this serves to help the offender to become invested in his or her own positive change. MI can also be an extremely useful tool for mental health clinicians working to rehabilitate offenders. Table 13.2 highlights the primary focuses of motivational interviewing.

Trauma-Informed Care

In addition to identifying individual motivators, part of effective responsivity is providing trauma-informed care (TIC) to inmates in prison and as they transition to the community. As mentioned earlier,

Table 13.2   Motivational Interviewing: Primary Objectives

1	Develop a collaborative relationship between the offender and the supervising officer.
2	Motivate the offender while holding him or her accountable.
3	Target dynamic (changeable) risk factors.
4	Decrease the offender's impulsivity by encouraging prosocial interests and developing natural talents.
5	Assist the offender in increasing his or her social support network.
6	Discourage the offender from associating with antisocial peers.
7	Adapt interventions and interaction-style to offender's learning style, cognitive ability, and motivating factors.

Source: Walters, S. T. et al., *A guide for probation and parole: Motivating offenders to change.* Retrieved from: https://www.victimsofcrime.org/docs/restitution-toolkit/c9_nic-motivating-offenders.pdf?sfvrsn=2, 2007.

many offenders have experienced significant exposure to violence throughout their lives and thus exhibit symptoms of posttraumatic stress. Abrupt detoxification or overbearing or punitive authority figures, in combination with the ongoing threat of physical harm, can result in re-traumatization. Therefore, officers should consider the impact of trauma on individuals trying to successfully reintegrate into society and incorporate trauma recovery principles into their supervision styles (Miller & Najavits, 2012).

TIC requires a paradigm shift from the traditional viewpoint that offenders are inherently bad people to the idea that they are psychically injured. Rather than characterizing their criminal acts as immoral, officers are challenged to view them as a result of early trauma. Furthermore, focus should be placed on collaboration instead of managing or controlling offender behavior, and POs should acknowledge reentrants' ambivalence to change as opposed to classifying them as "resistant." Additionally, addiction and other self-destructive behaviors should not be considered "evil" or "immoral" choices, but rather be recognized as maladaptive coping behaviors reflective of the need to survive underlying trauma (Levenson, 2016).

For some reentry professionals, this significant change in mindset may be difficult, as we are conditioned to believe that *perpetrators* and not *victims* are subject to community supervision. However, failing to approach offenders from a holistic standpoint, which takes into consideration the impact of trauma on their reentry, is insufficient at best. Community correctional officers should avoid viewing trauma as a singular event, but rather as a defining series of experiences that profoundly influences an individual's identity (Levenson, 2016). When this level of understanding and compassion is achieved, parole and probation officers are more likely to build a strong rapport with offenders under their supervision. As a result, these officers become instrumental in assisting offenders with creating lasting change and, in turn, achieving successful reentry.

REFERENCES

18 U.S.C. § 2331

Aasscher, J. J., van Vugt, E. S., Stams, G. J. J. M., Dekovic, M., Eichelsheim, V. I., & Yousfi, S. (2011). The relationship between juvenile psychopathic traits, delinquency and (violent) recidivism: A meta-analysis. *Journal of Child Psychology and Psychiatry, 52,* 1134–1143.

Adam Walsh Child Protection and Safety Act. (2006).

Ahern, A. (2001). A biography of Aileen Wuornos. Retrieved from: www.courttv.com/onair/shows/mugshots/indepth/wuornos.html.

Ainsworth, P. B. (2002). *Psychology and policing.* Portland, OR: Willan.

Alison, L. J., Bennell, C., Mokros, A., & Ormerod, D. (2002). The personality paradox in offender profiling: A theoretical review of the processes involved in deriving background characteristics from crime scene actions. *Psychology, Public Policy, and Law, 8,* 115–135.

Allen, C. (1991). *Women and men who sexually abuse children: A comparative analysis.* Brandon, VT: The Safer Society Press.

Alm, R. (1994, February 5). Hostage wounded by police. *Minnesota Law Review, 37,* 427–439.

American Institute of CPAs (AICPA). (n.d.). Conducting effective interviews. Retrieved from: http://www.aicpa.org/InterestAreas/ForensicAndValuation/Resources/PractAidsGuidance/DownloadableDocuments/10834-378_interview%20whiite%20paper-FINAL-v1.pdf.

American Psychiatric Association. (2013). *Diagnostic and statistical manual of mental disorders* (5th ed.). Washington, DC: American Psychiatric Association.

American Psychological Association. (1984). Text of position on insanity defense. *APA Monitor, 15,* 11.

American Psychological Association. (2014). Mental illness not usually linked to crime, research finds. Retrieved from: http://www.apa.org/news/press/releases/2014/04/mental-illness-crime.aspx.

An Abuse, Rape, and Domestic Violence Aid and Resource Center (AARDVARC). (2011). Abusers, batterers, domestic violence offenders. Retrieved from: http://www.aardvarc.org/dv/batterer.shtml.

Andrews, D. A., & Bonta, J. (2003). *The psychology of criminal conduct* (3rd ed.). Cincinnati, OH: Anderson.

Andrews, D. A., & Bonta, J. L. (2006). *The psychology of criminal conduct* (4th ed.). Cincinnati, OH: Anderson.

Andrews, D. A., Bonta, J., & Wormith, S. J. (2006). The recent past and near future of risk and/or need assessment. *Crime and Delinquency, 52,* 7–27.

Anne Arundel County Police Department. (2012). Responding to persons with mental illness, emotional crisis, or physical disability: Written directive 3.

Retrieved from: http://www.aacounty.org/Police/RulesRegs/Sections17-19/1830RespondPersonsWithDisabilties.pdf.

Arata, C. (2002). Child sexual abuse and sexual revictimization. *Clinical Psychology, 9*, 135–164.

Archambault, J., Eisenga, H., Lisak, D., & Keenan, S. (2001). Sex offenders: Dynamics and interview techniques. In National Center for Women and Policing (Ed.), *Successfully investigating acquaintance sexual assault: A national training manual for law enforcement.* Washington, DC: U.S. Department of Justice.

Ariz, D. (2006, April 14). *United States v. Curran*, No. 2:06cr277. *Forensic Report.* Springfield, MO: U.S. Medical Center.

Arrigo, B. A., & Griffin, A. (2004). Serial murder and the case of Aileen Wuornos: Attachment theory, psychopathy, and predatory aggression. *Behavioral Sciences & the Law, 22*, 375–393.

Arrillagaap, P. (2006, April 14). Does Eric Clark deserve life in prison? *Arizona Daily Sun.* Retrieved from: http://azdailysun.com/news/does-eric-clark-deserve-life-in-prison/article_29719067-fdfe-5880-b6a4-e77e3e1e9658.html.

Associated Press. (1986, May 12). A crime that doesn't pay. *Kansas City Star*, p. 5A.

Associated Press. (2012a, December 14). U.S. judge says victims' bodies can prevent rape. *USA Today.* Retrieved from: http://www.usatoday.com/story/news/nation/2012/12/13/judge-women-rape-victims/1768673/.

Associated Press. (2012b, December 14). Calif. judge reprimanded for telling rape victim she "didn't put up a fight" and that her body would have "shut down" if she didn't want to have sex. *New York Daily News.* Retrieved from:http://www.nydailynews.com/news/national/judge-told-rape-victim-didn-put-fight-article-1.1220328.

Bachman, R., & Saltzman, L. E. (1995). *Violence against women: Estimates from the redesigned survey.* Washington, DC: U.S. Bureau of Justice Statistics.

Bailey, J. E., Kellermann, A. L., Somes, G. W., Banton, J. G., Rivera, F. P., & Rushforth, N. P. (1997). Risk factors for violent death of women in the home. *Archives of Internal Medicine, 157*, 777–892.

Baillargeon, J., Williams, B. A., Mellow, J., Harzke, A. J., Hoge, S. K., Baillargeon, G., & Greifinger, R. B. (2010). Parole revocation among prison inmates with psychiatric and substance use disorders. *Psychiatric Services, 60*(11), 1516–1521.

Barbaree, H. E., Hudson, S. M., & Seto, M. C. (1993). Sexual assault in society: The role of the juvenile offender. In H. E. Barbaree, W. L. Marshall, & S. W. Hudson (Eds.), *The juvenile sex offender* (pp. 10–11). New York, NY: Guilford Press.

Bartol, C. R., & Bartol, A. M. (2008). *Criminal behavior: A psychosocial approach* (8th ed.). Upper Saddle River, NJ: Pearson Prentice Hall.

Bartol, C. R., & Bartol, A. M. (2012). *Introduction to forensic psychology: Research and application* (3rd ed.). Los Angeles, CA: Sage.

Becker, J. V., Harris, C. D., & Sales, B. D. (1993). Juveniles who commit sexual offenses: A critical review of research. In G. C. N. Hall, R. Hirschman, J. Graham, & M. Zaragoza (Eds.), *Sexual aggression: Issues in etiology and assessment, treatment, and policy* (pp. 215–228). Washington, DC: Taylor & Francis.

Becker, J. V. (1998). What we know about the characteristics and treatment of adolescents who have committed sexual offenses. *Child Maltreatment, 3*, 317–329.

Bekerian, D. A., & Jackson, J. L. (1997). Critical issues in offender profiling. In J. L. Jackson, & D. A. Bekerian (Eds.), *Offender profiling: Theory, research, and practice* (pp. 209–220). New York, NY: John Wiley.

Bennell, C., & Canter, D. V. (2002). Linking commercial burglaries by modus operandi: Tests using regression and ROC analysis. *Science & Justice, 42*, 153–164.

Bennell, C., & Jones, N. J. (2005). Between a ROC and a hard place: A method for linking serial burglaries using an offender's modus operandi. *Journal of Investigative Psychology and Offender Profiling, 2*, 23–41.

Bernard, M. (2013). Rihanna and Chris Brown are proof that domestic violence is everyone's business. *Washington Post.* Retrieved from: https://www.washingtonpost.com/blogs/she-the-people/wp/2013/02/11/rihanna-and-chris-brown-are-proof-that-domestic-violence-is-everyones-business/.

Berson, S. B. (2013, May). Beyond the sentence: Understanding collateral consequences. *NIJ Journal, 272*, 25–28. National Institute of Justice: Office of Justice Programs.

Biography.com Editors. (2016a). Ferdinand Demara biography. Retrieved from: http://www.biography.com/people/ferdinand-demara-20648861.

Biography.com Editors. (2016b). Gary Ridgway biography. Retrieved from: http://www.biography.com/people/gary-ridgway-10073409.

Biography.com Editors. (2016c). Ted Bundy biography. Retrieved from: http://www.biography.com/people/ted-bundy-9231165.

Biography.com Editors. (2016d). Seung-Hui Cho biography. Retrieved from: http://www.biography.com/people/seung-hui-cho-235991.

Bixby, L. (1995, July 2). "Mad bomber" of Waterbury terrorized New York for 17 years. *Hartford Currant*, p. A6.

Black, M. C., Basile, K. C., Breiding, M. D., Smith, S. G., Walters, M. L., Merrick, M. T., ... Stevens, M. R. (2011). *National intimate partner and sexual violence survey: 2010 summary report.* Atlanta, GA: National Center for Injury Prevention and Control; Centers for Disease Control and Prevention.

Blair, K. S., Newman, C., Mitchell, D. G., Richell, R. A., Leonard, A., Morton, J., & Blair, R. J. R. (2006). Differentiating among prefrontal substrates in psychopathy: Neuropsychological test findings. *Neuropsychology, 20*, 153–165.

Bonta, J., Law, M., & Hanson, R. K. (1998). The prediction of criminal and violent recidivism among mentally disordered offenders: A meta-analysis. *Psychological Bulletin, 123*, 123–142.

Borum, R., Deane, M., Steadman, H., & Morrissey, J. (1998). Police perspectives on responding to mentally ill people in crisis: Perceptions of program effectiveness. *Behavioral Sciences & the Law, 16*, 393–405.

Borum, R., & Strentz, T. (1992, August). Borderline personality: Negotiation strategies. *FBI Law Enforcement Bulletin, 61*(8), 6–10.

Brantingham, P., & Brantingham, P. (Eds.). (1981). *Environmental criminology.* Beverly Hills, CA: Sage.

Brigham, J. (1999). What is forensic psychology, anyway? *Law and Human Behavior, 23,* 273–298.

Brody, R. G., & Kiehl, K. A. (2010). From white collar to red collar crime. *Journal of Financial Crime, 17*(3), 351–364.

Broomfield, N., & Churchill, J. (Directors). (2003). *Aileen: Life and death of a serial killer.* [Documentary]. United States: Lafayette Films.

Brown, S. L., & Forth, A. E. (1997). Psychopathy and sexual assault: Static risk factors, emotional precursors, and rapist subtypes. *Journal of Consulting and Clinical Psychology, 65,* 848–857.

Browne, A. (1987). The legal system and battered women. In *When battered women kill* (pp. 159–177). New York, NY: Free Press.

Brussel, J. A. (1968). *Casebook of a crime psychiatrist.* New York, NY: Bernard Geis.

Buchanan, A., Fahy, T., & Walsh, E. (2002). Violence and schizophrenia: Examining the evidence. *British Journal of Psychiatry, 180*(6), 490–495.

Bullock, H. A. (1955). Urban homicide in theory and fact. *Journal of Criminal Law, Criminology, and Police Science, 45,* 565–575.

Bumby, K. M. (2000). Empathy inhibition, intimacy deficits, and attachment difficulties in sex offenders. In D. R. Laws, S. M. Hudson, & T. Ward (Eds.), *Remaking relapse prevention with sex offenders: A sourcebook* (pp. 143–166). Thousand Oaks, CA: Sage.

Bureau of Justice Statistics. (n.d.). *Drug and crime facts: Drug use and crime.* Retrieved from: http://bjs.ojp.usdoj.gov/content/pub/pdf/dcf.pdf.

Bureau of Justice Statistics. (2003). *Violent victimization of college students.* Washington, DC: U.S. Department of Justice.

Bureau of Justice Statistics. (2016). *Reentry trends in the U.S.* Washington, DC: U.S. Department of Justice, Office of Justice Programs.

Bureau of Prisons. (n.d.). About our facilities. Retrieved from: www.bop.gov.

Burgess, A. W., Groth, A. N., Holmstrom, L. L., & Sgroi, S. M. (Eds.). (1978). *Sexual assault of children and adolescents.* Lexington, MA: Lexington Books.

Burgess, A. W., Hartman, C. R., Ressler, R. K., Douglas, J. E., & McCormack, A. (1986). Sexual homicide. *Journal of Interpersonal Violence, 1,* 251–272.

Buss, M. (2000). *The dangerous passion: Why jealousy is as necessary as love and sex.* New York, NY: Simon & Schuster.

Butterfield, F. (1994, October 23). Historical study of homicide and cities surprises the experts. *New York Times.* Retrieved from: http://www.nytimes.com/1994/10/23/us/historical-study-of-homicide-and-cities-surprises-the-experts.html.

Cahill, T. (1986). *Buried dreams: Inside the mind of a serial killer.* New York, NY: Bantam Books.

Cahill, T. (1987). *Buried dreams: Inside the mind of a serial killer* (paperback ed.). New York, NY: Bantam Books.

Canter, D. (2003). *Mapping murder: The secrets of geographical profiling.* London, UK: Virgin Books.

Canter, D., & Larkin, P. (1993). The environmental range of serial rapists. *Journal of Environmental Psychology, 13,* 63–69.

Carlsmith, K. M., Monahan, J., & Evans, A. (2007). The function of punishment in the "civil" commitment of sexually violent predators. *Behavioral Sciences & the Law, 25,* 437–448.

Carroll, J. S., Nelson, D. A., Yorgason, J. B., Harper, J. M., Ashton, R. H., & Jensen, A. C. (2010). Relational aggression in marriage. *Aggressive Behavior, 36,* 315–329.

Carter, D. L. (2013). The "First 48." *Homicide process mapping: Best practices for increasing homicide clearances* (p. 33). Bureau of U.S. Justice Assistance, U.S. Department of Justice.

Cascardi, M., Mueser, K. T., DeGiralomo, J., & Murrin, M. (1996). Physical aggression against psychiatric inpatients by family members and partners. *Psychiatric Services, 47*(5), 531–533.

Cascio, M. (Executive Producer). (1995). Jack the ripper: Phantom of death [Television series episode]. In Biography. New York, NY: A&E Television Networks.

Catalano, S. (2005). *National crime victimization survey: Criminal victimization, 2004.* Washington, DC: U.S. Bureau of Justice Statistics.

Cauffman, E., & Skeem, J. (n.d.). The juvenile psychopath: Is there such a thing as an adolescent superpredator? Retrieved from: http://www. adjj.org/downloads/7893Microsoft%20PowerPoint%20-%20Juvenile%20 Psychopathy.pdf.

Ceci, S. J., Ross, D. F., & Toglia, M. P. (1987). Suggestibility of children's memory: Psycholegal implications. *Journal of Experimental Psychology, 116*(1), 38–49.

Center for Sex Offender Management (CSOM). (n.d.a.). Understanding sex offenders: An introductory curriculum. Retrieved from: http://www.csom.org/ train/etiology/3/3_1.htm.

Center for Sex Offender Management (CSOM). (n.d.b.). The legal and legislative response: How do registration laws apply to juvenile offenders in different states? Retrieved from: http://www.csom.org/train/juvenile/7/7_4.htm.

Center for Sex Offender Management (CSOM). (1999). *Understanding juvenile sexual offending behavior: Emerging research, treatment approaches and management practices.* Silver Spring, MD: Center for Effective Public Policy.

Center for Sex Offender Management (CSOM). (2001). *Community notification and education.* Washington, DC: Office of Justice Programs, USDOJ.

Center for Sex Offender Management (CSOM). (2002). Supervision of sex offenders in the community: A training curriculum. Retrieved from: http://www. csom.org/train/supervision/download/02.html.

Center for Sex Offender Management (CSOM). (2007). Female sex offenders. Retrieved from: http://www.csom.org/pubs/female_sex_offenders_brief. pdf.

Center for Sex Offender Management (CSOM). (2010). Understanding juvenile sexual offending behavior: Emerging research, treatment approaches and management practices. Retrieved from: http://www.csom.org/pubs/juv-brf10.html.

Centers for Disease Control and Prevention (CDC). (2015). Intimate partner violence: Definitions. Retrieved from: http://www.cdc.gov/violenceprevention/intimatepartnerviolence/definitions.html.

Cervone, D., & Shoda, Y. (Eds.). (1999). *The coherence of personality: Social-cognitive bases of consistency, variability and organization.* New York, NY: Guilford Press.

Chaffin, M. (2005). Can we develop evidence-based practice for adolescent sex offenders? In R. E. Longo, & D. Prescott (Eds.), *Current perspectives: Working with sexually aggressive youth and youth with sexual behavior problems* (pp. 119–141). Holyoke, MA: NEARI Press.

Chandler, A. (2014). How many cops die in the line of duty each year? *The Atlantic.* Retrieved from: http://www.theatlantic.com/national/archive/2014/12/how-many-cops-die-in-the-line-of-duty-each-year/384129/.

Chappell, D. (2010). From sorcery to stun guns and suicide: The eclectic and global challenges of policing and the mentally ill. *Police Practice and Research, 11*(4), 289–300.

Chin, P. (1991). A Texas massacre: George Hennard's mounting fury—and the lives of 23 victims—ends in a rampage that became a Texas massacre. *People, 36*(17). Retrieved from: http://www.people.com/people/archive/article/0,20111193,00.html.

Cialdini, R. (2008). *Influence: Science and applications* (5th ed.). Boston, MA: Allyn & Bacon.

Clark, M. D. (2006). Entering the business of behavior change: Motivational interviewing for probation staff. *Perspectives, 30*(1), 38–45.

Clarke, J. (1990). *Last Rampage.* New York, NY: Berkley.

Cleckley, H. M. (1976). *The mask of sanity* (5th ed.). St. Louis, MO: Mosby.

Cleckley, H. M., & Cleckley, E. S. (1988). *The mask of sanity: An attempt to clarify some issues about the so-called psychopathic personality.* St. Louis, MO: Mosby.

CNN. (2016, March 30). Virginia tech shootings fast facts. Retrieved from: http://www.cnn.com/2013/10/31/us/virginia-tech-shootings-fast-facts/.

Cochran, J. R. (1999). Fair play George Metesky. *New York Daily News,* October 27.

Cochran, S., Deane, M. W., & Borum, R. (2000). Improving police response to mentally ill people. *Psychiatric Services, 51*(10), 1315–1316.

Coid, J., Petruckevitch, A., Chung, W. S., Richardson, J., Moorey, S., & Feder, G. (2003). Abusive experiences and psychiatric morbidity in women primary care attenders. *British Journal of Psychiatry, 183,* 332–339.

Colorado v. Connelly, 497 U.S. 157(1986).

Community Education Centers, Inc. (2016). CEC website. Retrieved from: www.cecintl.com.

Connors, E., Lundregan, T., Miller, N., & McEwan, T. (1996). *Convicted by juries, exonerated by science: Case studies in the use of DNA evidence to establish innocence after trial.* Alexandria, VA: National Institute of Justice.

Cornell, D., & Sheras, P. (2006). *Guidelines for responding to student threats of violence.* Dallas, TX: Sopris Learning.

Cornell Law Review. (1982). *United States v. John Hinckley*: A recent successful use of the insanity defense. Retrieved from: https://www.law.cornell.edu/background/insane/hinckley.html.

Corry, B. (1993). *Understanding domestic violence: A recovery resource for battered women and those who work with them.* Beverly Hills, CA: CARE Program.

Costanzo, M., & Krauss, D. (2012). *Forensic and legal psychology: Psychological science applied to law.* New York, NY: Worth.

Cotton, D. (2004). The attitudes of Canadian police officers toward the mentally ill. *International Journal of Law and Psychiatry, 27,* 135–146.

Crick, N. R. (1995). Relational aggression: The role of intent, attributions, feelings of distress, and provocation type. *Developmental Psychopathology, 7,* 313–322.

Cronin, J. M., Toliver, J. I., Murphy, G. R., Weger, R. E., & Spahr, L. L. (2007). *Promoting effective homicide investigations.* Washington, DC: Police Executive Research Forum.

Curtiss, A. (1995). FBI expert offers mental profile of "spree killer." *Los Angeles Times.* Retrieved from: http://articles.latimes.com/1995-11-11/news/mn-1955_1_serial-killers.

Dale, R., Riley, D., & Charleston, F. (Producers). (2010). *Too young to kill: 15 shocking crimes* [Television movie]. USA: E! Entertainment Television.

Daly, M., & Wilson, M. I. (1982). Homicide and kinship. *American Anthropologist, 84,* 372–378.

Darves-Bornoz, J. M., Lempériére, T., Degiovanni, A., & Galliard, P. (1995). Sexual victimization in women with schizophrenia and bipolar disorder. *Social Psychiatry and Psychiatric Epidemiology, 30*(2), 72–84.

Davis, G. E., & Leitenberg, H. (1987). Adolescent sex offenders. *Psychological Bulletin, 101,* 417–427.

Davison, S., & Janca, A. (2012). Personality disorder and criminal behaviour. *Current Opinion in Psychiatry, 25*(1), 39–45.

DeAngelis, T. (2009, November). Understanding terrorism. *Monitor on Psychology, 40*(10), 60.

Dedman, B. (1998, August 9). Study of assassins concludes there is no common profile. *Kansas City Star,* p. A-15.

Denov, M., & Cortoni, F. (2006). Women who sexually abuse children. In C. Hilarski, & J. S. Wodarski (Eds.), *Comprehensive mental health practice with sex offenders and their families* (pp. 71–99). Binghamton, NY: Haworth Press.

Department of Homeland Security. (2015a). *Ideologically inspired violent extremists: A case study on Abdulhakim Mujahid Muhammad.* Washington, DC: United States Secret Service: National Threat Assessment Center.

Department of Homeland Security. (2015b). *Exploring the effect of stressors in threat assessment in investigations: A case study on Bart Allen Ross.* Washington, DC: U.S. Secret Service: National Threat Assessment Center.

Department of Justice. (1999). *Cyberstalking: A new challenge for law enforcement and industry. A report from the attorney general to the vice president.* Washington, DC: U.S. Department of Justice.

DeSilva, D., & De Silva P. (1999). Morbid jealousy in an Asian country: A clinical exploration from Sri Lanka. *International Review of Psychiatry, 11,* 116–121.

Dienst, J. (2015, May 19). 7 Rikers Island guards raped, sexually abused inmates: Lawsuit. *NBC 4 New York.* Retrieved from: http://www.nbcnewyork.com/news/local/Rikers-Island-Female-Inmates-Lawsuit-Rape-Sexual-Abuse-Correction-Officers-304332321.html.

Doerner, W. G. (1988). The impact of medical resources on criminally induced lethality: A further examination. *Criminology, 26,* 171–179.

Domestic Violence Solutions for Santa Barbara County. (2015). Cycle of violence. Retrieved from http://www.dvsolutions.org/info/cycle.aspx.

Douglas, J., & Burgess, A. (1986). Criminal profiling: A viable investigative tool against violent crime. *FBI Law Enforcement Bulletin, 55,* 9–13.

Douglas, J., Burgess, A. W., Burgess, A. G., & Ressler, R. (1992). *Crime classification manual.* Lexington, MA: Lexington Books.

Douglas, J. E., Burgess, A. W., & Ressler, R. K. (1995). *Sexual homicide: Patterns and motives.* New York, NY: Free Press.

Douglas, J. E., & Munn, C. (1992, February). Violent crime scene analysis: Modus operandi, signature, and staging. *FBI Law Enforcement Bulletin, 61*(2), 1–10.

Douglas, J. E., & Olshaker, M. (1998). *Obsession.* New York, NY: Scribner.

Douglas, J. E., Ressler, R. K., Burgess, A. W., & Hartman, C. R. (1986). Criminal profiling from crime scene analysis. *Behavioral Sciences & the Law, 4*(4), 401–421.

Douglas, K. S., Guy, L. S., & Hart, S. D. (2009). Psychosis as a risk factor for violence to others: A meta-analysis. *Psychological Bulletin, 135,* 679–706.

Douki, S., Nacef, F., Belhadj, A., Bouasker, A., & Ghachem, R. (2003). Violence against women in Arab and Islamic countries. *Women's Mental Health, 6*(1), 165–171.

Eagan, S. H., VosWinkel, F., Ford, J. D., Lyddy, C., Schwartz, H. I., & Spencer, A. (2014, November 21). *Shooting at Sandy Hook elementary school: Report to the office of the child advocate.* Office of the Child Advocate: State of Connecticut.

Edwards, J. B. (2005). Homicide investigative strategies. *FBI Law Enforcement Bulletin: Focus on Investigations, 74*(1).

Eher, R., Rettenberger, M., & Schilling, F. (2010). Psychiatric diagnoses of sexual offenders: An empirical investigation of 807 delinquents imprisoned for child abuse and rape [in German]. *Z Sexualforsch, 23,* 23–35.

Ellison, K. W., & Buckhout, R. (1981). *Psychology and criminal justice.* New York, NY: Harper & Row.

End Violence Against Women International (EVAWI). (n.d.). Start by believing. Retrieved from: http://www.startbybelieving.org/Default.aspx.

Engel, R., & Silver, E. (2001). Policing mentally disordered suspects: A reexamination of the criminalization hypothesis. *Criminology, 39*(2), 225–252.

Engel, R., Sobol, J., & Worden, R. (2000). Further exploration of the demeanor hypothesis: The interaction effects of suspects' characteristics and demeanor on police behavior. *Justice Quarterly, 17*(2), 235–258.

Entorf, H. (2013). *Criminal victims, victimized criminals or both? A deeper look at the victim-offender overlap.* IZA Discussion Paper 7686. Bonn: IZA.

Ewing, C. P., & McCann, J. T. (2006). *Minds on trial: Great cases in law and psychology.* New York, NY: Oxford University Press.

Fagan, J., & Wexler, S. (1988). Explanations of sexual assault among violent delinquents. *Journal of Adolescent Research, 3,* 363–385.

Farrell, A., McDevitt, J., & Fahy, S. (2008). *Understanding and improving law enforcement responses to human trafficking: Final report.* Washington, DC: National Institute of Justice, U.S. Department of Justice.

Farrell, A., McDevitt, J., Pfeffer, R., Fahy, S., Owens, C., Dank, M., & Adams, W. (2012). Identifying challenges to improve the investigation and prosecution of state and local human trafficking cases. Washington, DC: National Institute of Justice. Retrieved from: https://www.ncjrs.gov/pdffiles1/nij/grants/238795.pdf.

Farrell, G., & Pease, K. (1993). *Once bitten, twice bitten: Repeat victimization and its implications for crime prevention.* Crime Prevention Unit Paper 46. London, UK: Home Office 6–7.

Fazel, S., & Danesh, J. (2002). Serious mental disorder in 23000 prisoners: A systematic review of 62 surveys. *Lancet Psychiatry, 359,* 545–550.

Fazel, S., Wolf, A., Chang, Z., Larsson, H., Goodwin, G., & Lichtenstein, P. (2015). Depression and violence: A Swedish population study. *Lancet Psychiatry, 2,* 224–232.

Federal Bureau of Investigation. (1985). The men who murdered. *FBI Law Enforcement Bulletin, 54*(8), 2–6.

Federal Bureau of Investigation. (1992). *Killed in the line of duty: A study of selected felonious killings of law enforcement officers.* Washington, DC: U.S. Department of Justice.

Federal Bureau of Investigation. (1997). *Uniform crime reports.* Washington, DC: U.S. Department of Justice.

Federal Bureau of Investigation. (2003). *Uniform crime reports: 2002.* Washington, DC: U.S. Department of Justice.

Federal Bureau of Investigation. (2004). *Uniform crime reporting handbook.* Washington, DC: U.S. Department of Justice.

Federal Bureau of Investigation. (2005). *Crime in the United States 2004: Uniform crime reports.* Washington, DC: U.S. Department of Justice.

Federal Bureau of Investigation. (2012). *Law Enforcement Bulletin: Psychopathy, 81* (7). Retrieved from: https://leb.fbi.gov/2012/july/leb-july-2012.

Fein, R. A., & Vossekuil, B. (2000). *Protective intelligence and threat assessment investigations: A guide for state and local law enforcement officials.* Washington, DC: U.S. Department of Justice, Office of Justice Programs, National Institute of Justice.

Felitti, V. J., & Anda, R. (2009). The relationship of adverse childhood experiences to adult medical disease, psychiatric disorders, and sexual behaviors: Implications for healthcare. In R. Lanius, E. Vermetten, & C. Pain (Eds.), *The hidden epidemic: The impact of early life trauma on health and disease.* Retrieved from: http://www.acestudy.org/yahoo_site_admin/assets/docs/LaniusVermetten_FINAL_8-26-09.12892303.pdf.

Fernandez, Y., Harris, A. J., Hanson, R. K., & Sparks, J. (2012). *STABLE-2007 coding manual*. Ottawa, CA: Public Safety Canada.

Fine, R. (1997). *Being stalked: A memoir*. London, UK: Chatto & Windus.

Finkelhor, D. (1994). The international epidemiology of child sexual abuse. *Child Abuse & Neglect, 18*(5), 409–417.

Firestone, P., Bradford, J. M., Greenberg, D. M., & Larose, M. R. (1998). Homicidal sex offenders: Psychological, phallometric, and diagnostic features. *Journal of the American Academy of Psychiatry and the Law, 26*, 537–552.

Fischbach, R. L., & Herbert, B. (1997). Domestic violence and mental health: Correlates and conundrums within and across cultures. *Social Science and Medicine, 45*(8), 1161–1176.

Fisher, R. P. (1995). Interviewing victims and witnesses of crime. *Psychology, Public Policy, and Law, 1*, 732–764.

Fisher, R. P., Geiselman, R. E., & Raymond, D. S. (1987). Critical analysis of police interviewing techniques. *Journal of Police Science and Administration, 15*, 177–185.

Fitch, L. W. (1998). Sex offender commitment in the United States. *Journal of Forensic Psychiatry, 9*(2), 237–240.

Forbes, G. B., Adams-Curtis, L. E., & White, K. B. (2004). First- and second-generation measures of sexism, rape myths and related beliefs, and hostility toward women. *Violence Against Women, 10*, 236.

Ford, M. E., & Linney, J. A. (1995). Comparative analysis of juvenile sexual offenders, violent nonsexual offenders, and status offenders. *Journal of Interpersonal Violence, 10*, 56–70.

Foster, H. H. (1969). Confessions and the station house syndrome. *DePaul Law Review, 18*, 683–701.

Francia, C. A., Coolidge, F. L., White L. A., Segal, D. L., Cahill, B. S., & Estey, A. J. (2010). Personality disorder profiles in incarcerated male rapists and child molesters. *American Journal of Forensic Psychology, 28*(3), 55–68.

Frank, G. (1966). *The Boston strangler*. New York, NY: Signet.

Frederick, R. I., Mrad, D. F., & DeMier, R. L. (2007). *Examinations of criminal responsibility: Foundations in mental health case law*. Sarasota, FL: Professional Resource Press.

Freeman-Longo, R. E. (1986). The impact of sexual victimization on males. *Child Abuse & Neglect, 10*, 411–414.

Frick, P. J., & Marsee, M. A. (2006). Psychopathy and developmental pathways to antisocial behavior in youth. In C. J. Patrick (Ed.), *Handbook of psychopathy* (pp. 353–374). New York, NY: Guilford Press.

Friedman, S., & Harrison, G. (1984). Sexual histories, attitudes, and behavior of schizophrenic and "normal" women. *Archives of Sexual Behavior, 13*, 555–567.

Fulero, S. M., & Wrightsman, L. S. (2009). *Forensic psychology* (3rd ed.). California: Cengage.

Fuselier, G. D. (1988). Hostage negotiation consultant: Emerging role for the clinical psychologist. *Professional Psychology: Research and Practice, 19*, 175–179.

308

Gabbert, F., Memon, A., & Allan, K. (2003). Memory conformity: Can eyewitnesses influence each other's memories for an event? *Applied Cognitive Psychology, 17,* 533–543.

Galaif, E. R., Stein, J. A., Newcomb, M. D., & Bernstein, D. P. (2001). Gender differences in the prediction of problem alcohol use in adulthood: Exploring the influence of family factors and childhood maltreatment. *Journal of Studies on Alcohol, 62,* 486–493.

Garner, G. W. (2005, January 1). Fatal errors: Surviving domestic violence calls. *Police: The Law Enforcement Magazine.* Retrieved from: http://www.policemag.com/channel/women-in-law-enforcement/articles/2005/01/fatal-errors-surviving-domestic-violence-calls.aspx.

Gearon, J. S., Bellack, A. S., & Brown, C. H. (2003). Sexual and physical abuse in women with schizophrenia: Prevalence and risk factors. *Schizophrenia Research, 60,* 38.

Geberth, V. J. (1983). *Practical homicide investigation.* New York, NY: Elsevier.

Geberth, V. J. (2010). *Sex-related homicide and death investigation: Practical and clinical perspectives* (2nd ed.). Boca Raton, FL: CRC Press.

Gendreau, P., Little, T., & Goggin, C. (1996). A meta-analysis of the predictors of adult offender rehabilitation: What works. *Criminology, 34*(4), 575–608.

Gendreau, P., Goggin, C., Cullen, F., & Paparozzi, M. (2002). The common-sense revolution and correctional policy. In J. McGuire (Ed.), *Offender rehabilitation and treatment: effective programmes and policies to reduce re-offending* (pp. 359–386). Chichester, UK: John Wiley.

Gettleman, J. (2002, October 25). The hunt for a sniper: The profiling—A frenzy of speculation was wide of the mark. *New York Times,* p. A3.

Gigler, K. (2015). How brain science can help explain discrepancies in a sexual assault survivor's story. *Huffington Post.* Retrieved from: http://www.huffingtonpost.com/cognitive-neuroscience-society/how-brain-science-can-help-explain-discrepancies-in-a-sexual-assault-survivors-story_b_7421768.html.

Gil, E., & Johnson, T. C. (1992). *Assessment and treatment of sexualized children and children who molest.* Rockville, MD: Launch Press.

Gold, J., Wolan Sullivan, M., & Lewis, M. (2011). The relation between abuse and delinquency: The conversion of shame to blame in juvenile offenders. *Child Abuse & Neglect, 35*(7), 459–467.

Goldstein, S. (2015). LAPD hunts "Teardrop Rapist" responsible for 35 sex assaults spanning 16 years. *New York Daily News.* Retrieved from: http://www.nydailynews.com/news/crime/lapd-hunts-teardrop-rapist-responsible-35-sex-assaults-article-1.2076051.

Gottfredson, M. R. (1984). *Victims of crime: The dimensions of risk.* Home office research study no. 81. London, UK: Her Majesty's Stationery Office.

Gottfredson, M. R., & Hirschi, T. (1990). *A general theory of crime.* Stanford, CA: Stanford University Press.

Grayston, A. D., & De Luca, R. V. (1999). Female perpetrators of child sexual abuse: A review of the clinical and empirical literature. *Aggression and Violent Behavior, 4,* 93–106.

309

Greenfield, L. A., Rand, M. R., Craven, D., Klaus, P. A., Perkins, C. A., Ringel, C., ... Fox, J. A. (1998). *Violence by inmates: Analysis of data on crimes by current or former spouses, boyfriends, and girlfriends.* Washington, DC: U.S. Department of Justice.

Gretton, H. M., McBride, M., Hare, R. D., O'Shaughnessy, R., & Kumka, G. (2001). Psychopathy and recidivism in adolescent sex offenders. *Criminal Justice and Behavior, 28,* 427–449.

Groth, A. N. (1979). *Men who rape: The psychology of the offender.* New York, NY: Plenum Press.

Groth, A. N., Burgess, A. W., & Holmstrom, L. L. (1977). Rape: Power, anger, and sexuality. *American Journal of Psychiatry, 134*(11), 1239–1243.

Groth, A. N., Hobson, W. F., & Gary, T. S. (1982). The child molester: Clinical observations. *Journal of Social Work and Human Sexuality, 1,* 129–144.

Grubb, A. (2010). Modern day hostage (crisis) negotiation: The evolution of an art form within the policing arena. *Aggression and Violent Behavior, 15,* 341–348.

Gudjonsson, G. H. (1992). *The psychology of interrogations, confessions and testimony.* New York, NY: John Wiley.

Gudjonsson, G. H., & Copson, G. (1997). The role of the expert in criminal investigation. In J. L. Jackson, & D. A. Bekerian (Eds.), *Offender profiling: Theory, research and practice* (pp. 62–76). New York, NY: Wiley.

Guerette, R. T. (2002). Geographical profiling. In D. Levinson (Ed.), *Encyclopedia of crime and punishment.* Thousand Oaks, CA: Sage.

Hakkanen-Nyholm, H., & Hare, R. D. (2009). Psychopathy, homicide and the courts: Working the system. *Criminal Justice and Behavior, 36*(8), 761–777.

Hall, D. L., Miraglia, R. P., Lee, L. W., Chard-Wierschem, D., & Sawyer, D. (2012). Predictors of general and violent recidivism among SMI prisoners returning to communities in New York state. *Journal of the American Academy of Psychiatry and the Law, 40*(2), 221–231.

Haney, C. (2001). *From prison to home: The effect of incarceration and reentry on children, families, and communities. The psychological impact of incarceration: Implications for post-prison adjustment.* Washington, DC: Office of the Assistant Secretary for Planning and Evaluation.

Hardoon, L. (1995, January 24). Letters to the editor: The real darkness is child abuse. *Wall Street Journal.*

Hare, R. (n.d.). Psychopathy scales. Retrieved from: http://www.hare.org/scales/pclyv.html.

Hare, R. D. (1970). *Psychopathy: Theory and research.* New York, NY: Wiley.

Hare, R. D. (1991). *The Hare psychopathy checklist: Revised.* Toronto, ON: Multi-Health Systems.

Hare, R. D. (1993). *Without conscience: The disturbing world of the psychopaths among us.* New York, NY: Guilford Press.

Hare, R. D. (1996). Psychopathy: A clinical construct whose time has come. *Criminal Justice and Behavior, 23,* 25–54.

Hare, R. D. (2003). *The hare psychopathy checklist: Revised* (2nd ed.). Toronto, ON: Multi-Health Systems.

Hare, R. D. (2006). A clinical construct whose time has come. In C. R. Bartol, & A. M. Bartol (Eds.), *Current perspectives in forensic psychology and criminal justice* (pp. 107–118). Thousand Oaks, CA: Sage.

Hare, R. D. (2012). Focus on psychopathy. *FBI Law Enforcement Bulletin: Psychopathy, 81*(7). Retrieved from: https://leb.fbi.gov/2012/july/leb-july-2012.

Hare, R. D., Hart, S. D., & Harpur, T. J. (1991). Psychopathy and the DSM-IV criteria for antisocial personality disorder. *Journal of Abnormal Psychology, 100*(3), 391–398.

Hare, R. D., Harpur, T. J., Hakstian, A. R., Forth, A. E., Hart, S. D., & Newman, J. P. (1990). The revised psychopathy checklist: Reliability and factor structure. *Psychological Assessment: A Journal of Consulting and Clinical Psychology, 2*(3), 338–341.

Harenski, C. L., Edwards, B. G., Harenski, K. A., & Kiehl, K. A. (2014). Neural correlates of moral and non-moral emotion in female psychopathy. *Frontiers in Human Neuroscience, 8,* 741.

Hart, S. D., & Dempster, R. J. (1997). Impulsivity and psychopathy. In C. D. Webster, & M. S. Jackson (Eds.), *Impulsivity: Theory, assessment and treatment.* New York: Guilford Press.

Hart, S. D., & Hare, R. D. (1997). Psychopathy: Assessment and association with criminal conduct. In D. M. Stoff, J. P. Maser, & J. Breiling (Eds.), *Handbook of antisocial behavior.* New York, NY: Wiley.

Hayes, T. C. (1991). Gunman kills 22 and himself in Texas cafeteria. *New York Times.* Retrieved from: http://www.nytimes.com/1991/10/17/us/gunman-kills-22-and-himself-in-texas-cafeteria.html?pagewanted=1.

Hazelwood, R. R., & Burgess, A. W. (Eds.). (2001). *Practical aspects of rape investigation: A multidisciplinary approach* (3rd ed.). Boca Raton, FL: CRC Press.

Hepburn, J., & Voss, H. L. (1970). Patterns of criminal homicide: A comparison of Chicago and Philadelphia. *Criminology, 8,* 19–45.

Hickey, E. W. (2006). *Serial murderers and their victims.* Belmont, CA: Wadsworth.

Hiday, V. A., Swartz, M. S., Swanson, J. W., Borum, R., & Wagner, H. R. (1999). Criminal victimization of persons with severe mental illness. *Psychiatric Services, 50,* 62–68.

Hirschel, D. (2008). Domestic violence cases: What research shows about mandatory arrest and dual arrest rates. Retrieved from: https://www.ncjrs.gov/pdffiles1/nij/222679.pdf.

Holmes, R. M., & DeBurger, J. (1988). *Serial murder: Studies in crime, law, and justice, 2.* Newbury Park, CA: Sage.

Holmes, R. M., & Holmes, S. T. (1996). *Profiling violent crimes* (2nd ed.). Thousand Oaks, CA: Sage.

Holmes, R. M., & Holmes, S. T. (2000). *Murder in America* (2nd ed.). Thousand Oaks, CA: Sage.

Holmes, R. M., & Holmes, S. T. (2001). *Mass murder in the United States.* Upper Saddle River, NJ: Prentice Hall.

311

Holmes, R. M., & Holmes, S. T. (2002). *Profiling violent crimes* (3rd ed.). Thousand Oaks, CA: Sage.

Holt, S. E., Meloy, J. R., & Stack, S. (1999). Sadism and psychopathy in violent and sexual violent offenders. *Journal of the American Academy of Psychiatry and Law, 27,* 23–32.

Holtzworth-Munroe, A., & Stuart, G. L. (1994). Typologies of male batterers: Three subtypes and the differences among them. *Psychological Bulletin, 116*(3), 476–497.

Homant, R. J., & Kennedy, D. B. (1998). Psychological aspects of crime scene profiling. *Criminal Justice and Behavior, 25*(3), 319–343.

Hooley, D. (2010, March 29). Forward-thinking leadership. CorrectionsOne.com website.

Horowitz, I. A., & Willging, T. E. (1984). *The psychology of law: Integrations and applications.* Boston, MA: Little, Brown.

Huff, C. R., Rattner, A., & Sagarin, E. (1996). *Convicted but innocent: Wrongful conviction and public policy.* Thousand Oaks, CA: Sage.

Hunter, J. A., & Becker, J. V. (1998). Motivators of adolescent sex offenders and treatment perspectives. In J. Shaw (Ed.), *Sexual aggression.* Washington, DC: American Psychiatric Press.

Hunter, J. A., Figueredo, A. J., Malamuth, N. M., & Becker, J. V. (2003). Juvenile sex offenders: Toward the development of a typology. *Sexual Abuse: A Journal of Research and Treatment, 15*(1), 27–48.

IACP (International Association of Chiefs of Police). (n.d.a.). National law enforcement leadership initiative on violence against women. Retrieved from: http://dnn9ciwm8.azurewebsites.net/Portals/0/documents/pdfs/ResponsetoDomesticViolenceChecklist.pdf.

IACP (International Association of Chiefs of Police). (n.d.b.). Trauma informed sexual assault investigation training. Retrieved from: http://www.iacp.org/Trauma-Informed-Sexual-Assault-Investigation-Training.

IACP (International Association of Chiefs of Police). (2005). *Investigating sexual assaults: Concepts and issues paper.* Alexandria, VA: Author.

Ibn-Tamas v. United States, 407 A.2d 626 (1979).

Inbau, F. E., Reid, J. E., Buckley, J. P., & Jayne, B. C. (2004). *Criminal interrogation and confessions* (4th ed.). Boston, MA: Jones & Bartlett.

Inderbitzen-Pisaruk, H., Shawchuck, C. R., & Tamara, S. (1992). Behavioral characteristics of child victims of sexual abuse: A comparison study. *Journal of Clinical Child Psychology, 21*(1), 14–19.

Innocence Project. (2016). Damon Thibodeaux. InnocenceProject.org website. Retrieved from: http://www.innocenceproject.org/cases-false-imprisonment/damon-thibodeaux.

Interview with the Green River Killer [Video file], pp. 14–19. Retrieved from: https://www.youtube.com/watch?v=SdpUaf1XAh4.

Jackson, R. L., & Richards, H. J. (2007). Diagnostic and risk profiles among civilly committed sex offenders in Washington State. *International Journal of Offender Therapy and Comparative Criminology, 51*(3), 313–323.

Jacobs, B. A., & Wright, R. (2010). Bounded rationality, retaliation, and the spread of urban violence. *Journal of Interpersonal Violence, 25*(10), 1739–1766.

James, S. D. (2007, August 29). Selective mutism is paralyzing shyness, not psychosis. *ABC News.* Retrieved from: http://abcnews.go.com/Health/story?id=3534240&page=1.

Jayne, B. C., & Buckley, J. P. (2014). The Reid Technique. Reid.com website. Retrieved from: https://www.reid.com/educational_info/canada.html.

Jeanneau, Y., Le Goff, C., Poncet, D. (Producers), & de Lestrade, J. X. (Director). (2001). *Murder on a Sunday morning.* USA: Home Box Office.

Johnson, E. K., & Howell, R. J. (1993). Memory processes in children: Implications for investigations of alleged child sexual abuse. *Bulletin of the American Academy of Psychiatry and the Law, 21*(2), 213–226.

Johnson, K. (2006, July 7). Journals reveal ruminations of teenage Columbine killers. *New York Times.* Retrieved from: http://www.nytimes.com/2006/07/07/us/07columbine.html?_r=0.

Johnson-Reid, M. (1998). Youth violence and exposure to violence in childhood: An ecological review. *Aggression and Violent Behavior, 3*, 159–179.

Johnson, S. A. (2012). Interview strategies for police officers investigating sexual offenses. Retrieved from: http://lawenforcementtoday.com/2012/02/25/interview-strategies-for-police-officers-investigating-sexual-offenses/.

Johnson, S. D., & Bowers, D. J. (2004). The burglary as clue to the future: The beginnings of prospective hot-spotting. *European Journal of Criminology, 1*(2), 237–255.

Kahn, T. J., & Chambers, J. H. (1991) Assessing re-offense risk with juvenile sexual offenders. *Child Welfare, 19*, 333–345.

Kaminski, R., DiGiovanni, C., & Downs, R. (2004). The use of force between police and persons with impaired judgment. *Police Quarterly, 7*(3), 311–338.

Karlin, R. (2006). Forged transcript center of attention. Retrieved from: http://www.timesunion.com/news/article/Forged-transcripts-center-of-attention-580255.php.

Kassin, S. M. (1997). The psychology of confession evidence. *American Psychologist, 52*, 221–233.

Kassin, S. M., & Kiechel, K. L. (1996). The social psychology of false confessions: Compliance, internalization, and confabulation. *Psychological Science, 7*, 125–128.

Kassin, S. M., Leo, R. A., Meissner, C. A., Richman, K. D., Colwell, L. H., Leach, A. M., & La Fon, D. (2007). Police interviewing and interrogation: A self-report survey of police practices and beliefs. *Law and Human Behavior, 31*, 381–400.

Kassin, S. M., & McNall, K. (1991). Police interrogation and confessions: Communicating promises and threats by pragmatic implication. *Law and Human Behavior, 15*, 233–251.

Kassin, S. M., & Wrightsman, L. S. (1985). Confession evidence. In S. M. Kassin, & L. S. Wrightsman (Eds.), *The psychology of evidence and trial procedure* (pp. 67–94). Thousand Oaks, CA: Sage.

Kelleher, M. D., & Kelleher, C. L. (1998). *Murder most rare: The female serial killer.* New York, NY: Dell Publishing.

Kelly, L., Lovett, J., & Regan, L. (2005). *A gap or chasm? Attrition in reported rape cases.* Home office research study 293. London, UK: Development and Statistics Directorate.

Kendall, W., & Cheung, M. (2004). Sexually violent predators and civil commitment laws. *Journal of Child Sexual Abuse, 13*(2), 41–57.

Keppel, R. (2005). *The riverman: Ted Bundy and I hunt for the Green River killer* (Paperback ed.). New York, NY: Simon & Schuster.

Keppel, R. (2010). *The riverman: Ted Bundy and I hunt for the Green River killer* (kindle ed.). New York, NY: Simon & Schuster.

Kiehl, K. A. (2015). *The psychopath whisperer: The science of those without conscience.* Danvers, MA: Broadway Books.

Kilpatrick, D. G., & Acierno, R. (2003). Mental health needs of crime victims: Epidemiology and outcomes. *Journal of Traumatic Stress, 16*(2), 119–132.

Kilpatrick, D. G., Edmunds, C. N., & Seymour, A. (1992). *Rape in America: A report to the nation.* Charlston, SC: National Victim Center and the Crime Victims Research and Treatment Center, Medical University of South Carolina.

Kilpatrick, D. G., & Saunders, B. E. (1997). *Prevalence and consequences of child victimization: Results from the national survey of adolescents.* U.S. Department of Justice, Office of Justice Programs, National Institute of Justice.

Kind, S. S. (1987). Navigational ideas and the Yorkshire Ripper investigation. *Journal of Navigation, 40,* 385–393.

Kingsbury, S. J., Lambert, M. T., & Hendrickse, W. (1997). A two-factor model of aggression. *Psychiatry: Interpersonal and Biological Processes, 60,* 224–232.

Knight, R. A., & Prentky, R. A. (1990). Classifying sexual offenders: The development and corroboration of taxonomic models. In W. L. Marshall & D. R. Laws (Eds.), *Handbook of sexual assault: Issues, theories, and treatment of the offender* (pp. 23–52). New York, NY: Plenum Press.

Kocsis, R. N., & Irwin, H. J. (1997). An analysis of spatial patterns in serial rape, arson, and burglary: The utility of the circle theory of environmental range for psychological profiling. *Psychiatry, Psychology, and Law, 4,* 195–206.

Kocsis, R. N., Cooksey, R. W., Irwin, H. J., & Allen, G. (2002). A further assessment of circle theory for geographic psychological profiling. *Australian and New Zealand Journal of Criminology, 35*(1), 43–62.

Kovacs, M. (1996). Presentation and course of major depressive disorder during childhood and later years of the life span. *Journal of the American Academy of Child and Adolescent Psychiatry, 35,* 705–715.

Kropp, P. R., Hart, S. D., & Lyon, D. R. (2002). Risk assessment of stalkers: Some problems and possible solutions. *Criminal Justice and Behavior, 29,* 590–616.

Kubrin, C. E., & Weitzer, R. (2003). Retaliatory homicide: Concentrated disadvantage and neighborhood culture. *Social Problems, 50*(2), 157–180.

Lamb, M. E., Sternberg, K. J., & Esplin, P. W. (1995). Making children into competent witnesses: Reactions to the amicus brief In re Michaels. *Psychology, Public Policy, and Law, 1,* 438–449.

Langer, W. C. (1972). *The mind of Adolf Hitler*. New York: Basic Books.

Laws, D. R., & O'Donohue, W. T. (1997). *Sexual deviance: Theory, assessment, and treatment*. New York, NY: Guilford Press.

Lea, S. J., Lanvers, U., & Shaw, S. (2003). Attrition in rape cases. *British Journal of Criminology, 43*, 583–599.

Lee, A. M., Galynker, I. I., Kopeykina, I., Kim, H., & Khatun, T. (2014). Violence in bipolar disorder. Retrieved from: http://www.psychiatrictimes.com/bipolardisorder/violence-bipolar-disorder/page/0/3.

Leo, R. A. (2008). *Police interrogation and American justice*. Cambridge, MA: Harvard University Press.

Leund, R. (2004, December 10). Why did Eric kill? *Forty Eight Hours: CBS News*. Retrieved from: http://www.cbsnews.com/news/why-did-eric-kill-10-12-2004/.

Levenson, J. (2003). Policy interventions designed to combat sexual violence: Community notification and civil commitment. *Journal of Child Sexual Abuse, 12*(3/4), 17–52.

Levenson, J. (2016). *Trauma informed care*. Presentation for New Jersey Association for the Treatment of Sexual Abusers (NJ ATSA).

Levin, A. (2012, December 21). Mentally ill individuals more vulnerable in police interrogations. *American Psychiatric Association: Psychiatric News*. Retrieved from: http://psychnews.psychiatryonline.org/doi/10.1176/appi.pn.2012.12b16.

Lieb, R., & Matson, S. (1998). *Sexual predator commitment laws in the United States: 1998 update*. Washington, DC: Washington State Institute for Public Policy.

Lightfoot, L. O., & Barbaree, H. E. (1993). The relationship between substance use and abuse and sexual offending in adolescents. In H. E. Barbaree, W. L. Marshall, & S. W. Hudson (Eds.), *The juvenile sex offender* (pp. 203–224). New York, NY: Guilford Press.

Lindsay, R. C. L., Martin, R., & Webber, L. (1994). Default values in eyewitness descriptions: A problem for the match-to-description lineup foil selection strategy. *Law and Human Behavior, 18*, 527–541.

Linedecker, C. L. (1980). *The man who killed boys: A true story of mass murder in a Chicago suburb* (1st ed.). New York, NY: St. Martin's Press.

Lipian, M. S., Mills, M. J., & Brantman, A. (2004). Assessing the verity of children's allegations of abuse: A psychiatric overview. *International Journal of Law and Psychiatry, 27*(3), 249–263.

Lisak, D., Gardinier, L., Nicksa, S. C., & Cote, A. M. (2010). False allegations of sexual assault: An analysis of ten years of reported cases. *Violence Against Women, 16*(12), 1318–1334.

Lloyd, S., Farrell, G., & Pease, K. (1994). *Preventing repeated domestic violence: A demonstration project on Merseyside*. Police Research Group, Crime Prevention Unit Paper 49. London, UK: Home Office 2.

Loeber, R., & Stouthamer-Loeber, M. (1998). Development of juvenile aggression and violence: Some common misconceptions and controversies. *American Psychologist, 53*, 242–259.

315

Loftus, E. F. (1979). The malleability of human memory. *American Scientist, 67*, 312–320.

Loftus, E. F., Altman, D., & Geballe, R. (1975). Effects of questioning upon a witness' later recollections. *Journal of Police Science and Administration, 3*, 162–165.

Loftus, E. F., & Palmer, J. C. (1974). Reconstructions of automobile destruction: An example of the interaction between language and memory. *Journal of Verbal Learning and Verbal Behavior, 12*, 585–589.

Logan, T. K., Shannon, L., & Walker, R. (2006). Police attitudes toward domestic violence offenders. *Journal of Interpersonal Violence, 21*(10), 1365–1374.

Logan, T. K., Walker, R., Jordan, C. E., & Leukefeld, C. G. (2006). *Women and victimization: Contributing factors, interventions, and implications*. Washington, DC: American Psychological Association.

Lonsway, K. A., & Archambault, J. (2016, April). Start by believing: Changing attitudes toward sexual assault. *The Police Chief: The Professional Voice of Law Enforcement*. Retrieved from: http://www.policechiefmagazine.org/magazine/index.cfm?fuseaction=display&article_id=3300.

Los Angeles Police Department. (2016). Domestic violence: Reasons why battered victims stay with the batterers. Retrieved from: http://www.lapdonline.org/get_informed/content_basic_view/8877.

Love Is Respect. (2014). Break the cycle. Retrieved from: http://www.breakthecycle.org/how-we-help.

Lowencamp, C. T., Latessa, E. J., & Smith, P. (2006). Does correctional program quality really matter? The impact of adhering to the principles of effective intervention. *Criminology and Public Policy, 5*, 575–594.

Lykken, D. T. (2000). The causes and costs of crime and a controversial cure. *Journal of Personality, 68*(3), 559–605.

Maas, P. (1990). *In a child's name*. New York: Pocket Books. Television movie, CBS, November 17, 1991.

MacArthur Foundation. (2016). Assessing juvenile psychopathy: Developmental and legal implications. MacArthur Foundation Research Network on Adolescent Development and Juvenile Justice: Issue Brief 4. Retrieved from: https://www.macfound.org/media/files/ADJJPSYCHOPATHY.PDF.

MacFarlane, K., & Krebs, S. (1986). Techniques for interviewing and evidence gathering. In K. MacFarlane, & J. Waterman (with S. Conerly, L. Damon, M. Durfee, & S. Long) (Eds.), *Sexual abuse of young children* (pp. 67–100). New York, NY: Guilford Press.

Magnier, M. (2002, January 29). Battery, behind the Shoji Screen. *Los Angeles Times*. Retrieved from: http://articles.latimes.com/2002/jan/29/news/mn-25265.

Maher, G. (1977). *Hostage: A police approach to a contemporary crisis*. Springfield, IL: Charles C Thomas.

Maker, A. H., Kemmelmeier, M., & Peterson, C. (2001). Child sexual abuse, peer sexual abuse, and sexual assault in adulthood: A multi-risk model of revictimization. *Journal of Trauma and Stress, 14*, 351–368.

Marion County. (2015). *Specialized caseloads.* Retrieved from: http://www. co.marion.or.us/SO/Probation/Pages/SpecializedCaseloads.aspx.

Masten, A., & Garmezy, N. (1985). Risk, vulnerability, and protective factors in developmental psychopathology. In F. Lahey, & A. Kazdin (Eds.), *Advances in clinical child psychology* (pp. 1–52). New York, NY: Plenum.

Mathews, R., Matthews, J., & Speltz, K. (1989). *Female sexual offenders: An exploratory study.* Brandon, VT: The Safer Society Press.

Matson, S., & Lieb, R. (1997). *Megan's law: A review of state and federal legislation.* Olympia, Washington: Washington State Institute for Public Policy.

Mauro, M. (2010, February 13). Children who murder: Jordan Brown, Eric Smith and others. Retrieved from: https://www.psychologytoday.com/blog/take-all-prisoners/201002/children-who-murder-jordan-brown-eric-smith-and-others.

McClish, M. (2006, August 17). John Mark Karr and the JonBenet Ramsey murder: An analysis by Mark McClish. Statementanalysis.com website. Retrieved from: http://www.statementanalysis.com/ramseynote/update/.

McCorkle, R. (1992). Personal precautions to violence in prison. *Criminal Justice and Behavior, 19,* 160–173.

McCoy, D. (2005). Interrogating the psychopath. (Part 1). Retrieved from: http://www.policeone.com/health-fitness/articles/97850-Interrogating-the-psychopath-Part-1/.

McGough, M. (2016, April). The front line: Challenges for law enforcement in the fight against human trafficking. *The Police Chief, 81,* 44–46. Retrieved from: http://www.policechiefmagazine.org/magazine/index. cfm?fuseaction=display&article_id=3413&issue_id=72014.

McGuire, C., & Norton, C. (1988). *Perfect victim.* New York, NY: Dell.

McGuire, J. (2002). Integrating findings from research reviews. In J. McGuire (Ed.), *Offender rehabilitation and treatment: Effective programmes and policies to reduce re-offending* (pp. 3–38). Chichester, UK: John Wiley.

Meloy, J. R. (1992). *The psychopathic mind: Origins, dynamics, treatment* (2nd ed.). Northvale, NJ: Aronson.

Meloy, J. R. (1997). Predatory violence during mass murder. *Journal of Forensic Sciences, 42,* 326–329.

Meloy, J. R. (2001). Threats, stalking, and criminal harassment. In G. F. Pinard, & L. Pagani (Eds.), *Clinical assessment of dangerousness: Empirical contributions.* New York, NY: Cambridge University Press.

Meloy, J. R., Davis, B., & Lovette, J. (2001). Risk factors for violence among stalkers. *Journal of Threat Assessment, 1,* 3–16.

Meloy, J. R., & Hoffmann, J. (Eds.). (2013). *The international handbook of threat assessment.* New York, NY: Oxford University Press.

Meloy, J. R., & Meloy, M. J. (2002). Autonomic arousal in the presence of psychopathy: A survey of mental health and criminal justice professionals. *Journal of Threat Assessment, 2*(2), 21–34.

Melton, G. B. (Ed.). (1987). *Reforming the law: Impact of child development research.* New York, NY: Guilford Press.

317

Mercy, J. A., & Saltzman, L. E. (1989). Fatal violence among spouses in the United States. *American Journal of Public Health, 79,* 595–599.

Messman-Morre, T., Walsh, K., & DeLillo, D. (2012). Emotion dysregulation and risky sexual behavior in revictimization. *Child Abuse & Neglect, 34*(12), 967–976.

Meyers, L. (2008). Unfriendly skies. *APA Monitor, 39*(3), 36. Retrieved from: http://www.apa.org/monitor/2008/03/skies.aspx.

Miethe, T. D., & Drass, K. A. (1999). Exploring the social context of instrumental and expressive homicides: An application of qualitative comparative analysis. *Journal of Quantitative Criminology, 15,* 1–21.

Miller, A. (2014, February). Threat assessment in action. *Monitor on Psychology, 45*(2), 37.

Miller, L. (2007, May 22). Hostage negotiations: Psychological strategies for resolving crises. Retrieved from: https://www.policeone.com/standoff/articles/1247470-Hostage-negotiations-psychological-strategies-for-resolving-crises/.

Miller, W. R., Zweben, J., & Johnson, W. R. (2005). Evidence-based treatment: Why, what, where, when, and how? *Journal of Substance Abuse Treatment, 29*(4), 267–276.

Mischel, W. (1968). *Personality and assessment.* New York, NY: Lawrence Erlbaum Associates.

Modestin, J., Hugg, A., & Ammann, R. (1997). Criminal behavior in males with affective disorders. *Journal of Affective Disorders, 42*(1), 29–38.

Monahan, J., Steadman, H. J., Silver, E., Appelbaum, P. S., Robbins, P. C., Mulvey, E. P., ... Banks, S. M. (2001). *Rethinking risk assessment: The MacArthur study of mental disorder and violence.* New York, NY: Oxford University Press.

Morgan, R. D., Fisher, W. H., Dunn, N., Mandracchia, J. T., & Murray, D. (2010). Prevalence of criminal thinking among state prison inmates with serious mental illness. *Law and Human Behavior, 34,* 324–336.

Morin, J. W., & Levenson, J. S. (2002). *The road to freedom.* Oklahoma City, OK: Wood "N" Barnes Publishing & Distribution.

Morton, R. J., & Hilts, M. A. (Eds.). (2008). *Serial murder: Multi-disciplinary perspectives for investigators.* Quantico, VA: Federal Bureau of Investigation.

Moston, S., Stephenson, G., & Williamson, T. M. (1992). The effects of case characteristics on suspect behavior during police questioning. *British Journal of Criminology, 32,* 23–40.

Mulder, R. T., Wells, J. E., Joyce, P. R., & Bushnell, J. A. (1994). Antisocial women. *Journal of Personality Disorders, 8,* 279–287.

Mullen, P. E., Mackenzie, R., Ogloff, J. R. P., Pathé, M., McEwan, T., & Purcell, R. (2006). Assessing and managing the risks in the stalking situation. *American Academy of Psychiatry and Law Journal, 34*(4), 439–450.

Murphy, W. D., & Peters, J. M. (1992). Profiling child sexual abusers: Psychological considerations. *Criminal Justice and Behavior, 19*(1), 24–37.

Murray, J. (2009). Teen dating violence: Warning signs. *ABC News Online*. Retrieved from: http://abcnews.go.com/2020/teen-dating-violence-warning-signs/story?id=7783273.

Nathan, P., & Ward, T. (2002). Female sex offenders: Clinical and demographic features. *The Journal of Sexual Aggression, 8*, 5–21.

National Center for Victims of Crime. (2012). The trauma of victimization. Retrieved from: https://victimsofcrime.org/help-for-crime-victims/get-help-bulletins-for-crime-victims/trauma-of-victimization.

National Center on Addiction and Substance Abuse at Columbia University. (2003). *The formative years: Pathways to substance abuse among girls and young women ages 8–22*. New York, NY: Columbia University.

National Coalition Against Domestic Violence (NCADV). (2014). What is domestic violence? Retrieved from: http://www.ncadv.org/images/National%20DV%20Stats%20Sept%202014.pdf.

National Conference of State Legislatures. (2016). *E-bulletin: Sentencing and corrections policy updates newsletter*. Retrieved from: http://www.ncsl.org/research/civil-and-criminal-justice/issue-in-focus-risk-and-needs-assessment.aspx.

National Council of State Governments. (2002). Criminal justice mental health consensus project. Retrieved from: http://consensusproject.org/.

National Domestic Violence Hotline. (n.d.). What is digital abuse? Retrieved from: www.thehotline.org.

National Human Trafficking Resource Center. (2007). *What is human trafficking?* Retrieved from: https://traffickingresourcecenter.org/.

National Institute of Justice. (2003). *Youth victimization: Prevalence and implications*. Washington, DC: U.S. Department of Justice.

National Institute of Justice. (2007). *Stalking*. Washington, DC: Office of Justice Programs. Retrieved from: http://www.nij.gov/topics/crime/stalking/pages/welcome.aspx

National Institute of Justice. (2008). *Study of deaths following electro muscular disruption: Interim report*. Washington, DC: U.S. Department of Justice.

National Institute of Justice. (2015, February 15). *Offender reentry*. Washington, DC: Office of Justice Programs.

National Network to End Domestic Violence (NNEDV). (2013). 13 domestic violence counts: National summary. Retrieved from: http://nnedv.org/downloads/Census/DVCounts2013/DVCounts13_NatlSummary.pdf.

National Threat Assessment Center. (2015). *Attacks on Federal Government 2001–2013: Threat assessment considerations*. Washington, DC: U.S. Secret Service, Department of Homeland Security.

Naudts, K., & Hodgins, S. (2005). Neurobiological correlates of violent behavior among persons with schizophrenia. *Schizophrenia Bulletin*, 1–11.

New Jersey Division of Criminal Justice. (2003a). Legal aspects of domestic violence. Retrieved from: http://www.nj.gov/oag/dcj/njpdresources/dom-violence/dv-legal-aspects-stud.pdf.

319

New Jersey Division of Criminal Justice. (2003b). Interviewing techniques in domestic violence cases. Retrieved from: http://www.nj.gov/oag/dcj/njp-dresources/dom-violence/module-four-student.pdf.

New Jersey State Parole Board. (2007). *Division of release.* Retrieved from: http://www.nj.gov/parole/release.html.

New York City Alliance Against Sexual Assault. (2012). Factsheets: False allegations of sexual assault vs. "unfounded" sexual assaults. Retrieved from: http://www.svfreenyc.org/survivors_factsheet_84.html.

New York City Domestic Violence Fatality Review Committee. (2015). 2014 Annual Report. New York, NY: NYC Mayor's Office to Combat Domestic Violence.

New York Times. (1982, June 9). Ferdinand Waldo Demara, 60, an impostor in varied fields: Obituaries.

Note. (1953). Voluntary false confessions: A neglected area in criminal investigation. *Indiana Law Journal, 28,* 374–392.

Obeidallah, D. A., & Earls, F. J. (1999). *Adolescent girls: The role of depression in the development of delinquency.* Washington, DC: National Institute of Justice.

O'Brien, D. (1985). *Two of a kind: The Hillside Stranglers.* New York, NY: New American Library.

Office of Juvenile Justice and Delinquency Prevention. (2015, October 1). Statistical briefing book: Juveniles tried as adults. Minimum transfer age specified in statute, 2014. Retrieved from: http://www.ojjdp.gov/ojstatbb/structure_process/qa04105.asp?qaDate=2014&text=.

Office for Victims of Crime. (n.d.a.). Trauma-informed victim interviewing. Retrieved from: https://www.ovcttac.gov/taskforceguide/eguide/5-building-strong-cases/53-victim-interview-preparation/trauma-informed-victim-interviewing/.

Office for Victims of Crime. (n.d.b.). Victim-centered investigations. Retrieved from: https://www.ovcttac.gov/taskforceguide/eguide/5-building-strong-cases/51-victim-centered-investigations/.

Office for Victims of Crime. (n.d.c.). Child victims. Retrieved from: https://www.ncjrs.gov/ovc_archives/reports/firstrep/chldvics.html.

Office for the Prevention of Domestic Violence. (2016). Domestic violence: Stalking. New York State OPDV. Retrieved from: http://www.opdv.ny.gov/professionals/criminal_justice/stalking/stalking-infoguide.html#note1.

Office of the Public Advocate: Queensland. (2005). *Preserving life and dignity in distress: Responding to critical mental health incidents.* Brisbane, Australia: Attorney-General, Queensland Government; Department of Justice.

Office of the United States Attorneys. (2014). *Crime Victims' Rights Act.* 18 U.S.C. 3771. Washington, DC: U.S. Department of Justice.

Office on Violence Against Women. (2016). *Stalking.* Washington, DC: U.S. Department of Justice. Retrieved from: https://www.justice.gov/ovw/stalking.

Office on Violence Against Women. (2015). *Domestic violence.* Washington, DC: U.S. Department of Justice.

Ofshe, R. (1992). Inadvertent hypnosis during interrogation: False confessions due to dissociative state, misidentified multiple personality, and the satanic cult hypothesis. *International Journal of Clinical and Experimental Hypnosis, 40,* 125–156.

Ofshe, R., & Leo, R. A. (1997). Missing the forest for the trees: A response to Paul Cassell's "balanced approach" to the false confession problem. *Denver University Law Review, 74,* 1135–1144.

Ofshe, R., & Watters, E. (1994). *Making monsters: False memories, psychotherapy, and sexual hysteria.* New York, NY: Scribner's.

O'Hara, C. E., & O'Hara, G. L. (1980). *Fundamentals of criminal investigation* (5th ed.). Springfield, IL: Charles C Thomas.

Orion, D. (1997). *I know you really love me: A psychiatrist's journal of erotomania, stalking and obsessive love.* New York, NY: Macmillan.

Osgood, D. W., Wilson, J. K., O'Malley, P. M., Bachman, J. G., & Johnston, L. D. (1996). Routine activities and individual deviant behavior. *American Sociological Review, 61,* 635–655.

O'Toole, M. (2000). *The school shooter: A threat assessment perspective.* Quantico, VA: Critical Incidence Response Group (CIRG), National Center for the Assessment of Violence Crime (NCAVC), FBI Academy, Diane Publishing Co.

O'Toole, M. E., Logan, M., & Smith, S. (2012). Looking behind the mask: Implications for interviewing psychopaths. *FBI Law Enforcement Bulletin.* Retrieved from: https://leb.fbi.gov/2012/july/looking-behind-the-mask-implications-for-interviewing-psychopaths.

Overstreet, N. M., & Quinn, D. M. (2013). The intimate partner violence stigmatization model and barriers to help-seeking. *Basic Applied Social Psychology,* 35(1), 109–122.

Padget, D. K., & Struening, E. L. (1992). Victimization and traumatic injuries among the homeless: Associations with alcohol, drug, and mental problems. *American Journal of Orthopsychiatry, 62,* 525–534.

Pardini, D. A., & Loeber, R. (2007). Interpersonal and affective features of psychopathy in children and adolescents: Advancing a developmental perspective. *Journal of Clinical Child and Adolescent Psychology,* 36(3), 269–275.

Parry, H. (2015, April 17). "Girl in the box" psycho Cameron Hooker who kept kidnapped hitchhiker in a tiny box 23 hours a day for seven years is denied parole and told: "You'll spend 'at least' 15 more years in jail." *Daily Mail.* Retrieved from: http://www.dailymail.co.uk/news/article-3043291/Cameron-Hooker-kidnapped-young-hitchhiker-held-SEVEN-years-denied-parole.html.

Pathé, M., & Mullen, P. E. (1997). The impact of stalkers on their victims. *British Journal of Psychiatry, 170,* 12–17.

Pathé, M., Mullen, P. E., & Purcell, R. (2002). Patients who stalk doctors: Their motives and management. *Medical Journal of Australia, 176,* 335–338.

Pediatric Academy Societies. (2014). Scores of bullying victims bring weapons to school. Retrieved from: https://www.aap.org/en-us/about-the-aap/aap-press-room/pages/Scores-of-Bullying-Victims-Bringing-Weapons-to-School-.aspx?nfstatus=401&nftoken.

Perri, F. (2011). The flawed interview of a psychopathic killer: What went wrong? *Journal of Investigative Pyschology and Offender Profiling, 8*, 41–57.

Perri, F. S., & Lichtenwald, T. G. (2007). A proposed addition to the FBI criminal classification manual: Fraud detection homicide. *Forensic Examiner, 16*(4), 18–31.

Perri, F. S., & Lichtenwald, T. G. (2008). The arrogant chameleons exposing fraud detection homicide. *Forensic Examiner, 17*(1), 52–69.

Perri, F. S., & Lichtenwald, T. G. (2009). When worlds collide. *Forensic Examiner* (summer ed.), 52–69. Retrieved from http://www.all-about-forensic-psychology.com/support-files/criminal-profiling.pdf.

Perry, B. (2012). Supporting maltreated children: Countering the effects of neglect and abuse. Adoption Advocate. Retrieved from: https://www.adoptioncouncil.org/images/stories/documents/NCFA_ADOPTION_ADVOCATE_NO48.pdf.

Peterson, J. K., Skeem, J., Kennealy, P., Bray, B., & Zvonkovic, A. (2014). How often and how consistently do symptoms directly precede criminal behavior among offenders with mental illness? *Law and Human Behavior, 38*(5), 439–449.

Petrick, J. (2010, October 12). Convicted Passaic ax murderer gets life sentence. *Record.* Retrieved from: http://www.northjersey.com/news/convicted-passaic-ax-murderer-gets-life-sentence-1.1161309.

Phillips, H. K., Gray, N. S., MacCulloch, S. I., Taylor, J., Moore, S. C., Huckle, P., & MacCulloch, M. J. (2005). Risk assessment in offenders with mental disorders: Relative efficacy of personal demographic, criminal history, and clinical variables. *Journal of Interpersonal Violence, 20*, 833–847.

Pinizzotto, A. J., & Finkel, N. J. (1990). Criminal personality profiling: An outcome and process study. *Law and Human Behavior, 14*, 215–233.

Prentky, R. A. (1996). Community notification and constructive risk reduction. *Journal of Interpersonal Violence, 11*, 295–298.

Prescott, D. S. (2007). *Assessing youth who have sexually abused: A primer.* Holyoke, MA: NEARI Press.

Prison Rape Elimination Act. (2003). National PREA Resource Center, Bureau of Justice Assistance. Retrieved from: http://www.prearesourcecenter.org/about/prison-rape-elimination-act-prea.

Porter, S., Fairweather, D., Drugge, J., Herve, H., Birt, A. R., & Boer, D. (2000). Profiles of psychopathy in incarcerated sexual offenders. *Criminal Justice and Behavior, 27*, 216–233.

Porter, S., Woodsworth, M., Earle, J., Drugge, J., & Boer, D. (2003). Characteristics of sexual homicides committed by psychopathic and nonpsychopathic offenders. *Law and Human Behavior, 27*, 459–470.

Post, J. M. (1991). Saddam Hussein of Iraq: A political psychology profile. *Political Psychology, 12*, 279–289.

Pozzulo, J., Bennell, C., & Forth, A. (2013). *Forensic psychology.* New York, NY: Pearson.

Public Health Agency of Canada. (2004). *Canadian Incidence Study (CIS) of reported child abuse and neglect.* Ottawa, Canada.

Purcell, R., Pathé, M., & Mullen, P. E. (2002). The prevalence and nature of stalking in the Australian community. *Australia and New Zealand Journal of Psychiatry, 36*, 114–120.

Purposefully Scarred. (2015). Trauma and the brain: Understanding why a victim's story might change. Retrieved from: https://purposefullyscarred.com/2015/10/15/trauma-and-the-brain-understanding-why-a-victims-story-might-change/.

Pyszczynski, T., Greenberg, J., & Solomon, S. (1997). Why do we need what we need? A terror management perspective on the roots of human social motivation. *Psychological Inquiry, 8*(1), 1–20.

Pyszczynski, T., Solomon, S., & Greenberg, J. (2003). *In the wake of 9/11: The psychology of terror.* Washington, DC: APA.

Quay, H. C. (1965). Psychopathic personality: Pathological stimulation-seeking. *American Journal of Psychiatry, 122,* 180–183.

Quayle, J. (2008). Interviewing a psychopathic suspect. *Journal of Investigative Psychology and Offender Profiling, 5,* 79–91.

Quinsey, V. L., Rice, M. E., & Harris, G. T. (1995). Actuarial prediction of sexual recidivism. *Journal of Interpersonal Violence, 10,* 85–105.

Ramsland, K. (n.d.). The case of the seven year sex slave. *Crime Library on TruTV. com.* Retrieved from http://www.trutv.com/library/crime/criminal_mind/psychology/sex_slave/10.html.

Ramsland, K. (2014). Interview with the psychopath whisperer: A neuropsychologist explains why psychopaths don't fully grasp morality. Retrieved from: https://www.psychologytoday.com/blog/shadow-boxing/201404/interview-the-psychopath-whisperer.

Rape Abuse and Incest National Network (RAINN). (2009). Intimate partner sexual violence. Retrived from: https://www.rainn.org/public-policy/sexual-assault-issues/marital-rape.

Rattner, A. (1988). Convicted but innocent: Wrongful conviction and the criminal justice system. *Law and Human Behavior, 12,* 283–293.

Redlich, A. (2004). Mental illness, police interrogations, and the potential for false confession. *Law and Psychiatry, 55,* 19–21.

Reid, W. H. (2005). Law and psychiatry: Delusional disorder and the law. *Journal of Psychiatric Practice, 11*(2), 126–130.

Remen, R. N. (1996). *Kitchen table wisdom: Stories that heal.* New York, NY: Riverhead.

Ressler, R., Burgess, A., & Douglas, J. (1988). *Sexual homicide.* Lexington, MA: Lexington Books.

Ressler, R. K., & Shachtman, T. (1992). *Whoever fights monsters.* New York, NY: St. Martin's Press.

Reuland, M., & Margolis, G. (2003). Police approaches that improve the response to people with mental illness. *The Police Chief, 70*(11). Retrieved from: http://www.policechiefmagazine.org/magazine/index.cfm?fuseaction=display_arch&article_id=145&issue_id=112003.

Reuland, M., Schwarzfeld, M., & Draper, L. (2009). Law enforcement responses to people with mental illness: A guide to research-informed policy and practice. Retrieved from: http://csgjusticecenter.org/wp-content/uploads/2012/12/le-research.pdf.

Roberts, A. D., & Coid, J. W. (2010). Personality disorder and offending behaviour: Findings from the national survey of male prisoners in England and Wales. *Journal of Forensic Psychiatry and Psychology, 21,* 221–237.

Rodriguez, J. (2009, November 7). Rihanna details Chris Brown assault in "20/20" interview. *MTV News.* Retrieved from: http://www.mtv.com/news/1625783/rihanna-details-chris-brown-assault-in-2020-interview/.

Rogers, R. (1987). APA's position on the insanity defense: Empiricism versus emotionalism. *American Psychologist, 42,* 840–848.

Rogstad, J. E., & Rogers, R. (2008). Gender differences in contributions of emotions to psychopathy and antisocial personality disorder. *Clinical Psychology Review, 28,* 1472–1484.

Rosenfeld, B., & Harmon, R. (2002). Factors associated with violence in stalking and obsessional harassment cases. *Criminal Justice and Behavior, 29,* 671–691.

Rossmo, D. (1995). Targeting victims: Serial killers and the urban environment. In T. O'Reilly-Flemming, & S. Egger (Eds.), *Serial and mass murder: Theory, research and policy.* Toronto: University of Toronto Press.

Rossmo, D. K. (2000). *Geographic profiling.* Boca Raton, FL: CRC Press.

Rothman, E., Hathaway, J., Stidsen, A., & de Vries, H. (2007). How employment helps female victims of intimate partner abuse: A qualitative study. *Journal of Occupational Health Psychology, 12*(2), 136–143.

Ruiz, J. (1993). An interactive analysis between uniformed law enforcement officers and the mentally ill. *American Journal of Police, 12*(4), 149–177.

Ruiz, J., & Miller, C. (2004). An exploratory study of Pennsylvania police officers' perceptions of dangerousness and their ability to manage persons with mental illness. *Police Quarterly, 7*(3), 359–371.

Rule, A. (2000). *The stranger beside me* (20th anniversary ed.). New York, NY: Signet.

Russell, S. (1992). *Damsel of death.* London: BCA.

Safe Horizon. (2015). Domestic violence: Statistics and facts. Retrieved from: http://www.safehorizon.org/page/domestic-violence-statistics--facts-52.html.

Salekin, R. T. (2016). Psychopathy in childhood: Toward better informing the DSM-5 and ICD-11 conduct disorder specifiers. *Personality Disorders: Theory, Research and Treatment, 7*(2), 180–191.

Salekin, R. T., Rogers, R., & Sewell, K. W. (1997). Construct validity of psychopathy in a female offender sample: A multitrait-multimethod evaluation. *Journal of Abnormal Psychology, 106,* 576–585.

Sansone, R. A., & Sansone, L. A. (2010). Fatal attraction syndrome: Stalking behavior and borderline personality. *Psychiatry, 7*(5), 42–46.

Sattler, J. M. (1998). *Clinical and forensic interviewing of children and families: Guidelines for the mental health, education, pediatric, and child maltreatment fields.* San Diego, CA: Jerome M. Sattler.

Saunders, B. E., Kilpatrick, D. G., Hanson, R. F., Resnick, H. S., & Walker, M. E. (1999). Prevalence, case characteristics, and long-term psychological correlates of child rape among women: A national survey. *Childhood Maltreatment, 4,* 187–200.

Saunders, D. G. (1992). A typology of men who batter: Three types derived from cluster analysis. *American Journal of Orthopsychiatry, 62,* 264–275.

Saunders, D. G. (1995). The tendency to arrest victims of domestic violence: A preliminary analysis of officer characteristics. *Journal of Interpersonal Violence,* 10, 147–158.

Schell, B. H., & Lanteigne, N. M. (2000). *Stalking, harassment and murder in the workplace.* Westport, CT: Quorum Books.

Schmerler, K., Perkins, M., Phillips, S., Rhinehart, T., & Townsend, M. (2002). *Problem-solving tips: A guide to reducing crime and disorder through problem-solving partnerships.* Washington, DC: U.S. Department of Justice, Office of Community Oriented Policing Services.

Schwartz, B., & Cellini, H. (1995). Female sex offenders. In B. Schwartz, & H. Cellini (Eds.), *The sex offender: corrections, treatment and legal practice* (pp. 5-1–5-22). Kingston, NJ: Civic Research Institute.

Sears, D. (1991). *To kill again.* Wilmington, DE: Scholarly Resources.

Seto, M. C., & Barbaree, H. E. (1999). Psychopathy, treatment behavior, and sex offender recidivism. *Journal of Interpersonal Violence,* 14, 1235–1248.

Sexual Assault Prevention and Awareness Center. (2016). What is stalking? University of Michigan. Retrieved from: https://sapac.umich.edu/article/65.

Shaw, J., Hunt, I.M., Flynn, S., Meehan, J., Robinson, J., Bickley, H., … Appleby, L. (2006). Rates of mental disorder in people convicted of homicide: National clinical survey. *British Journal of Psychiatry, 188,* 143–147.

Sherman, L. W., & Berk, R. A. (1984). The specific deterrent effects of arrest for domestic assault. *American Sociological Review, 49,* 261–272.

Shroder, S. (2012, May 18). Wounded officer asked, "Is this my time?" *San Diego Union-Tribune.* Retrieved from: http://www.sandiegouniontribune.com/news/2012/may/18/shot-officer-asked-my-time/.

Sickmund, M., Snyder, H. N., & Poe-Yamagata, E. (1997). *Juvenile offenders and victims: 1997 update on violence.* Washington, DC: Office of Juvenile Justice and Delinquency Prevention.

Silva, J. A., Ferrari, M. M., Leong, G. B., & Penny, G. (1998). The dangerousness of persons with delusional jealousy. *Journal of the American Academy of Psychiatry and the Law, 26*(4), 607–623.

Silver, E., Arseneault, L., Langley, J., Caspi, A., & Moffitt, T. E. (2005). Mental disorder and violent victimization in a total birth cohort. *American Journal of Public Health, 95*(11), 2015–2021.

Singer, S. (1981). Homogeneous victim-offender populations: A review and some research implications. *Journal of Criminal Law and Criminology, 72,* 779–788.

Skeem, J., & Peterson, J. (2012). Identifying, treating, and reducing risk for offenders with mental illness. In J. Petersilia, & K. Reitz (Eds.), *Handbook on sentencing and corrections* (pp. 521–543). New York, NY: Oxford University Press.

Skeem, J. L., Winter, E., Kennealy, P. J., Louden, J. E., & Tatar, J. R. (2014). Offenders with mental illness have criminogenic needs, too: Toward recidivism reduction. *Law and Human Behavior, 38*(3), 212–224.

Skolnick, J. H., & Fyfe, J. J. (1993). *Above the Law.* New York, NY: Free Press.

325

Slomnicki, D. (2013, November 14). Rape by fraud, deception, or impersonation—An addition to New York's penal law: Rape in the first degree statute. Retrieved from: http://nysbar.com/blogs/lawstudentconnection/2013/11/rape_by_fraud_deception_or_imp.html.

Smith, W. R. (1988). Delinquency and abuse among juvenile sexual offenders. *Journal of Interpersonal Violence, 3,* 400–413.

Snyder, H. N. (2000). Sexual assault of young children as reported to law enforcement: Victim, incident, and offender characteristics. Retrieved from: http://www.bjs.gov/content/pub/pdf/saycrle.pdf.

Stagg, V., Wills, G. D., & Howell, M. (1989). Psychopathy in early child witnesses of family violence. *Topics in Early Childhood Special Education, 9,* 73–87.

Stalking Resource Center. (2012). Stalking information. National Center for Victims of Crime. Retrieved from: https://victimsofcrime.org/our-programs/stalking-resource-center/stalking-information.

Stanglin, D., & Bello, M. (2014, November 21). Sandy Hook killer carefully planned attack, study says. *USA Today.* Retrieved from: http://www.usatoday.com/story/news/nation/2014/11/21/sandy-hook-massacre-newtown-connecticut-adam-lanza/19343223/.

Starmer, K. (2011, December 4). Domestic violence: The facts, the issues, the future. Speech by the Director of Public Prosecutions for The Crown Prosecution Service, United Kingdom. Retrieved from: http://www.cps.gov.uk/news/articles/domestic_violence_-_the_facts_the_issues_the_future/.

Stevens, J. A. (1997). Standard investigatory tools and offender profiling. In J. L. Jackson, & D. A. Bekerian (Eds.), *Offender profiling: Theory, research and practice* (pp. 76–91). New York, NY: John Wiley.

Stratham, D. J., Heath, A. C., Madden, P. A., Bucholz, K. K., Bierut, L., Dinwiddie, S. H., … Martin, N. G. (1998). Suicidal behavior: An epidemiological and genetic study. *Psychological Medicine, 28,* 839–855.

Stuart, H. (2003). Violence and mental illness: An overview. *World Psychiatry, 2*(2), 121–124.

Substance Abuse Mental Health Services Administration (SAMHSA). (2004). *NSDUH report: Marijuana use and delinquent behaviors among youths.* Washington, DC: U.S. Department of Health and Human Services.

Sudbury-Wayland-Lincoln Domestic Violence Roundtable. (2008). *Safety planning.* Retrieved from: domesticviolenceroundtable.org.

Sullivan, T., & Maiken, P. T. (2000). *Killer clown: The John Wayne Gacy murders.* New York, NY: Pinnacle.

Szymanski, L. A. (2003). *Megan's law: Juvenile sex offender registration age limits,* 8(5). Pittsburgh, PA: National Center for Juvenile Justice.

Tanford, J. A. (1990). The limits of a scientific jurisprudence: The Supreme Court and psychology. *Indiana Law Journal, 66,* 137–173.

Tarullo, A. (2012). Effects of child maltreatment on the developing brain. *Child Welfare 360°: Using a Developmental Approach in Child Welfare Practice, 11.* https://www.bu.edu/cdl/files/2013/08/Tarullo-CW360-2012.pdf.

Taxman, F. S. (1999). Unraveling "what works" for offenders in substance abuse treatment. *National Drug Court Institute Review, 2*(2), 93–134.

Taxman, F. S., Shepardson, E. S., & Byrne, J. M. (2004). *Tools of the trade: A guide to incorporating science into practice.* Washington, DC: U.S. Department of Justice, National Institute of Corrections, and Maryland Department of Public Safety and Correctional Services. NIC Accession Number 020095.

Taylor, B., Woods, D., Kubu, B., Koper, C., Tegeler, B., Cheney, J., … Kappelman, K. (2009). *Comparing safety outcomes in police use of force cases for law enforcement agencies that have deployed conducted energy devices and a matched comparison group that have not: A quasi experimental evaluation.* Washington, DC: U.S. Department of Justice.

Teplin, L. A. (1983). The criminalization of the mentally ill: Speculation in search of data. *APA Psychological Bulletin, 94*(1), 54–67.

Teplin, L. A. (2000). Psychiatric disorders in youthful offenders. *National Institute of Justice Journal,* 30–32.

Teplin, L. A., & Pruett, N. (1992). Police as streetcorner psychiatrist: Managing the mentally ill. *International Journal of Law & Psychiatry, 15,* 139–156.

Terr, L. (1986). The child psychiatrist and the child witness: Traveling companions by necessity, if not by design. *Journal of the American Academy of Child Psychiatry, 25,* 462–472.

Texas Department of Criminal Justice. (2016). Parole division: Specialized programs. Retrieved from: https://www.tdcj.state.tx.us/divisions/parole/parole_specialized_programs.html.

Thompson, S. (2014). Sexting prosecutions: Minors as a protected class from child pornography charges. *University of Michigan Journal of Law Reform, 48.* Retrieved from: http://mjlr.org/2014/10/27/sexting-prosecutions-minors-as-a-protected-class-from-child-pornography-charges/.

Thompson, L., & Borum, R. (2006). Crisis intervention teams (CIT): Considerations for knowledge transfer. *Law Enforcement Executive Forum, 6*(3), 25–36.

Thomson Reuters. (2016). The recanting victim and domestic violence. Retrieved from: http://family.findlaw.com/domestic-violence/the-recanting-victim-and-domestic-violence.html.

Thornton, D., & Blud, L. (2007). The influence of psychopathic traits on response to treatment. In H. Herve, & J. C. Yuille (Eds.), *The psychopath: Theory, research and practice* (pp. 505–539). Mahwah, NJ: Lawrence Erlbaum Associates.

Tjaden, P., & Thoennes, N. (1998a). Full report of the prevalence, incidence, and consequence of violence against women. Retrieved from: https://www.ncjrs.gov/pdffiles1/nij/183781.pdf.

Tjaden, P., & Thoennes, N. (1998b). *Stalking in America: Findings from the national violence against women survey.* Washington, DC: U.S. Department of Justice, National Institute of Justice.

Tjaden, P., & Thoennes, N. (2001). *Stalking: Its role in serious domestic violence cases.* Washington, DC: National Institute of Justice.

Towers, J. (Executive Producer). (2009) *American justice* [Television series]. New York, NY: A & E Television Networks.

Treatment Advocacy Center. (2010). More mentally ill persons are in jails and prisons than in hospitals: A survey of the states. Retrieved from: http://www.treatmentadvocacycenter.org/storage/documents/final_jails_v_hospitals_study.pdf.

Truman, J. L., & Morgan, R. E. (2014). *Nonfatal domestic violence, 2003–2012.* Washington, DC: U.S. Bureau of Justice Statistics.

Urban Institute. (2008, May). The challenges of prisoner reentry: Facts and figures. Retrieved from: http://www.urban.org/sites/default/files/alfresco/publication-pdfs/411683-The-Challenges-of-Prisoner-Reentry-Facts-and-Figures.PDF.

U.S.C. 17 [U.S. Code: Title 17].

U.S. Department of Health and Human Services. (n.d.a.). Mental health myths and facts. Retrieved from: http://www.mentalhealth.gov/basics/myths-facts/.

U.S. Department of Health and Human Services. (n.d.b.). www.stopbullying.gov.

U.S. Department of Health and Human Services. (2003). *Child maltreatment, 2001.* Washington, DC: U.S. Administration on Children, Youth, and Families.

U.S. Department of Justice. (1988). *Report to the nation on crime and justice: The data* (2nd ed.). Washington, DC: USGPO.

U.S. Department of Justice. (1989). *Criminal victimization in the United States, 1987.* Washington, DC: USGPO.

U.S. Department of Justice. (2011). *Victims with disabilities: The forensic interview.* Retrieved from: http://www.ovc.gov/publications/infores/pdftxt/VictimsGuideBook.pdf.

U.S. Department of Justice. (2012). Attorney general Eric Holder announces revisions to the *Uniform Crime Report's* definition of rape: Data reported on rape will better reflect state criminal codes, victim experiences. Retrieved from: http://www.justice.gov/opa/pr/attorney-general-eric-holder-announces-revisions-uniform-crime-report-s-definition-rape.

U.S. Department of Justice. (2013). *National crime victimization survey: 2008–2012.*

U.S. Department of Justice. (2015). Sexual assault. Retrieved from: http://www.justice.gov/ovw/sexual-assault.

Valdes, C. M. (2010, July 2). Guilty verdict in ax murder case: News release. Retrieved from: http://pcponj.org/PDF/2010%20PR/Press%20RELEASE%20Chireno.pdf.

Van Hasselt, V. B., Flood, J. J., Romano, S. J., Vecchi, G. M., de Fabrique, N., & Dalfonzo, V. A. (2005). Hostage-taking in the context of domestic violence: Some case examples. *Journal of Family Violence, 20,* 21–27.

Viding, E., Blair, R. J. R., Moffitt, T. E., & Plomin, R. (2005). Evidence for substantial genetic risk for psychopathy in 7-year-olds. *Journal of Child Psychology and Psychiatry, 46,* 592–597.

Vizard, E., & Tranter, M. (1988). Helping young children to describe experiences of child sexual abuse: General issues. In A. Bentovim, A. Elton, J. Hildegrand, M. Tranter, & E. Vizard (Eds.), *Child sexual abuse within the family, assessment and treatment* (pp. 84–105). Bristol, UK: John Wright.

Verhovek, S. H. (1993, May 5). Investigators puzzle over last minutes of Koresh. *New York Times*, p. A10.

Vronsky, P. (2004). *Serial killers: The method and madness of monsters.* New York, NY: Berkley Books.

Vronsky, P. (2007). *Female serial killers: How and why women become monsters.* New York, NY: Penguin Group.

Walker, C. E., Bonner, B. L., & Kaufman, K. L. (1988). *The physically and sexually abused child: Evaluation and treatment.* New York, NY: Pergamon Press.

Walker, L. (1979). *The battered woman.* New York, NY: Harper & Row.

Walker, L. (1984a). Battered women, psychology, and public policy. *American Psychologist, 39:*1178–1182.

Walker, L. (1984b). *The battered woman syndrome.* New York, NY: Springer.

Walters, G. D. (2003). Predicting institutional adjustment and recidivism with the psychopathy checklist factor scores: A meta-analysis. *Law and Human Behavior, 27,* 541–558.

Walters, J. (2012, December 15). Sara Reedy, the rape victim accused of lying and jailed by U.S. police, wins $1.5m payout. *Observer.* Retrieved from: http://www.guardian.co.uk/world/2012/dec/15/sara-reedy-rape-victim-wins-police-payout/print.

Walters, S. T., Clark, M. D., Gingerich, R., & Meltzer, M. L. (2007). *A guide for probation and parole: Motivating offenders to change.* Retrieved from: https://www.victimsofcrime.org/docs/restitution-toolkit/c9_nic-motivating-offenders.pdf?sfvrsn=2.

Warner, S., & Wilkins, T. (2004). Between subjugation and survival: Women, borderline personality disorder and high security mental hospitals. *Journal of Contemporary Psychotherapy, 34*(3), 1573–3564.

Warren, J. I., & South, S. C. (2009). A symptom level examination of the relationship between Cluster B personality disorders and patterns of criminality and violence in women. *International Journal of Law and Psychiatry, 32,* 10–17.

Watson, A. C., Morabito, M. S., Draine, J., & Ottati, V. (2008). Improving police response to persons with mental illness: A multi-level conceptualization of CIT. *International Journal of Law and Psychiatry, 31*(4), 359–368.

Wells, G. L. (1993). What do we know about eyewitness identification? *American Psychologist, 48,* 553–571.

Wells, G. L. (1995). Scientific study of witness memory: Implications for public and legal policy. *Psychology, Public Policy, and Law, 1,* 726–731.

Wells, G. L., & Loftus, E. F. (2002). Eyewitness memory for people and events. In A. Goldstein (Ed.), *Handbook of psychology. Vol. 11, Forensic psychology* (pp. 149–160). New York, NY: John Wiley.

Wells, G. L., Small, M., Penrod, S., Malpass, R. S., Fulero, S. M., & Brimacombe, C. A. E. (1998). Eyewitness identification procedures: Recommendations for lineups and photospreads. *Law and Human Behavior, 22,* 603–647.

Widom, C., Czaja, S., Bentley, T., & Johnson, M. (2012). A prospective investigation of physical health outcomes in abused and neglected children: New findings from a 30 year follow-up. *American Journal of Public Health, 102*(6), 1, 135–144.

Wilson, C. (2000). *The mammoth book of history of murder: The history of how and why mankind Is driven to kill.* New York, NY: Carroll and Graf.

Wolff, N., Morgan, R. D., Shi, J., Huening, J., & Fisher, W. H. (2011). Thinking styles and emotional states of male and female prison inmates by mental disorder status. *Psychiatric Services, 62,* 1485–1493.

Wolfgang, M. E. (1958). *Patterns in criminal homicide.* Philadelphia, PA: University of Pennsylvania Press.

Wood, J. (2013). *Competency hearing for Puckett, who killed Avery sheriff's deputy ten years ago, delayed until evaluation.* HCR Press. Retrieved from: http://www.hcpress.com/news/near-10-year-anniversary-of-avery-sheriffs-deputy-glenn-hicks-murder-another-competency-hearing-for-puckett-to-take-place.html.

Woodsworth, M., & Porter, S. (1999). Historical foundations and current applications of criminal profiling in violent crime investigations. *Expert Evidence, 7,* 241–264.

Wright, L. (1994). *Remembering Satan.* New York, NY: Knopf.

Wrightsman, L. S., & Kassin, S. M. (1993). *Confessions in the courtroom.* Thousand Oaks, CA: Sage.

Yarmey, A. D., & Kent, J. (1980). Eyewitness identification by elderly and young adults. *Law and Human Behavior, 4,* 359–371.

INDEX

Bianchi, Kenneth, 58, 59
Bind Torture Kill Killer, 89, 91, 95
Bipolar disorders, 31–32
Bizarre delusion, 25
Black Widow, 93
BOP, *see* Federal Bureau of Prisons
Borderline personality disorder
(BPD), 37
Boston Strangler, 161–162
BPD, *see* Borderline personality
disorder
Brain dysfunction, 70
Brennan, William, 182
Brigham, Jack, 10
Brother John, 49–50
Broward Correctional Institution, 60
Brown, Chris, 125
Brown, Jordan, 234, 235
Brussel, James, 156, 161
Brutal facial injuries, 175
BSU, *see* Behavioral Science Unit
Bullying
and deadly violence, 268–272
Columbine, 269
Sandy Hook shooting, 272
Virginia Tech, 270–271
effects of, 268
types of, 267–268
Bundy, Ted, 86–87
Buono, Angelo, 58
Bureau of Justice Statistics, 101
Butler, Brenton, 199
BWS, *see* Battered woman syndrome

C

CAC, *see* Child Advocacy Center
California Commission on Judicial
Performance, 213
Callous-unemotional (CU)
dimension, 231
Carroll, Lewis, 85
Catch Me If You Can, 49
CDC, *see* Centers for Disease Control
and Prevention

CDS, *see* Controlled dangerous
substance
CED, *see* Conducted energy device
Center for Sex Offender
Management, 102
Centers for Disease Control and
Prevention (CDC), 128, 264
Central Park Five, 194–195
Champagne, Crystal, 181–182
Child abuse hysteria, 245–246
Fells Acres Day Care, 245–246
Kern County, 245
Child Advocacy Center (CAC), 249
Child molestation, 38, 100, 113–114
Child psychopathy, 231–233
immaturity and, 232–233
measuring, 232
Child sexual abuse (CSA), 243
Child victims, 243–244
Chireno murder, 3–4, 5–6
CITs, *see* Crisis intervention teams
Clark, Eric, 26–27
Classic mass murder, 82
Cleckley, Hervey, 52
Clinical psychology, 20
Closed-ended question, 200–201
Closed questioning phase, 253
Closing phase, 254
Clouser, Ronald, 208
Cluster A disorders, 35
Cluster C disorders, 35
Coakley, Martha, 246
Co-ed Killer, 92
Coerced-compliant confessions,
193–195
Coerced-internalized confessions,
195–197
Coerced sexual penetration, 128
Cognitive distortions, 20, 109
Cognitive impairments, 42
Cognitive psychology, 20
Collaborative supervision models, 120
Collateral consequences, 283–284
Collectivist mentality, 276
Collier, Kevin, 146